HARRIET'S LEGACIES

CARLETON LIBRARY SERIES

The Carleton Library Series publishes books about Canadian economics, geography, history, politics, public policy, society and culture, and related topics, in the form of leading new scholarship and reprints of classics in these fields. The series is funded by Carleton University, published by McGill-Queen's University Press, and is under the guidance of the Carleton Library Series Editorial Board, which consists of faculty members of Carleton University. Suggestions and proposals for manuscripts and new editions of classic works are welcome and may be directed to the Carleton Library Series Editorial Board c/o the Library, Carleton University, Ottawa K1S 5B6, at cls@carleton.ca, or on the web at www.carleton.ca/cls.

Harriet's Legacies

Race, Historical Memory, and Futures in Canada

Edited by
**RONALD CUMMINGS
AND NATALEE CAPLE**

Carleton Library Series 259

McGill-Queen's University Press
Montreal & Kingston · London · Chicago

© McGill-Queen's University Press 2022

ISBN 978-0-2280-1065-4 (cloth)
ISBN 978-0-2280-1219-1 (ePDF)
ISBN 978-0-2280-1220-7 (ePUB)

Legal deposit second quarter 2022
Bibliothèque nationale du Québec

Printed in Canada on acid-free paper that is 100% ancient forest free
(100% post-consumer recycled), processed chlorine free

Publication has been supported by the Dean's Discretionary Fund of
the Faculty of Humanities, Brock University.

We acknowledge the support of the Canada Council for the Arts.

Nous remercions le Conseil des arts du Canada de son soutien.

Library and Archives Canada Cataloguing in Publication

Title: Harriet's legacies: race, historical memory, and futures in Canada / edited
   by Ronald Cummings and Natalee Caple.

Names: Cummings, Ronald, editor. | Caple, Natalee, 1970– editor.

Series: Carleton library series; 259.

Description: Series statement: Carleton Library series ; 259 | Includes bibliographical
   references and index.

Identifiers: Canadiana (print) 20210371765 | Canadiana (ebook) 20210371870 |
   ISBN 9780228010654 (hardcover) | ISBN 9780228012191 (PDF) |
   ISBN 9780228012207 (ePUB)

Subjects: LCSH: Blacks—Canada. | LCSH: Blacks—Canada—History. | LCSH:
   Blacks—Canada—Social conditions. | LCSH: Blacks—Race identity—Canada. |
   LCSH: Tubman, Harriet, 1822-1913. | LCSH: Underground Railroad—Canada. |
   LCSH: Fugitive slaves—Canada. | CSH: Black Canadians. | CSH: Black
   Canadians—History. | CSH: Black Canadians—Social conditions.

Classification: LCC FC106.B6 H37 2022 | DDC 305.896/071—dc23

This book was typeset by Marquis Interscript in 10.5/13 Sabon.

Contents

Figures and Tables

FIGURES

TABLES

Acknowledgments and
a Brief Note on Editorial Choice

Our thanks to Lezlie Harper Wells for the inspirational tour of sites related to the Underground Railroad in Niagara that began our journey towards this book. Thanks as well to Gregory Betts, Kevin Gosine, and Tamari Kitossa for co-organizing the Harriet's Legacies conference at Brock University. And much gratitude to Shannon Kitchings, Jacob McArthur Mooney, Ryan Racine, and Melissa Roberts for assistance with the manuscript. We gratefully received funding from the Senator William McMaster Chair at McMaster University to support the creation of this book's index. Enormous thanks to Jeremy Leipert for ongoing support, technical and emotional, and on-call proofreading throughout the years of this project. And, of course, our greatest thanks to our contributors for their works.

Our contributors vary in their use of upper case and lower case regarding Black and black. Because this is a decision that is informed by many layers of political and social history, we respect the choices of individual writers and hope that the discontinuity causes thought rather than distraction.

Figure 0.1 Portrait of Harriet Tubman, 1868 or 1869.

Figure 0.2 Harriet Tubman, 1911, probably at her home in Auburn, New York.

HARRIET'S LEGACIES

On the Non-linearity of Legacy: Harriet Tubman and Our Current Historical Juncture

Ronald Cummings and Natalee Caple

Born enslaved on the shores of eastern Maryland, Araminta Ross was to become Harriet Tubman, the most famous conductor of the Underground Railroad. She later renamed herself Harriet, after her beloved mother, and Tubman was her married name. After fleeing Dorchester County, Maryland, in 1849, she settled in Philadelphia, before arriving in St Catharines, Canada West, in 1851 where she lived for almost a decade.[1] During her time in St Catharines, Tubman resided in a house on North Street across from the historic Salem BME Chapel,[2] founded by Black freedom seekers in 1820. This was where she attended services and was part of their community. Today there is a bust in tribute to her in the meditation garden outside of the chapel. The engraving on the tall marble platform beneath quotes Tubman saying "I wouldn't trust Uncle Sam with my people no longer, but I brought them clear off to Canada."[3] On 14 June 2020 a group of BIPOC high school students led a thousand protestors on a Black Lives Matters march from the statue of Harriet Tubman by the BME Chapel to City Hall in St Catharines to protest police violence in Canada and the US.

There are few sites of memory for and about Harriet Tubman's time in Canada. While Tubman has been largely claimed as an American cultural figure, this volume seeks to recuperate the significance of her time in Canada, not just as an interlude in her American narrative but, rather, as another site for thinking about Black diasporic mobilities, possibilities, and histories. We foreground the consideration of Tubman's time in Canada, as well as her numerous crossings of the border as inspiration and guidance to think about Black radical and transnational possibilities not confined to bounded national histories. This text thus participates in, revises, and extends a tradition of writings and representations about Tubman but also rethinks the complex historical and contemporary relationship between Blackness and Canada as one way of raising questions about potential futures.

HARRIET TUBMAN AND OUR CURRENT
HISTORICAL JUNCTURE

As a cultural figure, Harriet Tubman has returned forcefully to the public imagination since the turn of the century. Tubman's life and narrative has notably inspired numerous works of children's literature, plays, films, biographies, and other cultural texts. Historian Janell Hobson, for example, points to a rich visual archive that has emerged in popular culture and media today. In her work Hobson cites, as evidence of this resurgence of interest, the fact that "she won the popular vote for the *Women on the 20* competition" in which the American public voted for Tubman's image to appear on the US$20 bill.[4] Hobson also discusses among other visual texts, a "cameo appearance" on the short-lived television series *Underground* in which Tubman was played by the actress Aisha Hinds in an episode that consisted of a rousing hour-long monologue that sought to capture the spirit and fervour of anti-slavery speeches and meetings of the abolitionist era through the practice of testimony.[5] In building on Hobson's work, we might read this particular episode as not just merely a restaging of history but perhaps also an attempt to pass on this memory to future generations. This question of Tubman's powerful return to visual representation has also been materialized through the recirculation of images of her, as seen in the recent (re)discovery of a portrait of a younger Tubman in an album, once owned by Tubman's fellow abolitionist and friend, Emily Howland. In much the same way that this book aims to rethink and participate in the reassessment of the public narratives told about Tubman, this rediscovered photograph in many ways disrupts widely circulated and canonized representations of Tubman as an elderly "Aunt Harriet" or "Mother Tubman."[6] It reveals a younger figure but also serves to make visible a process of aging or one of becoming, rather than foregrounding a figure seemingly fixed in time in the cultural memory.

To add to this rich and generative contemporary archive, which Hobson mentions, in September 2019 the Hollywood feature film *Harriet* directed by Kasi Lemmons had its world premiere at the Toronto Film Festival.[7] Lemmons's film has since then continued to ignite public debates about Tubman's life and about the historical specificities of its narrative. The film, in a self-conscious way, calls attention to the very process of constructing representations and memory and reflects on the process of narrative making in the public imagination through its depictions of the circulation of narratives of Tubman as the liberator "Moses" – Tubman's codename – in antebellum times as part of its storylines. In the film, as frenzied panic and news spread among the planter class about the freedom journeys of the enslaved, the stories of the escapes are rendered rich through elaborations, including the gendered speculation that "Moses" was, in fact, a man. We also see as part of the film, Tubman composing herself and simultaneously being composed (the film notably calls attention to the duality of this process) in the now well-known picture portraits which have come to mark our imaginings and narratives of Harriet Tubman in the twentieth and twenty-first century.

In turning to Lemmons's film as part of the introduction to this book we read it as a text that reveals why the current volume is necessary and important. It also serves to highlight what the essays, poems, and discussions collected here potentially add to the public memory of Tubman. In Lemmons's film Canada, as part of Tubman's narrative, is notably absent in any significant way. The action of the film takes place primarily in the United States with the exception of a single scene set in St Catharines, Ontario. As one end point of the Underground Railroad, St Catharines seems unusually diminished by this representation. It was to St Catharines that Tubman brought her own family. In contrast, to the film's minor representation of Canada, the contributions to this volume serve to recall Tubman's time in Canada as central to articulating that Tubman's and, indeed, her passengers' lives did not end, nor did their struggles to be free, when they crossed the border out of America.

Attending to the question of the silencing of Canada as part of Tubman's narrative, we note how in Lemmons's film, the single scene set in Canada is particularly interesting for having no dialogue. In the scene Tubman is seen indoors, cooking before receiving a prophetic vision that urges her return to Maryland to rescue her parents. The scene is thus central to the culmination of the action of the film; however, it is, at the same time, rendered as a caesura in the unfolding action. The implication of the silent scene is that the story of slavery ends in Canada while also locating the articulations of Black lives only in relation to America.

Three things might be noted here about the treatment of this Canadian episode in the narrative. In the first instance, we might note how the very absence of dialogue performs and becomes representative of a discursive silencing that has attended Canada as part of Tubman's narrative. This

functions in the wider schema of representation as part of the singular
claims to Harriet Tubman's story as an African American narrative. This
serves to promote a troubling historical ownership of Tubman as an
American cultural figure, when any twentieth century national ownership
(American or Canadian) of Tubman elides the specificity and complexity
of her life and resistance. Second, in the film's representational frame, her
life in Canada is imagined not as part of her public activism. In spite of
the fact that we know Tubman continued in political life in Canada and in
the US, working with abolitionists, supporting suffrage, acting as a nurse,
cook, and spy for the Union army during the US Civil War, Tubman is
pictured after her Canadian arrival, as settled, indoors, in the space of the
domestic, baking. Our noting of this seemingly minor detail is meant to call
attention to the film's overwhelming work of gendering Tubman as part of
the telling of this narrative. This remarkable housewifing of a freedom
fighter implies a great revising of her public persona. Instead of continuing
to remember Tubman as the "General" she was called by fellow abolitionists,
who recognized her peership, she is consigned to a seemingly naturalized
role of "woman in Canada." However significant the gender bias here we
also want to note how, in many ways, this representation perpetuates and
relies on particular idealized narratives about Canada as a free utopia, as
a safe space, which functions here to efface and render not only invisible
but perhaps even improbable the ongoing need for the public work of
activism and anti-slavery agitation that Tubman and others carried out in
Canada and in St Catharines. In this way the film also performs a whitewash-
ing of Canada's own history of slavery and the racism that freed people
encountered in their new lives. Third, in the film's positioning of Tubman's
return to America, after her sojourn in Canada, as centred around the act
of rescuing her parents, the film locates the intergenerational and legacy
claims for Tubman firmly within and in relation to an African American
space. It is there that she is located in relation to kin, blood, and belonging,
as opposed to in Canada, where she is positioned as a lone figure in a private,
secluded, yet seemingly relatively comfortable, perhaps even pastoral, space.

The film notably closes with a postscript that not only firmly situates
Tubman, once again, within the context of American history but one might
even argue within a narrative of American state institutional formation
(thereby co-opting her acts for Black emancipation) by noting that she was
one of the only women in *US history* to lead an armed military expedition.
While she does function to challenge the white masculine narratives of
military conquests, Tubman's liberatory narrative becomes arguably (con)
scripted into the state neoliberal narrative. This posthumous conscription

of Tubman is also echoed in the tensions that attend the US Treasury announcement of plans to replace President Andrew Jackson, on the US $20 bill with her image.

Like the film's important work of representation, which, as we have noted above, has served in the process of recalling Tubman to public memory in a meaningful way by locating her on the big screen, the proposed inclusion of her image on the $20 bill would be, and should be, significant in terms of recognizing women and addressing the history of slavery in the US. Tubman's face as currency might additionally be seen as radical for promoting values that puncture the centrality of capitalist gains and highlighting the bodies that suffer under capitalism. Tubman's face on money does seem ironic if it is considered as one historic "face" of resistance to disaster economies, those economies that function through hierarchies of power that brutalize some bodies and elevate others away from harm.[8] Indeed, Tubman's life work and political practice worked directly against the slave-driven economies that built wealth in early America and that still inform its social-political landscapes and market economies. While the inclusion of her image on the American $20 bill potentially challenges foundational American capitalist values, it also embeds her in institutions that she worked to resist and subvert. A key challenge remains in terms of how we can make Tubman's power and representation visible and political without institutionalizing her.

In attending to the complexity of Tubman as a figure, this book argues for a much more expansive vision of Tubman's life and narrative beyond nationalist and nationalizing rhetorics and structures. We aim to reposition Tubman as transnational and diasporic rather than as a figure primarily of American significance. This repositioning, we argue, also opens up space for a more radical visioning of Tubman's legacies to be found beyond the bounded American national context. Yet, while this volume makes the claim for Tubman's connections to and life and experience in Canada to be taken more seriously in the recounting of her life and work, this should not be read as simply a mobilization of a particularly nationalizing Canadian claim to Tubman to exist alongside or as an alternative to an American one. Rather the attention to Canada here is meant to function within a broader dialogue about the multiple meanings of Tubman to and within Black diasporic networks of relation. In other words, this text should be read as a dialogical grappling with paradoxes and legacies made visible through various connections to a historical figure in and of the Black diaspora.

The location of this work within and in relation to networks of Black diasporic mobility as part of Tubman's legacy can be seen in the attention that is given to examinations of cross border histories, as in the account of the history of the Cataract House hotel in the Niagara River borderlands. We note how various essays in this volume also attend to the publishing and circulation histories of eighteenth-century texts, letters, photographs, and pamphlets. Alongside these are works that examine the continued transnational and diasporic formations and circulations of Black life such as Kaie Kellough's visual poem, "She Balances The Border," which explicitly maps connections between Canada, Haiti, and beyond. A critical commitment to Black diasporic connections can also be seen in the volume's attention to transnational forms such as dub poetry, which scholars like Phanuel Antwi have examined as a "Black Atlantic body-archive" and which connects Canada, to Kingston, Jamaica, and to London, England.[9] The anthology describes international movements that intertwine Black Canada with other Black diaspora locations and movements as one way of connecting Tubman's legacies of survival, freedom, and cultural expression to ongoing Black diasporic movement.

However, in situating Canada firmly within this complex diasporic network, we might also read this work as one response to earlier discursive mappings of the Black Atlantic that have sometimes elided Canada's contributions to and space within these networks. The publication of Paul Gilroy's landmark text *The Black Atlantic*, for instance, sparked a debate in Black Canadian studies about the ways and moments in which Canada can go missing from representations and theorizations of Black diasporas.[10] These debates have been summarized in Winfried Siemerling's book *The Black Atlantic Reconsidered*.[11] Our collection is thus directed specifically at articulating a new terrain for Tubman in relation to the Black Atlantic archive. This also provides a useful opportunity to trace key ways in which Tubman's historical legacies are also very much tied to geographical politics, economies, and cultures, even while acknowledging the wider circulation and significance of Tubman. In thinking about the multiple legacies of Tubman, this work also raises the question of what further lessons might Tubman's life hold for the political possibilities of freedom in Canada where questions of decolonization, justice, and freedom are pressing ongoing concerns. The essays in the volume disrupt and challenge longstanding narratives of Canadian freedom and utopic kindness and, instead, comment on the unfinished work of freedom in our present moment.

ON THE NON-LINEARITY OF LEGACY

Questions surrounding how to access or trace non-white legacies haunt us in the wake of the genocidal violence on Indigenous lands that was the founding of colonial North America. The deep wounds of this violence remain a lasting trauma of colonization. Legacy in Black histories is no less complex, especially when we consider how those histories have been so strangely shaped and erased by the theft of people for enslavement, the industries of colonialism, neocolonialism, and capitalism in overlapping ways. Indeed, as Hortense Spillers poignantly reminds us in her essay, "Mama's Baby, Papa's Maybe: An American Grammar Book," under the conditions of genocide, enslavement, and unfreedom central to the making of the Americas and, indeed, Canada, "the *vertical* transfer of a bloodline, of a patronymic, of titles and entitlements, of real estate and the prerogatives of 'cold cash,' from fathers to sons ... becomes the mythically revered privilege of a free and freed community" (74).[12] For those that are unfree (or in the case of Indigenous people, whose family histories belie the origin stories of colonizers) continuous lines of history, and thus inheritance and entitlement under law, are rendered more than uncertain. Where rights and relations are narrativized as visible emplacement, one's experience in and contributions to history are confounded or even rendered impossible. Spillers's work is marked by the search for a grammar through which to narrate this structure of relations while also revealing and unsettling the logics of "*vertical* transfer of a bloodline, of a patronymic, of titles and entitlements" or what she further terms "the press of a patronymic, patrifocal, patrilineal and patriarchal order."[13]

We might further suggest that it proves useful to understand Tubman's own dispersal, her transnational, interdisciplinary public meaningfulness, as a kind of multiplying of kinship and legacy that we might examine through Spillers's suggestive concept of "*feeling* of kinship" [emphasis in original] – a phrase that brings into mind a notion of legacy in terms of affiliation as opposed to filiation.[14] The mode of relation we foreground can already be observed in Canadian literature as involving Tubman. For example, in M. NourbeSe Philip's young adult novel *Harriet's Daughter*, the main character, a young Black girl in Canada named Margaret, renames herself Harriet, resolutely claiming, "I want a name that means something – important."[15] Her claiming of this right to name herself is positioned in explicit terms as a usurping of the patriarchal order or what we might understand in Spillers's work as the patronymic prerogative. The terms of her resistance and the simultaneous inscription of "the press of a patronymic, patrifocal, patrilineal and patriarchal order"[16] is foregrounded when she declares, as she contemplates the name she would like to have, "I'm sure HE would never let me."[17] This patronymic imperative is also inscribed by NourbeSe Philip in the account of Margaret's birth where we are explicitly told that, despite her mother's preference for another name, her father, "Cuthbert wanted Margaret, his mother's name."[18]

In strategizing her journey towards her own name or what we might frame in Spillers's grammar as an act of "claiming the monstrosity" of "a female with the potential to 'name,'"[19] Margaret decides that she will go "to the library and look up famous women to see what their names were."[20] In this turn to history she finds and situates herself in Harriet Tubman's legacy. In reflecting on Tubman and her significance, she tells the reader,

> She had to take care of people: babies, children, men and women – she had to bring them all the way up to Canada, and not get caught …
> I thought Harriet, Harriet Tubman … again I thought of changing my name to one that meant something – like Harriet. Harriet Tubman was brave and strong and she was black like me. I think it was the first time I thought of wanting to be called Harriet – I wanted to *be* Harriet.[21]

Philip's writing importantly allows us to think about legacy and relation beyond bloodlines. Her writing of Tubman not only pays attention to her revolutionary praxis of self-possession but also foregrounds a radical praxis of communal care. This also inspires Margaret's desire to *be* Harriet. Here the temporal logics of genealogical lineage are also revised to create a more capacious and non-linear relational structure that opens up different terms and modes of identification. Margaret's desire illustrates her sense of belonging to a kind or kinship of women in history that Tubman's existence continues to mark. Additionally, if we understand the patronymic order, in terms of the family name, as signifying "belonging," the claiming of the name Harriet, in this instance, becomes understood through a notion of longing to *be*. This is a rearrangement of the grammar and terms of relation. Desire rather than blood becomes the defining terms of intimacy. Spillers's concept of "*feeling* of kinship" is arguably performed in this moment. Margaret's reading of Harriet Tubman outside the straightforward chronological framework of historical linearity and her articulated transformative desire of wanting "to be Harriet" also provides a grammatical tense for thinking about the future in relation to legacies. While she locates her present Black-girl self in relation to the past, she also makes evident a wilful construction of futures that is expressed in the verb tense "to be."

In this way we might also understand the concept of historical memory, used in our title, as being not just about the past but also about the future. What we attend to in this volume is not just a remembering or a citation of the past but rather an attention to how this past might shape our present and future in more radical ways. Katherine McKittrick talks of the significance of NourbeSe Philip's work and its remembering and recalling of Tubman's legacy in this way in her essay "Freedom is a Secret': The Future Usability of the Underground," which is part of a critical genealogy of thought in response to Philip's novel Harriet's Daughter. In her discussion, McKittrick raises important questions (some of which are taken up by contributors to this volume) about how the narrative of the Underground Railroad has been utilized in the construction and consolidation of imaginings of Canada as "a finished emancipatory location" and the attendant discourses of "Canadian helpfulness, generosity and adorable impartiality."[22] McKittrick and others like Afua Cooper and Adrienne Shadd have challenged this myth highlighting the ways in which this not only erases histories of enslavement in Canada but also, importantly, delegitimizes ongoing freedom work and decolonization necessary in this time and space.[23] McKittrick also reads Philip's text as directly challenging this narrative in that it "refuses a unitary, linear or nationalist celebratory story."[24] Historical memory then is not to be understood in terms of a linear or genealogical chronology. Instead, she proposes that "Philip reminds us, there is no such thing as a 'last safe house,' for this linear progression towards liberatory finality refuses to attend to ongoing post-slave intercultural inequalities."[25] Historical memory is about remembering how to plot escape from the still "plantation time" of the present.[26]

However, McKittrick does more than insist on recalling legacies of struggle into the present. She writes of the future as a site of decolonial possibility and necessity. Her concept of "future usability" points towards "the ontological and psychic work we need to attend to in order to reimagine the livability" of the spaces we inhabit.[27] In locating the usability of these histories not just in relation to a present that is still "a location of continuing racisms"[28] and capitalist exploitations but also to the future, the idea of "future usability" marks a continued imagining and enactment of resistance and strategizing liberatory futures.[29] In thinking with McKittrick's work, we hope the freedom histories explored in this book might also function as "roadmaps" towards other kinds of futures.

Harriet's Legacies: A Road Map

We would argue for reading this book as an interdisciplinary and intergenerational volume. The contributors to this volume draw on the past and engage the question of Black intergenerationality and connectivity in a number of ways. They connect to and reflect on Harriet Tubman's life, work, and influence but they also each engage more generally with the question of legacy. This can be seen not just in relation to the topics they discuss but also in relation to their politics of citation, which serves as one way in which they situate themselves in the legacy of Black studies and cultural production and enact connections to a disparate field of discourse across history, film, literature, museum studies, and poetry. While we connect the work in this volume to the pioneering work of many Black scholars and artists, we also want to think about how the pieces collected here are related to each other. Indeed, alongside the politics of citation as a practice of legacy, we also want to think through a politics of relationality that operates among the pieces in this volume.

I. ON THE LEGACIES OF RADICAL MOBILITY

We turn now to our contributors and how their work relates to our exploration in this text of various concepts of legacy. In our opening section we use the concept of "legacies of radical mobility" as one way of organizing and thinking through works that describe the politics and practice of flight to freedom to which Tubman dedicated her life. Radical mobility might be understood as resistance to modes of unfreedom. It is radical because it defies the surveillance and enclosing strategies of power. While freedom might in fact name one desired legacy or outcome of radical mobility, it is not the singular or automatic outcome of flight, least of all flight to Canada, which has its own history of slavery and ongoing racism. Instead, in the following works, flight might also mean entry into an unsettled and continuing state of unfreedom negotiated in relation to ongoing practices of self-possession as resistance.

In the opening essay of this collection, Karolyn Smardz Frost discusses fugitive slave flight. Her discussion focuses on the Cataract Hotel in Niagara as a site through which we can map a history of flight across the Canadian-American border. Using borderland theory, Smardz Frost examines how "the Niagara border was an increasingly well-traveled site of Black transnationalism." While her essay offers us narratives of escape, it also charts the border as a tense and tenuous site of possibilities for freedom that might be at once possible but also foreclosed.

George Elliott Clarke's contribution to this volume is a long suite of poems from his project *Canticles*. In these "Meditations on Slavery and Imperialism" his vision of radical mobility shows parts of a system, highlighting connectedness but also profound disconnectedness. Herein, there is mobility for those who rise in wealth via slavery and those whose bodies are moved and abased to property and thus require radical tools to mobilize against imperial oppression. The economic enchantments portrayed have the historic cadence of white complaint in verse, as references to Elliott, Dante, Homer, and other canonized voices float in lines that bare power obsessed with itself in the midst of "*Time*" building.

Nele Sawallisch's work also examines questions of flight through her attention to the genre of the slave narrative. Taking the passage of the Fugitive Slave Law (FSL) of 1850 as part of the social context for her discussion, Sawallisch examines fugitivity as textual subject but also examines the figure of Thomas Smallwood as a fugitive narrator in his own text. Sawallisch's discussion is also interesting for its use of the concept of "radical legacies" which serves as one means for examining the complex, political alliances, identifications, and literary influences that shaped nineteenth-century Black Canada. In particular, she examines connections between Thomas Smallwood, David Walker, and Rev. Richard Allen, tracing a radical line of relation and influence which offers one contribution to the sprawling, complex outline of Black legacies and relations offered in this text.

While Sawallisch's discussion maps a masculine line and literary influence, Afua Cooper refocuses on a maternal line and on questions of motherhood for enslaved women and those engaged in fugitive flight. In one way, we might read her essay as attending to the condition that Spillers narrates in which the structures of Black family relation are constantly imperilled in the context of slave society. Her essay recounts the story of Ann Maria Jackson, a Black woman who fled slavery with her seven surviving children. Cooper reads Jackson's attempt at keeping her children together, through and while engaging in fugitive flight as a radical act and a refusal of this condition of the disruption of lineage. Yet we might also note the methodological challenge that Cooper offers to historians to engage with the problem of intergenerationality in the historiography of slavery.

Julie Crooks's discussion of photographic archives as sites of memory offers a meaningful discussion of the cultural work of art and its role in archiving Black lives. Crooks's chapter "*Free* Black North: Photography and Transnational Identities in Nineteenth-Century Southern Ontario" employs the concept of fugitivity as a means of analyzing historical photography. In her use of this concept (often theorized in relation to flight and diasporic

remaking) to examine photography, tensions between movement and stillness as registers of Black diasporic experience and histories are brought
into focus. Crooks also examines fugitivity in terms of "movement in and
out of the frame."[30] This becomes particularly significant in her examination of how these photographs survived, passed down to the present through
private family collections. The tensions between private archives and public
memory are also meaningfully explored in her examination of the curation
of these images as part of the exhibition *Free* Black North at the Art Gallery
of Ontario in 2017.

In the final essay from "Legacies of Radical Mobility," Carole Lynn
Stewart engages with the concept of cosmopolitan mobility, bringing
together a focus on "transnational and cosmopolitan civil societies and
networks" with ideas and narratives of mobility. Her essay challenges
utopian narratives of Canada. Stewart supports Nancy Kang's contention
that "the status of Canada West as a permanent home or 'promised land'
is often propagandistic."[31] Using this as a point of departure she explores
the tensions and mobilities that marked the narrative of agitator and abolitionist William Wells Brown and his refusal to settle in Ontario.

The background to all of these works is the practice of slavery and the slave
laws as legislation. This formed basis of nation-building as well as impacted
the narratives and experiences of Black individuals. These essays and poems
all offer a peek into the contemporary world of Tubman and examine the
complex formations of collectivities and communities that surrounded and
were part of Tubman's life. These chapters also, in several instances, track
the stories of particular individuals, always with an eye towards the social
possibilities, relations, and networks in which they participated and were
invested. In doing so, they each offer a kind of methodology for engaging the
historical world and narrative of Tubman relationally. These narratives
demonstrate a refusal to accept colonial practices of emplacement. They map
radical practices of flight and relation that challenge the law.

2. TRANSNATIONAL POETICS OF SPACE MAKING

In the second section of our book the language of roadmaps offers a useful
metaphor for connectedness but also for fugitivity and transnational praxis
in accounting for the legacies of Tubman. Instead of the rooted image of
the family tree, the image of the roadmap emphasizes both relation and
movement. Indeed, the relational lines between topics and works in this
book are not just intergenerational, they are also transnational. In thinking
about histories and representations of Tubman, we note the ways in which

she has been primarily claimed in and by African American studies. Her time in Canada needs to be better accounted for and could serve to complicate the discourses about Black mobility and histories. The papers in section 2 chart what we term as a "transnational poetics of space making." This includes, but also importantly exceeds, Tubman.

There is irony to the fierce embracing of Tubman as "American." In "Before the Bricks and Mortar: The Grassroots Development of the Harriet Tubman Underground Railroad National Monument," dann j. Broyld and Shaun Winton continue to challenge the imagining of Tubman in easy terms as a heroic "American" figure. Broyld and Winton pose the question "who has memorialized Tubman and why" and outline some of the reasons why Tubman must be understood as a transnational figure. They also note how a grassroots historical methodology might challenge grand national narratives, offering a layered understanding of the ongoing processes of memory involved in monuments and memorials. The focus on Tubman calls attention to the kind of interrelated thinking necessary to make sense of parts of Black history in North America, which have been scattered.

Tubman also pushes us to think about modes of Black mobility in different terms and in ways that account for gendered labour and movement in Black diasporic formations. In focusing on Tubman as central to imagining Black Canadian diasporic formation and Black life in Canada, we also hope to move from inscribing the chronotope of the ship as the dominant trope of Black diasporicity to discussing the movement of physical bodies that have had to cross actual borders. This attention to bodily and embodied mobility recalls the histories of maroon flight as important to Black diasporas and foregrounds not just oceanic movement but also flight and movement in relation to land.

Alexis Pauline Gumbs's contribution to this volume imagines and attends to embodied and "domestic diasporicity" in Black Atlantic life.[32] When Gumbs writes in "M is for Migrant" that "they say she carried a root in her pocket. a root in her pocket everyday," the root is not symbolic of the rooted narrative of identity that Édouard Glissant and others critique, but rather it functions simultaneously as a symbol of displacement and groundedness, of uprooting and survival.[33] We might also note Gumbs's attention to dirt and to ground as an attempt to honour a history of landed labour (as part of diasporic making) linked to the soil. Like the protagonist in M. NourbeSe Philip's *Harriet's Daughter*, Gumbs situates herself in a line of women thinkers and poets including M. Jacqui Alexander and Lucille Clifton, allowing us to imagine a complex genealogical line of relation that is non-linear, dispersed, and transnational (in this instance connected to Atlanta, Durham, Toronto, and Tobago).

Creative and critical works in section 2 focus on maps. They each invite attention to maps as metaphors but also importantly maps as material archives that signify and are about place and space making. They also each challenge the coloniality of cartography in their mappings of Black geographies. Kaie Kellough offers a hybrid of concrete and prose poetry that graph fugitive flight patterns with contemplations on what it means to occupy an indeterminate space as a body in motion. If Kellough begins with tracing maps of the Underground Railroad, these are in turn overlaid with maps that visibly chart coordinates of Jamaica, Cuba, Haiti, Cairo, Montreal. This recalls the Underground Railroad in meaningful relation to wider contexts and circuits of Black Atlantic geographies. In this way we can read his work in relation to the ongoing dialogues about Black Canada's place in Gilroy's Black Atlantic framework. Black Canada is recalled not just through the Underground Railroad but also the histories of Black Montreal.[34] However, Kellough's maps also invite us to meditate on time as well as space when he says, "The pattern doubles back on itself, it forgets or abandons parts of its design and has to return for them, and it is never complete." One legacy of the radical mobility mobilized by Tubman and others then might be an ongoing practice and experience of mobility and displacement for their descendants.

Nalini Mohabir also explores mapping and maps in her essay on political mapping in *Map to the Door of No Return*, titled, "Dionne Brand, Mapmaker." While scholarship on Brand's text has tended to engage with discourses of mapping in metaphorical terms, Mohabir in fact turns to the historical study of maps and engages with cataloguing the kinds of maps used in the text. Mohabir writes,

Black geographic knowledge is embedded in the concept "I write of the earth;" it is simultaneously a reminder of everyday directions and landmarks (e.g., "turn left at the mango tree") as well as profound flights (e.g. an ascendant north star). Furthermore, Black geographies cannot exist outside of history.

Like Gumbs, Mohabir highlights the connection of body to earth. Mapping, in this way, becomes part of a historic tracing of the complex and unsettled relationship between place, memory, stories, and embodiment. For Mohabir maps are not just "practical tools" they represent a potential archive for Black cultural memory of movement. In these regards, Mohabir's intervention, which literalizes mapping instead of only considering the metaphoric charge of maps in Brands work, represents a useful addition to the body of scholarship on Brand's writing while simultaneously raising important questions about how to think about mapping in relationship to Black Canadian geographies.

In his paper, "From Site to Sound and Film: Critical Black Canadian Memory Culture and Sylvia D. Hamilton's *The Little Black School House*," Winfried Siemerling takes up Sylvia D. Hamilton's documentary film *The Little Black School House* which examines the often forgotten history of segregated schools in Canada. Examining the film's structure and aesthetics, Siemerling notes how "*The Little Black School House* fittingly uses a brightly-coloured school bus as a kind of visual *leitmotif* that signals a communal journey serving to connect the past with the present." In his focus on the school bus as central to the film, tropes of the road, roadmaps, and of journeying, already signalled as important ones in this volume, recur. But this also becomes explicitly linked with history, temporality, and intergenerational memory. For example, Siemerling tells us how the 2006 journey which is documented (after a fire destroyed Hamilton's previous footage) is a restaging of a previous journey organized by Hamilton's mother when she secured "a bus (free of charge) when the members of a 1990 reunion of the Association of Retired Teachers of Segregated Schools Nova Scotia wanted to take a tour of their former schools." This information serves as a reminder that it wasn't "the first time" (to reference Alice Walker)[35] and functions to "serialize the event and its affect and also to elongate its temporality to stretch its time along the line of an unfolding series of moments of bearing witness."[36] Siemerling's examination of Hamilton's film in the context of this volume also reminds us of the significance of Nova Scotia to imaginings and narratives of Black Canadian history.

3. STRATEGIZING SURVIVAL AND RETHINKING COLONIAL ORDERING

The critical concern with the geographies of Black Canada returns in section three and also becomes linked with ideas of art and archives as themselves ways of mapping and making Black Canadian histories, legacies, and presence. We also note how the pieces in section 3 all draw on and engage a range of cultural texts and historical sources including, photography, film, monuments, poetry, plays among others. This is also true of the wider volume, which is likewise marked by a complex engagement with and inscription of a range of forms as sites of memory but also sites of innovation.

Natasha Henry explores the question and politics of Black public memory in her essay, "We Were Here: Reclaiming African Canadian History Through

Heritage Plaques." Henry argues that "as locations of public memory, plaqued historic sites allow visitors to interact with other members of the public and with archival information in front of the public out, in the open." This shared space, Henry argues, enables a specific kind of "unsettling" of a sense of the present in its political, geographic, and economic stability. Henry points out a collective public forgetting of Black presence by what we call Canada. The forgetting of a history of slavery in Canada necessarily erases the people who were here alongside the practices that state narratives may desire to forget. Henry argues that plaques do more than mark places, they also puncture the continuity of historical consciousness, creating an opportunity to think across narratives and counter-narratives.

Two works in this section address canonicity and problematize Shakespeare's legacy. Sonnet L'Abbé supplies an explanation of her practice, in which she innovates a new genre of poetry that returns to canonized works and fills them with new perspective. L'Abbé enacts a practice of remaking that revises Shakespeare's poetic archive through a transgressive overwriting of the sonnets. L'Abbé's rewritings challenge colonial order and power. They interrupt the performance of colonial ordering that might be read in the sonnet as a form. Both form and content of the text are revised. In the poems included here, canonized sonnets are overwritten with political critique about Black lives. The poems serve as texts that contain the colonial artworks inside texts that speak to the legacies of colonial history. In effect, Sonnet writes over Shakespeare, amplifying her postcolonial response, without releasing the other author's text from her testimony. The colonial script remains implicated in the ongoing structures of empire that continue to define our existence in later modernity. These pieces offer a meaningful exploration of the question of the Black body's relationship to colonial archives while also exploring the ongoing legacies of these archives. The pieces in this section all participate in a larger debate about public erasures and public memory that raises keen questions about the state of collective memory regarding Blackness in the public sphere in Canada.

Pilar Cuder-Domínguez's essay "Mobilizing the Bard: Joseph Jomo Pierre's *Shakespeare's Nigga* (2013)" describes the disruption and remaking of patriarchal and colonial legacies that Joseph Jomo Pierre's text performs in its attempt to think about race through Shakespeare's archive. Cuder-Domínguez argues that Joseph Jomo Pierre's *Shakespeare's Nigga* does not just appropriate Shakespeare's work but uses it as an archive to enact "specific realignments of race, power, and gender." This renegotiation of gender and power makes legible the "performance of two diverse and competing types of Black masculinities." Cuder-Domínguez's exploration of the tensions around race and masculinity are also positioned against Sylvia Wynter's contention that the Black woman is often obliterated in canonized literature.

The idea of strategizing survival names the long process of surviving colonialism which is addressed most directly in "Building Black and Indigenous Alliances for HIV Prevention and Health Promotion," where authors Wilson, Flicker, and Restoule note a history of collaborative resistance in the face of a long history of colonial oppression and genocide and call for a practice of community between Black and Indigenous peoples as one way of addressing HIV as crisis in these communities. They note how solidarities across these lines of relation can intervene in ongoing (neo)colonial state practices of death and they address how colonialism has produced tensions between Black and Indigenous communities. In their work, collaboration and community making for survival is not just thematized, it is also engaged as practice. We note their collaborative authorship as a model of producing work that is interdisciplinary and communally oriented.

In her essay "Blood is a politic of place-making: Blackness, Queerness and the Construction of the Donor," OmiSoore H. Dryden examines state practices of anti-Blackness in Canada through a study of Canadian Blood Services. Rather than offering a narrative of blood and belonging as synonymous or in which blood functions to mark belonging, Dryden traces a long colonial project in which blood has functioned to exclude and mark the limits of national belonging. She considers how this long history is re-inscribed in contemporary discourses and exclusions of the Canadian Blood Services in their blood donation policies. Her work highlights and interrogates the exclusionary practices of Canadian Blood Services as a way of charting how belonging is imagined and how the Canadian nation continues to be constructed as white, heteronormative, and exclusionary in law, policy, and practices. These exclusionary practices find articulation in the construction of the Black queer donor. According to Dryden, "Black people in Canada, including Black queers, continue to be in peril as a result of continued correlations between the abject and 'the black.'"

4. CREATION IS LEGACY: CREATIVITY AND FUTURES

Makeda Silvera writes in her essay "The Story of Sister Vision: Black Women and Women of Colour Press: We Had to Fight, Cuss and Kick Every Inch of the Way" about the motivations that made the work by Sister Vision Press on queer, Black, Indigenous, and multicultural writing in Canada historically significant and possible. Particularly useful to note is Silvera's outlining of the conditions of underrepresentation which continue to mark racialized writers and their writing in Canada. Her essay offers a detailed and inspiring narrative useful to scholars of Black voices in Canadian publishing as well as writers and future publishers. Silvera outlines, through a process of cataloguing, the interventions that Sister Vision made possible. But we also note in her title the emphasis on struggle as a condition of its making.

Many of the thinkers in this section emphasize orality and the power of the individual voice even as they map alternative traditions. In situating these discussions of creative practices rooted in Black community alongside Silvera's discussion of publishing queer Black, and Indigenous voices we aim to call attention to the rich diversity and legacies of Black literatures in Canada. Each of these essays and interviews call attention to the role of performance, poetry, and storytelling to Black literary traditions in Canada and in the wider diaspora.

Two interviews appear in this section. We use the mode of interviewing here as itself a kind of knowledge production that makes visible strategies of collaboration and thinking with each other. Its dialogic mode might be read as one methodology of "strategizing." This concern with collaborative thinking is also evident in the content of the discussion. "Political Acts: Dub and the Right to Exist" is a conversation between the "godmother of dub poetry" Lillian Allen and this volume's editors, Natalee Caple and Ronald Cummings. In this dialogue Allen reflects on and contextualizes her long career as a poet, teacher, administrator, and activist. Allen discusses her roles in multiple movements and how the dub poetry movement existed "with movements about equality, justice, the anti-apartheid movement, Black liberation movement, Black power, civil rights, women's movement, feminist movement, [and] union movement." The discussion ranges across her published work, her community activism, and the personal choices she made as a mother and as a writer. Allen also articulates a pedagogy of care for her students as whole people, as well as some of her hopes for future transformation in our university and government institutions.

In an extended interview with Ronald Cummings d'bi.young anitafrika talks about the challenges and possibilities of creative community. While d'bi.young anitafrika begins with examining the influence of her mother, she also reveals and reflects on an artistic community that is dispersed, international, and diasporic. She enacts a practice of listing names – what we might think of as a roll call – that attempts to gather a range of influences and map lines of connection and influence on her practice. She also examines how her work speaks to and about different communities, past and present, while also examining possibilities of futures by thinking about the work of mentorship as well as her own practice of mothering.

Andrea Thompson's critical creative essay, "Spoken Word: A Signifying Gesture Towards Possibility," offers one history of the development of spoken-word and slam poetry in Canada. Like Silvera and Allen, Thompson points to the institutional conditions that have made modes of creative production that exist outside of traditional institutions challenging. Yet she is keen to gesture to how those poetries connect to a long history of orality, drawing on storytelling traditions and structures. Thompson reminds us that "The First People of this land had deeply rooted traditions of orature, expressed through stories and myths passed down through generations." In doing so, Thompson's work, like Silvera's, calls attention to the sites of convergence, collaboration, and resistance to colonial and neocolonial thought and practices shared between Black and Indigenous people in this land. The form of Thompson's essay is also important to note. It is organized through a structure of call and response that functions to stage a dialogue with the work of Toni Morrison. She thereby demonstrates another way in which we might inhabit legacy – in responsive terms.

In our final section we return to the notion of legacy not only as inheritance but also as a politic of making or what Klyde Broox describes in terms of "creation." Klyde Broox provides a hybrid essay/performance text that, likewise, turns to the question of Black futures, situating that future as having been foreshadowed by the past. Broox asks us to think about the history of moments of creative flourishing in relationship to a violent past and present. For example, while raising questions about what our current moment might produce, he turns to the dub poetry revolution of the 1970s as already experimenting with modes of sound and textual production that were futuristic or rather invested in technological innovation while reinvigorating the "technology of the voice." Broox's formal experimentation with what he calls "performance writing" and his production of a "performance essay" or "textimony" is one of the rich innovations of this piece. It's a metatextual reflection that is rich and layered in conceptual and textual details.

Throughout this anthology we move across genre boundaries, bringing together creative works, interviews with artists and educators, and interdisciplinary scholarship to illustrate the enormous breadth of registers to Tubman's influence. However, we also engage this collective gathering in the spirit of breaking down hierarchies of research and work that goes on inside and outside of institutions. We do this in the hopes of reaching local, national, academic, and general readers. But we also seek to demonstrate how resistance is sometimes embodied in creative ways when access to institutional recognition is not forthcoming. We therefore bring together emerging and established scholars with creative artists as equal thinkers about Tubman's legacies, understanding that one of Tubman's legacies was the hand-to-hand support of peoples inside and outside of belonging in a collective striving for multiple freedoms.

This praxis of Black intergenerationality and connectivity is discussed and performed in different ways by the works in this volume. This book collects works that seek to reflect on and represent ongoing practices of strategizing freedom in the face of systemic oppression, a process described by Rinaldo Walcott as "the long Emancipation," in which particular rights were granted racialized subjects but without the state production or recognition of full citizenship or freedoms.[37] This book focuses a study of that ongoing struggle for liberation by returning to the figure of Tubman to reflect on her freedom work, its continuing significance, and on her various legacies. The works collected here show how Tubman represents a transnational challenge to the legal, governmental, and social regulation of Black bodies in Canada historically, but they also connect this challenge to ongoing state policing and other practices of the Canadian state. These unfreedoms continue into the present with practices like carding, which we might read as a legacy, if not a continuation of the cultures of policing, including anti-Black violence by police, legitimated by the Fugitive Slave Laws of the nineteenth century, discussed and critiqued in this volume by Nele Sawallisch, Karolyn Smardz Frost, and Afua Cooper. All of the works included here engage and grapple with the past, present, and future as sites of insecurity. The legacies of Harriet Tubman, we suggest, must be seen at once as ongoing, collective practices of antiracism and freedom seeking. Harriet Tubman herself continues to stand as a transnational symbol around which contemporary theorizing of resistance, community, and survival might be possible.

NOTES

1 Adrienne Shadd, Afua Cooper, and Karolyn Smardz Frost, *The Underground Railroad: Next Stop Toronto!* (Toronto: National Heritage Books, 2002).

2 There are two statues of Tubman in St Catharines: the bust on a pedestal at the BME Chapel and a full-length statue of her sitting with a book in her hands in front of Harriet Tubman Public School. The stone bust was vandalized in 2021. A public fundraiser enabled the remaking of the bust by the original

artist in bronze. Both are by sculptor Frank Rekrut. The latter created some local discussion about appropriate representation as Tubman could not read.

3 This quote on pedestal bearing the 2010 bust of Tubman by Rekrut is most likely a version of a quote from Sarah H. Bradford's 1868 book, *Scenes in the Life of Harriet Tubman*. In the 2018 e-book it appears on page 10: "[a]fter the passage of the Fugitive Slave law, she said, 'I wouldn't trust Uncle Sam wid my people no longer; I brought 'em all clear off to Canada.'" Sarah H. Bradford, *Scenes in the Life of Harriet Tubman* (Praha, Czech Republic: Madison & Adams, 2018), Kindle edition.

4 Janell Hobson, "Pictorial Manifestations: On a Younger Harriet Tubman," *Black Perspectives*, 15 January 2017, https://www.aaihs.org/pictorial-manifestations-on-a-younger-harriet-tubman.

5 Ibid.

6 Ibid.

7 *Harriet*, directed by Kasi Lemmons (2019; Beijing, China: Perfect World Pictures), DVD.

8 Naomi Klein, *The Shock Doctrine: The Rise of Disaster Capitalism* (Toronto: Vintage Canada, 2008).

9 Phanuel Antwi, "Dub Poetry as Black Atlantic Body-Archive," *Small Axe: A Caribbean Journal of Criticism* 19, no. 3 (48) (2015): 65–83.

10 Paul Gilroy, *The Black Atlantic: Modernity and Double Consciousness* (Cambridge, MA: Harvard University Press, 1993).

11 Winfried Siemerling, *The Black Atlantic Reconsidered* (Montreal and Kingston: McGill-Queen's University Press, 2015).

12 Hortense J. Spillers, "Mama's Baby, Papa's Maybe: An American Grammar Book," *Diacritics* 17, no. 2 (Summer 1987): 64–81.

13 Ibid., 74.

14 Ibid, 76.

15 M. NourbeSe Philip, *Harriet's Daughter* (Oxford: Heinemann, 1988), 26.

16 Spillers, "Mama's Baby, Papa's Maybe," 74.

17 Philip, *Harriet's Daughter*, 27.

18 Ibid., 22.

19 Spillers, "Mama's Baby, Papa's Maybe," 80.

20 Philip, *Harriet's Daughter*, 27.

21 Ibid., 37.

22 Ibid.

23 Katherine McKittrick, "Freedom is a Secret: The Future Usability of the Underground," in *Black Geographies and the Politics of Place*, ed. Katherine McKittrick and Clyde Woods (Toronto, ON: Between the Lines Press; Cambridge, MA: South End Press, 2007), 99. In addition to McKittrick's essay

"Freedom is a Secret," see Adrienne Shadd, "The Lord seemed to say 'Go': Women and the Underground Railroad Movement," in *We're Rooted Here and They Can't Pull Us Up: Essays in African Canadian Women's History*, ed. Peggy Bristow (Toronto: University of Toronto Press, 1994), 41–68; and Shadd, Cooper, and Smardz Frost, *The Underground Railroad*.

24 McKittrick, "Freedom is a Secret," 107.

25 Ibid., 110–11.

26 For a discussion of "plantation time" see Katherine McKittrick's "Plantation Futures," *Small Axe* 17, no. 3 (2013): 1–15.

27 McKittrick, "Freedom is a Secret," 111.

28 Ibid., 105.

29 Ibid., 110.

30 Fred Moten, "The Case of Blackness," *Criticism* 50, no. 2 (2008): 179.

31 Nancy Kang, "'As If I Had Entered a Paradise': Fugitive Slave Narratives and Cross-Border Literary History," *African American Review* 39, no. 3 (Fall 2005): 431–57.

32 For a discussion of domestic labour and diasporic life see Alexis Pauline Gumbs's essay "Dionne Brand: A Poetics of Diasporic Domestic Radicalism," in *The Routledge Companion to Anglophone Caribbean Studies*, ed. Michael Bucknor and Alison Donnell (London and New York: Routledge, 2011).

33 Édouard Glissant, *Poetics Of Relation* (Ann Arbor: University of Michigan Press, 1997).

34 See Afua Cooper, *The Hanging of Angelique* (Toronto: Harper Collins, 2006) and David Austin, *Fear of a Black Nation* (Toronto: Between the Lines, 2013).

35 Alice Walker, *In Search of Our Mother's Gardens* (New York: Harcourt, Brace, Jovanovich, 1983), xi.

36 Ian Baucom, *Specters of the Atlantic* (Durham, NC: Duke University Press, 2005),

37 Rinaldo Walcott, *The Long Emancipation: Moving Towards Black Freedom* (Durham, NC: Duke University Press, 2021).

SECTION ONE

On the Legacies of Radical Mobility

The Cataract House Hotel: Underground to Canada through the Niagara River Borderlands

Karolyn Smardz Frost

The 4 August 1841 issue of the New Orleans *Daily Picayune* included a letter to the editor describing the flight of a fourteen-year-old maidservant from the famed Cataract House hotel at Niagara Falls, New York. The author was James S. Evans, a prosperous hat merchant with a shop at 10 Rue Chartres. He and his wife had taken their enslaved nursemaid along on vacation with them to care for their young family. Sent to the hotel kitchens to acquire milk for the Evans baby, the young woman never returned.

Evans and some of his fellow hotel guests eventually located her, sequestered in a private home at the Canadian village of "Niagara" (Niagara-on-the-Lake) about twelve miles below the falls. Arriving at this "stronghold of Negroes," he and his supporters were confronted by an angry crowd who refused to let Evans communicate with his former "servant." Eventually the furious slaveholder and his friends crossed back to the American side of the river. The Evans family returned to New Orleans, but they did so without their maid.[1]

In his letter, James S. Evans accused the Cataract House staff of "enticing" the woman to run away and warned fellow slave owners that the hotel's owners had been complicit in her escape:

> The proprietors of the Cataract House keep in their employ, as servants, a set of free negroes, many of whom have wives and relatives in Canada, and they have an organized plan of taking off all slaves that come to the house. The Mesers. Whitney [*sic*] keep these fellows

in their employ, knowing them to be engaged in this business; therefore it behooves all Southern people traveling North to avoid the Cataract House at the Falls of Niagara.[2]

Evans's story was corroborated by a reporter for the *New York Herald*, who added, "Southern gentlemen who take their servants with them, should be careful where they lodge – and hotel keepers, who have colored persons for servants, should be careful of their inmates."[3] The *Madison County Abolitionist* took a different view. The editor assumed that the owners of the Cataract House had indeed been involved in "the poor girl's escape" and suggested that "every Northern man [should] see that they are patronized, by all means, for their consistency in freedom's cause."[4]

The details of this unnamed woman's flight to freedom offer fascinating insight into the mechanisms that facilitated antebellum Black transnationalism along the Niagara frontier. While such cross-border transfers were both illegal and dangerous, and became more so in the years leading up to the Civil War, the significance of the Cataract House as a nexus of Underground Railroad-era activism is well documented.[5] However, it was not the Whitneys but rather the African American staff of their popular hotel who were responsible for operating the highly efficient Underground Railroad station there. Furthermore, James Evans was quite right in suggesting that these anti-slavery-minded workers at that Cataract House depended on the support of African Canadian friends and relatives across the Niagara River for ensuring the successful escape of uncounted numbers of freedom seekers.[6]

This paper discusses African American and African Canadian Black-led Underground Railroad efforts undertaken in the Niagara River borderland. It describes several celebrated escapes orchestrated by Cataract House employees and highlights the leadership of the resourceful John Morrison who, from about 1840 through 1860, served as the hotel's head waiter. Referencing recent advances in borderland studies, it posits that links between Cataract House staff and both individuals and institutions on the other side of the border were crucial to their success. Thus, when the iconic Harriet Tubman traversed the Niagara River into Canada, accompanied by eleven refugees from bondage on her way to her adopted home of St Catharines in December 1851, she was entering a borderland with a long tradition of cross-border cooperation.[7] People of African descent on either side of the Great Lakes Basin had been collaborating for a generation and more to help formerly enslaved African Americans "make free."

Retrospective application of borderland theory to the antebellum era offers a useful lens through which to view the complex network of support for freedom seekers that developed along the Niagara frontier.[8] Borderland theory generally refers to the geopolitical and social construct of "bordered lands" in respect to modern globalization.[9] People living adjacent to major borders such as that dividing Canada from the US, may actually have more in common with each other than they do with their own compatriots residing further inland due to their shared experience of climate, economy, and culture. Residents of the Niagara River borderlands moved easily back and forth between the two adjacent political realities, sharing ties of family, faith, and experience with those on the opposite side of the boundary line.[10]

African Canadians and African Americans in the region also had a collective cause – ensuring that incoming freedom seekers safely reached Queen Victoria's domains. Underground Railroad stations did a lively business within these borderlands, the activities there were fostered by a notably resistant regional Black abolitionist movement. There were several major conventions organized by Black abolitionists within this borderland during the antebellum period. Held at such centres as Buffalo, Geneva, Rochester, and Syracuse on the US side and at Drummondville, Amherstburg, Ancaster, Toronto, and other towns in British Canada, these conventions drew delegates from a broad hinterland on either side of the border.[11]

During the years before the American Civil War, uncounted numbers of formerly enslaved African Americans found their way to the boundary between the US and Canada, a good many of them with little or no assistance.[12] However, crossing over into the British colony was complicated by the fact that Upper Canada (known as Canada West after the Act of Union was proclaimed in 1841) was divided from the United States by water. The Niagara and Detroit Rivers, the Great Lakes, and to the east the St Lawrence River presented formidable obstacles to such refugees. They needed help crossing over into Canada, and so African American and African Canadian communities on the two shores provided services essential to the flight of literally thousands of freedom seekers.[13] Much work remains to be done to identify the management and composition of what is broadly known as the Underground Railroad in the Niagara region, part of what was arguably the greatest social justice movement of nineteenth-century North America. I hope this paper points to some intriguing avenues for future research.[14]

Despite the impediment to their passage presented by the Niagara River and particularly by Niagara Falls, this part of the border was an increasingly well-travelled site of Black transnationalism during the nine decades

between the Revolutionary War and the 1865 passage of the Thirteenth
Amendment to the American Constitution that ended slavery. Small Black
communities had grown up over the years in both American and Canadian
border towns. Local residents included descendants of enslaved men,
women, and children imported to the region by French and British colonial
powers in the early years of European settlement. Slavery existed in colonial
Canada up to the time it was abolished throughout the British Empire by
the 1833 Imperial Act, made effective 1 August 1834. However, Upper
Canada had passed legislation in 1793 preventing further slave importation
and mandating a gradual abolition of the institution itself.[15] Thanks to a
subsequent decision by Upper Canada's Attorney General John Beverley
Robinson, the province's promise of liberty to the formerly enslaved was
confirmed in 1819. He set the precedent by refusing a request from the New
York governor to permit slave catchers to pursue their human prey into
Upper Canada. He wrote,

> whatever may have been the condition of ... Negroes in the Country
> to which they formerly belonged, here they are free – For the enjoy-
> ment of all civil rights consequent to a mere residence in the country
> and among them the right to personal freedom as acknowledged
> and protected by the Laws of England ... [must] be extended to these
> Negroes as well as to others under His Majesty's Government in
> this Province.[16]

This was a highly contested border. The Niagara region saw fighting in
the Revolutionary War, the War of 1812, and again in the 1837 Mackenzie
Rebellion. In each of these conflicts people of African descent served bravely
in the defence of British Canada.[17] Although small numbers of African
Americans had already made their way to Canada, it was American soldiers
fighting in the War of 1812 – or more likely the enslaved servants who
provided battlefield service to Kentucky and Virginia-born officers in the
invasion of Canada – who returned to the South with the news that "in
Canada, coloured men are free," as one song went.[18] Some African American
and African Canadian veterans settled in the Niagara region. There were
also free Black American immigrants who had voluntarily chosen life in
British Canada, including several clergymen and their families. Free African
Americans, they preferred to live under a regime where the legal system was
at least nominally colour blind, even if their neighbours were not. Still,
racism and discrimination remained daily, pernicious facts of life in both
Canada and the northern United States.[19]

The influx of freedom seekers from the United States into Upper Canada began in earnest soon after the end of the War of 1812, although the term "Underground Railroad" was not coined until after steam trains began their journeys across the North American continent in the early 1830s. People living in towns and villages on either side of the Niagara River endangered their own freedom and made substantial personal sacrifices to help freedom seekers fleeing bondage. On US shores they were first concealed and then assisted in making their way over the waters to Canada. In the forefront of such activism at Niagara Falls, New York, were the courageous African American waiters at the Cataract House hotel. On the Canadian side, in turn, their friends and relatives provided newcomers with shelter, nourishment, protection, and what comforts they could afford, until danger of pursuit had passed.

While some settled amongst their benefactors in the Niagara regions, fugitive slaves in imminent danger of recapture were sent on to points of greater safety and with more employment opportunities, such as Toronto or Hamilton. Alternatively, they travelled overland or later by rail to the flourishing agricultural colonies being established at Buxton, Dresden, and elsewhere in the southwestern part of the province.[20] This transborder covert rescue and reception system was managed with great ingenuity both by the fugitives themselves and by those dedicated to helping them achieve liberty. The result was an intricately woven network of borderland collaboration developed over time by African Americans and their Canadian counterparts working together in the cause of freedom.

By the 1840s the Underground Railroad was fully evolved along the Niagara boundary. Indeed, the entire Great Lakes Basin and the associated borderlands had become a passageway to liberty, with multiple crossing points. From Rochester, Buffalo, Lewiston, and smaller ports that lined the American shore, significant numbers traversed Lake Ontario on the sailing vessels and steam ships that made a regular circuit of the lake ports. Freedom seekers travelled thanks to sympathetic captains who carried their frightened, hopeful passengers for reduced fares and often for no fare at all, and with the aid of waiters, barbers, chambermaids, cooks, stokers, and other employees, nearly all of African descent, who worked on the lake boats in sailing season. In about 1848, British military engineer Sir Richard Bonnycastle travelled on one such vessel as far as Lewiston and remarked, "the stewards and waiters are coloured people, clean, neat, and active; and you may give seven pence-halfpenny or a quarter dollar to the man who cleans your boots, or an attentive waiter, if you like; if not, you can keep it, as they are well paid."[21]

The Detroit and Niagara River crossings, with their ferries and many small rivercraft, provided even more immediate and direct access to free soil. Some desperate fugitives swam the Niagara and Detroit Rivers or walked across the latter on the ice in the dead of winter. Transborder railways did not come into operation until the last decade prior to the American Civil War with the opening of the suspension bridge to rail traffic. It was a marvel of engineering, spanning the Niagara Gorge, and the brainchild of William Hamilton Merritt. Originally from Bedford, New York, he moved to St Catharines, Canada West, where he was also the driving force behind the establishment of the Welland Canal. The suspension bridge, completed by German engineer John Augustus Roebling, served first as a foot and carriage bridge starting in 1848 and then as a railroad bridge after 1855, the first of its kind in the world. Interestingly, William Hamilton Merritt was also personally involved in freedom seeker assistance efforts at St Catharines where he made his Canadian home. He sold at a steeply discounted price to the local African Canadian community the land on which Salem Chapel, now a Canadian National Historic Site, was built. This church was attended by Harriet Tubman and dozens of other freedom seekers.[22]

The Cataract House was a huge stone and frame edifice overlooking the Niagara Rapids above the falls and within sight of the opposite Canadian shore. Painted white with crisp green trim and latticed shutters opening out onto airy piazzas, the Cataract with its famously old-fashioned charm exemplified gracious living. Its owners were Parkhurst and Celinda Whitney, who had been among the early founders and promoters of Niagara Falls. Whitney's distinguished service in the War of 1812 had earned him the honorary title of "General," and it was he who operated the first ferry service across the river to Canada. Together with the powerful Porter family who owned most of the land on the American side, the Whitneys worked to improve the prospects of the falls, exploiting both its tremendous water power for manufacturing purposes and its natural beauty as a tourist attraction.[23]

Celinda and Parkhurst Whitney began their careers as Niagara hoteliers with the purchase of the rather humble Eagle Tavern in 1814.[24] Acquiring adjacent properties, they sold off the older log structure in favour of an adjacent three-storey frame building that they had originally purchased as an overflow facility. This became the nucleus of the Cataract House. They constructed a series of four- and five-storey additions over the years, so that by the 1840s, "General" and Mrs Whitney had established theirs as the preeminent hotel on the American side of the river.[25] By the mid-1850s, the hotel was expanding towards the riverfront, with a piazza for lounging,

Figure 1.1 Cataract House hotel from Goat Island in winter, n.d.

several dining areas, a noted taproom, and a spectacular ballroom. After Parkhurst and his wife retired, it was taken over by their son Solon M. Whitney and sons-in-law Dexter Ray Jerauld and James Fullerton Trott. The Cataract House was owned and operated by members of the same family through 1889.[26]

The Cataract House usually received guests only from late April or early May through October and stood on the site until 1945.[27] Over the 120 years of its existence, it hosted people from all parts of the globe including members of European nobility, famous scientists, future American president Abraham Lincoln, Canada's first prime minister John A. Macdonald, Father of Confederation George Brown, renowned Black abolitionist Frederick Douglass, and famous singer Jenny Lind, the latter of whom waxed eloquent about her enjoyment of feeling Niagara's waters rushing over her in the "current baths" in the hotel basement.[28] The Cataract House was in fact noted for its use of water and water power: the waters of the Niagara River were diverted to flush the hotel sewage, operate the great laundries located in the basement, and to fill stocked trout ponds for the entertainment of the anglers amongst the guests. The hotel also boasted the region's first elevator.[29]

Although the 1840 census for Niagara Falls lists only three people of African ancestry working for the Whitneys, the Evans incident and other sources suggest that as early as 1835 the Cataract's dining room was staffed by male waiters of African descent.[30] This was hardly accidental on the hoteliers' part: the tradition of African American service permeated

the North as well as South in antebellum America, and having Black servants
was a means hoteliers consciously employed for making Southern guests
feel more at home. With such familiar and sophisticated service and its
excellent cuisine, the Cataract House attracted a great many Southern guests.
Its expansive porches overlooking the rapids above the American falls and
breezy, comfortable rooms attracted everyone from individuals to entire
extended families, all anxious to escape the oppressive heat and threat of
epidemic disease that characterized summers below the Mason Dixon Line.[31]

Some guests even brought their own enslaved maids and valets when they
came to pass the fashionable "season" at Niagara, as the case of the Evans
family described above demonstrates. New York State had abolished slavery
in 1799 and revised the legislation in 1817, but it was a gradual abolition
law that left large numbers of bondspeople indentured to their former
enslavers. The final abolition of slavery in New York State did not come
until 4 July 1827. However, Southern tourism provided so large a percentage
of the profits at such resorts as Saratoga Springs and Niagara Falls that for
the next fourteen years, enslavers who entered the state could remain
unmolested for up to nine months. In fact, the New York law permitting
travellers to bring their enslaved servants with them was not struck down
until 1841. "As the case of Cecelia Jane Reynolds who fled in 1846 shows,
many slaveholders continued to bring their enslaved "servants" with them
even after that point."[32]

In the first half of the nineteenth century, Black hospitality workers
already were moving to professionalize the field. It is no coincidence that
not only the first but also the second published handbook of instruction for
household service in the United States was produced by African Americans.[33]
Some of the more elaborate customs suggested in such volumes were played
out to perfection at the Cataract House. Headwaiter John Morrison joined
the staff before 1840 and ran the dining room with military precision, as
one fascinated visitor recounted in her 1845 article published in *Godey's
Ladies Book*:

> It was amusing to see the manner in which this troop of well-drilled
> domestics brought in the dessert, and placed it on the table; or rather
> the tables, as there were two very long ones, and a set of waiters
> for each. At a signal from the major-domo (who was stationed at
> the upper end of the room between the tables,) the waiters took up
> the line of march in Indian file, and proceeded 'round with military
> precision, military step, and military faces. They were armed with
> japan trays or servers; each holding a different article.

One man carried all the dessert plates, which, as he passed along, he deposited in their places, slapping them down "with an air." A second had all the knives; a third the forks; a fourth the spoons, each article being put down with an air. Then came the pie-man; then the pudding-man; next the pudding-sauce man; then he of the calves-foot jelly; and he of the blanc-mange; and he of the ice cream – this last being the most popular. There were also some who had been detailed on the almond and raisin and motto secret service. Pine-apple and other fruit men brought up the rear. In this manner the whole dessert was placed on the tables in a very few minutes, and in the most complete order.[34]

Although seasonal in nature, the opportunity to work at the falls was sufficiently financially rewarding to attract skilled employees from throughout the Great Lakes Basin. According to the St. Catharines Journal, "Niagara is an expensive place. The coloured gentleman who does you a trifling service receives a shilling (and nothing less) not because he has earned it but because he is at Niagara!"[35] Some entrepreneurial souls earned an independent living as hack drivers, porters, hucksters, and housekeepers while others provided sewing, laundry, and hairdressing services to tourists. This continued through the end of the century. For instance, Levi A. Thomas of Rochester is listed in the 1891 city directory as a "teamster" at the Cataract House. This was also true on the Canadian side of the border, and the elegant Clifton House hotel begun in 1833 nearly opposite the Cataract also was also staffed predominantly by employees of African descent.[36]

The US census shows that by 1850, there were forty-four African Americans in the town of Niagara, with twenty-eight of them employed at the Cataract House during "the season." All but two of the waiters were listed as either African American or African Canadian.[37] A decade later, the Black population on the US side of the falls had grown to 244, of whom sixty were employed in the Whitney family business. At the same time, cross-border refugee traffic was escalating dramatically due to the passage in 1850 by the US Congress of the harsh new Fugitive Slave Law. For instance, the Buffalo Daily Courier of 7 October 1850, noted that fifteen people formerly resident at Rochester had crossed over to Canada a few days earlier. "We understand that there are some two hundred of this class of persons in [Rochester], and that they are not a little alarmed by the passage of the Fugitive Slave Law." By mid-century, the Provincial Freeman, published by the remarkable Mary Ann Shadd Cary first at Windsor, then in Toronto, and finally Chatham, carried warnings of slave catchers operating on the Canadian side of the border. There were also frequent notices in the same paper of people making their way to freedom via the Niagara River route.[38]

In the months of their employment, some members of the Cataract House staff lived in the hotel itself and possibly also in cottages scattered about the grounds. In the off-season, some of the Canadians resided in Lundy's Lane, Drummondville, St Catharines, and what today is Niagara-on-the-Lake, but others made their homes in Toronto, Brantford, and even more distant locations. Toronto was home to the Anti-Slavery Society of Canada, founded in 1851, and had the largest Black population of any urban centre in the province. Some African Americans who worked at the Cataract House spent the winter months away from Niagara, in upstate New York locations such as Rochester, Geneva, and Lockport, each of which places had vigorous anti-slavery organizations and Underground Railroad stations of their own. While home for the winter, they undoubtedly engaged in the life of their communities, attended church, participated in events mounted by fraternal orders and charitable organizations, and listened to lectures by visiting clergymen, and, of course, abolitionists.[39] That the Cataract House's African American employees had permanent homes in such hotbeds of anti-slavery as Rochester shows how far flung were the support networks that developed for freedom-seeker assistance on the US side of the border.

One tends to think of the Underground Railroad era as a unidirectional movement from the United States into Canada, but as their frequent employment at Niagara's famous hotels proves, some people traversed the Niagara River in both directions, migrating back and forth between colonial Canada and the United States. Even refugees from slavery living in the relative safety of British colonial Canada sometimes braved recapture on the American side of the Niagara River to work a "season" or more at Niagara's elegant hotels, attracted by their famously high wages and handsome gratuities, as the example of the Cataract House staff demonstrates.[40]

As a last stop before crossing over into Canada, the location of the Cataract House could hardly have been bettered. It stood at the very edge of the Niagara River above the falls and only a few hundred feet from Prospect Point. There was a long flight of steps leading to the ferry landing at river's edge, and in 1845 Parker Whitney constructed an "incline railway" (or funicular) that ran up and down the face of the gorge. From its base, long, heavy rowboats were used to ferry passengers across a less turbulent section below Niagara Falls. Starting in 1846, there was also a plucky little steamer called the "Maid of the Mist" that combined passage back and forth to Canada with a dramatic – and very damp – sightseeing voyage that ventured perilously close to the foot of the mighty torrent. Conveniently, too, there was a railway station directly opposite the Cataract House on Main Street from 1836 to 1850 on which at least some refugees likely reached the American side of the falls on their way to Canada. However, even after trains became a preferred method of transporting people across the Niagara River, the ferry and private boats continued to serve the same purpose.[41] There, headwaiter and Underground Railroad conductor John Morrison and others amongst the hotel wait staff used small boats to row freedom seekers across to Canada, usually under the cover of night.[42]

Queenston, which had its own African Canadian settlement complete with a small Baptist Church, was the northernmost safe landing place for steamers on the Niagara River, due to the strength of the current flowing down from the falls. From there Niagara-bound passengers were carried to the Canadian tourist district, at first by stage and later by rail.[43] Although the lake ships from Toronto and Hamilton stopped at Lewiston on the American side of the Niagara River to deliver tourists bound for the American village at the falls, sometimes particularly endangered freedom seekers had to be spirited overland to catch the steamboat at Queenston on the Canadian side. This was the case with Cecelia Jane Reynolds whose biography is detailed in my volume, *Steal Away Home*.[44]

Lake steamers travelled a regular circuit of ports, their times of sailing widely advertised in newspapers and city directories. One ship's officer notable for his assistance to freedom-seeking African Americans was Thomas Dick, the Scottish-born captain of the *City of Toronto* steamer and later of the *Peerless*. Another was Captain Hugh Richardson, who went on to become Toronto's first harbour master. In the 1840s Captain Richardson commanded the *Transit* and later the *Chief Justice Robinson*, which had been expressly built to ply the waters between Toronto and Niagara. Richardson once told British travel writer Harriet Martineau that the sublimest sight he had ever seen was the leap of a fugitive slave from his steamer to the free soil of Canada.[45]

As noted above, after 1855 refugees were able to travel by rail, crossing the Niagara Gorge via the new suspension bridge. Frederick Douglass and his wife, who operated a busy Underground Railroad station out of their second home on Rochester's outskirts, had originally sent their charges by steamboat from the port of Charlotte across Lake Ontario. After the advent of the railroad, however, they and their fellow Underground Railroad stationmasters could forward freedom seekers via Niagara. From there, it was up to local Underground Railroad operators such as John Morrison and his staff to see them safely across the river on "the cars."[46] On 22 September 1858, the *Niagara Falls Gazette* reported that "four highly colored chattels" had been sent to

Canada by the "mail train" by Frederick Douglass at Rochester and had safely
traversed the suspension bridge into Canada. In October 1859, Douglass
himself would pass this way to evade arrest in the immediate aftermath of the
John Brown raid on the military arsenal at Harper's Ferry, Virginia.[47]

It was across this same bridge that Harriet Tubman led Joe Bailey, his
brother, and two others to freedom in 1856.[48] Tubman herself lived for
several years in St Catharines on Canada's Niagara Peninsula, bringing her
aged parents and other relations rescued from Maryland there. She had close
ties with the same Rochester anti-slavery community of which both Frederick
Douglass and Cataract Hotel waiter John Morrison were a part. While no
stories connecting her to the Cataract House have come down to the present
day, she was on the board of the St Catharines branch of the Anti-Slavery
Society of Canada and would have known about John Morrison and the
well-organized Underground Railroad station he operated at the Cataract
House at Niagara Falls. Tubman moved back over the river in 1859, taking
her family members with her to a new home at Auburn, New York.[49]

Whether or not Parkhurst and Celinda Whitney along with their heirs
were themselves engaged in Underground Railroad activities remains an
open question. At the very least, the Whitneys did little to hinder the waiters
in their service to freedom's cause. The same policy was apparently followed
by their son and two sons-in-law who took over the business. Census records
show that a proportion of the waiters, chambermaids, and other hotel
workers had been born in the slave states, and, as it turned out, some were
refugees from bondage themselves, a fact that could hardly have escaped
their employers' notice. James Evans, whose letter to the editor of the New
Orleans *Daily Picayune* opens this chapter, believed that the Cataract House
owners knew exactly what was going on. Whatever the Whitneys' involvement in their flight may have been, Evans was certainly not the first guest of
the Cataract House to discover that "servants" taken to the very borders
of Canada sometimes preferred the view of the falls from the *other* side.

Nor could they be retrieved once they fled. Efforts to force the extradition
of freedom seekers back to the US on trumped up criminal charges were
first initiated in the case of Thornton and Lucie Blackburn, who were rescued in Detroit's first racial riot and crossed over into Canada in 1833.
Increasingly more sophisticated extradition demands in subsequent cases
were rebuffed by a long series of abolitionist-minded lieutenant governors.
Few refugees were successfully returned to their enslavers over the entire
antebellum period; in one instance, the magistrates who so ruled lost their
jobs; in another failed attempt to do so, the lieutenant governor received a
stiff reprimand from an infuriated British Colonial Office.[50]

Once safely delivered across the border, African Canadian families, churches, benevolent societies, and fraternal organizations all played a role in receiving the refugees. First, they provided for their immediate wants and hid them from possible pursuit. Secondly, they collaborated with like-minded members of communities located further inland in order to assist freedom seekers in finding homes, employment, friends, and churches to help them build new lives in freedom.[51] Faith centres included African Canadian churches such as the Methodist chapel located first at Murray Hill in 1836 and rededicated as a British Methodist Episcopal church on Peer Street at Gray in Niagara Falls; an African Canadian Baptist Church at Niagara-on-the-Lake founded in 1831; the St Catharines Zion Baptist Church established in 1838; and the Salem Chapel in St Catharines, built in its present form in 1855. Associated fraternal orders and benevolent societies were also important to the cause. Formally constituted organizations such as the Toronto-based Queen Victoria Benevolent Society headed since the late 1830s by the wife of Toronto's wealthiest African American immigrant, Ellen Toyer Abbott, and the Anti-Slavery Society of Canada which had both white and Black abolitionists on its board had branches across the province, including at Niagara.[52]

Freedom seekers reaching the town of Clifton, as the Canadian village at Niagara Falls was then known, thus found assistance awaiting them. Notable Black residents such as Burr Plato and Oliver Pernell (the latter of whom reputedly had swum the Niagara River to reach freedom) were there to help newcomers. As noted above, the great hotels on the Canadian side of the river also employed Black waiters, cooks, porters, and gardeners and a majority of hack drivers, and, as several travellers recorded, the guides at the famous Cave of the Winds leading behind the falls were also of African descent. There was also a Black-owned hotel at Niagara, operated by Samuel Hall, a formerly enslaved African American and his Scottish-born wife. Jane Ralston Hall had herself fled the St Thomas family to whom she had formerly been indentured, so both members of the couple had good reason to know the value of liberty.[53] Local Black families, too, were undoubtedly on the look out for newly arrived refugees and could be relied upon to see them on their way to Black communities in Lundy's Lane or Drummondville in the immediate vicinity or else either to Niagara or St Catharines.

Communities at Drummondville (the African Canadian settlement there was known as "Pollytown"), Lundy's Lane, Chippewa, Port Robinson, Fort Erie, and the modern Niagara-on-the-Lake, which had its own "Coloured Village," offered a haven for freedom seekers.[54] For those in particular danger of discovery, refugees might be transported to rural locations such as the small

Black settlement near McNab or to isolated farms in Grantham Township
between St Catharines and Welland. There, formerly enslaved men and
women such as Adam Nicholson and his family resided and had good cause
to identify with those with human bloodhounds on their heels. William
Steward, Harriet Tubman's brother, had a farm nearby as well.[55]

Of St Catharines, Quaker abolitionist Benjamin Drew wrote in 1856 that
out of a population of some six thousand people, about eight hundred were
refugees from bondage. Although documentation of their involvement is
lacking, individuals residing there such as Reverend Nelson Countee who
arrived in 1840 and Reverend Alexander Hemsley, both previously enslaved;
John W. Lindsay, who had been born free but was kidnapped at age seven
and enslaved at Washington, DC, and multiple other locations until he finally
escaped; free-born and prosperous barber Thomas O. Casey; and Oberlin
College-educated Elijah B. Dunlop who was a frequent delegate to Black
abolitionist conventions in the Great Lakes basin were all known for protesting mistreatment and discrimination and also were undoubtedly engaged in
fugitive freedom relief efforts.[56]

European American missionary Reverend Hiram Wilson also lived in
the Niagara region from 1849 on. He and his wife worked in tandem
with African Canadian activists, opening their home to freedom seekers
and providing them with clothing and other necessities collected for
the purpose. Wilson wrote in the 6 May 1852, edition of the *Voice of the
Fugitive* newspaper,

> I am happy to announce the formation of a Refugee Slaves Friends
> Society in St. Catharines which already numbers over seventy members
> and includes some of the most influential men in the place. Of these
> I would notice particularly the Honourable William Hamilton Merritt,
> M.P., Elias Adams, Esq., Mayor of St. Catharines, Colonel John Clark,
> Collector of Customs and James Lamb, Esq., Customs House officer
> and editor of the St. Catharines Journal ... Colored people here are
> heart in hand in the cause. Three of them are on the executive
> committee of five, of which Mr. Lamb is chairman. The object of the
> society is to bear testimony against slavery by extending sympathy
> and friendly aid to refugees from slavery who from time to time
> are taking shelter in this section of Canada and by promoting
> the education of their children.

Despite undoubted vigilance on the part of those who claimed their
service, a good number of the enslaved men and women brought by

their erstwhile owners to Niagara found their own way to the opposite, Canadian shore. One tale dates back even before the War of 1812. In 1898 a local historian interviewed Mary Ann Guillen of Queenston. Guillen recounted how her father, William Riley, escaped his Virginian enslaver during a trip to Niagara Falls in 1802. A coachman, he had driven his enslaver all the way from Fredericksburg, Virginia, to view the glory of the falls. Slipping away across the river, Riley hid in a cornfield for several days, undoubtedly with the collusion of local Black families, until his owner abandoned the search and went home. Settling in the "Coloured Village" at what is now Niagara-on-the-Lake, Riley married a German house servant and became a prosperous and respected local farmer.[57] Another early incident was reported in the *Freedom's Journal* on 21 December 1827. However, in that case the absconding girl was retrieved and returned to her enslaver. Her name was unfortunately not mentioned in the article.

Most freedom seekers crossed into Canada with as little fanfare as could be arranged, but over the years there were several escapes at the falls that drew the attention of the press. One such case involved the rescue of Solomon Moseby from the Niagara courthouse before he could be taken over the Niagara River for rendition to his previous owners. Interestingly, the petition for his extradition was entered by David Castleman, a horse breeder and slaveholder from Kentucky who was related by marriage to the Porters of Niagara Falls, New York, and he stayed with that family during the proceedings. What began as a peaceful demonstration on the part of the local Black populace ended in violence due to the actions of a trigger-happy soldier in an incident that saw the deaths of two men, both African Canadian. This took place on the eve of the 1837 Rebellion.[58] Other transitions from slavery to freedom were more peacefully accomplished; Kentucky fugitive Josiah Henson, who later worked with Hiram Wilson to found the Dawn Settlement north of Chatham, brought his family secretly to Canada by way of Black Rock, crossing the Niagara River in 1830 with the help of a kindly ship's captain. He remained at "Little Africa" in the Fort Erie area for some time, working and serving as a Methodist preacher.[59]

Lacking funds to go further and finding a warm welcome amongst the Black families living there, a substantial number of refugees settled near Niagara Falls. They, however, risked discovery by slave catchers, who did not scruple to enter Canada. That these formerly enslaved men and women would continue to support cross-border fugitive escapes was central to Underground Railroad operations at the Cataract House. Indeed, these hinged on the cooperation between John Morrison's wait staff and their friends and relations across the border in Canada. But there was a much broader hinterland for their activities. Morrison's skills made him indispensable to his employers, while his personal relationships illustrate the importance of international connections in borderland Black transnationalism. On the American side, the abolitionist network stretched throughout upstate New York and even as far as the eastern seaboard of the United States. Morrison not only organized the Cataract House wait staff into an efficient fugitive slave assistance force but also made it known throughout abolitionist circles that help could be found for freedom seekers at Niagara's famous Cataract Hotel.

This was accomplished in a remarkably creative way. Morrison chose as his vehicle the most widely read anti-slavery paper in the United States, William Lloyd Garrison's *Liberator*. The issue of 7 November 1845 bore an ad from a man who could only have been John Morrison, entitled "Wants a Situation:"

A most worthy, intelligent, and faithful colored man, who has had the superintendence of the Cataract House at Niagara as head waiter for the last four or five years, being desirous of spending the winter in Boston, wishes to obtain a situation in some private family, or public establishment. Application made by made to the Editor of the Liberator, 25 Cornhill. [60]

Antislavery-minded folk would easily read between the lines and understand that this "worthy, intelligent and faithful colored man" might be willing to undertake additional duties apart from his regular work at the Cataract House. By his own admission, his parents resided at Lundy's Lane on the Canadian side of the river, receiving freedom seekers in their homes and presumably helping others find similar accommodation.[61] According to a local historian, Michelle Anne Kratts, in October 1859, a daughter of Pennsylvania abolitionist Joseph Smith visited the Cataract House. John Morrison approached Rachel Smith with greetings for her father. He told her that a number of freedom seekers who had passed through his hands at the Cataract House were now living in neat little cottages near his parents' own home in Lundy's Lane, Canada West. Rachel Smith remembered that Morrison himself rowed fugitive slaves across the river by night twice during her sojourn at the Cataract House.[62]

John Morrison's clandestine efforts in freedom's cause seem to have been an open secret in the region. The *Niagara Falls Gazette* reported that at the Emancipation Day Ceremonies in Lockport, New York, in the first week of August 1856, Morrison was presented with a gold-headed cane in honour of his service to the community.[63] Interestingly, a notebook belonging to an anonymous visitor to the falls appeared on eBay a few years ago. It contains a pencil sketch labelled, "Head Waiter at the Cataract House." It also says he was "a Full Blood Indian," although the census records Morrison's ancestry as "Black" or "Mulatto." Evidence of the complexity of Black transnationalism in the region, one census, referencing the home at 8 Vine Street, Rochester, that he shared in the off season with his wife Flora, shows John Morrison as having been born in South America of mixed African and Indigenous parentage. He was listed in the US census for Niagara in the same year as a headwaiter for the Cataract House at Niagara Falls.[64]

Several of the other Cataract House employees were also engaged in Underground Railroad work elsewhere. Formerly enslaved Stepney Brown fled to Canada and settled first at Brantford and later Toronto. Spending his summers working as a waiter, he used the name "James A. Walkinshaw" to conceal his identity while employed at Niagara hotels. Brown was connected not only to the Toronto anti-slavery network, and the one in Philadelphia through which he had fled, but also to the Brantford, Canada West, Black community. In a letter addressed to William Still, secretary of the Pennsylvania Anti-Slavery Society at Philadelphia on 27 August 1857, he wrote that he was doing well and working "at the falls." By 1865, with the threat of capture and re-enslavement passed, Stepney Brown was listed under his own name in the New York census. He was working openly at the Cataract House on the American side.[65]

Likewise, Toronto-based waiter Moseby Hubbard (recorded as "Moses Hubbard" in the 1850 US census for Niagara, under the listing "Cataract House") had been born in Richmond, Virginia, and resided with wife Lavinia and family in a snug log cabin just north of Toronto's city limits of Bloor Street. He was part of a broad anti-slavery network that had established the British Canadian Anti-Slavery Society with branches across the province in the early 1830s, and his name appears on several petitions and as a participant at abolitionist and community meetings in Toronto over the years.[66] Hubbard continued working seasonally at Niagara through at least 1875, when, at age sixty-one, his name is to be found in the New York State Census in the list of waiters employed at the Cataract House, alongside that of Stepney Brown. To demonstrate how far the borderland network reached, Moseby Hubbard's brother owned a Toronto livery stable that carried people to and from the city wharves, a handy line of work for people engaged in welcoming refugees from American slavery to the largest city in Canada West. Moseby and his wife educated their several children at Toronto schools, and one, William Peyton Hubbard, would go on to become

Toronto's first elected African Canadian councillor and in 1903 its first Black deputy mayor.[67]

Underground Railroad leadership in Niagara Falls, New York, was also provided by another intrepid African American named (James) Samuel Patterson. Patterson had arrived in upstate New York from Virginia to seek his fortune in 1836. Beginning as a porter at the Cataract House, he and his wife Luvisa eventually saved sufficient funds to open their own smaller hotel. Undoubtedly a colleague of John Morrison's in anti-slavery work, this Patterson dubbed the "Free-Soil Hotel," in honour of the new Free Soil Party. The latter had grown up with the demise of the Whigs and in response to the rapid expansion of US territory into the American West, a place its adherents vowed would remain "free soil." Patterson established his hotel on Main Street in 1849, continuing in operation through the 1860s. The name of the hotel reflected Patterson's politics and also doubled as an advertisement to incoming freedom seekers that help might be available there, for after the Civil War when such assistance was no longer needed, the Pattersons renamed their inn the "Falls Hotel" and leased it out.[68]

A number of escapes directly involving the Cataract Hotel took place over the years. A fifteen-year-old lady's maid named Cecelia Jane Reynolds fled her Kentucky owners in 1846. The family of attorney Charles W. Thruston along with his adult son and daughter booked into the Cataract House in early May, bringing Cecelia with them. Having arranged with sympathetic abolitionists in Louisville to prepare her path to freedom even before she left Louisville, Cecelia found all in readiness upon her arrival. She was listed only as "servant" in the hotel register but by her full name was written by her owner, Fanny Thruston, in the Bath Island Register of tourists visiting that popular spot.[69] A young Virginian named Benjamin Pollard Holmes, a steamboat waiter living in Toronto and a fugitive slave himself, arranged for Cecelia's transport across the Niagara River to one of the African Canadian communities that dotted the Niagara Peninsula. She remained in hiding for a time, possibly in the household of Benjamin's friend, Elijah B. Dunlop, at St Catharines. Once the furor over her disappearance died down, she was taken to Toronto, most likely via Queenston. Cecelia went on to lead a very adventurous life, marrying her handsome rescuer and travelling off to Europe with him before he departed for the Australian gold rush. He went in order to raise the funds to purchase the beloved mother Cecelia had been forced to leave behind in Kentucky.[70]

Another, very risky rescue was attempted a year later by waiters at the Cataract House. This one was described by Samuel Ringgold Ward in the *Provincial Freeman* of 22 July 1847 and a story about the same incident also appeared in the *National Anti-Slavery Standard*.[71] Cruelly treated by her owners, a family named Stephens from Alabama, an enslaved young woman staying at the hotel begged the African American chambermaid for help in getting away. Her owner discovered the plot and carried her off by train, despite rescue attempts on the part of local Blacks, including a number of Cataract House waiters. One even jumped on the train to try to free her when it reached Lockport, but the enslaver evaded pursuit by going by way of Lewiston instead. According to historian Christopher Densmore, Cataract House headwaiter John Morrison, waiter Sandy Shamite, and future hotelier James Samuel Patterson (at the time working as a porter at the Cataract), along with Niagara Falls grocer John M. Anderson and a Charles Patterson were beaten for trying to rescue the girl.[72] The local African American community suffered as a result, for as the *Liberator* of 9 August 1847, reported, "A few drunken *Irishmen*, ripe for destruction, and several wicked young lads, commenced the work of destroying the little shanties of the poor blacks, and they would have burnt the whole of them if not fearful of setting fire to other houses. The mob made the slave case a pretext for attacking the colored people because they sell beer instead of brandy, and took away the custom from the grog dealers." The *Liberator* article did credit Lockport attorneys with volunteering to prosecute the vandals and recover damages for those who had been victimized.

Toronto's *Weekly North American* of 18 August 1853 reported another such incident but with a happier ending. An older woman named Martha and her husband were working at the Cataract House when, to her horror, she learned her former owner had just arrived for a visit. Recognizing Martha immediately, he offered a $100 reward for anyone who could catch her. Fleet of foot and fuelled by desperation, she ran two blocks to the ferry landing and all but threw herself down the steep flight of wooden steps that descended the gorge. Waiters from the Cataract House blocked pursuit while she and her husband jumped into the boat there and, with help from some of other members of the hotel staff, managed to row across to the Canadian village of Clifton and safety.[73]

The most famous rescue, however, was that of Patrick Sneed. The young man and his half brother had escaped from Savannah, Georgia, in 1849. They were arrested in Ohio and only Patrick managed to go on to Canada.[74] Sneed thereafter made his home in Toronto but he spent his summers working on the American side at Niagara under the assumed name of "George, or Joe Watson," and sometimes as Joseph Lewis, including at the Cataract House.[75] He was quite distinctive in appearance, being described as very light-skinned, "red-haired and freckled, a cooper by training, with a mixture

of African American, Jewish, and Native American ancestry." Sneed's owner
was a liquor merchant, broker, and possible slave dealer named David R.
Dillon. Dillon tracked his former human "property" down in 1853 after
being informed by a Savannah visitor at the falls who had recognized the
young man. The slaveholder was adamant about recovering his human
"property," whom he accused of murder to justify his arrest and a subsequent request for his extradition to Georgia to stand trial.[76] A US deputy
marshal accompanied by two Buffalo constables arrived to arrest Patrick
on 27 August 1853, at about four o'clock, while dinner was being served.
Interestingly, in an interview published in the *Buffalo Daily Courier* of
30 August 1853, Sneed explained that Cataract House managers Solon
Whitney, James F. Trott, and Dexter R. Jerauld had personally refused to
assist the constables in making his arrest, although the three Cataract
owners did not actively help Patrick Sneed evade the clutches of those in
pursuit either. Even such passive resistance was a brave act, undertaken as
it was in direct defiance of the federal Fugitive Slave Law.[77]

An important letter written to her brother by Susan Greeley, a young
woman who was a visitor to Niagara Falls in 1853, survives in the Rogers
Family collections at the Ontario Archives. Although it names neither the
freedom seeker nor the hotel from which he was fleeing, the letter was
recently recognized as offering a unique eyewitness perspective on the Sneed
incident. The officers of the law tried to capture the young man at about
4 p.m., while he was serving at table. The waiters sprang into action and
tore Patrick from the grasp of his captors. Others blocked the doors to the
dining room, trapping the constables inside. Patrick and some of his friends
fled to the incline railway and were transported down the face of the Niagara
Gorge to the ferry docks. The eyewitness account describes the waiters
arriving at the wharf with their serving dishes still in their hands; the writer
gives the number as between fifty and sixty.[78]

The ferryman was accustomed to carrying freedom seekers across the
river and began rowing his craft through the churning waters at the base
of the falls. However, when the constables shouted that Sneed was an
escaped murderer, the ferryman turned the boat around in midstream and
brought him back to the American shore. He landed down river at the docks
for the "Maid of the Mist" to avoid the crowd of hotel workers waiting at
the ferry landing to seize Patrick Sneed and carry him off to safety. The
newly discovered account suggests there were by this time between two and
three hundred people gathered at the docks.[79] This matches a rather odd
story copied from an unnamed American paper; the usually partisan Toronto
Globe reported on 30 August 1853 that although sixty Black waiters and

some 300 people who arrived from other hotels and from the town tried to free Sneed, US authorities bolstered by the arrival of three hundred Irish labourers prevented his rescue. The numbers are obviously exaggerated, but the fact that Sneed's would-be rescuers were confronted with overwhelming odds remains salient.[80]

The *Liberator* of 2 September 1853 reported that Patrick Sneed had been taken to Buffalo for trial. Local abolitionists were aware that slave catchers sometimes pressed false criminal charges so they could recover freedom seekers for their owners. Fortunately, Sneed engaged a local lawyer of some repute who managed to cast sufficient doubt on the Southern constables' claims that the judge freed Patrick. Despite the subsequent arrival of a new telegram from Savannah charging Sneed as a runaway under the Fugitive Slave Law, he was able to make his way over to Canada. He walked thirty miles to the Clifton House, presumably to ask assistance from the people he knew there so he could return home to Toronto. It took, however, the labour of several years for Sneed to pay off his Buffalo attorney's bill.[81]

The Patrick Sneed case was reported in newspapers from New York to New Orleans, and he gave his own detailed interview to Quaker abolitionist Benjamin Drew.[82] Neither the owners of the Cataract House, legally liable for harbouring the fugitive, nor the Cataract House waiters, for their attempt to help Sneed escape, were prosecuted under the Fugitive Slave Law. Frederick Douglass, in his own account in the *Frederick Douglass Paper* of 23 September 1855, praised the Cataract House waiters, writing that while the federal law might empower slave owners and their agents to capture and try him, "those brave colored men relied for their authority only, upon the rights of human nature, and the higher law of God that nullifies all oppressive enactments."

Headwaiter John Morrison left his position on the eve of the Civil War and died in Rochester on 21 November 1869.[83] After that conflict ended, Southern guests continued to flock to the Cataract House to pass their summers at Niagara Falls.[84] General Parkhurst Whitney died in 1862, and his son and sons-in-law went on to operate the hotel until it was sold in 1889. After that the venerable hostelry went through a series of hands, until on 15 October 1945 the *Niagara Gazette* reported that the hotel and most of its furnishings and beautiful objet d'art had been destroyed by fire. Fortunately, a pewter chandelier given to Parkhurst Whitney by the Marquis de Lafayette in honour of his 1825 visit, along with some fifty-three hotel ledgers, were sealed in a fireproof vault and survived. The current location of the chandelier is not known, but the surviving Cataract House registers bear the signatures of presidents and princes, famous actors and singers, world-famous musicians and thousands of tourists, some of whose notations include the words "and servants" beside their names. As we now know, those servants included enslaved men and women, some of whom took advantage of their proximity to Canada to cross the river in search of freedom.

Today, the former location of the Cataract House is a city park bordering Niagara Falls State Park. A native of Niagara Falls, the chair of the Underground Railroad Heritage Commission, Bill Bradberry, is tireless in his efforts to recover and publicize the secret work of the Cataract's brave African American waiters in the cause of freedom. With support from former mayor Paul Dyster and the local community, the Cataract House site has become the subject of extensive research efforts. Niagara's new Underground Railroad Interpretive Center is located in a restored 1863 warehouse seamlessly integrated with the spectacularly modern Amtrak Station. The centre stands just across Whirlpool Boulevard from a foundation of the old suspension bridge, across which so many freedom seekers made their way to Canada. Thanks to Director Ally Spongr and Director of Education and Development for the Niagara Falls Heritage Area Christine Bacon, its exhibits bring to life the stories of the Cataract House and its courageous African American staff for visitors and residents of the Niagara Region alike.

A major archival study is also underway, a project for which I have the honour to serve as historical archaeologist alongside historian Dr Judith Wellman with her vast knowledge of Underground Railroad in upstate New York. Our work is part of a multi-year program of research in support of an ambitious and highly significant archaeological excavation. The objective is to recover what evidence may survive of African American life and associated Underground Railroad-era activities at Niagara's celebrated Cataract House.[85] The dig is being carried out by Dr Douglass J. Perrelli and his team from the Archaeology Lab at the University at Buffalo and will undoubtedly shed much new light on the heritage of Black activism and transnationalism in this important boundary region.[86]

As the case of the Cataract House proves, the Niagara Region was a true borderland. Not only were communities of resistance engaged in fugitive slave assistance on both sides of the Niagara River but the Underground Railroad operations at Niagara had a figurative hinterland that stretched for miles on either side of the boundary. The multidisciplinary program of research now centred on the Cataract House provides a fascinating opportunity to reconstruct, at least in part, the complex web of relations between the Niagara River communities and those with which they were so closely allied in both upstate New York and, on the other side of the border, what is now the province of Ontario.

NOTES

I am grateful to Ronald Cummings and Natalee Caple, co-editors of this important volume, for their incredible patience, cogent editorial commentary on early drafts that much improved the final version, and their generosity in publishing this chapter. This work builds on groundbreaking research on the Cataract House and environs carried out by historian Dr Judith Wellman in her *Niagara Falls Underground Railroad Heritage Area Management Plan*. Conducted on behalf of the Underground Railroad Heritage Commission, this provides more than three hundred pages of detailed information about sites, people, and places relevant to the antebellum black experience in America's Niagara region. I am indebted to Underground Railroad Heritage Commission Chair Emeritus, William Bradberry, whose personal research and long series of fascinating articles about Niagara's role in the Underground Railroad are published in the *Niagara Gazette*. I am profoundly grateful to Dr Douglas J. Perrelli, Director of the Archaeological Survey for the SUNY University at Buffalo, site director Dr Kathleen Whalen, Heather Lackos, and their dedicated team for their hard work and deep personal commitment to uncovering and preserving the Cataract House Site. Much of the primary source material related to the Cataract House itself was recovered with the assistance of Courtney Geerhart, local history librarian, Niagara Falls Public Library; Catherine L. Emerson, Niagara County historian; Cynthia Van Ness, director of library and archives at The Buffalo History Museum; community historian Charles Lenhart; and countless librarians, archivists, and community historians in the region and beyond. Historian Christopher Densmore who worked for many years in the Buffalo area also provided both unpublished data and advice for the purposes of this study. I thank Judy Wellman, Christopher Densmore, Bill Bradberry, and Doug Perrelli also for kindly reading this paper in draft and providing insightful and cogent commentary.

This essay could not have been completed without the historical insights as well as the warm friendship I have shared over the years with Canadian community historians the late Wilma Morrison and my friend Donna Ford, both of whose ancestors arrived on the Underground Railroad. I am indebted to the work of local historians Michael Power and Nancy Butler; of scholars James St George Walker, Owen Thomas, David Murray, Daniel G. Hill, and Donald G. Simpson; and the remarkable research of genealogist Guylaine Petrin. Much of my thinking in respect to Underground Railroad activism in the borderlands was worked through in long conversations both virtual and actual with Dr Veta Smith Tucker on our coedited volume *A Fluid Frontier: Race, Slavery and the Underground Railroad in the Detroit River Borderland* (Detroit: Wayne State University Press, 2016) and in discussions over the years with Dr Afua Cooper,

the former James R. Johnston chair of Black Canadian Studies and a current
Killam Professor at Dalhousie University, Halifax.

1   In the newspaper article cited above, the young woman's name is never
    mentioned. According to the 1842 New Orleans City Directory, James Evans
    lived at no. 5 on the same street where his hat shop was located. *The New
    Orleans Picayune* of 13 July 1843 published ads for Evans' "City Hat Store,"
    which carried a wide range of fashionable headwear, including Panama hats.
    Evans may well have been an unscrupulous and possibly abusive owner. *The
    Times Picayune* of 30 September 1846 recorded the escape of another enslaved
    woman, who was then harboured by a free woman of colour named Marie
    Joseph. Five years later, when the City Hat Store burned to the ground, Evans
    was accused of overvaluing his stock for the purpose of insurance fraud. See
    "The Perjury Case," *New Orleans Times Picayune*, 28 March 1851.

2   Although the article about the Evans' maid's flight to Canada was widely
    reprinted in American newspapers, the *Boston Traveler* of 17 August 1841
    denied the "malicious libel upon Gen. Whitney & Son" stating that the
    Whitneys were known worldwide as respectable and honourable inn keepers
    and that General Whitney could never "interfere with the rights and privileges
    of his visiters [*sic*]." Furthermore, he could not be charged with harbouring or
    giving employment to "persons who have combined to abduct colored servants
    from families visiting his house."

3   Reprinted in the *National Antislavery Standard*, 26 August 1841.

4   This second clipping was brought to my attention by Charles Lenhart, for which
    I am most grateful, and appeared in the *Madison County Abolitionist* (Cazenovia,
    NY), 2 November 1841.

5   For the purposes of this paper, I am employing the term "Underground Railroad"
    in its broadest sense, as defined by the US Department of the Interior, US Park
    Service for its multiyear project *Underground Railroad Resources in the U.S.
    Theme Study* (Washington, DC: National Park Service, 1995), https://www.nps.
    gov/nhl/learn/themes/UndergroundRailroad.pdf.

> The Underground Railroad refers to the effort – sometimes spontaneous,
> sometimes highly organized – to assist persons held in bondage in North
> America to escape from slavery ... The period under consideration for this
> study is primarily the 1780s to 1865, with emphasis on the years from 1830
> to 1865 when most antislavery advocates abandoned their hope for gradual
> emancipation and adopted immediate abolition of slavery as their goal ...
> The term "Underground Railroad" had no meaning to the generations
> before the first rails and engines of the 1820s, but the retrospective use of the
> term ... is made so as to include incidents which have all the characteristics

of Underground Railroad activity, but which occurred earlier. These activities foreshadowed and helped to shape the Underground Railroad.

6   The most recent work is contained in Judith Wellman's superbly researched, "Site of the Cataract House," in *Niagara Falls Underground Railroad Heritage Area Management Plan, Appendix C: Survey of Sites Relating to the Underground Railroad, Abolitionism, and African American Life in Niagara Falls and Surrounding Area, 1820–1880, Historic Resources Survey Report* (April 2012): 48–78, http://www.niagarafallsundergroundrailroad.org/assets/ Uploads/NF-HAMP-Report-Appendix-C-1.pdf. The overall report is hereafter cited as Wellman, *Survey of Sites.*

7   Kate Clifford Larson, *Bound for the Promised Land: Harriet Tubman: Portrait of an American Hero* (New York: Random House, 2004), 107ff; William H. Seiner and Thomas A. Chambers, "Harriet Tubman, the Underground Railroad and the Bridges at Niagara Falls," *Afro-Americans in New York Life and History* 36, no. 1 (January 2012): 34–63; Dann J. Broyld, "The Power of Proximity: Frederick Douglass and His Transnational Relations with British Canada, 1847–1861," *Afro-Americans in New York Life and History* 41, no. 2 (July 2020): 3–34. Tubman eventually settled several members of her family in St Catharines and the surrounding area, including three of her brothers whom she rescued in 1854, and her aged parents in 1857. Larson, *Bound for the Promised Land,* 302.

8   For a discussion of the retrospective application of borderland theory to the US-Canadian border region relevant to the passage of enslaved African Americans in the Underground Railroad era, see "Introduction," in Karolyn Smardz Frost and Veta Smith Tucker, eds., *A Fluid Frontier: Slavery, Resistance and the Underground Railroad in the Detroit River Borderland* (Detroit: Wayne State University Press, 2016), 1–23.

9   The term borderlands is believed to have been employed in this way for the first time by Herbert Eugene Bolton in his landmark volume, *The Spanish Borderlands: A Chronicle of Old Florida and the Southwest* (New Haven: Yale University Press, 1921). Its application to historical contexts is suggested in the seminal article by Jeremy Adelman and Stephen Aron, "From Borderlands to Borders: Empires, Nation-States, and the Peoples in between in North American History," *American Historical Review* 104, no. 3 (1999): 814–41.

10 Victor Konrad and Heather N. Nichol, *Beyond Walls: Re-inventing the Canada–United States Borderlands* (Aldershot, Hampshire, UK, and Burlington, VT: Ashgate, 2008), 32; Randy Widdis, "Migration, Borderlands, and National Identity," in *The Great Lakes Basin as Transnational Region,* ed. John Bukowczyk et al. (Pittsburgh: University of Pittsburgh Press, 2005), 152–74, esp. 154.

11 A full list of such conventions can be found at "Colored Conventions: Bringing
    Nineteenth-Century Black Organizing to Digital Life," a project of the University of
    Delaware, accessed 12 December 2021, http://coloredconventions.org/conventions.

12 In the words of the US Parks Service Network to Freedom program, "While
    most runaways began their journey unaided and many completed their self-
    emancipation without assistance, each decade in which slavery was legal in
    the United States saw an increase in the public perception of a secretive network
    and in the number of persons willing to give aid to the runaway." US
    Department of the Interior, US Park Service, *Underground Railroad Resources
    in the U.S. Theme Study*.

13 See for example Keith P. Griffler, *Front Line of Freedom: African Americans
    and the Forging of the Underground Railroad in the Ohio Valley* (Lexington:
    University Press of Kentucky, 2004); Cheryl Jannifer LaRoche, *Free Black
    Communities and the Underground Railroad: The Geography of Resistance*
    (Urbana and Chicago: University of Illinois Press, 2014); and J. Williamson,
    "Review Essay: The Underground Railroad in the Midwestern Borderlands,"
    The Public Historian 36, no. 3 (August 2014): 154–7.

14 My own comprehension of the importance of borderland community collabora-
    tion in Underground Railroad-era slave rescue is particularly influenced by the
    work of Afua Cooper ("'Doing Battle in Freedom's Cause': Henry Bibb,
    Abolitionism, Race Uplift, and Black Manhood, 1842–1854" [PhD diss.,
    University of Toronto, 2000]; "The Fluid Frontier: Blacks and the Detroit River
    Region, 1789–1854; A Focus on Henry Bibb," *Canadian Review of American
    Studies* 30, no. 2 [2000]: 129–49), the late J. Blaine Hudson (*Fugitive Slaves and
    the Underground Railroad in the Kentucky Borderland* [Jefferson, NC, and
    London: MacFarland & Co., 2002]), and Gregory Wigmore ("Before the
    Railroad: From Slavery to Freedom in the Canadian–American Borderland,"
    Journal of American History 98, no. 2 [September 2011]: 437–54).

15 *An Act to Prevent the Further Introduction of Slaves and to Limit the Term of
    Contracts for Servitude within This Province, Cap. 7, 33 George III*, (Upper
    Canada: 9 July 1793), Archives of Ontario, http://www.archives.gov.on.ca/en/
    explore/online/alvin_mccurdy/big/big_03_anti_slavery_act.aspx. This gradual
    abolition law was passed, thanks to the bravery of a single woman. At Queenston,
    the struggles of the gagged and bound Chloe Cooley had been observed as her
    owner carried her off to a small boat to be sold across the Niagara River into ups-
    tate New York. The event was witnessed by Peter Martin, a Black Loyalist, and
    his white comrade, William Grigsby. Martin, taking his friend with him, repaired
    to the military barracks at Niagara to report what they had seen to Upper
    Canada's new lieutenant governor, John Graves Simcoe. Simcoe had served in the
    British forces during the American Revolution alongside African American troops.

Profoundly impressed with their courage, he developed a personal loathing
for slavery. He charged his attorney general with creating a legal solution to the
ongoing problem of slavery in Upper Canada. Having previously practised law in
slaveholding Dominica, John White knew there was no possible recourse against
Adam Vrooman, Chloe Cooley's owner, but looking to the future he proposed a
law that freed not a single slave but rendered their children free at age twenty-five,
and their children at birth. Vrooman presented a petition to Simcoe protesting
that his actions were not illegal and providing proof he owned Chloe Cooley, in
Upper Canada Land Petitions, "u-v" Bundle 1, 1792–1796 (RG 1, L3, vol. 514,
p. 8a), a reference for which I am grateful to Guylaine Petrin and her detailed
research. For the case see Robin W. Winks, *The Blacks in Canada: A History*,
2nd ed. (Montreal and Kingston: McGill-Queens University Press, 2007), 96–8;
William Renwick Riddell, "The Slave in Upper Canada," *Journal of Negro
History* (October 1919): 372–86; and Adrienne Shadd, "Chloe Cooley and the
1793 Act to Limit Slavery in Upper Canada," (unpublished report to Ontario
Heritage Trust, 2007), accessed 12 May 2016, http://www.heritagetrust.on.ca/
CorporateSite/media/oht/PDFs/Chloe-Cooley-ENG.pdf. See also William Renwick
Riddell, "Upper Canada, Early Period," *Journal of Negro History* 5, no. 3 (1920):
324. Nonetheless, early chronicler T. Watson Smith noted that ads for the purchase and sale of slaves in the Niagara region continued to appear in the *Upper
Canada Gazette* and *American Oracle* through the end of the first decade of the
nineteenth century. T. Watson Smith, "The Slave in Canada," *Collections of
the Nova Scotia Historical Society* 10 (1899): 1–161.

16 John Beverley Robinson to Lieutenant Governor Sir Peregrine Maitland, 8 July
1819, Upper Canada Sundries, Library and Archives Canada. Despite its antiquity,
Judge William Renwick Riddell's "Notes on Slavery in Canada" (*Ontario
Historical Society Papers and Records* 4 [1919], 396–411) and his other articles
on the subject remain the authoritative Canadian source on the legal history of
slavery and slave escape in what is now Ontario. See also his important "The
Fugitive Slave in Upper Canada," *Journal of Negro History* 5 (June 1920): 343–5.

17 Primary sources relating to African Canadian military service are contained in the
collections of Library and Archives Canada. See "Military Heritage," Library and
Archives Canada, accessed 21 September 2017, http://www.bac-lac.gc.ca/eng/dis-
cover/military-heritage/Pages/military-heritage.aspx. See also Ernest Green,
"Upper Canada's Black Defenders," *Ontario History* 37 (1931): 365–91; Daniel
G. Hill, "Early Black Settlements in the Niagara Peninsula," 1981, Proceedings of
the Third Annual Niagara Peninsula History Conference entitled Immigration and
Settlement in the Niagara Peninsula, 25–6 April 1981; David Meyler and Peter
Meyler, *A Stolen Life: Searching for Richard Pierpoint* (Toronto: Natural Heritage
Books, 1999), esp. chap. 5; Wayne Kelly, "Race and Segregation in the Upper

Canada Militia," *Journal of the Society for Army Historical Research* 78, no. 316 (Winter 2000): 264–77; Fred Landon, "Canadian Negroes and the Rebellion of 1837," *Journal of Negro History* 7, no. 4 (October 1922): 377–9; Gareth Newfield, "Upper Canada's Black Defenders? Re-examining the War of 1812 Coloured Corps," *Canadian Military History* 18, no. 3 (2009): 31–4; and James W. St G. Walker, *The Black Loyalists: The Search for a Promised Land in Nova Scotia and Sierra Leone, 1783–1870* (New York: Africana Publishing and Dalhousie University Press, 1976), esp. chap. 1.

18 Michael Power and Nancy Butler, *Slavery and Freedom in Niagara* (Niagara, ON: Niagara Historical Society, 1993), 13–15; James Cleland Hamilton, "Slavery in Canada," *Transactions of the Canadian Institute* 1 (1889–90), 102–8; Smith, "The Slave in Canada"; Winks, *Blacks in Canada*, 34, 48. According to T. Watson Smith, there were three hundred people of African ancestry as well as a few Native people (known as *panis*) enslaved at Niagara in 1791.

19 See Roy F. Fleming, "Negro Slaves with the Loyalists in Upper Canada," *Ontario History* 44 (1952): 27–30; Winks, *Blacks in Canada*, 146, 148–52. The venerable but still authoritative legal history of slavery in the colony is William Renwick Riddell, "Notes on Slavery in Canada," *Journal of Negro History* 4 (January 1919): 396–408; "The Slave in Upper Canada," *Journal of Negro History* 4 (October 1919): 372–95; "The Slave in Canada," *Journal of Negro History* 5 (1920): 261–375; "Some References to Negroes in Upper Canada," *Ontario Historical Society Papers and Records* 19 (1922), 144–6; and Winks, *Blacks in Canada*, 146, 148–52.

20 Sources on the Underground Railroad and the importance of local community involvement on the Canadian side of the Niagara River include Power and Butler, *Slavery and Freedom in Niagara,* and Owen Thomas, *Niagara's Freedom Trail: A Guide to African-Canadian History on the Niagara Peninsula* (Niagara, ON: Niagara Economic & Tourism Commission, 1997). For more general works featuring Niagara as one of the main crossing points, see Hill, *Freedom-Seekers*, 48ff; Donald G. Simpson, Paul E. Lovejoy, eds., *Under the North Star: Black Communities in Upper Canada Before Confederation* (Trenton, NJ: Africa World Press, 2005), 188–94; and James St George Walker, *A History of Blacks in Canada: A Study Guide for Teachers and Students* (Ottawa: Minister of State for Multiculturalism, 1980), esp. chap. 4.

21 Sir Richard Bonnycastle, "A Journey from Montreal to Toronto," *Canada and the Canadians* (1849), reproduced in *The Canadian Antiquarian and Numismatic Journal* 4–5 (1875): 60–4.

22 J.J. Talman, "William Hamilton Merritt," *Dictionary of Canadian Biography*, accessed 11 September 2017, http://www.biographi.ca/en/bio/merritt_william_hamilton_1793_1862_9E.html. This was the first successful suspension bridge

in the world, spanning some 825 feet. John A. Roebling, *Report on the Condition of the Niagara Railroad Suspension Bridge, August 1, 1860* (Trenton, NJ: Murphy and Bechtel, Printers, 1860), https://dr.library.brocku.ca/bitstream/handle/10464/4856/reportonconditionniagararailway1860.pdf. For its importance to Harriet Tubman and the Underground Railroad, see Thomas Chambers and William Siener, "Harriet Tubman, the Underground Railroad, and the Bridges at Niagara Falls," *Afro-Americans in New York Life and History* 36, no. 1 (January 2012): 34–48. William Hamilton Merritt's involvement in UGRR activities is noted in Winks, *Blacks in Canada*, 258; and Mary Ellen Snodgrass, *The Underground Railroad: An Encyclopedia of People, Places, and Operations*, vols. 1 and 2 (New York and London: Routledge, 2008), 263–4.

23 Again, the most recent work is by Judith Wellman, "Site of the Cataract House," *Survey of Sites*; and "Niagara Falls Underground Railroad Heritage Area Management Plan," *Historic Resources Survey Report* (June 2012), accessed 15 June 2017, http://niagarafallsundergroundrailroad.org/assets/Uploads/NF-HAMP-Report-Chapter-01.pdf; and Karolyn Smardz Frost and Judith Wellman, *Cataract House, Niagara Falls, New York: Development, 1825–1945*, (Unpublished report for the Niagara Falls Underground Railroad Heritage Commission, 4 July 2017). There is a superb account of the Cataract House history in the "Papers of James Fullerton Trott" in the Special Collections at the Niagara Falls Public Library.

24 It was at the Eagle Tavern that the Marquis to Lafayette would disembark in 1825 from his fabled red coach. The French hero of the American Revolution then visited the terminus of the newly completed Erie Canal in the company of Parkhurst Whitney and Whitney's young, Solon. See Ann Marie Linnabery, "Niagara Discoveries: Solon Whitney, Niagara Falls Community Leader," *Lockport Union-Sun & Journal*, 11 July 2015, http://www.lockportjournal.com/news/lifestyles/niagara-discoveries-solon-whitney-niagara-falls-community-leader/article_0baa9473-f51b-5dcc-b6e6-c6983702d23b.html.

25 Albert H. Porter, "Niagara from 1805 to 1875, by an old resident," privately printed pamphlet, 1875, Buffalo and Erie County Public Library; *History of Niagara County, N.Y.* (New York: Sanford & Co., 1831), 301, 304; Josephine Hardwick, "Silhouettes," *New York Times Herald* (Olean, NY), 23 May 1936; Wellman, "Site of the Cataract House," *Survey of Sites*, 48–52; and William Bradberry, "A Better Glimpse into the Cataract House's Past," *Niagara Gazette*, 2 February 2013, https://www.niagara-gazette.com/opinion/bradberry-a-better-glimpse-into-cataract-houses-past/article_43550e05-7537-57f0-9f15-4621764483f9.html.

26 There was a huge addition to the southwest wing in 1853 that included the hotel's celebrated "River Parlour," with broad porches and luxurious guest rooms directly

overlooking the American rapids. This addition was demolished in 1885 when the entire riverfront was expropriated for the Niagara Falls Reserve, providing visitors with free access to the waterfront and eliminating private ownership there. With minor changes to outbuildings and such, the hotel retained the 1886 footprint until it was destroyed by fire on 14 October 1945.

27 Newspapers across the US advertised that the Cataract House would stay open in the winter months of 1854 and 1855; however the size and ethnicity of the staff employed over the winter are not known. The hotel lost money through the experiment, which was not repeated until later in the century.

28 Their names are recorded in the Cataract House ledgers, some fifty-three of which survived the 1945 fire that destroyed the hotel. These are preserved today in the Special Collections of the Niagara Falls Public Library. Frederick Douglass and his bride stayed at the Cataract House following his second marriage. See *Buffalo Morning Express and Illustrated Buffalo Express* (Buffalo, New York, United States of America), 5 Aug 1884. For Jenny Lind's recollections of the current baths, see "Letters to the Editor, continued," *Niagara Falls Gazette*, 7 June 1935, 21. The use of diverted Niagara waters is described in Thomas Holder, *A Complete Record of Niagara Falls & Vicinage* (Niagara Falls, NY: by the author, 1882), 83; and in the fascinating, firsthand account of the history of the Cataract House by James Fullerton Trott, referenced above.

29 The fire was widely reported. For local examples, see "Cataract House Destroyed by Fire," *Press & Sun-Bulletin* (Binghamton, NY), 15 October 1945, 2; "Famed Cataract House Burns," *Star-Gazette* (Elmira, NY), 15 October 1945, 2; "Blaze Destroys Cataract House at Niagara Falls," *Dunkirk Evening Observer* (Dunkirk, NY), 15 October 1956, 1.

30 There were eighteen men and two women living in the household of William Murray, and another four men in the home of Cornelius Griffin. The Whitneys had a small house nearby. My thanks to Judy Wellman for this detailed information.

31 Analysis of the identified names within the Cataract House ledgers suggests that about 20 per cent of the antebellum guests were of Southern origin, Wellman, "Site of the Cataract Hotel," *Survey of Sites*, 59. The popularity of the hotel with Southerners is reiterated in a nostalgic note on the front page of the *Time-Picayune* published at New Orleans, 9 July 1858: "CATARACT HOUSE, NIAGARA. – Of the many delightful summer resorts to which those in search of health or recreation annually flock from the South, we recall none that possesses superior attractions to those delivered at that far-famed – and justly so, too – hotel, at Niagara Falls, the Cataract House."

32 An Act for the Gradual Abolition of Slavery, 29 March 1799, New York State Archives, New York (State). Dept. of State. Bureau of Miscellaneous Records.

Enrolled acts of the State Legislature. Series 13036-78, Laws of 1799, chapter 62, accessed 14 July 2017, http://digitalcollections.archives.nysed.gov/index. php/ Detail/ Object/ Show/object_id/10815; Nathaniel Paul, *An Address, Delivered on the Celebration of the Abolition of Slavery, in the State of New-York* (Albany: J.B. Van Steenbergh, 1827), accessed 14 July 2017, http://www. blackpast.org/1827-rev-nathaniel-paul-hails-end-slavery-new-york; Edgar J. McManus, *A History of Negro Slavery in New York* (Syracuse: Syracuse University Press, 1966). Insight into the life and times of a man who had been first a slave and then a free man in upstate New York is provided by Austin Steward, *Twenty-Two Years a Slave, and Forty Years a Freeman* (Rochester: William Ailing, 1857).

33 The first such volume was by Robert Roberts, *The House Servant's Directory: A Monitor for Private Families* (Boston: Monroe and Francis, 1827), which was also the first commercial publication by an African American in the United States. The second was written by Tunis Gulic Campbell. Published in 1848 it was entitled *Hotel Keepers, Head Waiters, and Housekeepers' Guide* (Boston: Coolidge and Wiley, 1848).

34 Miss Leslie, "Niagara," *Godey's Ladies Book*, December 1845, accessed 31 July 2012, http://www.accessible.com/accessible/print?AADocList=11&AADocStyle= STYLED&AAStyleFile=&AABeanName=toc1&AANextPage=/printFull DocFromXML.jsp&AACheck=2.38.11.0.6n.

35 Cited in Power and Butler, *Slavery and Freedom in Niagara*, 56–7.

36 Judy Wellman, "People and Sites Relating to the Underground Railroad, Abolitionism, and African American Life, 1820–1880, Niagara Falls and Niagara County," accessed 10 July 2017, http://niagarafallsundergroundrailroad.org/assets/ Uploads/Niagara-Falls-Underground-Railroad-Project-Database.pdf. For the Clifton House see S. De Veaux, *The Falls of Niagara, or Tourist's Guide to this Wonder of Nature* (Buffalo: William B. Hayden, 1839), 135.

37 John Morrison became headwaiter in about 1840, effectively bringing an end to white employment in the Cataract House dining rooms, although some white waiters would have continued in cafe and salon service. Because of the racially discriminatory dictates of the day, all the men Morrison directly supervised would have been of African ancestry.

38 See "Close Work," *Provincial Freeman*, 26 August 1854, and "Underground from Delaware to Niagara Falls," *Provincial Freeman*, 11 July 1857. Important information for would-be fugitives and their conductors was also provided. "A Hint to Niagara Visitors," *Provincial Freeman*, 22 July 1854, a chatty piece of tourist advice, informed visitors that hiring a waiting conveyance, most of "which belong to coloured men, the only reasonable persons there" to take them to the bridge and then walking across was better than taking a coach over

into Canada. Ostensibly this was to avoid paying tolls but it also gave useful information to fugitives wary of waiting slave catchers: that the Black drivers were sympathetic to their plight and would help them on their way in safety. With thanks to Christopher Densmore for pointing this out, personal communication, 16 April 2008.

39 The likelihood of their boarding with local families is suggested by the extensive research on this subject within African American urban communities conducted by James Oliver Horton and Lois E. Horton, *In Hope of Liberty: Culture, Community, and Protest Among Northern Free Blacks, 1700–1860* (New York and Oxford: Oxford University Press, 1997), 96–9, 114, 123; and James Oliver Horton and Lois E. Horton, *Black Bostonians: Family Life and Community Struggle in the Antebellum North* (New York: Holmes and Meier, 1999), 17–18, 37ff. Former Niagara Falls City Historian Michelle Anne Kratts and Peter Ames, historian at the Oakwood Cemetery, have done a remarkably detailed study of John Morrison. See Michelle Anne Kratts and Peter Ames, "Bringing Lost Souls Home: John Morrison, a Hero of Niagara," accessed 12 May 2016, http://myoakwoodcemetery.com/kratts-korner/2013/3/26/bringing-lost-souls-home-john-morrison-a-hero-of-niagara.html; and Wellman, "Site of the Cataract House," *Survey of Sites*, 61, 66–9.

40 Carol Mull, "The McCoys: Charting Freedom from Both Sides of the River," in *A Fluid Frontier: Slavery, Resistance and the Underground Railroad in the Detroit River Borderland*, ed. Karolyn Smardz Frost and Veta Smith Tucker (Detroit: Wayne State University Press, 2016), 215–25, provides an excellent example of a family that crossed the Detroit River into Canada but, despite the danger, returned to the US before the Civil War to gain economic advantages. See below for examples including Cataract waiters and freedom seekers Stepney Brown and Patrick Sneed who both lived in Canada during the winter months.

41 Wellman, *Survey of Sites*, 171. The ongoing use of boats and skiffs to take people across to Canada is documented in a number of celebrated cases and most notably in Robert Clemens Smedley, *History of the Underground Railroad in Chester and the Neighboring Counties of Pennsylvania* (Lancaster, PA: Office of the Journal, 1883), 231–2. This account of the daughter of a Pennsylvania abolitionist and Underground Railroad stationmaster who visited the Cataract House and encountered John Morrison includes a description of his taking at least two freedom seekers across the Niagara River in his own boat during her stay.

42 Kratts and Amers, "Bringing Lost Souls Home," 231–2. An illustration of the long, heavy rowboats used as ferries below the falls appears in "View from the Ferry," Samuel Geil, *Map of the Vicinity of Niagara Falls* (Philadelphia: J.L. Delp, 1853).

43 For instance Rowsell's *City of Toronto and County of York Directory*, 1850–51 (Toronto: Henry Rowsell, 1850), 35: "FOR NIAGARA AND LEWISTON. – The

steamer Chief Justice Robinson leaves Toronto for Niagara and Lewiston, daily, (Sundays excepted) at half-past 7 o'clock A.M. Returning, leaves Lewiston at 1 o'clock P.M. The steamer Sovereign leaves Toronto for Niagara and Lewiston, daily, (Sundays excepted) at 2 o'clock P.M., and Lewiston for Toronto at half-past 7 every morning."

44 Karolyn Smardz Frost, *Steal Away Home* (Toronto: HarperCollins Canada, 2017), esp. chap. 2.

45 Samuel Ringgold Ward, Freemason's Hall, London, England, 1856, quoting Captain Hugh Richardson, in C. Peter Ripley et al., eds., *The Black Abolitionist Papers*, vol. 2, *Canada, 1830–1865* (Chapel Hill: University of North Carolina Press, 1986), 158–9, hereafter cited as *BAP*. Also Samuel Ringgold Ward, *Autobiography of a Fugitive Negro* (London: John Snow for Samuel Ringgold Ward, 1855), 158; and Frederick H. Armstrong, "Captain Hugh Richardson and Toronto's Lake Communications," in *Toronto: A City in the Making: Progress, People & Perils in Victorian Toronto* (Toronto: Dundurn, 1988), 202–11.

46 Jermain Loguen returned to Syracuse the following spring, but Ward remained in Canada as an agent of the Canadian Anti-Slavery Society. Frederick Douglass's Underground Railroad activities at Rochester are well documented. Perhaps the most famous fugitives he put on the lake boats were William Parker and his party, who had been involved in the Christiana Riots. They arrived in September 1851. See William Parker, "The Freedman's Story in Two Parts," *Atlantic Monthly*, XVII (February 1866): 152–66; and (March 1866): 276–95; Frederick Douglass, "Freedom's Battle," *Frederick Douglass Paper*, 25 September 1851.

47 Frederick Douglass wrote a letter on 27 October 1859, to his friend and colleague in UGRR work, Amy Post at Rochester. He was staying at Clifton (Niagara Falls) on the Canadian side of the falls. See Frederick Douglass to Amy Kirby Post, 27 October 1859, *Post Family Papers Project*, University of Rochester Rare Books and Special Collections, accessed 1 November 2017, https://rbsc.library.rochester.edu/items/show/1157. A second letter from Douglass, dated 31 October 1859, was written to the *Toronto Globe*. Published on 4 November 1859, it avowed his innocence in the John Brown incident.

48 Sara Bradford, *Harriet: The Moses of Her People* (New York: Geo. R. Lockwood & Son, 1886), 48; William Bradberry, "Colorful Characters, Amazing Stories Define Niagara's History," *Niagara Falls Gazette*, 30 August 2017, http://www.niagara-gazette.com/opinion/bradberry-colorful-characters-amazing-stories-define-niagara-s-history/article_9a08fboe-8dd7-11e7-ace4-3746733d6a5f.html.

49 Two years later, the outbreak of the American Civil War demanded a different type of service in the cause of freedom. Tubman became a spy and nurse for the Union Army. See Larson, *Bound for the Promised Land*, chap. 10.

50 Bryan Prince, "The Illusion of Safety: Attempts to Extradite Fugitive Slaves from
    Canada," in *A Fluid Frontier: Slavery, Resistance and the Underground Railroad
    in the Detroit River Borderland*, ed. Karolyn Smardz Frost and Veta Smith Tucker
    (Detroit: Wayne State University Press, 2016): 67–79. This builds on earlier work
    by such scholars as Alexander L. Murray, "The Extradition of Fugitive Slaves
    from Canada: A Re-evaluation," *Canadian Historical Review* 43, no. 4 (December
    1962): 298–314; Roman J. Zorn, Criminal Extradition Menaces the Canadian
    Haven for Fugitive Slaves, 1841–1861," *Canadian Historical Review* 38 (1957):
    284–94; Robert C. Reinders, "The John Anderson Case, 1860 – 1, A Study in
    Anglo-Canadian Imperial Relations," *The Canadian Historical Review* 56, no. 4
    (December 1975): 393–415; and the more recent work by David Murray on the
    Niagara region published in *Colonial Justice: Morality, and Crime in the Niagara
    District* (Toronto: Osgoode Hall, 2002); "Criminal Boundaries: the Frontier and
    the Contours of Upper Canadian Justice, 1792–1840," *American Journal of
    Canadian Studies* 26, no. 3 (Autumn, 1997): 341–66; and "Hands Across the
    Border: The Abortive Extradition of Solomon Moseby," *Canadian Review of
    American Studies* 30, no. 2 (2000): 187–209. The 1833 case of Thornton and
    Lucie Blackburn set the precedent for all fugitive slave cases up to the time of the
    Civil War and resulted in the creation of Canada's first articulated refugee
    reception policies. See Karolyn Smardz Frost, *I've Got a Home in Glory Land:
    A Lost Tale of the Underground Railroad* (Toronto: Thomas Allen, 2007), esp.
    chaps. 9–11.

51 The role of such organizations in helping freedom seekers become established in
    their new homes is discussed extensively in both Frost, *I've Got a Home in Glory
    Land*, esp. chaps. 7 and 13; and in my more recent volume, *Steal Away Home*,
    esp. chaps. 5 and 6.

52 Hill, *Freedom-Seekers*, 179; Ripley, BAP, 222n; Winks, *Blacks in Canada*, 253–8,
    329.

53 Thomas, *Niagara's Freedom Trail*, 15; Isabella Bird, *The Englishwoman in North
    America, 1856* (1856; reissue, Carlisle, MA: Applewood Books, 2007), 232. The
    latter source employs shockingly discriminatory language. The Hall family's story
    is told in June Payne Flath, "Indentured Servants in Canada," *The Country
    Connection Magazine* 50 (Summer 2005), accessed 12 October 2017 http://www.
    pinecone.on.ca/MAGAZINE/stories/IndenturedServants.html; and Peggy
    McCarthy, "Tracing His Black Roots: Port Hope Resident Forges a Connection
    with His Past," *Northumberland News*, 13 February 2008,
    https://www.northumberlandnews.com/news-story/3766061-tracing-his-black-
    roots; Larry Hill, "Our Ancestors Gave Us Genuine Freedom," *The North
    Country Lantern*, 11 (Summer/Fall 2009), 3, http://northcountryundergroun
    drailroad.com/newsletters/Newsletter-SummerFall-2009.pdf.

54 Natasha L. Henry, *Emancipation Day: Celebrating Freedom in Canada* (Toronto: The Dundurn Group, 2010), 144–5; Hill, *Freedom-Seekers*, 50–1; Thomas, *Niagara's Freedom Trail*, 19–20.

55 See "Adam Nicholson," *Breaking the Chains*, Harriet Tubman Institute, York University, http://tubman.info.yorku.ca/educational-resources/breaking-the-chains/toronto/adam-nicholson; also personal communication, Donna Ford, 12 September 2011.

56 Benjamin Drew, *A North-side View of Slavery: The Refugee; or, The Narratives of Fugitive Slaves in Canada, Related by Themselves, with an Account of the History and Condition of the Colored Population of Upper Canada* (Boston: John P. Jewett, 1856), 17–18, 32–40; "Report by Samuel Ringgold Ward," in Ripley, BAP, 256–64. There was a major convention held at Drummondville in 1847 to discuss resistance and fugitive slave assistance efforts. See Report of the Convention of the Colored Population, Held at Drummondville, August 1847, Victoria University Digital Collection, accessed 14 September 2017, http://coloredconventions.org/items/show/451. For John W. Lindsay, see dann J. Broyld's excellent article, "John W. Lindsay: Finding Elements of American Freedoms in British Canada, 1805–1876," in *Ontario History* 109, no. 1 (Spring 2017): 27–59. For biographical details regarding Elijah B. Dunlop, see Frost, *Steal Away Home*, 67, 76, 155, 318n6.

57 This story was recounted in 1896, by Mary Guillan, in Janet Carnochan, *A Slave Rescue in Niagara Sixty Years Ago* (1897). Also quoted in Nancy Butler, "Starting Anew: The Black Community of Early Niagara," in Power and Butler, *Slavery and Freedom*, 48.

58 Peter B. Porter, whose father had been Parkhurst Whitney's first Niagara Falls employer, was David Castleman's brother-in-law. For his involvement in the incident see Wellman, "The Site of the Peter B. Porter House, *Survey of Sites*: Murray, *Colonial Justice*, 198–201, 214; and Murray's "Hands Across the Border," 187–209. Also Carnochan, *A Slave Rescue in Niagara*, which includes interviews with elderly eyewitnesses to the Moseby rescue.

59 Josiah Henson, *The Life of Josiah Henson, Formerly a Slave, Now an Inhabitant of Canada, as Narrated by Himself* (Boston: Arthur D. Phelps, 1849), 58–9; William H. Pease and Jane H. Pease, "Josiah Henson," Dictionary of Canadian Biography Online, accessed 26 August 2017, http://www.biographi.ca/009004-119.01-e.php?BioId=39700.

60 I am indebted to Christopher Densmore for sharing the unpublished text of a talk he gave at the Niagara County Historical Society, in Lockport, NY, on 24 February 2000, entitled "Fugitive Slave Cases in Niagara County: A Glimpse into the Underground Railroad." He suggests the ad was possibly a coded notice, placed in the abolitionist paper with the widest circulation in the US,

that assistance might be found at the Cataract House if freedom seekers were
passing through Niagara. Christopher Densmore, personal communication,
16 April 2008.

61 John Morrison first appeared in the Rochester "Directory of Colored Persons,"
    in the *Daily American Directory of the City of Rochester, 1851–2* (Rochester: Lee,
    Mann & Co., 1851), 278. The US Census for 1850 shows him as working at the
    Cataract Hotel in Niagara, aged forty and illiterate, no birthplace given. The New
    York State Census of 1855 for Rochester, Monroe County, shows Morrison as
    aged forty-five and married to Flora A. aged thirty. It says they were both "Black
    or mulatto" and that he had been in the city seven years (since 1848) and she two
    years. Interestingly this census states he was born in Maryland while his wife was
    from Pennsylvania. He was a waiter and owned his own rather modest frame
    home (those of most neighbours were valued between $1,000–$2,000 but theirs
    only at $600).

62 Michelle Anne Kratts, "Bringing Lost Souls Home: John Morrison, a Hero of
    Niagara," accessed 12 May 2016, http://myoakwoodcemetery.com/kratts-
    korner/2013/3/26/bringing-lost-souls-home-john-morrison-a-hero-of-niagara.
    html; Smedley, *History of the Underground Railroad in Chester and the
    Neighboring Counties of Pennsylvania*, 231–2.

63 *Niagara Falls Gazette*, 5 August 1856, cited in Kratts, "Bringing Lost Souls
    Home."

64 The reference to John Morrison's South American birth comes from US Census
    for 1860, Monroe County, Rochester, NY, 10th Ward. His age varied between
    censuses, and here he was listed as a "mulatto," aged forty-five, as was his
    Pennsylvania-born wife, incorrectly named wife "Clara," aged thirty-seven. The
    pencil sketch believed to be of John Morrison shows a man in perhaps his forties,
    with the words "Headwaiter at the Cataract House, a full-blooded Indian, a tall
    man." See "Lot 1272: 1853: Pencil Sketches, Niagara Falls," accessed
    22 September 2017, https://www.liveauctioneers.com/
    item/230699_lot-1272-1853-pencil-sketches-niagara-falls.

65 James W. Dungy to William Still, 6 March 1860, in "Letters of Negroes, Largely
    Personal and Private, Part 4," *Journal of Negro History* 11, no. 1 (January 1926):
    172–3. In the census listing, Moseby's place of birth was circled, with the words
    "Don't know." Falsifying or leaving out the birthplace in such records was a
    common way that fugitive slaves used to conceal their identities and particularly
    their legal status while on American soil.

66 For Hubbard, see US State Census, Niagara Falls, 1865, "Cataract Hotel."

67 The life of William Hubbard is detailed in Catherine Slaney, *Family Secrets:
    Crossing the Colour Line* (Toronto: Dundurn Group, 2003), 207–8, and
    Stephen L. Hubbard, *Against All Odds: The Story of William Peyton Hubbard:*

Black Leader and Municipal Reformer (Toronto: Dundurn, 1997). Moseby Hubbard's son, William Peyton Hubbard, invented a bake oven, the patent for which made him independently wealthy. A chance encounter with the *Globe* publisher George Brown, who had initiated the founding of the Anti-Slavery Society of Canada in 1851, encouraged him to enter politics. William P. Hubbard's own son would become a senior officer in the Toronto Transit Commission.

68 Wellman, "Site of the Free Soil Hotel," *Survey of Sites*, 84–5; William Bradberry, "Meet James Patterson and his Free-Soil Hotel," *Niagara Gazette*, 6 April 2016.

69 I am grateful to Christine Bacon, director of education and development for the Niagara Falls Heritage Area, for sharing this recent discovery with me. "Cecelia Jane Reynolds" was written out in full, in the hand of Fanny Thruston, whom she served as lady's maid. The Bath Island Registers are in the Special Collections at the Niagara Falls Public Library. According to an article entitled "A Ramble at Niagara," first published in the *True Wesleyan* and reprinted in the *Colored American* of 22 September 1838: "On Bath Island, which is 24 rods long, and contains about two acres, is the Toll House, where every visitor is expected to record his name, and pay 25 cents for the privilege of being enrolled on this immortal record."

70 Cecelia's Niagara adventures are recounted in Frost, *Steal Away Home*, chap. 2.

71 "Riot At Niagara" was published in the *National Anti-Slavery Standard*, copied to the *Liberator* of 6 August 1847. The story also appeared in the *True Wesleyan* of 14 August of the same year.

72 Christopher Densmore, "Fugitive Slave Cases in Niagara County"; see note 60 above.

73 Extensive research on this incident is provided in Wellman, *Survey of Sites*, 1–2, 159.

74 Barry Sheehy, Cindy Wallace, and Vaughnette Goode-Walker, *Civil War Savannah: Savannah, Immortal City* (Austin: Greenleaf Book Group, 2014), 51. David Ruth Dillon who was Sneed's owner was a broker, tradesman, developer, and sometimes a slave dealer. Paradoxically he went so far as to have an act of state legislature passed in Georgia to legitimize his own marriage to a woman of mixed ancestry named Rachel, who bore him seven children. During the Civil War Dillon ran the blockades on his ship *Amazon* for the Confederacy, until he turned his coat and began shipping supplies for the Union. Noted as a cruel slaveholder, he left large sums and land to his former slaves when he died in 1880. See David Dixon, "A Dash of African Blood: Straddling Savannah's Color Line," *Georgia Backroads* (Spring 2016): 14–16. While Patrick's surname is variously spelled, his collateral descendant Tony Cohen now has definitive proof that the "Sneed" spelling is correct. Tony Cohen, via personal email, 16 August 2017.

75 The name Joseph Lewis is cited for Patrick Sneed in the transcripts of his Buffalo trial in early September 1853 under Judge Shelton. The transcripts survive and were recently rediscovered by archivist Cynthia Van Ness in the William Hodge papers at the Buffalo History Museum. Interestingly, the commitment of the prisoner to trial listed the case as that of "The People vs. Joseph Watson" on 5 September 1853, but the final opinion in the case given on 8 September 1853, states the case title as "The People vs. Patrick Sneed." See MSS ADO-596 William Hodge Papers, Folder 5, Various Topics, Buffalo History Museum Research Library.

76 Christopher Densmore, "Crossing Niagara: Stories of Fugitive Slaves in Western New York," delivered on 14 February 2002, at the Great Works Symposium on "The Underground Railroad," Drexel University, Philadelphia, Pennsylvania.

77 The *Buffalo Daily Courier* of 30 August 1853 reported the collusion if not the active participation of the Whitney family in his escape, as cited in William Bradberry, "A Better Glimpse into the Cataract's Past," *Niagara Falls Gazette*, 5 February 2015, http://www.niagara-gazette.com/opinion/bradberry-a-better-glimpse-into-cataract-house-s-past/article_43550e05-7537-57f0-9f15-4621764483f9.html.

78 Letter, Susan Greeley, Hamilton, Canada West, to James P. Greeley, Colborne, Canada West, in Rogers Family Papers, Early Correspondence and Documents, Archives of Ontario, F 533-1-0-1, Reel 522. The letter is dated only 2 September with no year listed but was surely written in 1853; it describes the flight of a fugitive slave from a Niagara Falls, NY, "Hotel" who, from the detailed description of his flight and recapture after his accusation of murder and the return of the ferry in midstream, could only have been Patrick Sneed.

79 Patrick Sneed was charged with murdering James W. Jones at Savannah in the course of making his own escape from Georgia in July 1849. Carter Godwin Woodson, Rayford Whittingham Logan, "Some Undistinguished Negroes," *Journal of Negro History* (1918): 145.

80 There was frequent tension between Irish immigrants and people of African ancestry on both sides of the border. The Irish competed with Black workers for low-paying jobs, arousing ill feeling that not infrequently ended in bloodshed. One notable incident took place during the building of the Welland Canal. African Canadian soldiers of the famous "Coloured Corps" that defended Niagara in the 1837 Mackenzie Rebellion (known to American readers as the "Patriot War") remained enlisted and were charged with maintaining peace amongst Welland Canal workers. One attempt to suppress a melee in 1849 resulted in a racist attack on the soldiers. Winks, *Blacks in Canada*, 152.

81 Sneed was interviewed several times regarding the incident, but the fullest account in his own words comes from Drew, *A North-side View of Slavery*, 99–104.

Sneed says the two waiters who tore him from his captors' grasp were named Smith and Graves.

82 In a fascinating footnote to the tale, Underground Railroad historian Tony Cohen who is Patrick Sneed's great-great-grand nephew has retraced his ancestor's flight from Savannah to Canada by way of the Cataract Hotel. An account of the case including the text of telegrams between Georgia and Niagara and the actual court proceedings was printed in full in the Frederick Douglass Paper under the title " Slave and Not a Murderer. – The Case of Patrick Sneed. – His Examination," 30 September 1853. Melissa Pachikara, "Author's Journey Reveals Ancestor's Escape," *The Gazette*, 15 February 2006, accessed 25 June 2016, http://www.gazette.net/stories/021506/olnenew211024_31951.shtml. Tony Cohen made a video documentary detailing his ancestor's escape, entitled "Patrick and Me,' available on YouTube at https://www.youtube.com/watch?v=nAgGnKPfGDk. I am indebted to my former student Marquis Clayton, of Dartmouth, Nova Scotia, for this important reference.

83 Kratts, "Bringing Lost Souls Home," and obituary of John Morrison, *Niagara Falls Gazette*, 24 November 1869.

84 The *Quad-City Times* (Davenport, Iowa) carried a notice about Niagara in the 15 May 1866 edition, p. 2: "Niagara: At Niagara Falls the note of preparation for the fashionable season is heard on every hand. The Cataract House is already opened, and will be patronized principally by southern families."

85 Anne Neville, "Dig aims to unearth Underground Railroad's daring history at old Cataract House Site," (6 and 8 September 2017), http://buffalonews.com/2017/09/06/freedoms-history-daring-intrigue-old-cataract-house-site.

86 Douglas J. Perrelli and Nathan Montague, "Phase 1A Literature Search and Sensitivity Assessment for the Former Location of the Cataract House City of Niagara Falls, New York, Niagara County, New York," *Report to the Underground Railroad Heritage Commission*, October 2015.

2

A Selection of "Canticles"
(Meditations on Slavery and Imperialism)

George Elliott Clarke

THE FOUNDING OF LUNENBURG
BY COL CHARLES LAWRENCE, OVERSEER

Abreast of Samborough Island –
wind not unfair,
waves mixing dingy and sparkly,
nigh 8 o'clock,
8th of June, 1753,
with sails rippling so lightly,
the creaking keying light music:

I drifted off to that fairy singing,
so elegant,
compared to Negro grunts
in the slaving *Commerce.*

At 3h, I had to wake to order
the Commodore to discharge a gun
to warn adjacent vessels
too close they were
to the lurking, submarine rocks,
able to gnaw timbers to the quick,
and let in the surf
as bodies can let
bloodletting out.

By 4 and 5 a.m., we were across
from Cross Isle,
then, at 7h, the first rosy rays –
Dawn –
occupied the offing.

Now, let go did we of our anchor,
at Merliguash,
vessels being two leagues astern.

The final anchorage of our lot
was at 9 a.m. and ½ an hour.

Come 10h, the Brit ships berthed.
I signalled masters to board,
and make over the boats
with a disposition for landing.

At 11 a.m., I dispatched Rangers
and regulars ashore,
to assume what beach
settlers could secure by Arms.
Ashore, rangers marched,
herding settlers behind,
to the Harbour Head,
taking pains to occupy also
head and haunch of a hill.

Reconnoitring accomplished,
I planned the future, troop fixture,
stationed round blockhouses,
to discourage Indian or French assault.

Capt. Morris, the Surveyor,
laid out streets and forts,
in less than four hours,
so that, at 4 p.m.,
soldiers, settlers
(soon to be "citizens"),
re-embarked the vessels,

it being too late now –
night coming on –
to strike a camp.

Consulted I with the Militia captain,
at 5 p.m.,
to number the settlers available
at 3 a.m.
to begin to settle the town.
He settled on "120":
No more could be prevailed upon
to work more than every second day

(not like slaves).

Provisions were dressed by dusk
to distribute by dawn
because *Time* is building.

Landed 120 men at 3 a.m.
to carry up blockhouses,
furnished with arms,
and guided by Rangers.

More Regulars and Rangers shored at dawn;
a Sergeant secured the summit
of the South East Hill.
Officer and Rangers guarded the landing party.
A Corporal's Guard watched the fresh water brook
at Harbour Head.
Other soldiers took up posts
where the upper blockhouse goes.

These measures –
protecting the extremities of cleared earth –
let settlers come and go,
in vast squads,
labouring in safety,
"speaking even of Michelangelo."

At 6 p.m. of this second day,
I commanded Cap'n Joe Rouse
to take gondolas (canoes)
and larger boats
to ferry the blockhouses to land
and get them towed to their stands.

Men filled the gondolas with timbers
and extra lumber,
now cut into rafts,

complete by 9 p.m.,

and the whole towed to high water by 2h.

A lumber vessel,
protected by the sloop *York*,
followed,

to protect the rafts and the blockhouses,

and the gallows,

set up at once.

[Lunenburg (Nova Scotia) 8 août mmxiv &
Dartmouth (Nova Scotia) 10 août mmxiv]

"SAM SLICK" CONTRADICTS HARRIET BEECHER STOWE

Regard, coldly, the streaming black ink of Homer
and the clotted, red ink of Dante,
both agree:
Slavery improves the slave,
civilizes the master.

Hoi polloi – riff-raff – scalawags,
lack all the dignity
and charity
the Ancients grant th'Ethiopes.

Because of the Impeccable Institution,
Slavery,
there are no Ethiopian bastards,
no Ethiopian beggars,
no Ethiopian dregs
and drags on the public purse,
for they have toil,
may feast and drink,
and every one of em
literally
has *Value*.

But the white poor are real niggers,
the dirtiest niggers,

and all you hissing abolitionists –
bellicose as pepper,
earnest as vomit –
should attend to the piss-ass party

that be the indigent Caucasians,
whose lives mock our civilization.

Miss Stowe, as a political philosopher
and humorist,
but no novelist
(though critics rank me with you,
Trollope, Dickens),

I hope you'll dissociate yourself
from the smug tongues that cast *Slavery*
as an orchestra of screams,

as a gang of white sadists
whipping the backs and buttocks
of whimpering, buck-naked blacks,

as if we were silly enough
to damage lucrative livestock!

Those who mumble such asinine fantasies –
worthy of any opium-addled poet
(Coleridge) –
should be stuck in the ass
with hatpins.

Succulent conversation, heroic chatter:
That's what you Sunday School types produce.

But *Slavery* is not so trite
as a saga of do-gooders versus evil-doers.
Nope.

Masters are not jaunty satyrs;
slaves are not bullwhipped martyrs.

If no hypocrite, one admits earthy facts:
To eat is to murder;
Taxation is *Theft.*
The moral?
Civilization is the exercise of discreet *Violence*,
legal *Violence*,
an arrangement mirroring Divine design.

Anti-Slavery is pro-hallucination –
the despotic notion that *Society*
(genteel, orderly, cultivated, educated)
rests upon unambiguous *niceties.*

But no idyll is unprepared.

If *Slavery* is "mischievous, malicious, and ungodly,"
why, so much worse are the factories –
a Dead Sea of Consciousness –
where capitalists' engines, machines, tools,
blacken white workers with soot, dirt, ash,
and make em stink,
and drink emselves dead.

Compared to these *avant-garde* evils –
of which only Marx mumbles a bit –
and for whom you abolitionist rabble
care not,
Slavery is operatic Venus,
comic Ceres,
and love affairs amid magnolia,
strolls amid peach trees and apple blossoms,
and much milk, much wine, much honey,
and scenes pleasing a water-colourist
or simple, frivolous poems.

Nor should you blame me for naming
Anti-Slavery
as bogus *Philanthropy*, ample blubber,
whose heartless speakers care zilch for blacks!

Rather, your sermons espouse the Utopian Sadism
of Adam Smith and his ilk.

Why don't you rescue the lowly whites
from the dirty mills?

True-blue bluebloods and bluestockings
care
for our black "help."

                    [Helsinki (Finland) 28 juin mmxiii]

PAPERS OF EDWARD MITCHELL
BANNISTER,[1] BARBIZONIAN

I.

No Christian can praise Aubrey Beardsley!
The dwarf drafts pen-and-ink *Terror* –
just clear-black, blue-black, real black, pitch-black
blotches of women,
twigs of men.

His *Kitsch* bewitches Ruddy Kipling, Dicky Burton –
faces as disfigured as an Empire's squiggle cross a map.

Rather treasure Tennyson's rapids of light.
Cast aside Beardsley's pitcher of smoke.

Tennyson is radiant drink –
gold-leaf mead –
letters that equal unequalled liqueurs.

To follow Beardsley, though,
is to play Golliwog in a gutter:

The fiend's drawings splay rats in high-heels –
haughty, axe-faced rodents with dirty tits

(the middle-class is necessarily unoriginal) –
the boudoirs plumped on *Plunder*.

His sickly figures are sycophantic cocksuckers;
his madonnas show cunts bumpy with herpes.

(Indifferent winter freezes their postures –
prostrate, supine, crucified.)

All his subjects require face transplants.

II.

Coming from Nouveau-Brunswick –
Saint Andrews by-the-Sea, New Brunswick –
I paint – exult in – bovine pathos –
oxen moving as unhurried as sunset.

I stroll amid oiled sunlight,
democratic gold,

and loll in grass
and lounge in moss –

democratic as Whitman.

Why should I copy the puny excretions
of Beardsley?

I expect to depict efficiently marbled water –
such as the waves of Passamaquoddy Bay –
or reset th'Acropolis, but in a cornfield.

Being the first African artist in America,
unfulfillable *Excellence* –
never painstakingly pallid or piebald execution –
is my wont.

IV.

Let Beardsley, Toulouse-Lautrec, *et al.*,
spelunk in the abysses of the brothel,
retrieve bodies that are metallic smoke.

Rather, there's *Beauty* in a weather-beaten boat,
or in flame-polished eves,
and in pastoral scenes as honest as manure.

Gaze upon ivory moon and sable night!

But open Tennyson and sound silvery music,
golden in the hearing –
level, yet exalting.

His sonnets are stained-glass texts.

God is, for him, a medieval *Brilliance*,
and one reaches Him when caught up in wine.

But Toulouse-Lautrec, Beardsley, their ilk,
contemplate *Pestilence* that eats through cosmetics –
so Austen's *Emma* is unmasked
as Flaubert's *Emma Bovary*.

Their pens surrender bastard scum –
racailles –
gutless lice –
that daylight ought to incinerate.

Just like Baudelaire, these so-called *artistes*
mooch off Can-Can whores –
the malicious peddlers of tuberculosis.

Discard their rabbit-like anatomies!
Serve em a rinse of wine-like fire –
a stringent cleansing!

Reading Tennyson,
I'm captive of *Magnificence* –
as unfenced as sunrise.

And I enjoy the intoxicating honey that's Virgil,
the dreamy nobility of *paysans* in Millet,
the facts of absolutely fat cows
in Maine or in Massachusetts,
their sincere mooing.

Art is arrogant.
My narcissism is accidental.

Give Toulouse-Lautrec his buffoon Hell;
grant Beardsley his peep-show divinity.

I will prove as rigorous or as whimsical
as my signature.

[Saint Andrews by-the-Sea (New Brunswick)
Noël mmxi & Niagara Falls (New York) 1 janvier mmxii]

BANNISTER REFLECTS

To breakfast on pollen, in filtered light,

until night's sooty finality
along the brash North Atlantic –
the cold, bare, rude rocks –
the shallow vantage point of boulders –
and to spy Anglo-Saxon moors
reborn in this Moorish New Scotland –
is to suffer hard-edged hallucinations,
stumble among bric-a-brac architecture
of brackish puddles and tumbled pines –
or amble into settler churches,
the cast-offs of cathedrals –
and inhale the giddy smell of molten ice,
all April,
all over mud-flat Fundy ...

Against the epic whiteness
of this cold, uncivil, asexual, ruinously European America,
we Blackamoors seem foolhardy silhouettes –
despite our strutting, top hat, Creole pose,
and our niggardly muses,
too narrow in thought to loudly blot out
chalked-up Yellow Journalism,
what refuses our Art to be hung,
but insists our selves be lynched.

I view Audubon's almost audible Art –
his atypical signature –
the dead-end spectacle,
the obsessive gutting,
the self-satisfied craftsmanship,
of his frigid, morbid aviary,
imprisoned in painting's rigid frames.

The artist is an appropriate usurper
of animate Nature –

it suits our adventurous instinct,
to relocate the wild to a parlour –
or a library –
with saintly imperiousness.

My task: To paint Classical Music,
cut with Country n Western,
so that banjo and fiddle
violently displace harp and violin.

To ramble, not rampage,
and commune with spume,
driftwood, snow-foam,
or spill an elixir of silken willows
from paint pots onto canvas,

and to imagine cattle sauntering through an orchard,
sudden as blossoms.

Or I can try thinking like a horse,
and activate snorts or whinnied
by mottling clear blue
with gaseous white,
the breathy emissions of a chilly pastoral dawn,
a journey in chalk.

Paint pinpoints a picnic setting for a rape
(see Manet),
or the iconic, royal black shadows
where assassins lurk as saints are born.

I don't have an odd-job brain.
I paint so I can buy milk
or gasp at wine's insouciance
and lose my balance.

Nor do I exhibit Audubon's casual grisliness –
his hyperbolic slaughters that please
the salacious elites
of America's venomous imperium,

its symbol being an eagle (vulturous)
as inflexible as rigor mortis.

Nor am I as smug as a savant –
or purse-proud as Midas.

No, as an "African" outta
Saint Andrews by-the-Sea,
I see my canvasses,
pliant as light,
drafting an unmistakeably
Negro Renaissance.

[Baltic Sea: Tallinn (Estonia) – Helsinki (Finland) 29 mai mmxiv]

WILLIAM HALL, VC, REMEMBERS

I.

I swept the fort – the Mosque – with bursts,
volleys, the cannon spat.

First –
out of respect for his sacrifice –
I had to scrape the raw brains
of Lt Cape
from the weapon's side.

I did next all I could –
to copy Nietzsche's superhuman Negro –

to maim the Mosque,
to tumble the temple into wreckage.

II.

Blood – dust – a kind of smegma
smeared the battery, streaking it.

My firing was sprays of shot.

As Her Majesty's emissary,
I meant to bash and crush faces –
bronze and copper –
like so much tin;
to batter and cave in skull bones.

Death would be the heathens's impartial *Disgrace*.

III.

Sweat flopped – slapped – from all my pores
as I did my level utmost
to scalp

the scoundrels, pulp em;
to tussle over the yellow dust of Lucknow –
all that cow-dung
showing an overlay of gold.

Vultures came on thick as crows, squabbling,
bolting clots of blood.

IV.

Eventually triumphant (as ordained),
our Marines surged into the breach
I broke open.

They scuffled, veered, stirred up dust,
teaching the rebel Injuns
their reward is only dung –
just more and more dung in their mouths –

that we have the strength to slaughter our opponents:

All those who'd mob Whitehall,
besiege Buckingham Palace,
overturn the House of Commons,
threaten the Empress,
widow every wife,
rape every virgin,
sack every treasury,
and make London a city of cannibals
and cadavers,
and scholars tutored in the cringing of slaves ...

But such *Victory* – *Anarchy* – the rabble win,
if we'd let the Mosque remain stuck
in Indo-satanic hands.

Any true Briton must fling down and outhurl tyrants –
serve them deathless, mirthless, tireless *Disaster*.

V.

Dusty and dustier, dirty and dirtier, bloody and bloodier
was my solo *Action*,

and so,

though I'm a Coloured Nova Scotian,
I obtained this splendid, bronze trophy.

[Smiths Cove (Nova Scotia) 20 aout mmxv]

CHRONICLE OF THE TRIUMPH OF WILLIAM HALL, VC, AT THE RELIEF OF LUCKNOW, INDIA

Cannon-splintered, the air caved in
as his being – one muscle flexed, reflexed,
careered behind cannon,
careened the machine,
so that the brawnzy, bronze Nova Scotian,
now a slick sheen,
a shining automaton,
or a living carcass,
all nerves dedicated to Sepoy rout,
battered em from ramparts.

The noise was banshee shriek
and rampaging barking,
the lead balls howling
as they hurtled down
and splashed down rebels,
stamping *Carnage* about.

The balls struck with thundering *Terror*.
Each splash-down
rendered a Sepoy trench a mass grave.

As Hall ramped up each ball,
tamped in morsels of powder
to the belly of the cannon,
and kept yammering, hammering, at the mosque –
like breakers bashing, smashing rock,
then splintering into sprinkles –
he looked masoned in bronze.
His form was steel, steely,
as Hall greased the sky with fire,
or shrank it with raucous blooms of smoke.

Eventually, after hours of single-handed
loading, firing,
Hall conceived a gaping breach,
and British troops swarmed finally

into the blood-smeared, black-scorched rubble –
that grim shattering of stone,
and now wrangled over the turf,
rampaging past avalanching bits of wall,
into the tense depths,
where khaki bodies perched berserk in pieces
over a glint of fire still flying, leafing up,
or stone-skewered eyes popped out, dangled,
or men who'd been doubly lopped
formed quadriplegic corpses,
or a foe sprawled,
his head jutting from his shoulders,
but ejected from his neck,
an enormous wound sprawling his brains ...

Disciplined troops –
a dusty bastion –
disintegrated into shambled timbers and stone,
amid the scurrying of unthrottled cries,
thanks to Hall's buckets packed with gunpowder,
his almost reckless *Combat*,
the scattered flashes of his strategic aim.

Thus, the Injuns wept as they bled
and dripped down gore –
Vagabonds were trampled –
for our militants did not slink
through the blazing ruin of the mosque,
but grabbed the grisly crown of *Triumph*,
glistening in the *Slaughter* –
thanks to Able Seaman Hall.

Hall, heroic, was blank-eyed in the skirmish,
uncaring, save for his Queen and The Empire.

[Stratford (Ontario) 4 août mmxv]

THE TRUE HISTORY OF JESSE WILLIAMS[2]

I.

Fresh out from Scotland, the boyish clerk,
too young to accumulate multitudinous sins,
beamed snow-clean, stood lily-upright ...

But the left hand of Jesse Williams, 43 –
ex-slave, Civil War vet, late of Texas –

hacked up the kid with a razor,
then whacked im with an axe.

The feeble backing for this *Murder*
was Williams' staggering drunkenness:

Led him to guess a mercantile transaction
was a *Fraud* perp'd by Adams.

Thus the lad's skull spluttered open.

A hash cook, extra sinister
thanks to his twitchy left eye,
Negro Williams put on no show of *Industry* –
to plod after the creeping plough.

Nope. Instead, he dismayed Adams
via cutting, castrating, and decapitating *Butchery*,

emphasizing roguish *Dexterity*,

leaving po' boy Adams an abiding ruin –
like wintering trees –[3]

statuesque, but dislimbed.

II.

The scene is Calgary, North West Territories,
Dominion of Canada, 1884:
As disorderly as a market,
the city's as policed as a cemetery.

(The *Telephone* is now arrivin.)

Proof?

White dudes jumped on horses –
a stablekeeper passed the posse free reign –
to gallop after Williams –

and "Religious" –
the comical wench Williams claimed his "wife" –

and deliver both *Spite*.

The lynch mob schemed *un cinquain* of *Slaughter*:
1) "nigger" Williams, 2) two half-breeds, 3) two squaws.

The Sarcee lady and buffalo-black dude
trampled snow as they ambled,

and so were custodied –
four miles outta town –
in the Sarcee camp.

The pair faced "blasts of magnitude,"
if they'd not heed
the tenacious facts:

Outmaneouvered & outgunned.

III.

"Judge Lynch" is *de facto* American President.
In Canada, though, niggers
get a trial and a stalwart *Defence*,

despite their bare-face *Guilt*.

Though men brewed, spewed, dark words,
plotting Williams' black-ass fall
(outside of *Law*),

such caustic *Carnage*
be Un-Canadian.

Still, Williams' trial was taut,
was minstrel-banjo *Minimalism*:

Just one day,
including five mins for the jury
to confirm their *Bias*.

Even Religious was not – well – faithful,
for she denounced her "husband."

(Williams was, ironically, a bit like Christ:
Abandoned by all
in His last hours.)

IV.

Passing "smoke-browned, picturesque" teepees,
en route to Calgary,
Williams confessed he'd wanted
"grub and coin"
when he cut young Adams into string.

He blamed "vials of violent spirits"
for his "damned vile fix ...

"A drunkard's house
is a merry universe."[4]

Said he only needed two six-shooters
to scatter the posse
that lasso'd him.

Perfectly *sang-froid* in his cell,
Williams waxed in *Gall*:
succeeded to half-sunder his chains ...

Next, got shackled down,
thanks to a 30-pound ball-and-chain.

V.

A 16-foot scaffold will uphold *Justice*,
letting Williams dangle,
strangling as he hangs.

That "Black Tower" cannot be escaped
easily.

His hanging will be
weightless *Choreography*.

(The jailhouse preacher lisps 2¢ wisdom
clasped by $10 words.)

Williams pledges he'll see his victim, Adams

(from whom blood flew
as if from hog slaughter),

in Heaven.

[Hull (Québec) 14/7/14]

NOTES

"The Founding of Lunenburg By Col Charles Lawrence, Overseer" appears in *Canticles I (MMXVI)*, Guernica Editions, 2016. "'Sam Slick' Contradicts Harriet Beecher Stowe," "Papers of Edward Mitchell Bannister, Barbizonian," "Bannister Reflects," "William Hall, VC, Remembers," and "Chronicle of the Triumph of William Hall, VC, at The Relief of Lucknow, India" appear in *Canticles I (MMXVII)*, Guernica Editions, 2017.

1 Born in Saint Andrews by-the-Sea, New Brunswick, Bannister (1828–1901) was the first significant African Canadian artist, but had his career in the United States, where he is celebrated as being among the first significant African American artists.

2 Cf. Thomson.

3 Cf. Plath.

4 *The Calgary Herald*, 2 April 1884.

3

Radical Legacies in Black Nineteenth-Century Canadian Writing

Nele Sawallisch

The Fugitive Sláve Law (FSL), passed by the United States as a part of the Compromise of 1850, had a substantial effect on the Black communities in North America around mid-nineteenth century. The law represented a new attempt to regain control over Black lives, their movements, and their status, which, in turn, fuelled the discussions on emigration. Canada figured as one prominent destination of flight alongside Haiti, Mexico, and Africa. However, as much as the passage of the FSL seemed a setback in the fight against slavery, the opposition to the law that erupted also showed how active and vocal Blacks in Canada had become by the 1850s. They had always closely observed the goings-on in the neighbouring republic of the US and cooperated with Black and white abolitionists in the United States, England, and Canada itself. Blacks in Canada participated in and provided a space for much groundbreaking work, which included, selectively, the publication of the first newspapers by people of African descent in Canada, *The Voice of the Fugitive* (1851–54), and *The Provincial Freeman* (1853–57), or the international North American Convention in Toronto in 1851. Blacks in Canada openly engaged with radical ideas that were put forth at that time: radical because they put into question white supremacist stereotypes by resolutely participating in shaping a liveable future. In the same way that Harriet Tubman defied the white slaveholding system and its geographical space of control through her radical cross-border movements, numerous other women and men complemented this work by using radical writings to undermine the system through words.

One significant example is Thomas Smallwood's *Narrative of Thomas Smallwood, (Coloured Man),* published in Toronto in 1851. Smallwood's often polemic, always political narrative builds on genre expectations surrounding the slave narrative but quickly sets out to appropriate them to create an idiosyncratic politico-ideological manifesto that takes a stance on prominent topics of his time. In doing so, Smallwood establishes a radical cross-border allegiance with David Walker and his *Appeal in Four Articles* of 1829 by drawing on some of Walker's central ideas. In fact, Walker becomes an underlying presence in Smallwood's account of radical ideas of citizenship, the Black community, and their place in Canada. I argue that Smallwood accepts Walker as his paragon and fashions himself as a living example of Walker's arguments. In doing so, Smallwood puts forth a claim to leadership within Canada West's Black community through the lineage of a Black intellectual genealogy.[1]

This paper will first look at how Smallwood's experiments with a highly successful genre, the slave narrative, enable him to explore alternatives for Black life writing. This allows him to intervene in several contemporary debates. In sketching both the discursive and ideological overlaps and the differences between Smallwood and Walker, it becomes possible to see how Walker ultimately gains the status of a role model whose ideas are still important in the discussions of the Black community's future twenty years after his death. Finally, the paper outlines how Smallwood's establishment of a paragon reflects a strategy in Walker's own *Appeal* and can thus be read as a part of creating a genealogy of Black intellectuals and radical thinkers.

BEYOND THE SLAVE NARRATIVE

Smallwood was born a slave in Maryland in 1801. Freed at around the age of thirty, he became one of the founders of the Underground Railroad (UGRR) in Washington, DC, together with abolitionist Charles Turner Torrey (1813–1846). The two created what Stanley Harrold has called a "biracial antislavery community" in the city.[2] He settled in Canada West in 1843 but led a restless life going back and forth across the border. He engaged in work with fugitives and also became actively involved in political practice on Canadian soil. This involved discussions, debates, petitions, conventions, and meetings. The international North American Convention, for example, which convened in Toronto's St Lawrence Hall in September 1851 as a direct response to the passage of the FSL, adopted resolutions against the FSL, as well as resolutions on gratefulness to the British crown, and on supporting Canada as an emigration destination – all of which were issues Smallwood had addressed in his *Narrative*, which had appeared only a few months before the convention took place.

It appears that Smallwood's foremost quality – which translates into what Sandrine Ferré-Rode has termed his "all-powerful" voice in his narrative[3] – was his directness in dealing with others. It seems that Smallwood always and openly spoke his mind, while showing somewhat less regard for authority, which made him unpopular at times with some.[4] I argue that Smallwood saw himself as a leader, underlining his aspirations through his constant cross-border engagement for Black fugitives in the United States and Canada and, most fiercely, in his *Narrative* of 1851.

Nevertheless, both Thomas Smallwood and his text remain somewhat elusive. Richard Almonte, editor of the 2000 edition of his *Narrative*, claims that there are only "five published sources" through which one can approach him at all.[5] In the same way, the *Narrative* seems to have confused scholars, although at first sight, its outline appears straightforward: the main body of text follows an elaborate preface without further subdivisions; an appendix of four documents serves to complement several of Smallwood's episodes.[6] The main body, the actual "Narrative of Thomas Smallwood," is challenging, however. Almonte laments the brevity of Smallwood's introductory paragraph as basically the only part that "can rightly be said to deal with biographical matters."[7] Indeed, this paragraph summarizes Smallwood's birth into slavery, the regulations of his own and his sister's freedom, and briefly mentions his marriage. Very quickly thereafter, Smallwood moves on to his post-slavery life and hastens to the more immediate present of his writing. Consequently, a large focus of his *Narrative* is placed on his involvement with Torrey in Washington, DC's, Underground Railroad.

Smallwood is not a coherent narrator and digresses often, revisiting many fugitive slave cases that illustrate his work as an UGRR organizer. These episodes deromanticize the UGRR by focusing on the danger involved in organizing, planning, and executing the escapes. Additionally, they point to the conflicted relationship Smallwood entertains with what he portrays as a "perverted" Black community.[8] The abundance of traitor figures and the numerous attacks on his personal reputation, which he is intent on restoring, underline Smallwood's delicate position within the community in Washington, DC. Once he has officially settled in Canada in the fall of 1843, it becomes increasingly difficult for readers to follow his numerous border crossings, which multiply the number of names, character constellations, and fugitive episodes in the *Narrative*.

The confusion scholars have felt when analyzing the text, this paper argues, might also stem from its uncertain genre status. Almonte's call for aid ("Where then do Smallwood as a writer, and the *Narrative* as a nineteenth-century text, find a home?") is paradigmatic in this respect.[9] Upon first sight, in fact,

Smallwood seems to have written a slave narrative. This is no unlikely classification since his text appeared at the outset of a significant literary decade for the genre. The genre of the slave narrative enjoyed great popularity throughout the antebellum era, but after political conditions focused public attention more and more on the figure of the fugitive slave, the genre continued to gain additional momentum.[10] As George Elliott Clarke has demonstrated in his seminal article "'This is No Hearsay': Reading the Canadian Slave Narratives" (2005), slave narratives were greatly relevant in Canadian literature of the nineteenth century as well. Clarke offers a tentative list of such Canadian slave narratives, containing eighteen titles, "almost half" of which were published in Canada, including Smallwood's.[11] Following this argument, the *Narrative*, too, should be considered a part of "Victorian-era Canadian literature (1837–1901)" and should therefore be placed alongside other notable publications from the 1850s, such as Samuel Ringgold Ward's *Autobiography of a Fugitive Negro* (1855), Benjamin Drew's interview collection *The Refugee* (1856), Austin Steward's *Twenty-Two Years a Slave, and Forty Years a Freeman* (1857), and Jermain W. Loguen's *The Rev. J. W. Loguen, As a Slave and As a Freeman* (1859).[12]

While the *Narrative* shows some affiliations with the slave narrative, it also deviates from the genre in significant ways. Given Smallwood's work with the Black community in Canada West, it is likely that he was aware of the popularity of the genre. Indeed, his own title reads like an attempt to capitalize on reader expectations by securing their attention:[13] *A Narrative of Thomas Smallwood, (Coloured Man) Giving an Account of His Birth – The Period He Was Held in Slavery – His Release – and Removal to Canada, etc. Together With an Account of the Underground Railroad. Written by Himself* contains all the elements that would align his work with even its most prominent predecessors. It identifies his name and emphasizes that he is a Black man, lists the different stages of his life until he reaches freedom, and announces his claim to authorship.

On the other hand, however, Smallwood assumes control over his writing and his story in a way that defies the genre conventions. In this respect, Ferré-Rode has foregrounded the ubiquity of Smallwood's "self-defined and self-determined voice" in his text.[14] Smallwood's narrative is indeed striking for the absence of introductory or appended letters by white sponsors. The preface is Smallwood's own, and free from self-humbling justifications or explanatory remarks. He proves that he is writing independently of any white outside influence – a remarkable, even radical, fact, heightened by the contemporary pressures Black authors were under from abolitionist influence and control. Moreover, his bold defiance of the genre's focus on the protracted story of suffering of the protagonist under slavery speaks to Smallwood's "originality" in reframing his priorities.[15] Ultimately, he produces his own, idiosyncratic text that reads more like a manifesto in the line of Walker than the teleological journey of an enslaved individual to freedom.

We might also take this search for where to insert Smallwood as an opportunity to reconsider our understanding of a genre that is open to a lot more creativity and ingenuity than we have recognized.[16] Smallwood's text, a manifesto in the guise of a life narrative, is also an indicator of how Black authors around mid-nineteenth century were exploring possibilities of life writing that exceeded the classic slave narrative. Clearly, Smallwood is not writing as a former slave but a free Black man in Canada West. In fact, he declares that "[i]t is needless for me to go into a detail of the vicissitudes through which I passed during that period [of enslavement]."[17] Instead, he transcends the confines of the slave narrative to focus on his cross-border life in freedom, using his text to reflect the challenges of this life, and create a forum to voice his opinions on current debates within the Black community.

SMALLWOOD AND WALKER

If Smallwood's voice dominates his text from the outset, as Ferré-Rode has demonstrated, there is nevertheless evidence of an influential subtext. The first version of David Walker's famous *Appeal in Four Articles* was published in 1829, with two revised editions following in 1830, "each increasingly militant and inflammatory in tone," according to one biographer.[18] Walker's *Appeal* has become an iconic document of resistance to white dominance and has been influential in shaping the later discourse on Black nationalism.[19] The outrage and upsurge of white fear in the South following the publication were met with Walker's sudden death in 1830, the conditions of which remain a mystery but have contributed to his image as a martyr. In 1848, Henry Highland Garnet reprinted the *Appeal*, adding a preface and biographical sketch of Walker. It is this edition that Smallwood references and partly includes in his text. For Smallwood, Walker is an ideological role model whose radical language he employs, as Clarke has suggested.[20] Additionally, he uses Walker to substantiate his own claims by presenting himself, indirectly, as the living example of some of Walker's assertions (see below). This forms the basis for Smallwood to insert himself in a genealogy of Black leaders such as Walker, whose legacy he tries to both restore and continue.

Smallwood begins by inserting Walker prominently in his *Narrative*. After his own preface, he reproduces, verbatim, Garnet's biographical sketch and introduction from the 1848 edition of the *Appeal*. This instance of life writing within life writing further extends Smallwood's intertextual strategy of his preface. This highly complex opening section recreates a sense of living in "stirring times," following the sense of urgency that is visible in Walker.[21] For Walker, as much as for Smallwood, the question of slavery was irrepressibly pushing the United States to a possibly violent resolution.[22] His *Appeal* thus appeared at a crucial moment to raise awareness amongst his fellow slaves and freemen to take a stand, a call that Smallwood follows in his *Narrative*. Moreover, Smallwood connects what he perceives as an "age of epochs" to the notion of great representative men.[23] Positioning Walker directly following this preface, Smallwood inserts him into the line of extraordinary – this time, *African American* – men of the age.

Smallwood's inclusion of Henry Highland Garnet's two short pieces on Walker also serves the purpose of authentication. In addition to reintroducing Walker to public attention, Smallwood is also eager to restore authorship and authenticity to his *Appeal* and to his person in the middle of a plagiarism scandal. Smallwood makes explicit reference to Paola Brown, who first appeared in Upper Canada in 1828, who had unabashedly copied large passages from the *Appeal* in the "Address ... on the Subject of Slavery" he gave in Hamilton's City Hall in February 1851 (notably, shortly before Smallwood published his *Narrative*).[24] Smallwood calls attention to Brown's plagiarism while at the same time acts to ensure that his readers know the true origin of the text.

Restoring this intellectual property, for Smallwood, is a way of paying respect to Walker but also introduces one of the major concerns he shares with his role model. Through his criticism of the figure of Paola Brown, Smallwood alludes to the complex relationship he entertains with the Black community early on in his text. In fact, Smallwood treats fellow African Americans with even harsher judgments and language than Walker twenty years prior. While Walker, too, had been seriously concerned with "the colored people [who] are now, in the United States of America, [disunited],"[25] Smallwood seems almost obsessed with the treachery and disunion amongst the community. These topoi reappear throughout his narrative, giving way to numerous instances in which Smallwood feels sabotaged by other Blacks. The detailed account of his UGRR work with Torrey, for example, is interspersed with several "remarkable pieces of treachery" featuring traitor figures like George Lee and Benjamin Lannum.[26] Smallwood marks them as social and moral outcasts who take advantage of the suffering of Black fugitives. Additionally, Smallwood portrays himself as a victim who fights the more vague menace of rumours that are spread about his person. In a dispute with the preacher Abraham Cole, for example, Smallwood reports that "his friends strove to do me all the injury they could by ... mak[ing] it appear among the respectable portion of my own colour, that I was a great traitor to my race."[27] Such a verdict posed a great danger to Smallwood's fugitive work, in the same way that the number of his traitor episodes showcase the threat individuals like Lee and Lannum represented when they turned against their own community.

Against the background of disunion, Walker's *Appeal* is committed to overcome internal division as a result of white-induced "ignorance" in order to bring about the betterment and improvement of Black people.[28] Walker's language is as incendiary as it is empowering, since he seems optimistic with regard to possible betterment: "we can help ourselves ... if we lay aside abject servility, and be determined to act like men."[29] Smallwood, on the other hand, does much to reveal what he, too, perceives as self-inflicted harm of the Black community but overall seems pessimistic at the thought of fundamental change. He accuses "the coloured men of the present generation" of lacking "energy [and] courage" to overcome imitations of the white man.[30]

What is more, both writers connect impressions of Black division and strife to their "scathing" critique of the United States as a place of broken promises and self-righteous idolatry of freedom.[31] Certainly, one reason why Walker's *Appeal* created such an outrage among white (pro-slavery) Americans was his decided rejection of their monopoly to interpret the Declaration of Independence. Walker is instrumental in lucidly dissecting this ur-American document, exposing it not as the origin of democratic self-definition but as the root of a hypocritical politics of white supremacy. After citing the declaration's famous beginning, Walker's *Appeal* gains a performative quality that highlights its inherent discrepancies: "See your declaration, Americans!! Do you understand your own language? ... Compare your own language above ... with your cruelties and murders inflicted by your cruel and unmerciful fathers on ourselves on our fathers and on us [*sic*]."[32]

Walker thus radically challenges the young nation's self-understanding of being free and equal; yet, he includes white citizens in a discourse of necessary change.[33] Walker asks white Americans to stand true to their overtly inclusive promise, which implies self-awareness ("understand your own language") as well as fundamental societal and political changes. Although Walker calls out white racism and oppression as features of the "natural enemies" to Black people, it seems that it is necessary to face this enemy on the same soil.[34] Walker's equally radical stance on colonization, which he had situated as a key issue by 1829, serves as an example here.

His demand to "tell us now no more about colonization, for America is as much our country, as it is yours" implies the indisputable right of African Americans to lay claim to a home that they had helped build and sustain for over two centuries.[35]

Smallwood's conclusion on the situation for Black people in the United States, however, is unfavourable and his outlook on race relations in the country, more finalized than Walker's. He heightens Walker's denunciation of racism and oppression into a more polemical and more hostile final judgment by concluding that "[t]he United States is the most hypocritical, guileful, and arrogant nation on the face of the earth."[36] Later, he predicts that "the people of the United States will never voluntarily grant the African race among them freedom."[37] A form of dialogue with white Americans seems impossible for Smallwood. Faced with an incorrigible *nation* (see below), he pushes for viable alternatives and powerfully constructs his allegiances to Canada and Great Britain. In contrast to Walker, these allegiances constitute Smallwood's true focus. His *Narrative* is largely concerned with his personal feuds with the Black community in the United States, which flare up again each time he re-crosses the border and position him at the heart of Black disunity. Ultimately, this position is connected to his disdain of a nation that he experiences as threatening, chaotic, and conflict ridden, whereas Canada seems to provide a safer, more harmonious place of residence.

The impression of stability and security finally invites us to consider how both Walker and Smallwood conceptualize the *other* space, Great Britain and Canada, in their texts. Both authors make use of the powerful binary opposition that has become a common argument in abolitionist discourse, plotting a slavery-free Britain against the slavery-ridden United States. In the end, however, Walker and Smallwood arrive at ambiguous positions of Britain and its North American *dépendance*, Canada. Walker powerfully begins by portraying Great Britain as reliable and representing the "best friends the colored people have upon earth."[38] At the same time, the former English implication in the slave trade is played down. In fact, the British abolition of the slave trade in 1807 weighs more heavily for Walker and is seen as more beneficial to Black Americans than the "little cruel" oppression of Black people through slavery.[39] Walker underlines his radical political trajectory, having already voiced his claim that Black people were as rightfully "American" as whites,[40] by calling on his fellow Blacks to form an alliance with Britain: "There is no intelligent *black man* who knows any thing [*sic*], but esteems a real English man."[41] What is more, he specifically uses the term "nation" to identify British support for Blacks, possibly also to contrast it to the often-cited "American slave Republic": "as a nation, the English are our friends."[42] If ever Walker was to consider emigration, he seems to imply, "the hospitable shores of Canada," being closest to Britain on the North American continent, are a promising option.[43]

Against this argumentative background, Smallwood's allegiances to Walker (and Great Britain) are obvious. Smallwood inserts himself in the rampant discussion on the possible emigration goals for Black people in the 1850s by pursuing Walker's ideas. The Toronto Convention of 1851 would openly endorse loyalty to Great Britain and its monarchy, while Mary Ann Shadd Cary would follow, in 1852, with her *Plea for Emigration* to promote Canada as a destination.[44] Smallwood, too, supports both Britain and Canada for offering Black people the only "true freedom" which the United States failed to provide.[45] When he visits the Black pioneer settlers in the Queen's Bush in 1843 and 1846, he praises their "resolution" and achievements as self-made men who "had settled there with no means whatever." Real[46] change for the community, Smallwood suggests, only seems possible in Canada, the "*true* land of opportunity" for Black people.[47]

Similar to Walker, Smallwood sees Britain as providing "the best national freedom" for Black people despite its slaveholding past.[48] The convert status of Great Britain after the Slavery Abolition Act of 1833 from slaveholder to abolitionist is extended to Canada, where the past of slavery is blotted out. In this respect, Smallwood confirms Clarke's observation that many narratives which discuss Black life in Canada are "so rich with almost bombastic praise for Canadian/British 'liberty,' that the more negative, earlier accounts of white settler racism are obscured to the point of erasure."[49] Therefore, I would argue, there is no conclusive answer in the *Narrative* on the question of what status Britain and Canada should have for the Black community. The chaos and conflict Smallwood describes every time he re-crosses the border into the US do not seem to end when he returns to Canada, a place apparently filled with opportunity for Black emigrants. The class bias he evidences in putting Black settlers in the Canadian wild hierarchically above Blacks who remain in the US does not contribute to settling the conflict with the community. The fact that he admits "a prejudice equal to any thing [sic] I have ever experienced in the south [sic]" in his "Preface" complicates Smallwood's image of the Canadian haven and precludes a sense of resolution in the *Narrative*.[50]

BLACK INTELLECTUAL GENEALOGIES

If Smallwood sees Walker as a role model, he also both identifies with and authenticates Walker as a part of a Black intellectual and activist genealogy in which he ultimately seeks to insert himself. This strategy, too, finds its origin in Walker's *Appeal*, which openly addresses the question of a Black intellectual tradition, an issue that is subsequently mirrored in Smallwood's *Narrative*. In the *Appeal*, Walker himself identifies with the Rev. Richard Allen (1760–1831), founder of the African Methodist Episcopal Church in Philadelphia. He inserts Allen's letter on the question of colonization, originally published in the *Freedom's Journal* on 2 November 1827,[51] as a clear and decided refusal of the "Colonizing of Africans in Liberia."[52] Allen's final verdict – "This land which we have watered with our tears and our blood, is now our mother country, and we are well satisfied to stay"[53] – foreshadows Walker's own rejection of colonization by claiming that "America is as much our country, as it is yours."[54]

Walker is also the scribe of Allen's homage, portraying him as an exemplary member of the Black community and a fighter for the betterment of its condition. Allen even becomes a "godly," "entirely pre-eminent" man, and a hero who "has done more in a spiritual sense for his ignorant and wretched brethren than any other man of colour has, since the world began." Yet, Allen is not only a man of superlatives but also one who is at the heart of Black disunity, assailed by his critics, and "now in obscurity in degradation." Walker pictures him as a man who nevertheless prevails and foresees justice for Allen's reputation in the future, no less at the hands of "coloured historians in succeeding generations" who will provide the "gazing world" with the yet missing perspective of Black people on slavery. As such, Walker predicts the rehabilitation and acknowledgment of Richard Allen as one of "the greatest divines who have lived," while at the same time, his figure serves to foretell with assuredness the rise of Black scholars and authoritative Black historiography. This radical challenge to white history writing, though seemingly future oriented, underlines yet again the performativity of Walker's text which is actively engaged in laying the foundations for Allen's place in "the pages of history."[55]

Smallwood continues this genealogy of notable Black men by focusing on Walker. He authenticates him through the reproduction of Garnet's sketch and the introduction in his own preface, defending Walker against Brown's "diabolic" appropriation and plagiarism.[56] He endorses Garnet's biographical portrait of Walker's moral respectability as "an estimable man."[57] In the same way that Walker described Allen, Garnet builds on Walker's predictions of a future Black historiography by establishing him as an exceptional African American hero who has made the essential "boldest and most direct" contribution to the early anti-slavery effort: "When the history of the emancipation of the bondmen of America shall be written, whatever name shall be placed first on the list of heroes, that of the author of the Appeal [sic] will not be second."[58]

This assessment reflects Smallwood's control in his *Narrative* in the sense that what is at issue here is the continuation of a Black intellectual, activist tradition through the voices of Blacks themselves. Smallwood's principle of being independent of outside white authenticators is being maintained in his appraisal of Walker through Garnet. Walker, like Richard Allen, becomes a martyr-like figure whose reputation awaits restoration. Incidentally, both would die in brief succession, in 1830 and 1831 respectively. In turn, the attacks on Walker mark the grounds of identification for Smallwood: his *Narrative*, too, focuses on the perceived abuse of his public reputation and how he prevails. His portrayal of a conflicted Black community that is made up of enemies who attack his work and character is set against his attempts to rectify, correct, and restore his image as a fighter for Black fugitives. Therefore, a genealogy emerges in which David Walker stands on the shoulders of Richard Allen and in which both Garnet and Smallwood single out Walker as a leader and role model. Although he never utters the claim directly, Smallwood's *Narrative* stands as testimony to his willingness to continue radical discussions within the Black community and to aspire to becoming one of its outstanding leaders like Richard Allen and David Walker before him.

NOTES

1 Upper Canada and Lower Canada existed from 1791 until 1841 when the Act of Union created the Province of Canada, which was subsequently divided into Canada East and Canada West. The Province of Canada ceased to exist upon Confederation in 1867. Although Thomas Smallwood lived and published mainly in Canada West, I will use "Canada" and "Canada West" interchangeably for mere simplicity's sake. It should also underline the presence of Black people in all the different provinces that make up Canada today.

2 Stanley Harrold, *Subversives: Antislavery Community in Washington, D.C., 1828–1865* (Baton Rouge: Louisiana State University Press, 2003), 67.

3 Sandrine Ferré-Rode, "A Black Voice from the 'Other North': Thomas Smallwood's Canadian Narrative (1851)," *Revue Française d'études américaines* 137 (2013): 27.

4 The *Narrative* mentions several personal feuds, including the traitor figures George Lee and Benjamin Lannum, or the minister Abraham Cole. Additionally, Almonte notes that Smallwood was among the shareholders who sued the

Provincial Freeman. Richard Almonte, "Introduction," in *A Narrative of Thomas Smallwood (Coloured Man)* (Toronto: Mercury Press, 2000), 11.

5 Almonte, "Introduction," 9. He lists the five sources as 1) the *Narrative* from 1851; 2) the Report of the Convention of the Coloured Population, Held at Drummondville (1847); 3) the Toronto City Directory after 1846, in which Smallwood and his family are listed; 4) passages in Mary Ann Shadd Carey's biography; and 5) brief passages in *The Slave's Narrative*, edited by Charles T. Davis and Henry Louis Gates Jr (1985). To this relatively short list, we could add a few more primary documents that highlight Smallwood's involvement in the Black community, such as the "Address to the Colored Citizens of Canada" (1863) in *Black Abolitionist Papers*, vol. II, *Canada, 1830–65*, ed. C. Peter Ripley (Chapel Hill: University of North Carolina Press, 1986), 513–14.

6 Smallwood's appendix contains a rectification on a financial transaction, two short pieces on slavery and Blacks in Canada, and a letter to the Albany *Weekly Patriot*, signed with his alias "Samuel Weller, Jr."

7 Almonte, "Introduction," 9.

8 Ferré-Rode, "Black Voice," 31.

9 Almonte, "Introduction," 16.

10 In her foundational study *The Slave Narrative* (1988), Marion Wilson Starling has described the antebellum period as the golden age of the slave narrative. Marion Wilson Starling, *The Slave Narrative: Its Place in American History*, 2nd ed. (Washington: Howard University Press, 1988), 1.

11 George Elliott Clarke, "'This is No Hearsay': Reading the Canadian Slave Narratives," *Papers of the Biographical Society of Canada* 43, no.1 (Spring 2005): 17. In the article, Clarke convincingly argues that Canadian slave narratives have for too long been misconceived as an "exotic species of Americana" (7). In Canadian academia, this attitude has led to the discarding of a whole body of texts. These are instructive on the conditions for Black refugees, exiles, and activists, many of whom were fugitives from US-American slavery, their pioneer lives in the Canadian "wild," as well as race relations, discrimination, and prejudice before the Constitution Act of 1867 created the Dominion of Canada.

12 Clarke, "This is No Hearsay," 7.

13 See Almonte, "Introduction," 9.

14 Ferré-Rode, "Black Voice," 28.

15 Ibid., 27.

16 John Ernest's *Oxford Handbook of the African American Slave Narrative* offers new approaches to the genre. In the collection, for example, Winfried Siemerling considers it from the angle of hemispheric studies. John Ernest, ed., *Oxford Handbook of the African American Slave Narrative* (Oxford and New York:

Oxford University Press, 2014), 344–61. In his own recent monograph, Siemerling moves toward a cross-border approach to Black Canadian literature of the nineteenth century. Winfried Siemerling, *The Black Atlantic Reconsidered. Black Canadian Writing, Cultural History, and the Presence of the Past* (Montreal and Kingston: McGill-Queen's University Press, 2015).

17 Thomas Smallwood, *A Narrative of Thomas Smallwood, (Coloured Man:) Giving an Account of His Birth – The Period He Was Held in Slavery – His Release – and Removal to Canada, etc. Together With an Account of the Underground Railroad. Written by Himself* (Toronto: James Stephens, 1851), http://docsouth.unc.edu/neh/smallwood/smallwood.html.

18 John C. Inscoe, "Walker, David," *Dictionary of North Carolina Biography*, 6 vols., ed. William S. Powell (Chapel Hill: University of North Carolina Press, 1979–96; NCpedia, 1994), http://ncpedia.org/biography/walker-david.

19 Thabiti Asukile, "The All-Embracing Black Nationalist Theories of David Walker's Appeal," *The Black Scholar* 29, no. 4 (Winter 1999): 16, http://www.jstor.org/stable/41068837. As Asukile explains, Walker's "radicalism," much like the term "black nationalism," as discussed in the reading of Walker by Sterling Stuckey (1972, 1987), has been debated among scholars (see 17). Asukile points out that while many think the terminology in reference to Walker is anachronistic and usually applied to later figures like Delany, it is important to note that Walker's *Appeal* "would become an ideological foundation for what Sterling Stuckey interprets as black nationalist theory" (17).

20 George Elliott Clarke, review of *A Narrative of Thomas Smallwood (Coloured Man)*, by Thomas Smallwood, ed. Richard Almonte, *University of Toronto Quarterly* 71, no. 1 (Winter 2001–2): 271, http://doi.org/10.1353/utq.2001.0305.

21 Smallwood, *Narrative*, iii.

22 David Walker, *Walker's Appeal: With a Brief Sketch of His Life*, ed. Henry Highland Garnet (New York: Printed by J.H. Tobitt, 1848), Project Gutenberg, 2005, 61, http://www.gutenberg.org/files/16516/16516-h/16516-h.htm.

23 Smallwood, *Narrative*, iii. In all, Smallwood's "Preface" references a mosaic of no less than twenty-nine writers, politicians, and some of their most representative works from all ages. They include a wide variety of personalities from John Milton to William Shakespeare, from Napoleon to Lord Brougham, from William Wordsworth to Robert Burns and, not least, the British abolitionists Thomas Clarkson and William Wilberforce.

24 John C. Weaver's biography of Brown does not note the plagiarism of the speech, which he summarizes as "fus[ing] in prophetic rhetoric his passion for black freedom in the United States and his vision of divine justice." John C. Weaver, "Brown, Paola," *Dictionary of Canadian Biography*, vol. 8 (Toronto: University of Toronto/Université Laval, 2003), http://www.biographi.ca/en/bio/brown_paola_8E.html.

25 Walker, *Appeal*, 30.
26 Smallwood, *Narrative*, 28.
27 Ibid., 32.
28 Walker, *Appeal*, 30.
29 Ibid., 73–4.
30 Smallwood, *Narrative*, 55.
31 Clarke, review, 271.
32 Walker, *Appeal*, 85–6.
33 Asukile suggests a parallel between Frederick Douglass and Walker in that both "desired to live in a society where free Africans and white Americans could coexist as a nation," "The All-Embracing," 20. Consequently, Asukile refuses to call Walker a Black nationalist in the sense that he did not explicitly strive for a separate Black nation.
34 Walker, *Appeal*, 71.
35 Ibid., 80.
36 Smallwood, *Narrative*, 46.
37 Ibid., 48.
38 Walker, *Appeal*, 53.
39 Ibid.
40 Ibid., 80.
41 Ibid., 53 (original emphasis).
42 Ibid.
43 Ibid., 61.
44 Mary Ann Shadd Cary, *A Plea for Emigration, or, Notes of Canada West* [1852], ed. Richard Almonte (1852; reissue, Toronto: Mercury Press, 1998).
45 Smallwood, *Narrative*, 33.
46 Ibid., 55.
47 Clarke, "This is No Hearsay," 26 (original emphasis).
48 Smallwood, *Narrative*, 44.
49 Clarke, "This is No Hearsay," 18.
50 Smallwood, *Narrative*, vii.
51 The original document can be accessed via the Wisconsin Historical Society at http://www.wisconsinhistory.org/Content.aspx?dsNav=N:4294963828-4294963805&dsRecordDetails=R:CS4415.
52 Quoted in Walker, *Appeal*, 67.
53 Ibid., 68.
54 Ibid., 80.
55 Ibid., 69.
56 Smallwood, *Narrative*, ix.
57 Ibid.
58 Quoted in Walker, *Appeal*, iii.

4

The Miracle of Ann Maria Jackson, Slave Fugitive and Heroine of the Underground Railroad

Afua Cooper

Canada has been long hailed and mythologized as the "final stop" on the Underground Railroad and has also been called "the promised land," "Canaan's land," "glory land," and a "haven and refuge." However, this perspective of the Railroad privileges an Anglo-American continental context that focuses on a south-to-north movement of enslaved fugitives. It does not take in account the *north-to-south* passage of runaway slaves from places like the Carolinas and Georgia, to the Spanish colony of Florida for more than a full century before 1793. The Spanish government, hostile to Anglo-American encroachment on southern territories, and fighting various religious and political wars with both England and colonial America, offered refuge and freedom to enslaved Africans from the Anglo-dominated territories to the north. Hundreds of enslaved Blacks seeking freedom spirited themselves away to Florida where they set up free communities under Spanish rule.[1] Enslaved Africans also found refuge in Florida among such Native tribes as the Seminole and Creek and became part of these nations, and together, Blacks and Natives also organized collective resistance.[2] A major part of Canada's allure was because, as a British territory, in Upper Canada for example, the process of the abolition of slavery had begun in 1793, when that province passed an act to limit slavery. Finally, in 1834, Britain abolished slavery in its colonies including Canada. This made Canada most attractive to enslaved African Americans who liberated themselves from slavery and wanted to leave behind permanently a slavery-soaked soil.[3] It has been estimated that at least 35,000 enslaved African Americans successfully made it to Upper Canada on the Underground Railroad (UGRR).

It is important to underscore that there would not have been an Underground Railroad had it not been for enslaved Africans who actively sought their liberation by emancipating themselves from slavery. There are certain stock images associated with the Railroad. The fugitive is usually a male; he is pursued by hound dogs; he sprints across the border into Canada in just the nick of time; he falls on his knees and kisses the ground. He lives happily ever after. This image of Canada welcoming the fleeing fugitive has lodged itself in Canadian consciousness and has become part and parcel of Canadian national identity.[4]

Within this frame there has been little space for imagining the women and children who also fled slavery. However, recent Underground Railroad research has begun to pay serious scholarly attention to the imbrication of gender within such field of study.[5] This paper contributes to this work by examining the story of Ann Maria Jackson. I read Jackson as an Underground Railroad heroine and highlight how the details of her story offer important possibilities for rethinking UGRR narratives through attention to gender, motherhood, and Black women's embodied resistance. Here attending to gendered risk as the starting point for telling this story allows us to examine the surprising and rich details of Ann Maria Jackson's flight in a fresh light to foreground her experiences as a woman with children fleeing slavery.

Though the UGRR's most famous conductor, and the name we associate most frequently with the Railroad, is that of a woman – Harriet Tubman – it is only in the last two decades that a scholarly biography of her life has been published.[6] Tubman, herself a fugitive from slavery, is chiefly remembered for her role as an indomitable conductor guiding runaways to freedom. Legend has it that she conducted more than three hundred enslaved Americans to freedom in Canada. The actual number of persons Tubman escorted to freedom is approximately seventy.[7] Nevertheless, in both fact and legend, Tubman stands as a towering figure in Black history on both sides of the border.[8] She has been honoured with plaques and monuments in both countries because of her formidable legacy.[9] We do not know if Harriet Tubman personally aided Jackson in her quest for freedom. But the Wilmington–Philadelphia–New York–St Catharines route that Jackson took on her freedom journey was the route Tubman employed when she took fugitives to freedom. Along this path she partnered with such abolitionists as Thomas Garrett (Wilmington), William Still (Philadelphia), and Hiram Wilson (St Catharines) – the very people who aided Jackson. Jackson's freedom route matches the one Tubman frequently used to transport her fugitives.

Ann Maria Jackson of Delaware fled slavery for Canada in the fall of 1858. With the help of supporters and friends, Jackson and her seven children reached St Catharines, Ontario. Soon after Jackson's arrival in St Catharines she was sent to Toronto, which was felt to be safer.[10] There she built a life for herself and her seven children. Her youngest child, Albert, grew up to become Canada's first Black postman.[11] Tubman's own accounts of her journeys from Wilmington, Delaware to Ontario, gives us some sense of the circumstances of Jackson's own flight to Canada. Wilbur Siebert, one of the first scholars to write about the UGRR, interviewed Harriet Tubman and learned from her one of the principal routes she took from Philadelphia leading fugitives to the north and to Canada. Tubman notes that she travelled by train from Philadelphia to New York City. From NYC, she once again used a real train to Albany, where UGRR helper Stephen Myers welcomed and looked after her and the runaways. Refreshed, she and her group boarded another train from Albany to Rochester "where the fugitive slave, Frederick Douglass, would see that she got on the train for the Suspension Bridge and St Catharines in Canada."[12] Did Jackson and her seven children ride the train on the suspension bridge from New York to St. Catharines, Ontario? It seems likely. The coincidences and crossings of these narratives potentially prove illuminating.

The Jackson story is not just one of triumph. Tragedy is the other thread that holds this narrative together. Jackson was a mother of nine children, and just before her flight to freedom, her slave owner seized two of her older children and put them for sale on the slave market. Jackson's husband went mad on account of losing his children. He died in the mental asylum. It was the loss of her two children and the death of her husband that prompted Jackson to flee from Delaware slavery.

As an Underground Railroad scholar, the story of Jackson and her escape has always intrigued me. It was difficult for anyone to escape slavery, let alone for a woman to escape with seven children. I wrote a poem for Jackson (see "Seven Children") and later featured her "startling" story in the *Underground Railroad: Next Stop, Freedom* exhibit I co-curated for the federal government. A book with a similar title followed.[13] I returned to Jackson's story in another exhibit, *A Glimpse of Black Life in Victorian Toronto*, commissioned by the City of Toronto Museums. Ann Maria Jackson's story is part of the global story of Black emancipation rooted in particular American and Canadian historical circumstances. My interest in the Underground Railroad is not about the national myths enshrined of Canada as the "last stop" on the Underground Railroad. Instead, I am drawn to the narratives of strength, resilience, struggles, sufferings, and bittersweet triumph of freedom seekers. These men, women, and children endured much in their bid to escape conditions that robbed them of dignity, humanity, and family and caused them to

be in danger of losing life and limb.[14] Additionally, I am interested in exploring the tensions inherent in Canadian history being both a slaveholding and
slave-rescuing country simultaneously. To bring Jackson's history to light I
consulted census records, street directories, letters, headstones on graves,
obituaries, and published accounts. The following is the resulting story.

DELAWARE AT THE CROSSROADS OF SLAVERY AND FREEDOM

Since the colonial period, slaveholding legislators clashed with each other
over the future of slavery in Delaware. Some who were anti-slavery were of
the view that slavery discouraged free labour, and took away jobs from
Whites. These legislators were concerned more with the economic future of
poor Whites and thus were not necessarily pro-Black. Proslavery politicians
and their supporters felt that the labour of the enslaved was vital to the state's
economy, and that if the enslaved were freed they and the rest of the free
Black community would desire and clamour for social equality with Whites.
These men believed in the superiority of the White race, and would not and
could not countenance racial equality in the state. Furthermore, many White
proslavery Delawareans believed that if the enslaved were liberated they
would turn against Whites in a Nat Turner like bloodbath.[15]

Sitting on the Mason-Dixon line, Delaware was the recipient of and
caught between two models of slavery. Some legislators looked to the north,
favouring the Pennsylvania model of gradual abolition, while others turned
their gaze south, viewing the Maryland framework of continued and
expanded bondage for Black people as ideal. Debates on the future of
slavery in the state continued through the colonial, Revolutionary, early
Republic, and antebellum eras. In the end slavery was finally abolished by
the 13th Amendment to the Constitution, ushering in the triumph of the
Union during the Civil War.[16]

At the same time – due to the surplus of enslaved Africans as a result of
the change in the economy (from tobacco to wheat and corn), the outlawing
of slave importation, and the manumission by Whites who took seriously
the Revolutionary ideal of freedom – slavery began to decline in Delaware.
By 1840 only 13 per cent of the state's Blacks were enslaved, and slaves
made up a mere 3 per cent of the total population. This meant that there
were more freed Blacks than enslaved people "in proportion to its population than any state in the union."[17] By 1861, three years after Ann Maria
Jackson's flight, there were less than 1,800 enslaved Blacks in Delaware
and around 20,000 free Blacks.[18]

Even with the majority of freed people in the Black population, slavery was still important in Delaware because it was a source of wealth for those who owned human bodies. Slaves were property. They and their labour were owned by others, who therefore reaped the fruits of their labour. Enslaved bodies were also literally money. Enslavers could sell them for cash (for example to pay debts and mortgages), use them as collateral, exchange them for other goods, and/or gift them to their heirs. The children that issued from the bodies of the enslaved were also owned by the enslaver. As was the case with two of Ann Maria's offspring, children were often hired out by their owners who collected their pay, and they too were frequently sold for cash.[19] Enslaved children thus provided another income stream for slave owners.[20] The experience of the Jackson family demonstrates that familial bonds could be broken up at any moment by slaveholders who desired cash for their slaves.[21]

Bondswomen and men resisted slavery everyday in diverse ways. Most never passively accepted their bondage and sought to undermine the system that dehumanized them. Flight was a significant act of resistance. In every slave state, in every time period, tens of thousands of enslaved people ran away or attempted to run away from slavery. Research reveals that more men than women ran and that the men who took flight tended to be in their prime – between the ages of fifteen and thirty-five. Men from this age group made up 70 per cent of all runaways.[22]

Why is it that more men than women attempted to escape or escaped from slavery? The answer probably lies in the fact that men had more access to the outside world through the kinds of occupation in which they were engaged. Men dominated almost all the skilled jobs, such as carpentry and masonry; they were also coach and carriage drivers. And more men than women were hired away from the plantation to work in urban areas or on other plantations. Additionally, many men had wives who lived on other plantations and were permitted by their owners to visit their wives. All this meant that men had a better sense of the geography around them, a knowledge that would become very useful if and when one decided to flee.[23]

Perhaps even more importantly the prime age for running away, that is between the ages of fifteen and thirty-five, covered "a woman's peak childbearing years." Put another way, it was during these years that women who might have considered running were either pregnant, nursing, or raising children. Children tied up a woman's leg. Instead of running, many women stayed put – with their children.[24]

Escape was dangerous and physically demanding – even for men. Escapees often had to cross or hide out in swamps and forests, fight off insects, and encounter snakes in their flight from slavery. Escapees were vulnerable to extreme weather conditions, were prone to diseases, hunger, thirst, and starvation, and were often than not tracked down by slave catchers and their hounds. These risks were multiplied for women with babies and infants.[25] Underground Railroad scholar J. Blaine Hudson notes, "Thus, given the risks of flight, escapes by pregnant women with small children seemed particularly desperate and suggested either the operation of some powerful triggering event – or, perhaps, the expectation of significant assistance along the escape route that off-set the impracticalities of flight."[26]

Yet many women did run – and were successful. And that so many escaped – and with young children – was an especial miracle. Ann Maria Jackson was one such woman. The event that "triggered" her flight was the sale of two of her children and the further threat of sale of four of the others.

MY CHILDREN, MY CHILDREN, HE SOLD MY CHILDREN

Sometime before her escape, Ann Maria Jackson lived with John Jackson, her husband, who was a blacksmith, a free man, and father to their nine children.[27] Her slave owner was one Joseph Brown of Milford, Kent County. Brown hired out Mrs Jackson to other Whites to work as a washerwoman. It was hardly a benevolent act on the part of Brown to allow Jackson and her husband to live together with their children on his property. The fact is that Brown collected most of Jackson's wages, and it was she and her husband who supported the children, so allowing them to live together, meant lower costs for him. Although John Jackson, the children's father, was in the picture, Brown still owned Jackson's children. He hired out several of Jackson's children and collected the wages they earned. Thus, Brown was not even supporting the enslaved children, even though he collected the wages of those who worked. He could do this because he owned their bodies. Additionally, he could sell them if he wished. The Jackson children who were hired out most likely worked as house servants, babysitters, or field hands.[28]

Through her work, Jackson had a modicum of independence. She lived with her family (was allowed to live with her husband) and probably learned the geography of the land through Brown's practice of hiring her out. The fact that the Jacksons lived in a nuclear family setting was unusual. It was the norm for Delaware enslaved families to live in extended family units consisting of mothers, grandmothers, and children. Most enslaved children grew up without fathers. If the father was Black, whether free or enslaved, he tended to live elsewhere and would exercise his spousal and parental duties as a visiting husband and father. Sometimes the fathers of enslaved children were White men, whether these were their owners or other planters, and such cases paternity would never be acknowledged. It is not known how many Black enslaved Delawarean families lived in nuclear family settings like that of the Jacksons but what is known is that only a small percentage of Black men had that privilege or possibility.[29]

We learn more about women, slavery, and work in Delaware from the words of one Mrs Ellis of St Catharines, Ontario. Mrs Ellis was an escaped Delawarean who was interviewed by Boston journalist Benjamin Drew on his tour of the Black communities of Canada West. Mrs Ellis notes that the triggering event for her flight was her master's threat of selling *her* away from her children. With the threat of sale hanging over her, she fled through the Underground Railroad with her two children. Ellis spoke of the oppression of slavery and the work she did in her home state.

> I felt put down – oppressed in spirit. I did a great deal of heavy out-door work, such as driving team, hauling manure, etc. I have been whipped with a wagon whip and with hickories – have been kicked and hit with fists. I have a bunch on my head from a blow my master gave me, and I shall carry it to my grave.[30]

Ellis was brutalized by her owner and traumatized by the kind of work she did. It was hard and heavy labour. Driving team and hauling manure was considered to be men's work. But under slavery, a gender division of labour sometimes was not obtained. Women were foremost units of production, in other words, they were seen as labourers, before they were gendered as women. Bernard Moitt in his work on women and slavery in the French sugar island explained that women did the hoeing, weeding, and cutting of sugar cane as much as men did. "Feminine protection" from hard labour and physical abuse was reserved for White women. While many enslaved women like Jackson worked primarily as washerwomen, this type of labour was also physically demanding.[31]

Being a mother of nine children made Jackson a slaveholder's delight because she was seen as a "good breeder." Slavery dictated that children born of slave women, even in a patriarchal society like the slaveholding United States, inherited the status of their mother. The principle *partus sequitur ventrem*, which meant that children followed the condition of their mothers, came from old Roman civil law, which was adopted by many of the New World slave regimes. This was one instance in which western slave owners turned patriarchy on its head to accommodate the commodification of Black women's wombs. This was so even if the fathers of slave women's children were free persons. Thus, Mr Jackson, though a free man, had no legal rights over his children.[32] Sometime before Ann Maria Jackson's escape, her master "snatched and sold" two of her children. It seemed that these were two he was in the practice of hiring out. When Joseph Brown sold Jackson's children, her husband and father of the children turned his grief inward and went mad. Surely, he must have felt great love and affection for his children and was supremely angry and frustrated that he could do little to protect them. William Still notes, he was "rendered a fit subject for the mad-house." Mr Jackson later died in the mental asylum "a raving maniac."[33]

Ann Maria Jackson was forlorn at the loss of her two children. We can imagine both her and her husband, grief stricken about the loss of their children and furious at the slaveholder Joseph Brown for what he did: *my children, my children, he sold my children! My children, my children, he stole my children!*[34] Ann Maria's grief knew no bounds when her husband died in the madhouse. Desperation added another dimension to her grief when she learned that her master was going to sell four more of her children. Thus, she began to plan for her freedom and that of her remaining children.

Jackson in 1858 must have known about the UGRR, which had been in operation through the upper South for at least thirty years prior. Delaware had several stations on the UGRR, and Jackson most likely saw and knew of fugitives who escaped through the state. When Joseph Brown violated her bonds of motherhood and parenthood, she began her quest for liberty. The state capital, Wilmington, was one of the last stops on the Underground Railroad before arriving at the Pennsylvania border. For enslaved Delawareans fleeing north, Pennsylvania, a free state, was the promised land. Many fugitives however, did not settle permanently in Pennsylvania It was too close to the slave states and thus was a hunting ground for slave catchers working at the behest of slave owners who paid them to seek out and capture their runaway slaves. Thus, many self-emancipated slaves continued their journey north, until they eventually reached the Canadian provinces.

Free Blacks, Whites, and even enslaved Africans formed a solid network of freedom workers within the state of Delaware. They linked to other freedom activists in the neighbouring states of Maryland and Pennsylvania. Thomas Garret for example, a White Quaker abolitionist in Wilmington, Delaware was a known stationmaster who was arrested and jailed in 1847 for his UGRR activities. Additionally, within Wilmington itself there were several free Blacks who were active as Underground Railroad helpers.

Some of these included Black laborers Comegys Munson and Severn Johnson, mulatto laborer Joseph Walker, and black brickmaker Henry Craig. Joseph Hamilton of Wilmington offered his home as a "regular stopping place" for slaves fleeing to Pennsylvania. Abraham Shadd, a mulatto shoemaker who also lived in Wilmington, was a leading abolitionist and undoubtedly helped fugitives from Delaware and other slave states escape to the North. In Camden, just south of Dover, William Brinkley aided fugitive slaves.[35]

Historian William H. Williams also notes that "free blacks aided escaping fugitives from both Delaware and other slave states by guiding them along the freedom trail, providing them with food and shelter, and obstructing the attempts by white authorities to apprehend them."[36] Mention must also be made of Samuel Burris, a Delaware-born free Black who lived in Pennsylvania. Burris often ventured south into Delaware to escort fugitive slaves to freedom. In 1847, Burris was arrested for aiding fugitives. He spent ten months in jail after which he was put on the auction block to be sold as a slave. Fortunately for Burris, some White abolitionists, pretending to be slave buyers, showed up at the auction, made the highest bid, bought him, and then ferried him to free soil[37]

Through a network of freedom workers, Ann Maria Jackson and her seven children were able to flee from Joseph Brown's plantation in central Delaware. We do not know how Jackson made contact with the Underground Railroad. However, by 21 November 1858, she had made it north to Wilmington and was in the "care" of Thomas Garrett. Garrett's home was a refuge for thousands of fugitives on Delaware's UGRR.[38] Garrett in Wilmington would then pass them along to William Still in Philadelphia. On 21 November 1858 Garrett forwarded the following letter regarding Mrs Jackson and her children to Still (and J. Miller McKim) of Philadelphia.[39]

Wilmington

11th Mo, 21st, 1858

Dear Friends, I write to inform you that on the 16th of this month, we passed on four able bodied men to Pennsylvania, and they were followed last night by a woman and her six children, from three of four years of age, up to sixteen years; I believe the whole belonged to the same estate, and they were to have been sold at public sale. I was informed yesterday, but preferred seeking their own master; we had some trouble in getting those last safe along, as they could not travel on foot, and could not safely cross any of the bridges on the canal. Either on foot or in carriage. A man left here two days since, with a carriage, to meet them this side of the canal, but owing to spies they did not reach him till 10 o'clock this morning in a second carriage, on the border of Chester county, where I think they are all safe, if they can be kept from Philadelphia. If you see them they can tell their own tales, as I have seen one of them. May He, who feeds the ravens, care for them, Yours Thomas Garrett.[40]

We glean several things from Garrett's letter regarding the specifics of Jackson's journey as well as the wider network and formation of the UGRR. As a document it reveals a complex network of communication and movement. From this account, Garrett and other helpers on the UGRR had made contact with Jackson or vice-versa. One of the older children was taken from the larger family group and sent by himself along the freedom path. (It seems that the family was reunited in Philadelphia.) Garrett and his helpers determined that the family could not travel on foot because the children were very young and would not be able to walk the long distances required. Garrett and his friends procured a carriage to take the family to freedom. However, there was a problem. Jackson's owner, once learning of her flight, had sent slave trackers on her heels. They watched all the bridges and canals they thought she and her family would cross in order to get to Pennsylvania. Thus, even with the carriage procured, the family still could not continue their journey. However, that was remedied when another helper procured an additional carriage and the family was able to successfully cross over from Delaware into Philadelphia, Pennsylvania, where William Still met them. Garrett expressed the view that the family might be safe in Philadelphia if the slave catchers "can be kept away."

The importance of Philadelphia and its freedom network in the Underground Railroad cannot be overstated. William J. Switala notes that

Philadelphia was at a pivotal point on the Eastern Route of the Underground Railroad in Pennsylvania. Fugitives coming from the South arrived there over land and sea routes. In addition, many of the routes of the Southeastern corridor converged on the City. It was also a dispersal center from which fugitives were send northward to New York City and the towns of New England ... Without Philadelphia, the Eastern Route network would not have been successful as it was.[41]

Philadelphia was the first "free" station north of the Mason-Dixon line and hence a crucial stop on the Underground Railroad escape route. Thousands of fugitives from upper South and lower South states passed through Philadelphia. The city was home to a strong abolitionist and an active and vibrant Black community.

The indefatigable Still was Philadelphia's chief stationmaster. He would become known as the "father of the Underground Railroad." He was also one of the founders and leaders of the Philadelphia Vigilance Committee, an anti-slavery organization dedicated to helping fugitive slaves as they arrived in Philadelphia and other parts of Pennsylvania. Still and the committee helped to send more than a thousand runaways, including his own brother, to freedom and safety in other northern states and Canada.

In his book, *The Underground Railroad*, published in 1872, seven years after slavery's abolition, Still, in the role of historian, recorded for posterity the stories of more than six hundred runaway slaves that he assisted once they arrived in Philadelphia. Still interviewed the fugitives who sought refuge at this station. He noted their names, their places of birth and residences, the names of their owners and locations of their plantations, and he recorded other pieces of vital information. It was through this method of questioning that Still was able to determine that one Peter Still, a fugitive from slavery who had sought his aid in Philadelphia was his own brother.[42] Still was impressed with the fact that Jackson, with her many children, had the courage to flee from slavery. He writes, "The fire of freedom obviously burned with no ordinary fervor in the breast of this slave mother, or she never would have ventured with the burden of seven children to escape from the hell of slavery."[43] In his account, he describes Jackson in the following way:

> Ann Maria was about forty years of age, good-looking, pleasant countenance, and of a chestnut color, height medium, and intellect above the average. Her bearing is humble, as might have been expected, from the fact that she emerged from the lowest depths of Delaware slavery.[44]

Still then goes on to relate how her master snatched two of her children from her and sold them and the subsequent descent of her husband into madness. The narrative Jackson relates is rich and poignant:

> Prior to the time that the two children were taken from their mother, she had been allowed to live with her husband and children, independently of her master, by supporting herself and them with the

white-wash brush, wash tub, etc. For this privilege the mother
doubtless worked with double energy, and the master, in all probability,
was largely the gainer, as the children were no expense to him in their
infancy; but when they began to be old enough to hire out, or bring
high prices in the market, he snatched away of two of the finest articles,
and the powerless father was immediately rendered a fit subject for the
madhouse; but the brave hearted mother looked to God, resolved to
wait patiently until in a good Providence the way might open to escape
with her remaining children to Canada ... Under her former lot she
scarcely murmured, but declared that she had never been at ease in
slavery a day after the birth of her first-born. The desire to go to some
part of the world where she could have the control and comfort of her
children, had always been a prevailing idea with her. "It almost broke
my heart, she said, "when he came and took my children as soon as
they were big enough to hand me a drink of water. My husband was
very kind to me, and I had often wanted him to run away with me
and the children, but I could not get him in the notion; he did not
feel that he could, and so he stayed, and died broken-hearted, crazy.

I was owned by a man named Joseph Brown; he owned property
in Milford, and he had a place in Vicksburg, and some of his time he
spends in there, and some of the time he lives in Milford. This Fall
he said he was going to take four of my oldest children and two other
servants to Vicksburg. I just happened to hear of the news in time.
My master was wanting to keep me in the dark about taking them,
for fear that something might happen."[45]

We learn several facts from Jackson's narrative. She looked after herself
and family in slavery. Her master hired her out, and she worked as a washerwoman. The hiring out of enslaved people by their owners was a common
practice. Many times slaveholders did not have "enough" work on their
farms to give to their enslaved property, so they hired them to other White
families and plantations. In spite of the "independence" Jackson had by
being allowed to live with her husband, she lived in constant fear, every day
since the birth of her first-born, that her owner would sell her children. Her
fears came true. Her master played a cat and mouse game with her, watching her and plotting when was the best time to snatch her children. She
described her master as a depraved individual. He was a hard drinker, he
swore, and he was in thrall to money. But slavery dictated that he could get
richer on the backs of his enslaved property.

What shone through Still's narrative about Jackson was her strength, courage, and resilience. When she discovered her master's plot to kidnap four of her other children, she knew the time was right to leave. Still continues Jackson's story:

On the road, the poor mother with her travel-worn children became desperately alarmed, fearing that they were betrayed. But God had provided better things for her; her strength and hope were soon fully restored and she was lucky enough to fall into the right hands. It was a special pleasure to aid such a mother.[46]

We picture Ann Maria with her children, glancing furtively over her shoulder. The children weary, fretting, and fearful. She was a desperate woman yet she persevered and thus, determined to escape from slavery, her master, and his spies and slave catchers, Jackson related to Still that, once in flight, she feared she was betrayed. However, she was not, and her "flight attendants" conducted her to the home of William Still.[47]

TO ST CATHARINES, ONTARIO

William Still sent Mrs Jackson on to St Catharines, Ontario. St Catharines is located close to the American border, not far from Niagara Falls. This made it a significant site for the Underground Railroad crossing. From Philadelphia to Canada, there were several routes one could take. One of those routes went through Pennsylvania itself, through the Allegany mountains, then into western New York, with an important stop at Buffalo. From Buffalo, the fugitive could hurry on to Niagara Falls, Ontario and then into St Catharines. Alternatively, Still could have sent Jackson through the route that went from Philadelphia through northern Pennsylvania to Scranton, from Scranton to Ithaca, then Syracuse (a vibrant station on the UGRR), from Syracuse to Rochester (where abolitionist Frederick Douglass lived), from Rochester to Buffalo (where UGRR agent Jermain Loguen lived), and from Buffalo to St Catharines. Central and western New York was filled with UGRR stations and this latter route seems the more likely one through which Still sent Jackson.

In St Catharines, Jackson and her children were received by abolitionist, teacher, and missionary Hiram Wilson. The New Hampshire-born Wilson had been in Canada for more than twenty years working as an agent of the American Missionary Society. In Canada, Wilson had opened several schools for Black children. He was also instrumental in founding the

Dawn Settlement with famed fugitive abolitionist Josiah Henson. After his work at Dawn, Wilson relocated to St Catharines where he continued his work to further Black liberation.[48]

St Catharines had a strong and active Black community at the time Jackson arrived. UGRR heroine and conductor, Harriet Tubman established a home at St Catharines during this period, and though there is no evidence, Tubman might have been instrumental in conducting Jackson out of Delaware and into St Catharines. We know that, in Delaware, Garrett worked closely with Tubman and we also know that, in St Catharines, Wilson worked hand-in-glove with Tubman. Once Jackson arrived safely in St Catharines, Wilson wrote the following letter to William Still.

Niagara City

Nov. 30th, 1858
    Dear Bro. Still: I am happy to inform you that Mrs. Jackson and her interesting family of seven children arrived safe and in good health and spirits at my house in St. Catharines, on Saturday evening last. With sincere pleasure I provided for them comfortable quarters till this morning, when they left for Toronto. I got them conveyed at half fare, and gave them letters of introductions to Thomas Henning, Esq., and Mrs. and Dr. Willis, trusting that they will be better cared for in Toronto than they could be at St. Catharines. We have so many coming to us we think it best for some of them to pass on to other places. My wife gave them all a good supply of clothing before they left us. James Henry, an older son is, I think, not far from St. Catharines, but has not as yet reunited with the family. Faithfully and truly yours, Hiram Wilson.[49]

Toronto was inland, far enough from border points, and thus, it was felt to be safer for fugitives. Border towns like St Catharines were hotbeds for slave catchers and bounty hunters. Toronto also had a strong abolitionist network and a vigilant Black community that assisted new Underground Railroad immigrants. The Anti-Slavery Society of Canada exemplified this network of UGRR support. A coterie of Scotch Presbyterians dominated the leadership of the Assc. Rev. Michael Willis, principal of Knox College, was president of the society. Thomas Henning was secretary. And Mrs Agnes Willis (wife of the president of the ASC) was president of the Ladies' Fugitive Aid Society, an auxiliary to the ASC. The Ladies Society was organized to assist fugitives in Toronto.[50] With aid from Toronto abolitionists, including the Black community, Ann Maria and her "interesting family" settled down to life in Toronto. Another surprising turn of this story is that the two children, sons who were taken by the family's slave owner Joseph Brown and put on the slave market, were themselves able to escape on the Underground Railroad and made it to Toronto where they were united with their family.[51] The two boys, James Henry and Richard M. Jackson passed through the hands of William Still in Philadelphia, made it to St Catharines, and then on to Toronto.[52]

There were close to 50,000 people living in Toronto at the time of Jacksons' arrival. Of this number, close to 1,500 were Africans or Blacks. Most were Americans, and a good percentage, like Jackson, had roots on the Underground Railroad. Blacks in Toronto pursued a number of different occupations, had established several churches of diverse denominations, fraternal organization, anti-slavery and Black rights associations, and were making a contribution to the rise and growth of the city.[53]

Jackson took up residence in the St John's ward, around the area of today's City Hall. According to the 1861 census, she was living on Edward Street in a one-storey frame house.[54] In 1868, according to the City of Toronto Directory, Mrs Jackson was still living on Edward Street. The 1871 census finds her living on Elizabeth Street in St Patrick's ward. Six of her nine children, ages ranging from twenty-nine to twelve were still living with her. The census also records Jackson as continuing to work as a washerwoman.[55] Over time the children grew and they too became workers; some married.[56]

Even as the Jackson family members established themselves in Toronto and became Canadian, they did not forget John Jackson, husband to Ann Maria and father of the nine children. On 19 December 1867, in the very year the Canadian nation state was born as a confederated polity, Mary Jackson, now twenty-two years of age, and daughter of Ann Maria, married Daniel Carter. On the marriage record, Mary's origin is listed as Delawarean, and Daniel Carter, age twenty-seven, was a Virginian who had lived with his parents Daniel and Isabella Carter. The father of the bride is listed as John Jackson. It must have been a poignant moment for the bride to list the name of her father on her marriage certificate. Mary Jackson was a teenager when she fled Delaware with her mother and siblings and must have grieved the death of her father even as she made her escape from slavery.[57] At the time of her marriage, she had been in Canada for nine years and thus had become an adult on Canadian soil. But she did not forget her father and his tragic demise in the United States. At her marriage, she had no father to "walk her down the aisle" as tradition demanded, and this would have saddened her. The inclusion of John Jackson's name on his daughter's marriage certificate, though a normalized practice, could also be read as a memorial to him.[58]

Ann Maria Jackson became well known in the Toronto Black community. Her flight on the UGRR, with her seven children, was a topic of much conversation. In Toronto, Jackson established a close network of friends and supporters. She was neighbour to Charles Freeman and Martha Davey, Black civil rights activists. Freeman was a member of the British American Anti-Slavery Society, a local abolitionist society dominated by Blacks.[59] We also know that wealthy Black entrepreneurs Thornton and Lucy Blackburn befriended Jackson and her children. Jackson and the Blackburns became lifelong friends. The friendship continued into death. In 1880, Mrs Jackson died from "dyspepsia." She was buried in the Toronto Necropolis inside Thornton Blackburn's tomb.[60]

THE MEANING OF JACKSON IN HISTORY

What does it mean to write the history of enslaved and fugitive Black women, who, by their very status, were made historiographical outcasts in Canadian history? Doing Black women's history is still a work of excavation. And, in the case of Ann Maria Jackson, it means putting together disparate pieces of written artefacts to construct as much as possible a coherent story. Three male abolitionists wrote two letters and a report that somewhat document the history of Ann Maria Jackson's escape with the seven children and their journey "on the road." These three documents form the basis upon which I was able to construct a partial history of Jackson, both of her life in slavery and freedom. Once she arrived in Toronto, her presence and that of her children were noted in archival documents such as censuses, city directories, newspaper articles, and marriage and death records.

In recent times, the story of the Jackson family gained further prominence in a public history poster designed for Canadian public schools and the public at large. The "North Star to Freedom: Women on the Underground Railroad" poster published and printed in 2012 by Green Dragon Press, pays homage to eight fugitive Black women who escaped to the Northern states and Canada on the Underground Railroad. The women featured on the poster are Ann Maria Jackson, Ellen Craft, Deborah Brown, Lucie Blackburn, Ann Maria Weems, Charlotte Giles, Harriet Eglin, and Harriet Tubman. But prominence is given to Ann Maria Jackson and her seven children. Jackson is placed at the centre of the poster. She sits serenely, a bonnet on her head, surrounded by seven children, with the youngest, the toddler Albert, sitting on her lap.[61] It is not known who took the time to sketch Jackson and her family. Perhaps it was William Still or someone from the Philadelphia Vigilance Committee as this image appears in Still's narration of the Jackson family in his book *The Underground Railroad*. Did Jackson and the children "sit" for an artist or did the drawing come from the memory of its creator? In the drawing, Jackson looks hopefully at the artist. The children appear happy. And no doubt they and their mother were both hopeful and happy, given that they had escaped slavery.

But there was a pain in the heart of Jackson and the children. She had lost her husband, and the children had lost their father to slavery's vicious grip. I would submit that, throughout their lives, the pain of losing a husband and father stayed with them. It is worth noting that every triumphant Underground Railroad story like that of Jackson's was coloured by loss and sorrow. For every fugitive who was successful in their bid for freedom, there were countless others who were not. Runaways almost always left behind family and friends. And some family members, like Jackson's husband, died of grief and depression upon losing their kinfolk.

Ann Maria Jackson made a desperate, heroic, and successful dash for freedom on the Underground Railroad. By this act, the fugitive Jackson crossed the forty-ninth parallel and established a Canadian familial history. Descendants of Ann Maria Jackson and her children now live all over Toronto, other parts of Ontario, and beyond. Jackson's son and youngest child, Albert, grew up to be Canada's first Black postman. Albert's distinction was punctuated with struggle because the White men who ran the postal service did not want to train or work with a Black man. It took the intervention of Prime Minister John A. Macdonald for Albert to be confirmed in his role as postman.[62] The year in which this controversy over Albert Jackson's role blew up, 1882, was an election year, and Macdonald wanted the Black vote. The Liberals were already gaining ground in Black communities. As prime minister and leader of the Conservative Party, MacDonald personally intervened to order the postal service to train Jackson as a postal worker and integrate him in the service. This was done, and the Conservatives won the election and the Black vote in Toronto. Historian Colin McFarquhar notes that though Blacks in Toronto in the 1880s lacked economic and social equality they had some political clout – they could make a politician lose or win an election – and thus, politicians, even known afrophobes like John A. Macdonald, would sometimes open their ears to Black plight, as is illustrated in the case of the Albert Jackson affair.[63]

Stories such as Ann Maria Jackson's are still little known within Canadian history or women's history. We know about White pioneering women like Laura Secord, Madeleine de Vercheres, Elizabeth Simcoe, and other "founding mothers" from Canada's colonial past. Jackson arrived in Toronto when the future of the two territories on either side of the forty-ninth parallel were to be decided by their politicians. The American Civil War, which would decide whether enslaved Africans would be freed or continue in bondage, was three years from its commencement, and Canadian Confederation, which would usher in the new Canadian national polity that would be premised on the idea of a "white man's country," was nine years away. Jackson's story provides an important opportunity for research on the complexity of the Underground Railroad at this juncture and its meaning to both American and Canadian concepts of freedom. The Jackson narrative also highlights the critical and continuing importance of gender and Black women's histories to Canadian studies. Putting the story of poor, marginalized, and fugitive Black women like Jackson at the centre of our historical inquiry would create a revolution in our civil consciousness.

NOTES

1 Jane Landers, "Southern Passage: The Forgotten Route to Freedom in Florida," in *Passages to Freedom: The Underground Railroad in History and Memory*, ed. David Blight (New York: Smithsonian Books and HarperCollins, 2004), 117–31.
2 Ibid.
3 There is a veritable genre of what I call "Canada as haven" literature. Two examples will suffice. *Freedom's Land: Canada and the Underground Railroad*, TV, Canadian Broadcasting Corporation Documentary (2004; Toronto, CBC, 2004); Joyce Pettigrew, *A Safe Haven: The Story of the Black Settlers of Oxford County* (South Norwich Historical Society, 2006).
4 Canadian historian and professor Fred Landon has perhaps been the chief architect of this particular framing of the Underground Railroad to Canada. He published dozens of articles on the topic and is perhaps responsible for cen-tring the "glorious heroism" of the Railroad into the Canadian psyche. Karolyn S. Frost, et al., *Ontario's African-Canadian Heritage: Collected Writings by Fred Landon, 1918–1967* (Toronto: Dundurn, 2009). For my critique of the UGRR as mythology and ideology see Afua Cooper, *The Hanging of Angélique: The Untold Story of Slavery in Canada and the Burning of Old Montreal* (Toronto: Harper Collins, 2006), 69. See also Abigail B. Bakan, "Reconsidering the Underground Railroad and Racialization in the Making of the Canadian State," *Socialist Studies* (Spring 2008): 1–27.
5 For a very recent American treatment on women on the Underground Railroad see, Erica Armstrong Dunbar, *Never Caught: The Washingtons Relentless Pursuit*

of their Runaway Slave, Ona Judge (New York: Atria, 2017). For a Canadian perspective, see Adrienne Shadd, in Peggy Bristow, et al., *We're Rooted Here and they Can't Pull Us Up: Essays in African Canadian Women's History* (Toronto: University of Toronto Press, 1999); and Anthony Patrick Glesner, "Laura Haviland: Neglected Heroine of the Underground Railroad," *Michigan Historical Review* 21, no. 1 (1995): 19–48. Novelist Colson Whitehead also recently published the brilliant *The Underground Railroad* (New York: Doubleday, 2016). Though he hints at Canada, the novel takes place within continental United States. In this work, Colson has a real train running underground. The main protagonist is a woman.

6 The biography of Tubman is that by Kate Clifford Larson. See her *Bound for the Promised Land: Harriet Tubman, Portrait of an American Hero* (New York: Ballantine, 2004). Other scholarly works include Catherine Clinton, "'Slavery is War': Harriet Tubman and the Underground Railroad," in *Passages to Freedom: The Underground Railroad in History and Memory*, David Blight, ed. (New York: Smithsonian Books and HarperCollins, 2004), 195–209.

7 Kate Clifford Larson combed the historical records to arrive at an estimation of how many people Tubman led to freedom. She arrives at the figure of seventy and states that Tubman gave directions to an additional fifty. Larson, *Bound for the Promised Land*, xvii. It was Tubman's first biographer, Sarah Bradford, who exaggerated the number of enslaved Blacks that Tubman led from slavery. Bradford claimed that Tubman made nineteen trips to the South and freed three hundred persons even though Tubman herself believed she freed about fifty. Bradford's number began to be repeated time and time again until it became "true." Sarah Bradford, *Scenes in the Life of Harriet Tubman* (1869; reissue, Auburn, NY: W.J. Moses, 2015), reprint 2015.

8 See Ron Stodghill, "Harriet Tubman's Path to Freedom," *New York Times*, 24 February 2017.

9 Larson, *Bound for the Promised Land*. On 11 March 2017, The United States' National Park Service and the Maryland State Park Service honoured Tubman by opening the Harriet Tubman Underground Railroad Visitor Center. A stretch of the highway on Maryland's eastern shore (where Tubman was born) was also named after Tubman. On 27 May 2011, Parks Canada named Harriet Tubman "a Person of National Historic Significance" and unveiled a plaque in her honour in the town of St Catharines, Ontario, where Tubman once lived. The Ontario Heritage Trust has also unveiled a separate plaque in Tubman's memory. In addition, the Harriet Tubman Institute for Research on the Global Migrations of African Peoples, York University, Toronto, is named after Tubman. There are numerous other memorials to Tubman on both sides of the border.

10 William Still, *The Underground Railroad* (Medford, NJ: Plexus Publishing, 2005), 371–3.

11 In February 2019 Canada Post unveiled a commemorative stamp featuring Albert Jackson – Canada's first black letter carrier – more than one hundred years after his death.

12 See Larson, *Bound for the Promised Land*, 94. The Suspension Railway Bridge was built across the Niagara River in 1855 to connect via rail Niagara Falls, New York to Niagara Falls, Ontario. Numerous fugitive slaves rode on the train across the bridge from the United States into Canada. Wilbur H. Siebert, *The Underground Railroad from Slavery to Freedom* (New York: MacMillan, 1898; reissue, North Stratford, NH: Company Publisher, 2000).

13 This exhibit was commissioned by Parks Canada of the Canadian federal government. It opened at the Royal Ontario Museum in 2002 and went on to be showcased at several museums across the country. Adrienne Shadd and Karolyn Smardz Frost were the other curators. We later published a book inspired by the exhibit. See, *The Underground Railroad: Next Stop, Toronto* (Toronto: Natural Heritage Press, 2002; reissued in 2005 and reprinted in 2022 by Dundurn Press).

14 Bryan Prince does this with his *A Shadow on the Household: One Enslaved Family's Incredible Struggle for Freedom* (Toronto: McClelland & Stewart, 2009).

15 William H. Williams, *Slavery and Freedom in Delaware 1639-1865* (Lanham, MD: 1996), 74–5.

16 Ibid., 176.

17 Ibid., xvii. See also 141, 143.

18 Ibid., 174–5.

19 Henry Bibb was an enslaved child who was hired out and whose earnings were kept by his slaveholder. See *Life and Adventures of Henry Bibb, An American Slave* (Madison: University of Wisconsin Press, 2000), introduction by Charles J. Heglar. Bibb's young life has been immortalized in fiction by Afua Cooper. See *My Name is Henry Bibb: A Story of Slavery and Freedom* (Toronto: Kids Can Press, 2009).

20 For insights into the experience of children in slavery, see Wilma King, *Stolen Childhood: Slave Youth in Nineteenth-Century America* (Bloomington: Indiana University Press, 1995); Colleen A. Vasconcellos, *Slavery, Childhood, and Abolition in Jamaica, 1788–1838* (Athens: University of Georgia Press, 2015).

21 A book that elucidated the "property principle" of slavery, which was essentially the commodification of Black people's bodies, is Walter Johnson, *Soul by Soul: Life Inside the Antebellum Slave Market* (Cambridge, MA: Harvard University Press, 1999).

22 Shadd, in Bristow et al., *We're Rooted Here*, 42.

23 Ibid.

24 Ibid., 43.

25 Henry Bibb, a famous slave runaway cogently describes the dangers self-emancipated slaves faced on their runaway journeys. See Bibb, *Life and Adventures*.

26 J. Blaine Hudson, *Fugitive Slaves and the Underground Railroad in the Kentucky Borderland* (Jefferson, NC: McFarland, 2002), 56.

27 On John Jackson, see http://breakingthechains.tubmaninstitute.ca/sites/breakingthechains.tubmaninstitute.ca/files/ann %20maria %20jackson %20report_o.pdf.

28 It was William Still who recorded Mrs Jackson's history when she arrived in Philadelphia in November 1858. William Still, *The Underground Railroad: A Record of Facts, Authentic Narratives, Letters, &c., Narrating the Hardships, Hair-breadth Escapes and Death Struggles of the Slaves in their Efforts for Freedom as Related by Themselves and Others, or Witnessed by the Author* (1872; reissue, Medford, NJ: Plexus Publishing, 2005), 372.

29 Williams, *Slavery and Freedom*, 111–12.

30 Benjamin Drew, "Mrs. Ellis," *Narratives of Fugitive Slaves in Canada* (Boston: n.p., 1856), 44.

31 Bernard Moitt, "Behind the Sugar Fortunes: Women, Labour and the Development of Caribbean Plantations during Slavery," in *African Continuities*, ed. S. Chilungu & S. Niang (Toronto: Terebi, 1989), 410–17.

32 Ned and Constance Sublette have plumbed the depths of enslaved Black women's subjugation through the commodification of their womb in their book *The American Slave Coast: A History of the Slave Breeding Industry* (Chicago: Lawrence Hill, 2016). See Jennifer Morgan, *Laboring Women: Reproduction and Gender in New World Slavery* (Philadelphia: University of Pennsylvania Press, 2004), 72.

33 Still, *Underground Railroad*, 372.

34 These lines echo the Negro spiritual "Lord, How Come Me Here." Some lines of this song are as follows: "They sold my children away Lord, they sold my children away, I wish I never was born, I wish I never was born." The author(s) of this song are unknown, but the song is part of the large body of Negro spirituals produced by enslaved Africans as they expressed their grief and trauma at the destruction of their families by slaveholders.

35 Williams, *Slavery and Freedom*, 165.

36 Ibid.

37 Ibid., 166.

38 For the friendships among Black freedom workers such as Garrett, Tubman, Still, McKim, and others, and the network they created, see James A. McGowan, *Station Master on the Underground Railroad: The Life and Letters of Thomas Garrett* (Jefferson, NC: McFarland, 2005), 98–114, 115–28, 134–53.

39 J. Miller McKim was a friend and colleague of Still. McKim was also on the executive of the Philadelphia Vigilance Committee. Additionally, he was the

publishing agent of the Pennsylvania Anti-Slavery Society. McGowan, *Station Master on the Underground Railroad*, 137.

40 Ibid., 149.

41 William J. Switala, *Underground Railroad in Pennsylvania* (Mechanicsburg, PA: Stackpole Books, 2001), 141. See in addition 142–51.

42 See Larry Gara, "William Still and the Underground Railroad," *Pennsylvania History* 28, no. 1 (1961): 33–44.

43 Still, *The Underground Railroad*, 372.

44 Ibid.

45 Ibid.

46 Ibid.

47 William Still's life and work as stationmaster on the Underground Railroad was heroic. He lived a life devoted to Black liberation. He not only worked for the Pennsylvania Anti-Slavery Society as head of the Vigilance Committee, he also used his own wealth to help fugitive slaves and other Blacks in need. See Larry Gara, "William Still"; James Oliver Horton, "A Crusader for Freedom: William Still and the Real Underground Railroad," in *Passages to Freedom: The Underground Railroad in History and Memory*, ed. David Blight (New York: Smithsonian Books and HarperCollins, 2004), 175–93. Although intended for the young adult audience, Judith Bentley's work on William Still's collaboration and friendship with Thomas Garrett, is useful as a scholarly source. See Bentley's *"Dear Friend": Thomas Garrett & William Still, Collaborators on the Underground Railroad* (New York: Cobblehill Books, 1997).

48 On Hiram Wilson and his Black freedom work, see Bryan Prince, *One More River to Cross* (Toronto: Dundurn Press, 2012), 79.

49 Still, *Underground Railroad*, 372–3. It seems that one of the older children, John Henry, was separated from the family, for safety reasons, between Philadelphia and St Catharines.

50 The Anti-Slavery Society of Canada, headquartered in Toronto, helped Jackson and her family settle in Toronto. For a discussion of the Anti-Slavery Society of Canada and the roles of Rev. Michael Willis, Thomas Henning and Agnes (Mrs Willis) see Allen P. Stouffer, *The Light of Nature and the Law of God: AntiSlavery in Ontario, 1833–1877* (Montreal and Kingston: McGill-Queen's University Press, 1992).

51 "Ann Maria Jackson," The Harriet Tubman Institute, last modified 2016, http://tubman.info.yorku.ca/educational-resources/breaking-the-chains/toronto/ann-maria-jackson.

52 Still, "James Henry Jackson," *Underground Railroad*, 344. See also Hiram Wilson's letter to William Still, 373; Karolyn Smardz Frost, *I've got a Home in Glory Land: A Lost Tale of the Underground Railroad* (Toronto: Thomas Allen, 2007), 302.

53 Black abolitionist and author William Wells Brown toured Toronto in 1861
    and gave a breakdown of the city's Black population with regards to residential
    pattern, occupation, and social and political advancement. See his "The Colored
    People of Canada," in *Black Abolitionist Papers*, vol. II, *Canada, 1830–1865*, ed.
    C. Peter Ripley (Chapel Hill: University of North Carolina Press, 1986), 461–3.
54 Census of Canada, for Toronto, 1861, http://data2.collectionscanada.gc.ca/1861/
    jpg/4391542_01148.jpg.
55 1871 Census of Canada, Toronto West, St Patrick's Ward, Online at ancestry.ca
    https://search.ancestry.ca/cgi-bin/sse.dll?_phsrc=fZM141&_phstart=successSource
    &usePUBJs=true&indiv=1&db=1871canada&sin=C0000006&siv=4396300_00
    670&gss=angs-d&pcat=35&fh=39&h=61934&recoff=&ml_rpos=40.
56 A brief history of Ann Maria Jackson is included in Adrienne Shadd, Afua Cooper,
    and Karolyn Smardz Frost, *The Underground Railroad: Next Stop, Toronto!*
    (2002; reissue, Toronto: Natural Heritage Books, 2005), 74–5.
57 There is some discrepancy in Mary's age. The 1861 census lists her as twenty-two
    years of age. Her marriage certificate, done six years after the census, still lists her
    as twenty-two.
58 Mary Jackson, County Marriage Registers of Ontario, Canada, 1858–1869,
    Toronto City, vol. 2, p. 34, Archives of Ontario. The bride's mother's name is
    also listed (as Maria Jackson). This information resource can also be found online
    at ancestry.ca
59 Census of Canada, 1861; St John's Ward, Toronto. The Jackson's were living
    in the ward on Edward St, alongside African American neighbours Charles
    Freeman and Martha Davey.
60 Death record of Ann Maria Jackson, Schedule D, County of York, Division
    of Toronto, "Ontario Deaths, 1867–1937," #1257, Archives of Ontario. See
    also The 1880 Toronto Necropolis Burial Records, #8244, Archives of Ontario.
61 Pat Staton, "North Star to Freedom: Women on the Underground Railroad,
    Stories of Courage and determination – Black women follow the North Star
    seeking freedom in Canada," (Toronto: Green Dragon Press, 2012). I was a
    consultant on the Jackson story for this poster.
62 On Albert Jackson and his trajectory, Colin McFarquhar, "Blacks in 1880s
    Toronto: The Search for Equality," *Ontario History* 99, no. 1 (Spring 2007): 64–72.
63 Ibid.

5

Free Black North:
Photography and Transnational Identities
in Nineteenth-Century Southern Ontario

Julie Crooks

When I reached St. Catharines I was enfeebled in health. I had come to a small inferior place; there were pines rowing all about here where you now see brick houses. I rented a house, and with another man took five acres of cleared land, and got along with it very well. We were then making both ends meet. I then made up my mind that salt and potatoes in Canada, were better than pound-cake and chickens in a state of suspense and anxiety in the United States. Now I am a regular Britisher. My American blood has been scourged out of me; I have lost my American tastes.

Reverend Alexander Hemsley, 1855[1]

I have no opportunity to see my friends in my native land. We would rather stay in our native land, if we could be as free there as we are here.

Harriet Tubman, 1855[2]

In 1855 Benjamin Drew, journalist and abolitionist, set out to document the narratives of self-manumitted slaves who had escaped to Canada. Among the persons whose narratives Drew collected were the Reverend Alexander Hemsley and Harriet Tubman. For Reverend Hemsley, Canada West (southwestern Ontario), despite the precarious nature of freedom and belonging, offered the possibility of self-fashioning an identity as a "Britisher." He seemed well into the process of "becoming"[3] a Canadian "citizen" in the pre-confederation British colony. Stuart Hall's critical notion of identity formation as bound up in a process of becoming, as well as being, is useful for articulating the complex subjectivities of self-emancipated Black Americans who escaped to Canada and their process of adoption of Canada as their new "home." Hall refers to the notion of becoming in relation to identity formation as a "production which is never complete." Harriet Tubman (who lived in St Catharines for a brief period), viewed Canada as a liminal, political, and transient site of abolitionism and freedom. Unlike Reverend Hemsley, Tubman's outlook underscores the notion of fugitivity, which is "not only escape but also separate from settling."[4] Here, fugitivity is not only about escape but also a *refusal* to accept anything but full subjecthood.

As Americans, both Hemsley and Tubman, illustrate the complicated transnational existence and related border crossings of thousands of Blacks who sought refuge in Canada from the mid-to late nineteenth centuries. My aim in this paper is to discuss the ways in which two photography collections featured in the *Free* Black North exhibition at the AGO are transnational in scope and highlight a range of subjects who used photography as a way of marking their identities across both borders.[5]

Free Black North ran from 29 April 1 to October 2017 at the AGO (Art Gallery of Ontario). The exhibition featured the photographs of men, women, and children, descendants of former slaves with familial ties to Black settlements in St Catharines and Amherstburg, Ontario in the mid to late 1800s. (figure 5.1, installation view). Such ties can be traced to the collectors of the material who were themselves descendants of African Americans who had escaped to the north. Their formidable archives are illustrative of Black visuality and transnationality across the US-Canadian border.

Richard Bell's collection (the Bell-Sloman collection), which is housed at Brock University's James A. Gibson Library, constitutes a rich archive of photographic materials and ephemera dating from the 1850s to 1970s. Bell's family have deep roots in the Niagara region. Members of the Bell family escaped from Culpepper, Virginia in the mid-nineteenth century and eventually settled in St Catharines, Ontario. The Sloman family are descended from a former slave who settled in the Wilberforce Colony (a colony founded by escaped slaves from Cincinnati, Ohio in the 1830s).[6]

The second archive was assembled by Alvin McCurdy over several decades beginning from the 1950s. McCurdy was born and raised in Amherstburg in southwestern Ontario. The area was the main entry point for the Underground Railroad which allowed fugitives access along the narrowest point on the Detroit River between Canada and the USA. McCurdy's paternal grandfather Nathan, a freeman, settled in Amherstburg in the 1830s and brought a succession of fugitive slaves across the border, assisting others in their quest for freedom. His maternal grandmother had been enslaved in Kentucky. Following her manumission, she made her way to Canada.

Both the Bell and McCurdy narratives evidenced notions of fugitivity and migration familiar amongst the descendants of countless self-manumitted Blacks and "free" Blacks who fled to small communities in southern Ontario. The notion of flight and fugitivity forms an essential trope (particularly in African American print and media culture), which is embodied in the experience of removal from Africa, escape from slavery, and the journey to the free states or Canada.[7] *Free* Black North uses the notion of fugitivity as a framework for exploring, in the first instance, the idea of disruption whereby the runaway "ultimately transgressed the law of property."[8] In the second instance, fugitivity as a framework here highlights how Blacks and their descendants used photography not only for their own personal pleasure but also to "disrupt" fixed notions of the objectified Black body, thereby cultivating a range of subjectivities. As Fred Moten succinctly lays out, "What's at stake is fugitive movement in and out of the frame ... a movement of escape, the stealth of the stolen that can be said to break every enclosure."[9] What registers in these images are how these chiefly unknown individuals asserted this break through the use of the medium as a strategy to make themselves visible in hostile environments. Both Hemsley and Tubman reacted to the hostile border environments to which they fled with differing viewpoints. Hemsley's attitude of adaptation and visibility viewed future possibilities (though tenuous) of citizenship in Canada. Tubman offered a more sceptical outlook revealing both her longing and insistence on self-possession within a "free" United States.

The exhibition design provoked discussions of self-hood, biography, and presence by situating the objects in smaller jewel cases (figure 5.2, installation view). Each portrait was given its own space in order to tell a specific, unique counternarrative to the prevailing stereotypical notions of peoples of African descent. The tintype process was itself unique: producing a positive image, one of photograph on metal that could not be reproduced. The process lends itself to deeper reflections about its uncanny suitability as singular photo-object for a range of Black subjects and heterogeneous communities along the Canada-US border. The special attributes of the tintype formed variant tones of dark purple, brown, and grey on the metal which, when enhanced by the studio lighting, enriched the natural skin tones of the sitters (figure 5.3). For both the free and self-emancipated, portrait photographs became "fugitive images" that defied and transgressed archetypal representations of Black bodies.

Self-representation through the act of photography did little to address the firsthand encounters with racism for those who sought freedom and equality in the north. For example, Reverend Horace Hawkins (figure 5.4) escaped Kentucky and lived in Amherstburg. Hawkins experienced ongoing systemic racism towards him and recalled such hostility stating, "A coloured man cannot get accommodated at any of hotels in Canada or on any line of the railroad … I think the root of the prejudice is to be found in the fact that the coloured people came in here rapidly and the whites got the impression that the coloured people would become a majority in the Western county."[10] Hawkins sentiment runs counter to the narrative of Canada as the benevolent place of refuge for escaping Blacks and also rebukes Reverend Helmsley's pronouncements of faith in his new found "home."

One of the concerns of the exhibition relates to the dearth of identifiable subjects. Unlike Reverend Hawkins, we know precious little about the unidentified woman featured in a tintype from the Bell Collection (figure 5.5). She wears a distinctive white pinafore, which may designate her status as a domestic worker. Staring resolutely at the camera, her pose suggests complete ease with the photographic process. For African American statesman and abolitionist Frederick Douglass, the camera could be used as a weapon to control one's image. He observes, "The servant girl can now see a likeness of herself, such as noble ladies could not purchase fifty years ago. But now … such pictures are placed within easy reach of the humblest members of society."[11] Douglass confirms the democratization of photography through this reference to the portrait of a "servant girl" who used the medium to shape the way she wished to be seen. Douglass himself was passionate about photography and became the most photographed man of the nineteenth century. Due to the indexical nature of the photograph, he believed that camera told the "truth" about the subject captured before it. While Douglass's image circulated widely in the public sphere, images found in both the McCurdy and Bell collections reveal the formidable amount of portraits of Black women for private consumption – including that of the "servant" girl. The overwhelming gendered presence in Black archives reflects Black women subjects eager to document their self-possession. The images of Hawkins and the unknown "servant girl" represent the complexities and ambiguities of transnational identities, black visuality, and mobility in the racialized frontier of Canada West and the United States in the nineteenth century.

All of the photographs are portraits indicating that they were private and intimate commissions to be shared with friends and loved ones and were not primarily intended for public consumption. Thus, many of the photographs remain unlabelled and the sitters' names unknown. It was common for family members on both sides of the border to share photographs thus creating a widely circulating network of objects over one hundred and fifty years. Harvey Young argues that such circulation of photographs, has "allowed the past to be assessed in the present and the present to be captured for the future."[12] bell hooks further notes, "for black folks, the camera provided a means to document a reality that could, if necessary, be packed, stored, moved from place to place. It was documentation that could be shared, passed around. And, ultimately, these images, the worlds they recorded, could be hidden, to be discovered at another time."[13] Here fugitivity is linked to temporality where the future is at stake within acts of reclaiming such lost or hidden histories using photographs. So, while little is known about the many of the subjects featured in the exhibition, it opens the possibilities for further research and future discoveries.[14]

The collections from which these objects were culled and their formation engender notions of an absent presence within the larger narratives of the histories of Canada and histories of photography. Alvin McCurdy amassed his voluminous collection of photographic material in the 1950s. Over the span of forty years he endeavoured to preserve the history of a community, which he felt had been erased or relegated to invisibility. Richard Bell "rescued" a large amount of materials (including photographs and ephemera), destined for a junk heap from his mother's attic in St Catharines. Both collections trouble and disrupt the dominant narrative of settlement, forced movement and migration from a white/British colonial perspective. Both Richard Bell and Alvin McCurdy were participants in the wilful collection and recovery of photographic material that attempts to redress the skewed historic narrative. Art historian and queer activist David Deitcher argues that defiance is the crucial component for any project of historical reclamation and suggests "resistance compels the historian to unearth precious traces of the past. Through such acts of recuperation ... the historian helps to ensure the continued availability of that past as a source of validation."[15] *Free* Black North assisted in recuperating both "absent subjects," histories, and photo objects along Canada-US borderlands. The images underscore the importance of portrait photography, which played a critical role in asserting a range of states and diverse conditions: African American, British, "free," transitory, fugitive or expatriate.[16] They are also illustrative of nineteenth-century Black photography histories within broader narratives about the history of photography in Canada.

Figure 5.1 Installation view 1, *Free* Black North exhibition, 2017, Art Gallery of Ontario.

Figure 5.2 Installation view 2, *Free* Black North exhibition, 2017, Art Gallery of Ontario.

Figure 5.3 Unidentified man (circa 1865–75).

Figure 5.4 Westlake brothers, [Reverend?] Horace Hawkins, circa 1890s.

Figure 5.5 Unidentified woman (circa 1865–75).

NOTES

1 Benjamin Drew, *A North-Side View of Slavery. The Refugee: or the Narratives of Fugitive Slaves in Canada. Related by Themselves, with an Account of the History and Condition of the Colored Population of Upper Canada* (Boston: J.P. Jewett and Company, 1856), 39

2 Ibid., 30.

3 Stuart Hall, "Cultural Identity and Diaspora," in *Colonial Discourse and Post-colonial Theory: A Reader*, ed. Patrick Williams and Laura Chrisman (New York: Harvester Wheatsheaf, 1993), 394.

4 Fred Moten, "The Case of Blackness," *Criticism* 50 (2008): 179.

5 Steven Kasher, "The Personal Tintype," *America and the Tintype* (New York: ICP and Steidl, 2008), 40.

6 A detailed genealogy of the Bell-Sloman can be found on the Brock University Library and Special collections website.

7 Lawrence Rodgers, *Canaan Bound: The African American Migration Novel* (Urbana: University of Illinois Press, 1997), 3.

8 Saidiya V. Hartman, *Scenes of Subjection: Terror, Slavery, and Self-Making in Nineteenth-Century America* (New York: Oxford University Press, 1997), 69.

9 Fred Moten, "The Case of Blackness," 179.

10 Horace Hawkins, "American Freedmen's Inquiry Commission Interviews, 1863," in *Slave Testimony: Two Centuries of Letters, Speeches, Interviews, and Autobiographies*, ed. John W. Blassingame (Baton Rouge: Louisiana State University Press, 1977), 443.

11 Frederick Douglass, "Pictures and Progress," in *The Frederick Douglas Papers, Series One: Speeches, Debates, and Interviews, Volume III*, ed. John W. Blassingame (New Haven: Yale University Press, 1979), 379.

12 Harvey Young, *Embodying Black Experience: Stillness, Critical Memory, and the Black Body* (Ann Arbor: The University of Michigan Press, 2010).

13 bell hooks, *Art on My Mind: Visual Politics* (New York: The New Press, 1981), 60.

14 During the run of the exhibition, an individual with roots in Windsor and Amhertsburg recognized a descendant whose photograph was part of the Alvin McCurdy Collection.

15 David Deicther, "Looking at a Photograph, Looking for History," in *The Passionate Camera: Photography and Bodies of Desire*, ed. Deborah Bright (New York: Routledge, 1998), 34.

16 See Heike Paul and her discussion of the Canada-US border and the formation of transnational diasporic Black subjects in "Out of Chatham: Abolitionism on the Canadian Frontier," *Atlantic Studies* 8 (2011): 165–88.

6

Colour-Phobia in Canada: William Wells Brown's Cosmopolitan Mobility

Carole Lynn Stewart

According to escaped slave and author Henry Bibb, in an 1851 editorial of his paper *The Voice of the Fugitive,* "The most obnoxious and fatal disease has made its way into [Ontario] where it is destined to make havoc among the ignorant and vicious if speedy remedy is not applied." This "disease" was "color-phobia," and it plagued the United States. Bibb claimed colour-phobia was most prominent "among the lowest class of white people, who are used as mere stepping stones or political hobbies for the more refined and enlightened to ride into office upon." Derivative of "old Capt. Slavery," colour-phobia halted the "spread of knowledge" and used the "rum shop" as "the school house," leading to "kidnapping, man stealing, breaking up the bands of human affections by selling children from parents and husbands from their wives."[1] While most white Americans suffered from the illness, "In Canada, it gets hold of the very dregs of society. It makes them shudder at the idea of 'negro settlement,' 'they will ruin the country' &c." Fears of miscegenation, "amalgamation," and job stealing were prominent in Canada West.[2] Most reformers seemed to agree, and Samuel Ringgold Ward wrote to Henry Bibb (1851), "Rum and Negro-hate, the two great evils of our adopted land, shall receive undying fight from me during my life."[3] Arriving in a "free land" did not mean the space was temperate or cosmopolitan, and a legal definition of freedom was not enough to nourish a sense of community or identity.

Another prominent African American author-reformer, William Wells Brown, shared this uncanny experience as a fugitive who perceived a troubling lack of distinction between the mythical Canada (a Canaan of liberty) and the northern United States. Indeed, as Brown would remark in his 1861 report titled "The People of Canada," "Canada has so long been eulogized as the only spot in North America where the Southern bondsman could stand a freeman, and the poetical connection of its soil with the fugitive, the 'North Star,' and liberty, had created such an enthusiastic love in my heart for the people here, that I was not prepared to meet the prejudice against colored persons which manifests itself wherever a member of that injured race makes his appearance."[4] Both Bibb and Brown indicate that the experience of freedom on the hemispheric American continent was achieved through transnational and cosmopolitan civil societies and networks. These reformers also show that a sense of diasporic identity for some African Americans and Canadians, particularly escaped slaves in the nineteenth century, relied more on transnational structure and civil societies, such as temperance reform, than it did on any host's civil or national identity and political constitution. Still, Brown remained critical of most modern nation-states, including that of the mythical Promised Land of Canada.

The regions of southwest Ontario, or Canada West from 1841 to 1867, were some of the more prominent destination points for fugitive slaves by way of the Underground Railroad in the decades preceding the American Civil War. From the 1820s forward, many fugitive slaves arrived in the Niagara region and St Catharines from Buffalo, as well as crossing to Canada through the Detroit-Windsor border. While white Canadians generally like to view themselves as not racist (compared to Americans), the status of Canada as a Canaan for black liberty has been criticized since studies like Robin Winks' *The Blacks in Canada*.[5] Many fugitives did come to these regions to either settle or stay temporarily; for instance, in 1851 Harriet Tubman would make St Catharines her residence for abolitionist activities for the next seven years; other famous figures like Josiah Henson, long thought to be the model for Harriet Beecher Stowe's *Uncle Tom's Cabin*, settled in the area of Dresden, Ontario, and helped establish the all black Dawn Settlement. To be sure, many also returned to the United States or made the area their temporary refuge for abolitionist activities or protection. Henson, whose association with Uncle Tom, as Robin Winks points out, is more based on legend than fact, by virtue of "embrac[ing] the legend" became the pious Uncle Tom who followed the mythical North Star and fled to the promised land of Canada. By extension, "Canadians came increasingly to congratulate themselves upon their lack of prejudice and to contrast themselves favorable with the immoral and once slave-ridden United States."[6] As Nancy Kang contends, the status of Canada West as a permanent home or "promised land" is often propagandistic.[7]

David Blight and others have also troubled received notions of the Underground Railroad, such as its reputation as an advanced network with primarily white helpers aiding fugitives, the idea that Canada was free from slavery, or the idea that Canada was the primary destination for escaped slaves.[8] Moreover, African Canadians had already settled in many areas, given that Canada was part of the transatlantic economy and institutions of slavery. However, many free blacks immigrated for better opportunities or for legal protection and "refuge" following the fears of being captured after the passing of the 1850 compromise between US North and South. The 1850 Fugitive Slave Law (FSL) mandated the hunting, capture, and return of runaway slaves (or those suspected of being).[9] Winfried Siemerling has also recently documented the history of early Canadian black diasporic experience in order to "implicate Canada in hemispheric and transatlantic stories of modernity."[10] My discussion will focus on Brown's imagination and representation of the region of southern Ontario in the 1850s and 1860s, which Siemerling discusses in a more positive register as a possible space of counterhegemonic activity.[11] I do not mean to disregard the significant advancements made by nineteenth-century black Canadian communities. I do, however, want to consider the sources of colour-phobia as they affect what it means for Canada to be implicated in the transatlantic and hemispheric "American" story of freedom and racism.

Bibb's description of colour-phobia anticipates the criticisms of Canadian exceptionalism and suggests his own ambivalence toward the national boundaries, particularly those of the US and Canada. Afua Cooper argues that Henry Bibb's fugitive position as one who continued to cross borders between the US and Canada a number of times, rather than following the traditional journey from US slavery to Canadian freedom, troubles the notion that Canada was the utopian promised land. His multiple crossings suggest a "fluid frontier." In a parallel way, the Detroit River which runs through Detroit (US) and Bibb's Canadian home of Sandwich (Canada), which is part of Windsor (Canada), displays the fluidity and arbitrariness of national boundaries.

Contrary to the image of Canada as a free country opposing US slavery, as Cooper notes, in 1793 while blacks were still enslaved in Canada, slavery was outlawed in Detroit by the Northwest Ordinance and a reverse underground railroad existed.[12] This escape to the US from Canadian slavery also occurred along the Niagara Frontier into New York. Detroit and Buffalo remained havens for many fugitives up until the passage of the FSL when many crossed over into Ontario. Bibb first escaped to Canada from Kentucky in 1837 but then returned to search for his wife and child, and he made numerous passages across the borders. He remained in Detroit for many years, and not until 1850 did he cross into Sandwich, where he founded the newspaper and eventually a settlement with Mary Bibb while continuing to lecture in the US. Even Bibb's death marked his freedom as existing on a "fluid frontier," with friends and black abolitionists memorializing his death on a cruise boat on the Detroit River.[13]

Like Bibb, Brown was a prominent fugitive slave and abolitionist, as well as author of the first published novel by an African American, *Clotel; or the President's Daughter* (1853), plays, histories, and travel narratives. In 1854, Brown's freedom was purchased by Ellen Richardson from former Missourian owner Enoch Price, and he would no longer be a "fugitive," making it relatively safe for him to settle on the American continent. *Clotel* went through four versions, and it was first published in Britain, during his travels abroad in Europe. He initially went as a delegate for the International Paris Peace Congress and ended up remaining for the years of 1849–54, primarily in London and Edinburgh. *Three Years in Europe; or Places I Have Seen and People I have Met,* the first travel narrative by an African American, was published in 1852 in London and later revised for an 1854 American edition. Previous to leaving for Europe, Brown was a steamboat operator living in Buffalo for nine years and transporting fugitive slaves across the border during the 1830s and 1840s. Given Buffalo's proximity to the Canadian border, Brown's decision to remain there seems strategic, as a result of the potential need for his own flight.[14] Later, in 1861, he toured southern Ontario to promote Haitian immigration. Brown had visited Haiti, Cuba, and the West Indies in 1840.[15]

Brown's life captures the transnational experience of escape and freedom, the desired freedom of movement and mobility, for many who came through slavery. Even so, after Brown's escape he never displayed a desire to settle in Canada for any length of time. In 1861 he would tour southern Ontario not to settle in or promote Canadian settlements but, rather, to promote Haitian immigration. To be sure, Brown's imaginative renderings of southwest Ontario in the earlier *Clotel* are somewhat more positive and typical of the Promised Land mythos than those in his historical and journalistic accounts of 1861. Brown reported on the regions of southern Ontario in 1861, after delivering lectures associated with James Redpath's Haitian colonization program; these lectures resulted in seven articles entitled "The Colored People of Canada," published in *Pine and Palm.*

While he avoided settling in Canada, Brown romanticized the image of Canada as a symbol of freedom and sometimes the setting, such as the crossing of the Niagara River in his farcical 1858 play *The Escape; or A*

Leap for Freedom and in his early works.[16] However, in general he provides few fictional images of Canada even though the idea of Canadian freedom serves as a deferred promise. His 1847 slave narrative, that prefaces his novel *Clotel*, echoes the abolitionist belief in the promise of the "new Canaan" of Canada and free soil. He there recounts persuading his mother to attempt an escape with him to Canada, though she "did not wish to leave her children in slavery." They had "nothing but the North Star to guide them."[17] Brown indicates that his escape north disappointed, and "what crushed the poor slave's heart in his flight most was, not the want of food or clothing, but the thought that every white man was his deadly enemy. Even in the free states the prejudice against color is so strong that there appears to exist a deadly antagonism between the white and coloured races."[18] Nonetheless, he only ventures so far as Buffalo and upstate New York. In the first version of his slave narrative, the narrative desire is to move north to Canada – the reader anticipates his crossing into the "promised land." Yet, just within reach of the Canadian border, he arrives in Cleveland and says, "I had no money, and the lake being frozen, I saw that I must remain until the opening of the navigations, or go to Canada by way of Buffalo. But believing myself to be somewhat out of danger, I secured an engagement at the Mansion House, as a table waiter, in payment for my board." He stays there "until spring" and then finds "good employment on board a lake steamboat."[19] At this point Brown became involved with the Underground Railroad and abolitionism, combining his skills as a steamboat pilot with his anti-slavery interests, while remaining in Buffalo and becoming active in organizing temperance societies.

This avoidance of settling is in part because Brown appears to locate his freedom as one of mobility; in Stephen Lucasi's words, Brown's freedom becomes expressive of a "traveling subjectivity." Lucasi examines the way in which Brown's first slave narrative overlaps with and revises the traditional travel narrative genre (and indeed, Brown also wrote travel narratives). In his role as steamboat operator aiding in the delivery of fugitives to "free soil" in Canada, Brown reverses the earlier path that he took down to New Orleans as a steamboat operator while hiring his time in slavery, a role that forced him to witness an internal middle passage of slavery to the ports and auctions.[20] As a fugitive and steamboat operator aiding his fellow travellers to freedom, he is able to reclaim his freedom because of his mobility and agency on the water, in contrast to being a slave aiding in the internal trade while hiring out his time on a steamboat. According to Lucasi, "By coming into control of his own labor and body, he replaces the earlier reproduction of the slave economy along the Mississippi with this resistance to it on Lake Erie."[21]

Brown was proud of the number of slaves he transported across the border. He claimed in his slave narrative, "During the season of 1842, this fugitive slave conveyed no less than *sixty-nine* runaway slaves across Lake Erie, and placed them on the soil of Canada."[22] Brown's slave narrative, in emphasizing Brown's mobility, disrupts the typical arc of journeys and arrivals and "reflects a broadening of those conventions through its hybridization of the slave narrative and travel narrative."[23] A "traveling subjectivity" and a mobile subject position capture much of Brown's life and the potential energy of many reformers who escaped from slavery. Yet, although Brown's life accounts emphasize travelling and movement, the celebration of the "soil" and land itself recurs in his work in a more sacred register reminiscent of the imaginative aesthetic and sacred spaces of pilgrimage. Brown's constant travels, from his escape from slavery, his movement to Buffalo crossing to Canada, to his travels through Europe and then back to Massachusetts – a continuous crossing of boundaries and borders – as well as his contemplated (though this is speculation) emigration to Haiti, and his final return "home," in his autobiography *My Southern Home* (1880). These travels imitate the structure of a pilgrimage, complete with ambiguous tragic liminalities that indicate missed possibilities and deferrals of freedom. His search and reflection is informed by Romantic concepts of the folk, the meaning of tradition, and the nature of civil society in a cosmopolitan democracy. The sense of being rooted to the land and to the histories and memories connected to space, as well as participating in larger civil structures, such as the Temperance and Abolitionist movements that also facilitate cosmopolitan mobility, emerges as a desirable meaning of freedom that includes community and movement. Canada, as another colonial space, offers Brown the "freedom of British soil" or "Victoria's shore"[24] in his imaginative work, but the culture was not rooted for him, as American culture was in his generational history in the US or as African culture was through his connections with larger populations from the African diaspora through slavery. Nor was Canada cosmopolitan enough to enable the freer cultural exchange that Europe (and especially France) would afford. As someone who lived on the periphery of the Canadian border for some time, and who was light skinned enough to pass as white in certain contexts, Brown characterizes the problems and possibilities with these areas as locations for local and yet cosmopolitan communities.

On the one hand, Brown's subjectivity is constantly in motion and he appears to value that mobility as a modality of freedom, along with the cosmopolitan sensibility it inheres. On the other hand, while he transports others to Canadian soil, Brown does little to promote the area of Canada

West. Unlike Bibb, who remained committed to promoting Canadian settlements, and could be said to claim Canada West as his ambiguous "home" of freedom, along the Detroit–Windsor border, Brown's mobility still located its roots in Buffalo during the time he operated the steamboat. Moreover, it is difficult to ignore the fact that most of his published descriptions of Canada end with a critical tenor, suggesting the nation fell short of his ideal. Indeed, Canada becomes a detour, or reprieve, for Brown until the ideal space for a rooted, yet cosmopolitan subjectivity should become available. Brown investigates many international possibilities, including Europe, Haiti, the West Indies, and finally, his "Southern Home." Nonetheless, after returning from Europe to the United States in 1854, Brown chose to reside in Boston.

Not surprisingly, in his 1861 report, Hamilton and Toronto garner more praise than do the more rural farming areas. Rural areas were typically more segregated, and immigrants to the American continent seemed to form communities out of ethnic or racial (white) identification. As Robin Winks points out, "If Negroes in Amherstburg, along the Niagara frontier, and at Oro, enjoyed a degree of equality in the initial years of settlement, most observers reported that the degree diminished as time passed."[25] The metropolitan areas fared a little better in this regard due to cultural activity and integration. Brown remarks on Toronto, "The number of colored people in Toronto is about 1400. Every Southern state of the American Union is here." Various colours and "dialects" are "amalgamated into one conglomerated mass; and these are scattered in every part of the city."[26] Brown praises the "educational institutions as "the finest" of any city "in America," noting that many professions are present, with physicians and business men, as well numerous "benevolent associations" and "temperance" organizations.[27]

Brown also comments in a neutral tone on the issue of "passing" as European by "some of our class," which is a theme in his literature. He writes that African descendants who are light-skinned in Toronto often "pass for foreigners, and under that guise, almost any mulatto may push himself through the crowd, if he can rattle off a little French, German, or Spanish. With some of our class, this is an inducement to study the languages."[28] George Green, a main character of *Clotel,* will also pass while in Europe, though not while in St Catharines, Ontario. One might speculate that the fluidity of racial identification in Toronto versus more strongly demarcated racial identifications in rural areas encourages, for Brown, the positive desire to study languages and cultures. However, the need to deny any African heritage and "pass" as white, serves as a negative reminder of the limitations of freedom in these more cosmopolitan centres. Brown, while very light-skinned, never passes or indicates a desire to deny his African heritage.

The brief appearance of Canada as a setting in Brown's novel *Clotel* is located in the more rural area of St Catharines. The region was more segregated than Toronto and was also lacking in many of the educational opportunities. Brown comments in his 1861 report on "The Colored Settlement," where most blacks in St Catharines resided, with "about 100 houses, 40 of which lie on North Street, the Broadway of the place. The houses are chiefly cottages."[29] The area is close to Geneva Street and according to Leavey et al "Blacks primarily lived around the Geneva, Niagara, Cherry, and Williams Street area, although some lived where they were employed throughout St. Catharines or in nearby farming areas."[30] Although George Green escapes from prison and slavery to Canadian soil in St Catharines, this is a temporary asylum. In a brief paragraph, the narrator mentions George's quaint "abode in the little town of St. Catharines" while employed "on the farm of Colonel Street," where he "attended a night-school, and laboured for his employer during the day." His is a dignified reprieve, though "the climate was cold," because "he was in a land where he was free, and this young slave prized [this freedom] more than all the gold that could be given." George also teaches others "what he could" – and we are told that "there are many" other fugitives.[31]

The actual numbers in St Catharines, and major settlements like Chatham, Dawn, or Elgin, have been debated. Benjamin Drew in his famous recounting of statistics and numbers of blacks in Canada West, who were thought to be primarily fugitive slaves, notes that there were about 800 of the total population of 6,000 in St Catharines.[32] In his 1861 report, Brown follows Drew's statistics when he writes, "In the village and its environs, there are not far from eight hundred colored people, representing every Southern State in the late American Union, scattered around, and within five miles, are a large number of farmers, many of whom have become wealthy since escaping into Canada." Brown visits the market where he receives some news about the population from vendors. He provides a neutral, and even positive, assessment of St Catharines at this time: "The houses in the settlement are all owned by their occupants, and from inquiry I learned that the people generally were free from debt. Out of the eight hundred in St. Catharines, about seven hundred of them are fugitive slaves."[33] Given that Brown is promoting Haitian immigration in this 1861 tour, the fact that he notes the property of former slaves in St Catharines is an acknowledgment of progress in the region. However, property ownership and the development of a "community of negro farmers" in St Catharines was also a limitation in Brown's view, given that he was attempting to recruit people who could easily leave for Haiti.[34] Brown's positive (or neutral) remarks are countered by his general conclusions after visiting London, Ontario: "The more I see of Canada, the more I am convinced of the deep-rooted hatred to the negro."[35]

Brown made clear that even the wealthiest black farmers he encountered were excluded from civil society: "Whenever a colored man is employed by a white man, the former is invariably put to a side table to take his meal; in the farming districts it is the same; and even when a white man works for a colored person, he demands a side-table, for he feels himself above eating with his master. The Rev. William King, of Buxton, is the only white person who has yet invited me to partake of his hospitality."[36]

In *Clotel*, St Catharines appears as a place for labouring and "asylum" – not a space for civil society or cultured (and cultural) exchanges. Indeed, in an 1849 welcome speech in Britain published in the *North Star*, Brown gives thanks to God that "there was an asylum still left for the slave and that the Canadas, at the present moment, were the land of refuge for more than 20,000 escaped bondmen (cheers). Nor could he convey to that meeting the feelings which came over him when he landed at Liverpool and felt that he was really free. Then he could indeed adopt the language of the poet, and say – 'Old England! old England! thrice blessed and free!'". George Green, Brown's protagonist, follows the same route to Old England and then France, after spending some time labouring in what he clarifies as the cold climate of southern Ontario. In the 1860 revision, his two lovers (Green and Clotelle) are reunited just outside Geneva, while in the 1867 version *Clotelle* would become an "Angel of Mercy"[37] working to support black communities throughout parts of the Southern states, first working in New Orleans and eventually purchasing "Poplar Farm," which was also one autobiographical home for Brown as a child enslaved near St Louis, Missouri. Poplar Farm will also figure prominently as a re-conceptualized place for home and community in his final autobiographical work *My Southern Home* (1880). The Canadian ending for *Clotel* was never written.

While Brown's fictional depictions of Canada suggest a landscape that is sparse and cold, his letter promoting West Indian emigration published in the London *Times* on the fourth of July 1851[38] shows that he did not romanticize Europe as an alternative to Canada. He clearly warns African Americans against coming to England because of a lack of employment for them.

Nevertheless, Brown's representation of the climate also supported ideas of Canada as a wilderness made for labour rather than a space conducive to cultural development. Echoing the more negative sentiments given by slaveholders who depicted Canada as a desolate and cold wilderness and some of the scientific racism of the nineteenth century that argued certain races were suited to specific climates, Brown writes, "Although a residence in Canada is infinitely preferable to slavery in America, yet the climate of that country is uncongenial to the constitutions of the Negroes, and their lack of education is an almost insuperable barrier to their social progress."[39] Though Brown notes that he "attempted to remedy" and make the best of the situation "by the establishment of Manual Labour Schools in Canada for fugitive slaves," the school was not well supported. In *Clotel*, George Green also attempts to "obtain education for himself" and teach other fugitive slaves "what he could."[40] While George spends "nearly six months' labour at St Catharines," as soon as he receives news that Mary had been sold to the New Orleans market and he loses "all hope of getting the girl," he "resolved to quit the American continent for ever" and depart for Liverpool.

Why such a drastic and final decision? One reason is the lack of opportunity for education, and the narrator remarks, "With little or no education, he found many difficulties in the way of getting a respectable living." George works as a "porter" in Manchester and manages to pursue "private lessons at night" over the course of three years. These are not lessons in manual labour, such as in St Catharines. George becomes a "clerk" and eventually a "partner in the firm" and is set "on the road to wealth" while passing as white, being "somewhat ashamed of his African descent."[41] George vacations in northern France and, while in Dunkirk, he encounters his long lost love Mary, who was purchased by a Frenchman because she reminded him of his sister; the Frenchman and Mary marry, but he dies, and she is now living with her father-in-law. Presumably, the reunion in France highlights the fact that European governments have already ended slavery at this time, as the narrator remarks, "We can but blush for our country's shame when we recall to mind the fact, that while George and Mary Green, and numbers of other fugitives from American slavery, can receive protection from any of the governments of Europe, they cannot return to their native land without becoming slaves."[42]

Canada, while still a European government, is on the North American continent, and according to his 1861 report, is therefore not the ideal place for former slaves to establish their freedom and independence. George views the northern hemisphere as affected by the legacy of slavery: prejudice and colour-phobia. While England is preferable for economic and cosmopolitan mobility over Canada, George's need to pass serves as a criticism of England as well.[43] Nonetheless, the reader is uncertain whether George's shame is self-imposed or a necessary condition for economic and social advancement.

Whereas ambiguity about the degree of racial prejudice exists in representations of Europe, the first reason Canada, according to Brown's 1861 report, is not an ideal place to establish freedom and independence is "the prejudice" there. "The prejudice" results from two reasons: self-imposed segregation, such as experienced in "forming separate churches, taking back seats in public meetings, and performing menial offices of labor, and thereby giving the whites an opportunity to regard [blacks] with a degree of inferiority."[44] This issue may look like an attempt to blame the victims, and Brown's criticism seems somewhat ironic given that Brown had, in an introductory letter upon arriving in London quoted earlier, claimed that he desired to establish a manual labour school for blacks in the region. However, Brown also shares this view with others, like Mary Shadd, who, as Robin Winks points out, were critical of the mismanagement of the Dawn Settlement in Dresden, Ontario, which "began in Ohio" and was founded by the Anti-Slavery Society through charitable help from Oberlin in the 1830s and through other sponsors, including "Quaker philanthropist" James Cannings Fuller.[45] The settlement became associated with Josiah Henson (the presumed source for the fictional Uncle Tom). In this context, Brown also directly criticized the segregated settlement,[46] the issue of white philanthropy rather than mutual help (or self help), and other examples of voluntary segregation that were not culturally empowering.[47] And while Brown promoted black independence and segregated civil and cultural societies in some contexts, such as in his promotion of Haiti or in his final reflections in *My Southern Home*, he still indicated that in situations where African Canadians were a minority population, integration, or to use his word, "amalgamation"[48] – presumably without "passing" or needing to deny one's heritage to succeed – would be a more empowering strategy than segregated independence.

The second reason, which echoes Bibb's depiction of colour-phobia and perhaps became more pronounced after Brown's five years in Europe, was, in his words, "the main body of the population of Canada appears to be made up of the lower class of the people of England, Scotland, and Ireland. As I walk the streets here, I look in vain for that intelligent portion of the middle classes that I used to meet in London, Edinburgh, and Dublin. This lower stratum, coming from the old world, and feeling keenly their inferiority in education and refinement, and being vulgar and rude themselves, try, like the editor of the *London Free Press*, to draw attention from their own uncouthness, by directing the public eye to the other degraded class."[49] Brown acknowledges that this is not the case everywhere in Canada. Still, even New England with the threats of the FSL seems preferable. Segregation and lack of educational opportunities were worse than the situation in New England:

"The equality meted out to colored persons in the hotels of New England, are unknown in Canada. No where here, are our people treated with any kind of respect in the hotels; they are usually put off into inferior rooms by themselves, fed at separate tables from the whites, and not permitted to enter the common sitting rooms of the inn. Most of the towns have excluded the colored children from the common schools."

One might conclude that most of the northern regions of the American continent displayed cultural and intellectual limitations as a result of prejudice – but London, Ontario, seemed to Brown the worst. Notably, while the white immigrants emit the disease of racism, along with copious amounts of "bad beer and poor whisky," Brown says, "I have not yet seen a colored inhabitant intoxicated."[50]

The tensions noted presage complaints of African Americans in the latter nineteenth and early twentieth century when race "riots" broke out as a result of resentment from competing lower-class immigrant workers who believed whiteness should provide a level of superiority and entitlement. Brown's remarks on the poor show class tensions increasing racial resentment in Ontario. A fair labouring situation for the former slaves, he reasons, could mainly be achieved in majority black populated areas, like Haiti. In a different context, the focus has to be on integration and the establishment of educational and civil societies that can facilitate more cosmopolitan, cross-cultural exchanges.

While southern Ontario may have fallen short for the development of Africanist civil societies that could integrate without whitening into a larger cosmopolitan setting, there is some indication that the limitations Brown assesses relate to population deficiencies, including a lack of long-term indigenous connections that could solidify immediate cultural memory, and the segregation of black civil societies. Some of his criticisms also indicate his own ambivalence toward adopting any national identity imposed by statehood. When he returned from his tour of southern Ontario (August–October 1861), Brown still promoted Haitian emigration even when much support for the cause was waning. However, it soon became clear that the American Civil War would become a major struggle for liberty and along with other black abolitionists he turned his attention to the achievement of freedom within the United States for the enslaved populations. From the time of Reconstruction forward, he remained committed to black civil societies working in support of temperance organizations throughout the Southern states, while also continuing to travel abroad and promote international alliances. Although Canada did not appear as an ideal area to resettle in flight from US slavery, one assumes that with Brown's recommitment to the American continent, to the causes of reconstruction and temperance, the possibilities for Canadian cosmopolitanism were still open. Canada remained an important location in the network of black temperance organizations, specifically the Sons of Temperance, and civil societies with which Brown was involved. As Farrison points out, following the Civil War in 1866 the National Division of the Sons of Temperance desegregated, which included branches in Ontario. Brown would soon become chief officer of the John Brown Division of the Sons of Temperance in Massachusetts.[51] Nevertheless, he committed himself more exclusively to the internationalism of the Good Templars in the 1870s. Brown's answer to the problems of segregation and racism in the South in his final autobiography *My Southern Home* (1880) recommend a degree of "black pride,"[52] and a desire for justice, civil rights, and the acquisition of wealth in the form of land settlements that are productive not only of labour but of temperance, cultural development, civil exchange, and advanced education. Yet, he acknowledged that if the tragedies of southern violence and lynching could not be halted, blacks should emigrate. The location of home and global, cosmopolitan citizenship remained in movement. Brown's many peripatetic life and fugitive cosmopolitan mode of freedom suggests that the cultural effort of meaningful remembrance and cross-cultural exchanges between citizens must be rooted in the land, as well as in structural changes to institutions and civil societies.

NOTES

1 Portions of this chapter are reprinted with permission from Pennsylvania State University Press and from Carole Lynn Stewart, *Temperance and Cosmopolitanism: African American Reformers in the Atlantic World* (University Park: Penn State University Press, 2018).
   Henry Bibb, "Editorial by Henry Bibb, 21 May 1851: Color-phobia in Canada," in *The Black Abolitionist Papers: Volume II*. ed. Peter Ripley, et al. (Chapel Hill and London: University of North Carolina Press, 1986), 136.
2 Ibid., 136.
3 "Samuel Ringgold Ward to Henry Bibb 16 October 1815," in *The Black Abolitionist Papers*, 179.
4 William Wells Brown, "The People of Canada," in *The Black Abolitionist Papers*, 458–98, 466.
5 Robin Winks, *The Blacks in Canada: A History*. (Montreal and Kingston: McGill-Queen's University, 1997).

6 Ibid., 194.
7 Even Henson was more "cosmopolitan" than is often noted: "Others, like Josiah
   Henson, whose 1849 autobiography has popularly accrued the distinction of
   being 'the archetypal fugitive experience' [Winks, *The Blacks in Canada*, 115],
   were cosmopolites, traveling frequently between their Canadian settlements and
   American cities for the purpose of abolitionist campaigning." Nancy Kang,
   "'As If I Had Entered a Paradise': Fugitive Slave Narratives and Cross-Border
   Literary History," *African American Review* 39, no. 3 (Fall 2005), 443.
8 David Blight, ed., *Passages to Freedom: The Underground Railroad in History
   and Memory* (New York: Harper Collins Reprint, 2006).
9 While the more negative aspects of Canadian settlements, racism and segregation, have been recently the subject of criticism, many fugitives, according to
   Michael Wayne, stayed in Ontario because even if racism existed, it was not
   condoned by law. Moreover, Wayne points out, "it was in the interests of
   abolitionists to exaggerate the number of fugitives. As well, the prejudices of
   the times led most white Canadians to assume that any black person they
   encountered was a runaway slave." Wayne concludes,

   > By 1861 blacks had made their way to all corners of Canada West and had
   > become an integral part of the provincial economy. A great many – more
   > than half – were from the United States. Contrary to popular opinion,
   > however, they were mainly free blacks, not runaway slaves – immigrants not
   > fugitives ... Although entitled to equality before the law, they experienced
   > persistent discrimination ... Canada was not all they had hoped for, perhaps,
   > but, despite what their white neighbours may have believed, it had become
   > home. For the 40 per cent of the black population who had been born in the
   > province, it had never been anything else. (481)

   Michael Wayne, "The Black Population of Canada West on the Eve of the
   American Civil War: A Reassessment Based on the Manuscript Census of 1861,"
   Social History 28, no. 56 (1995): 465–85, http://pi.library.yorku.ca/ojs/index.
   php/hssh/issue/view/698.
10 Winfried Siemerling, *The Black Atlantic Reconsidered: Black Canadian Writing,
   Cultural History, and the Presence of the Past* (Montreal and Kingston: McGill-
   Queen's University, 2015), 8.
11 Though Siemerling's discussion is filled with qualifications and mitigations,
   he views Brown's 1861 report, which I will discuss, in "very positive terms"
   (ibid., 121). That being said, he does not spend much time analyzing the report
   and notes, "Brown sprinkles his generally positive comments with a few more
   critical observations" (127). I am not disputing the positive nature of some of

Brown's remarks. However, about a third of the report is critical, and the source of that criticism is rooted in the classed and racial composition of white Europeans who have settled the area, as well as a general structure of segregation. A more extensive discussion of Brown regarding the broader view of Canada West leads not to a positive but a highly ambiguous understanding of the area and its place in transatlantic discussions of the diaspora.

12 Afua Cooper, "The Fluid Frontier: Blacks and the Detroit River Region: A Focus on Henry Bibb," *Canadian Review of American Studies* 30, no. 2 (2000): 129–49, 133.

13 Ibid., 143.

14 See William E. Farrison, "William Wells Brown in Buffalo," *The Journal of Negro History* 39, no. 4 (October 1954): 298–314, 299.

15 Farrison comments, "In 1840 Brown visited Haiti and Cuba and possibly other islands in the West Indies." Brown had remarked that he was looking for a place to raise his two daughters where they would not experience discrimination, and he admired the Haitian Revolutionaries and the efforts to create the first black Republic. He was also "interested in the possibilities of life unhampered by race prejudice ... [K]nowing that slavery still existed in Cuba and that it had been only recently abolished from the British West Indies, he could scarcely have expected to find better prospects in the former than in the United States or as good opportunities in the latter as in Canada." William E. Farrison, *William Wells Brown: Author and Reformer* (Chicago: University of Chicago, 1969), 74. After this trip, which does not have extensive documentation, Brown returned to Buffalo to continue his work as a conductor for the Underground Railroad.

16 William Wells Brown, *The Escape: Or, A Leap for Freedom: A Drama in Five Acts*, ed. John Ernest (Knoxville: University of Tennessee, 2001). While Brown's play ostensibly leads to an "escape," a "leap" to cross the Niagara River, this is at the close of the play and few images of Canada as a civil space for freedom exist.

17 William Wells Brown, *Clotel; or, The President's Daughter: A Narrative of Slave Life in the United States*, ed. Robert S. Levine (1853, reissue, Boston: Bedford and St Martin's, 2000), 57.

18 Ibid., 61.

19 Ibid., 80, 79.

20 While a slave in Missouri (1814–34), Brown was hired out to James Walker and spent time working on a steamboat that shipped slaves internally down the Mississippi to New Orleans. Lucasi's paper addresses Brown's ambiguous situation as both witness and participant in what historian Ira Berlin has called the "Second Middle Passage," or what I have referred to as an internal middle passage. In Lucasi's words, "He undertook (or, more accurately, was forced to undertake) these travels because of the Lower South's renewed demand for

slaves from the states in the Upper South. His travels emerged from the period that Ira Berlin dubs the 'Second Middle Passage – the domestic slave trade' that 'would eventually bring millions of slaves to the Lower South' (131). This era was one, Berlin points out, of 'massive forced migration which informed every aspect of black life during the middle years of the nineteenth century' and 'shredded the planters' paternalist pretenses in the eyes of black people and prodded slaves and free people of color to create a host of oppositional ideologies and institutions that better accounted for the realities of the endless deportations, expulsions, and flights that continually remade their world' (18)" (Stephen Lucasi, "William Wells Brown's Narrative & Traveling Subjectivity," *African American Review* 41, no. 3 (2007): 528). See Ira Berlin's discussion of generations and various manifestations of slavery in *Generations of Captivity: A History of African-American Slaves* (Cambridge, MA: Belknap, 2003).

21 Lucasi, "William Wells Brown's Narrative & Traveling Subjectivity," 521–39, 532.
22 Brown, *Clotel*, 66.
23 Lucasi, "William Wells Brown's Narrative & Traveling Subjectivity," 523.
24 See, for instance, Brown's play, *The Escape*, which ends on crossing the Niagara Falls (Brown, *The Escape*, 25).
25 Winks, *The Blacks in Canada*, 148. Winks notes that churches were segregated as well and the Common School Act of 1850 would be passed to legislate segregated schools in St Catharines. Early black immigration patterns (prior to the FSL) were also in smaller numbers, which encouraged greater integration patterns than after 1850 (153). Winks traces increasing patterns of segregation in various rural parts on Canada West in his chapter "The Coming of the Fugitive, 1815–1861," in *Blacks in Canada*, which generally became the norm. In some areas this is a result of all black settlements organized by white philanthropy (such as Elgin). However, in some cases, segregation resulted from racism (white fears of crime), ethnic civil associations, and worsened as time passed. For example, in the three towns of Amherstburg, Colcester, and Sandwich, prior to 1851, the census data does not indicate segregation: "They lived together in blocs of forty or less with many whites interspersed into these communities. On the whole, they seem to have been accepted until the Irish began settling near Amherstburg in the late 1840s" (145).
26 Brown, "The People of Canada," *The Black Abolitionist Papers*, 458–98, 461.
27 Ibid., 462.
28 Ibid.
29 Ibid., 465.
30 Rosemary Sadlier, "Arriving in Canada," in *Canadian Cultural Heritage 4-Book Bundle: Molly Brant / Louis Riel / Harriet Tubman / Simon Girty*, ed. Peggy Dymond Leavey et al. (Toronto: Dundurn ebook, 2015).

31 Brown, *Clotel*, 216.
32 Drew writes, "Of the population of about six thousand, it is estimated that eight hundred are of African descent. Nearly all the adult coloured people have at some time been slaves." Benjamin Drew, *A North-Side View of Slavery. The Refugee: or the Narratives of Fugitive Slaves in Canada. Related by Themselves, with an Account of the History and Condition of the Colored Population of Upper Canada*. (Boston: J.P. Jewett and Company, 1856), 41. Michael Wayne points out that these numbers are somewhat exaggerated, and the census gives 601 in "The Black Population of Canada West on the Eve of the American Civil War: A Reassessment Based on the Manuscript Census of 1861," *Histoire sociale/Social History* 28, no. 56 (1995): 469; while Samuel Gridley Howe in 1863 estimates 700 (470) for St Catharines. More significant for Wayne's argument, is the issue of fugitive slave background because he contends that persons of African descent had been more widely "dispersed" throughout the province than either Brown or Drew consider.
33 Brown, "The People of Canada," 464.
34 As Farrison noted, "Having long been an important terminus on the Underground Railroad, Saint Catharines had become the center of a community of prosperous Negro farmers. Brown arrives there on August 23, and during a sojourn of several days, he lectured four times. Principally because of his efforts, many negroes in the community seemed to have become interested in immigrating to Haiti, but most of them were prevented from doing so because they owned property which they could not sell advantageously." William Edward Farrison, *William Wells Brown: Author and Reformer* (Chicago: University of Chicago, 1969), 342–3.
35 Brown, "The People of Canada," 479. Peter Ripley points out, "Brown understood the antislavery message inherent in discussing black success in Canada. A temperate, pious, and industrious black community made an eloquent statement against slavery and racial prejudice. Brown's positive description of black Canadian life seemed to contradict his efforts for Haitian immigration: If life was good in Canada, why would blacks decide to emigrate? His personal ambiguity reflected the debate between those who wished to build a model black community in Canada West and those who wanted to create a black nation in the Caribbean. Whatever their purpose, Brown's writings offer a rich look at black life in Canada" (*The Black Abolitionist Papers*, 461).
36 Brown, "The People of Canada," 480.
37 Brown, *Clotel*, 316.
38 Levine, *Clotel*, ft40, 77.
39 Brown includes an account of his attempt to established a manual labour school in Canada and its lack of support which resulted in his promotion of West

Indian immigration in 1851, "from Canada to the West Indies" (*Narrative of the Life in Clotel*, 77).

40 Brown, *Clotel*, 216.

41 Ibid., 217.

42 Ibid., 225.

43 Ibid.

44 Brown, "The People of Canada," 496.

45 Winks, *The Blacks in Canada*, 179, 180.

46 Ibid., 204.

47 Ibid., 219.

48 Brown uses the word amalgamation as the freedom of association and inter-mingling. For example, in *My Southern Home*, he writes, "amalgamation is the great civilizer of the races of men. Wherever a race, clan, or community have kept themselves together prohibiting by law, usage, or common consent, intermarriage with others, they have made little or no progress" (293).

49 Brown, "The People of Canada," 496

50 Ibid., 467, 469.

51 Farrison, *William Wells Brown*, 424.

52 He will end *My Southern Home* appealing to black pride in the midst of a context of lynch mob violence following Southern Reconstruction: "Black men, don't be ashamed to show your colors, and to own them." If this strategy was unsuccessful, and whites could only accept blacks in a servile role, Brown also left open the command for emigration: "Black men, emigrate." William Wells Brown, *My Southern Home; or, The South and its People*, ed. John Ernest (Chapel Hill: University of North Carolina, 2011), 186, 182.

SECTION TWO

Transnational Poetics of Space Making

7

Before the Bricks and Mortar:
The Grassroots Development
of the Harriet Tubman Underground
Railroad National Monument

dann j. Broyld and Shaun Winton

> I have always been most drawn to the study of ordinary people, those whose names are not on buildings we consider historic landmarks, but who put the bricks and mortar together so they could stand to this day.
> Archaeologist and historian Karolyn Smardz Frost, *Steal Away Home*[1]

On 25 March 2013, the Harriet Tubman Underground Railroad National Monument (HTURNM) was signed into existence by Barack Obama's Presidential Proclamation under the Antiquities Act. This monument formally recognizes Harriet Tubman,[2] who worked as an abolitionist, Civil War scout, women's rights activist, and humanitarian. Despite her honourable work, it took one hundred years from her 10 March 1913 death for the United States to acknowledge her with an official park.[3] This momentous development materialized because of immense grassroots local public work, annual commemorations and activities, as well as broad-based mobilization that provoked the National Park Services and the Maryland state authorities to erect a Harriet Tubman monument. These efforts deserve to be chronicled and acknowledged as the groundwork that the bricks and mortar of the HTURNM rest upon.

This chapter will first demonstrate that the grassroots actions in the "field" can cause power holders to concede and legislation to be passed to ensure that important legacies are formally memorialized. It will address important questions such as who has memorialized Tubman and why? Can the grassroots actions be directly responsible for causing Maryland authorities and the NPS to build a monument? Who are the major players, events, and organizations that need to be accredited? In wake of the National Monument's opening, are there threats of overlooking the community contributions? Moreover, is the quest for tourism dollars a danger to the integrity of the advocates and site, and how will a "national" park interpret Tubman as an American–Canadian transnational?

Furthermore direct attention will be given to the pioneers in the greater Dorchester, Maryland area[4] that navigated the social and political terrain to memorialize Harriet Tubman. The HTURNM is located on 25,000 acres of land between the Edward Brodess and Anthony Thompson plantations where Harriet Tubman initially toiled as an enslaved person and which is still largely open woodlands and marsh. The "Dorchester County landscape of Harriet Tubman's homeland," President Obama explained, remains "much as they were in her time there. If she were to return to this area today, Harriet Tubman would recognize it."[5] Nonetheless, Maryland lacks the physical Tubman-specific buildings that St Catharines, Ontario and Auburn, New York possess. From 1851 to 1858, Tubman lived in St Catharines with many others from Maryland and fellowshipped at the local Salem Chapel, British Methodist Episcopal Church (BME), which is still standing today. Also Auburn has three edifices of significance she left behind: the Tubman Home for the Aged, the Tubman's Residence, and the Thompson African Methodist Episcopal (AME) Zion Church.[6] Tubman spent more than fifty years of her life in Auburn doing the honourable work of feeding, clothing, and caring for the destitute and fighting for women's suffrage and greater rights for Blacks. In the 2000s, both Dorchester and Auburn waged a joint campaign to solicit the National Park Service to craft official sites in Tubman's honour. In the end, Dorchester managed to stake claim to Tubman first with the establishment of the HTURNM.

Although, political pundits, professional historians, and tourism agents have played a key role in the formation of the new monument, the less familiar accounts of grassroots activism in Dorchester have led the way. The *Dorchester Star* explained: "The idea to share the Eastern Shore's story of the Underground Railroad started as a grassroots effort from a group of residents and local historians who were involved in giving Harriet Tubman tours."[7] In greater Dorchester the commemoration of Tubman took on several mediums including Tubman Day, annual celebrations on 10 March to mark her death, to plays and parades, the building of the community-based Harriet Tubman Organization (HTO) and their storefront museum, and even an annual scholar's Tubman Conference. Such events and mobilization, which often grows meagre in the public's memory, ultimately attracted the attention of power holders to authorize a formal national monument in Tubman's honour. Moreover, the success of the Dorchester community has sent a "Message to the Grassroots"[8] of an effective means of creating needed museums and monuments.

The efforts in Dorchester were not totally unlike those in St Catharines or Auburn. However, the results have been quite different. In fact, community members in St Catharines, for instance, have fought to erect historical markers to Tubman, hosted countless events in her honour, and have helped to propel wider recognition of the esteemed leader and the BME Church in the region. The house of worship, which had a wealth of members from Tubman's Eastern Shore of Maryland, is a popular stop on the Niagara Black Heritage Tours. People are intrigued with its original American Southern-style architecture and the church's basement has been fashioned with an exhibit of pictures and memorabilia to engage visitors. Keeping Tubman's legacy alive in this manner created the context that inspired the District School Board of Niagara to establish the Harriet Tubman Public School in 2014 and to later place a bronze statue of her outside of the building. Trustee Dalt Clark of the school-naming committee explained, "There was no question Harriet Tubman was the first choice."[9] The school serves students kindergarten to eighth grade, and like the HTURNM will impart knowledge of Tubman to ensure her memory will be passed onto future generations.[10]

An element of this transfer of information needs to be centred on the ordinary people in the communities Harriet Tubman inhabited, particularly greater Dorchester County. Members of the Maryland memorialization movement do not want to be compromised by historical commemoration propaganda, masquerading as an opportunity to amass tourist dollars once the HTURNM opens.[11] They desire to maintain a sense of ownership and to make certain that their efforts are not in vain.[12] In the spirit of the immediate Dorchester community, this article will employ a grassroots historical methodology by privileging their voices and narrative via source materials such as local newspapers and oral interviews. This theoretical focus provides a window into their "bottom-up history" and direct reactions to HTURNM developments as they unfolded. In sum, as the public masses visit the finished museum to Harriet Tubman it is befitting that they grasp the grassroots efforts and common people that toiled in the shadows to lift Tubman's history and memory to the light of wider understanding and recognition.

Dorchester's grassroots ordinary citizens in Maryland devoted themselves to the conservation of Tubman's cultural heritage. It is their work that made the HTURNM ultimately a reality. For instance, local historian Addie Clash Travers, in the 1970s and 1980s actively persuaded community members to celebrate the legacy of Tubman at the Bazzel Methodist Episcopal Church in Bucktown where area Blacks had traditionally worshipped. Travers with the help of a modest group, including relatives of the Rev. Richard D. Jackson, were able to pull together an event they called "Harriet Ross Tubman Day," which became an annual celebration. Thereafter, the Harriet Tubman Organization, Inc. (HTO) began to develop. It evolved into the centrepiece, which much of the commemoration in greater Dorchester revolved around. The HTO went through several stages and name changes before the group took its current status as one of the oldest community organizations dedicated to the memory of Tubman.[13]

The HTO was formed as the amalgamation of two groups: the Harriet Tubman Association (HTA) and the Harriet Tubman Committee (HTC). On 24 September 1972, the HTA was established as a community-based organization at the 1032 Pine Street home of Rev. Blanch Bailey in Cambridge and cofounders Addie Clash Travers and Rev. Richard D. Jackson ran the group. On 31 January 1983 the HTC was organized at the Waugh Chapel United Methodist Church.[14] This meeting was key in transforming Harriet Ross Tubman Day into an entire weekend. The groups, which held a common interest in maintaining the memory of Tubman and Travers, were instrumental in the formation of each. In fact, Addie Clash Travers was "The lady to contact about Harriet Tubman."[15] Inquisitors were directed to her home to learn the local history. In 1989, the HTA sought to develop a community cultural centre to provide educational and social programs and to continue to promote and preserve the history of Tubman. The following year, area activism helped in turning 10 March into being nationally recognized as Harriet Tubman Day. At the time, Sen. Joseph Biden of Delaware explained, "It's a great tribute to the legacy of Harriet Tubman's moral strength and courage that Congress quickly passed this commemorative."[16]

In 1996, the association's board of directors elected to change the name of the group to the Harriet Tubman Organization to better reflect the membership's new vision for the future. They also revised their mission. The objective of the HTO was now to cultivate programs and services directed at children, youth, and families and to provide the community with interpretive history of Tubman's achievements to yield sustainable interest. A key goal of the HTO's mission statement and purpose was to help in the "erection of a State Park in her honor."[17] The HTURNM is something that the HTO actively strived to create. Before the building of the federal and formal site to Tubman, the HTO established its own storefront Harriet Tubman Museum and Educational Center (HTMEC). The Harriet Tubman Organization has been able to engender interest in protecting Tubman's legacy from the municipal, county, state, and national government. Evelyn Townsend, former president of HTO, was noted for her tenacity when it came to acquiring support from the community and stakeholders at all levels. Delegate Rudolph Cane, D-37A, remembered, "She called at least every 90 days," and Townsend contacted Cambridge Councilman Gilbert Cephas shortly after he took office to see that the museum was established.[18]

In the 1990s, the HTO built the HTMEC with assistance from the city. It is a storefront museum located at 424 Race Street in the heart of downtown Cambridge, Maryland. Historically, Race Street was a focal point of Jim Crow racial discrimination, tension, and protest. Retired educator and HTO board member Bill Jarmon explained that some dislike the HTMEC's location and suggested it be moved to nearby Pine Street a noted Black area.[19] Yet, the HTO was unwavering, and their act of faith yielded fruit. The centre has become a staple in Cambridge. It possesses an exhibit that focuses on Tubman, and it hosts an array of community and educational events. All of this on a street where Black civil and human rights protesters once marched and were jeered at, hit with eggs, rocks, and, the "weapon of choice," balloons filled with urine. The situation was so grave that scholar Peter B. Levy titled his book *Civil War on Race Street*, though it is about the Civil Rights Movement in Cambridge.[20] The location of the HTMEC is symbolic of the organization's desire to confront bigotry and guide progress. Kisha Petticolas of the Eastern Shore Network for Change asserted that "Harriet was the first civil rights leader in our community that we are aware of"[21]; thereby, Tubman's work is a continuation of what the HTO battled and undertakes. The president of the organization since 2006, Donald Pinder explained, "we provide a museum and a place for people to come to find out about the life and legacy of Harriet Tubman and the sites and activity of the Underground Railroad."[22] Pinder's words have outright gravity when the past and place on Race Street are put into context.

Like the 1960s Black museum movement in Chicago, Detroit, Philadelphia, and Washington, DC, highlighted in Andrea A. Burns award-winning book *From Storefront to Monument*, the HTMEC was crafted in the same vein. As a result of Black history being omitted or modestly told at the major cultural centres, communities found creative ways to present their heritage at establishments they oversaw. The Black museum movement ultimately induced mainstream institutions to integrate African American history and culture into their own exhibits and educational programs. The

HTMEC's struggle has been much the same as its early counterparts, as they have navigated the lack of funds and resources so readily available to principal state and federal sites. Despite challenges, the HTMEC and other Black "storefront" institutions served their constituencies as best they could and can, providing them with thought-provoking exhibits and programming, while simultaneously advocating for more inclusion, equity in tax distribution to cultural sites, and outright pushing for formal "monuments."[23]

By the mid-1990s, the NPS completed the broad-based *Underground Railroad Special Resource Study* that identified sites important to runaways and recommended a more in-depth investigation of sites significant to Harriet Tubman. Subsequently, Congress also formed the Network to Freedom Program to coordinate preservation and education efforts with institutions associated with the Underground Railroad throughout the country and abroad. In 2000, President Bill Clinton signed the *Harriet Tubman Special Resource Study Act* to determine the practicability of devoting a National Park to Tubman. After a rigorous eight-year resource examination was completed, the NPS requested that Congress designate two parks in the name of Tubman that worked cohesively together, one on the Eastern Shore of Maryland and another in Auburn, New York. Each American community was limited in the manner it could work with St Catharines due to the national border. The US legislation was called the Harriet Tubman Underground Railroad National Historical Park Act or S. 247. The bill had backing from representatives from each of the sites in Maryland and New York supporting its approval. S. 247 was introduced to Congress but was not voted on for six years.[24]

In the meantime, the HTO kept up its work to commemorate Tubman as the federal government was undecided on its objectives to honour the deserving leader. Since 2000 the organization has hosted annual Harriet Tubman Day Banquets. HTO President Donald Pinder acknowledges that "this banquet keeps the HTO involved and connected to community." He also asserted that as a community "we want to educate and promote Harriet Tubman and let everyone know she fought for justice during her time at Bucktown, during the Civil War and until her death in 1913."[25] This banquet helps keep the HTO's programming funded and the community engaged. One attendee who had been attending for many years began bringing her granddaughters. She explained, "I support the HTO. It's an important celebration. It's a way to keep Harriet Tubman's spirit alive. I think it's important for my grandchildren to experience it."[26] The annual celebrations have created a space where members of the community shared their appreciation and admiration for Tubman across generations.

For decades, the rank and file of the all-volunteer HTO has been filled with active community members. John Creighton, for example, had a mind "layered with Dorchester heritage." In January 2001, he started a discussion group that concentrated on Tubman and the Underground Railroad through genealogical and primary documentation.[27] In 2015, when Creighton died, Dorchester County Historical Society Executive Director Ann Phillips explained, "Dorchester is a much poorer place without him."[28] Other endeavours, like "Tubman Tours" conducted by Bill Jarmon and local aficionados show visitors the landscape where Tubman was born, enslaved, escaped, and helped other freedom seekers. These tours can last forty-five minutes to two hours depending on the level of details desired. Tourists arrive from all over the country and world to see the sites associated with Tubman. In addition, Royce Sampson of the HTO brought about the idea to host an annual Harriet Tubman Underground Railroad Conference to further engage academics, local researchers, and experts to get more in-depth interpretations of Tubman, the Underground Railroad, and related topics.[29] He explained, "we needed to do something bigger."[30] Sampson has a great heart for the community. He once highlighted, "My first responsibility is to my family; the second is to my community."[31] Ellen Mousin, a longtime "Harriet" enthusiast who has lived in both Auburn and Cambridge, has been instrumental in the execution of the Tubman Conference from its theme to booking keynote speakers. One participant informed Mousin that she "goes to conferences all over the country" but took exception to the "friendly" atmosphere and "receptive attendees"[32] at the Tubman Conference.

The Tubman Byway budded out of local efforts as well. It was initially completed in 1999, the sixty-four-mile byway stretched from Bucktown in Dorchester County, through Caroline County along Choptank River to the border at Sandtown, Delaware. The byway was revised in 2005 to encompass a total of 125 miles, and today it covers some 200 miles. In 2009, it received an All-American Road designation from the federal National Scenic Byways Program and many desire that the project's route be expanded again to reach more locations where Tubman ventured in Delaware, New York, and even to Canada.[33] What is now a scenic drive through the countryside of Maryland was once a landscape filled with the enslaved, marred with cruelty and blood, and skilfully navigated by Tubman. The Tubman Byway features some thirty stops including historic homes, meeting houses, mills, fields, and waterways which are highlighted with signage that collectively uncover the history of enslavement and the quest for freedom. "I think the byway is awesome," Patricia Ross-Hawkins explained, "because we're connecting the dots again."[34] She described the linking of places significant to Tubman "as a string of pearls."[35] The HTO also supported education through the Harriet Tubman Underground Railroad Byway Tour Certification Training, which was sponsored by Maryland State Tourism, in order to create a more formal network of people educated on Tubman's history in the region.

Grassroots organizers have endured pushback, but it did not deter them. In the summer of 2009, residents of Cambridge, Maryland became aware that the Harriet Tubman mural painted in 2000 in the Harriet Tubman Memorial Garden along Route 50 had been vandalized with racial epithets and iconography. "I was furious," recalled Victoria Jackson-Stanley, Cambridge's first Black woman to serve as mayor. Dorchester County was appalled by this senseless act and rallied the community together in an effort to ensure that the legacy of Tubman remained protected. Charlie Ross, a great-great-great-grand-nephew of Tubman, created two murals that now sit behind vandal-proof covering in the Harriet Tubman Memorial Garden. The new mural, unveiled on 29 July 2011, was highly lauded. "Exuberantly joyful," is how Jackson-Stanley described her reaction to the new piece of art; she commented that Ross possessed "the passion and commitment needed to get the job done." Valerie Ross-Manokey, a great-great-grandniece of Tubman and the artist's aunt remembered seeing "people here crying" as they watched Ross's painting come into being. After seeing the portrait of Tubman, Manokey proclaimed, "the lady is here."[36] The community response to the vandalization of the mural was merely an apparition of the work that has been going on behind the scenes in Dorchester County for a long time. In an article titled "Racial Progress Unclear in Cambridge," Bill Jarmon, who had participated in Civil Rights protest on Race Street, explained that, "things have changed ... but in some ways, very little has changed."[37] His statement underscores the rigid social environment that Tubman advocates were forced to navigate. The efforts of the HTO, Mayor Jackson-Stanley, and other members of the community were starting to materialize in more substantial ways.

The Harriet Tubman National Historic Parks Acts, S. 247, gained steam as it churned through Congress. Senators Ben Cardin and Barbara Mikulski were joined by people from around the country such as Sen. Lisa Murkowski from Alaska, Sen. Jeff Bingaman from New Mexico, and others to pass the bill after it had been introduced in 2008 and reintroduced in 2011 and 2012.[38] Elected officials sensed perhaps that the United States was engaging in a "Memorial Mania" as scholar Erika Doss suggested and did not see the value of this costly trend of creating new publicly supported sites particularly when it came to honouring a Black woman. The HTURNM is the 399th NPS site and is one of thirty-six that focus directly on African American themes and one of three that recognizes an African American woman.[39] Doss argued in her book *Memorial Mania* that American's thousands of new memorials to executed "witches," victims of terrorism, along with those that pay tribute to everyone from civil rights leaders to organ donors, and the eradication of Communism, underscores a national obsession to express and claim political issues in visible public contexts. These memorials, like the HTURNM, were grouped as a part of the same "excessive, frenzied, and extreme" push for more sites. Doss emphasized that the "growing number of memorials represent heightened anxieties about who and what should be remembered in America."[40]

Utah Republican Representative Rob Bishop, for instance, asserted that President Obama's actions in forming the HTURNM, along with four other parks[41] "promotes a certain type of unilateral governance and sets a dangerous precedent" and that "the costs associated with these new designations ought to be considered openly."[42] Bishop's statement highlighted the reluctance to approve new sites and a perceived phenomenon that needed to be checked and eradicated. Some used the "Mania" to counter parks supported by the oppositional party. Whatever the case, it took elected officials time to pass S. 247. However, the grassroots pressure remained stout.

The HTO was able to harness the enthusiasm of the Dorchester community to organize "Harriet on the Hill Day" on 14 September 2011. The HTO managed to "recruit local citizens to act as lobbyists on behalf of the National Park Service proposal."[43] Sally Kenyon Grant, also a "key organizer of the event," forewarned, "We are going to storm Capitol Hill," and "We are going to let them know we're not fooling around anymore." Grant's goal for Harriet on the Hill Day was "to get as much national exposure for this as possible."[44] The community and Grant understood that the work they had done to preserve the legacy of Tubman's life, brought about the bill, but it would take a movement of people to get the legislation passed. Harriet on the Hill Day brought their demands directly to Washington, DC, and gave Tubman supporters, including a score of people from Auburn, the chance to have their voices heard in regards to a formal monument.

Although the grassroots were getting the needed support of elected officials, they shaped the overall message that was put forth. Thereby, Harriet on the Hill Day was not hijacked by leaders and distorted from its intended purpose like the 28 August 1963 March on Washington during the Civil Rights Movement. Malcolm X, in his "Message to the Grass Roots" speech given on 10 November 1963 in Detroit, Michigan criticized the March on Washington, describing it as "a picnic" and "a circus." He condemned civil rights leaders for diluting the original purpose of the march, which had been to show the strength and anger of Black people, by allowing White people and the President John F. Kennedy administration to help organize and oversee the march. The uniformity in signage from permitted posters to buttons was stifling to the initial grassroots push. In addition, the speech of US Congressman John Lewis had to be censored and writer James Baldwin could not speak at all. This forced Malcolm X to explain, "They controlled it so tight, they told those Negroes what time to hit town, how to come, where to stop, what signs to carry, what songs to sing, what speech they could make, and what speech they couldn't make; and then told them to get out town by sundown."[45] The March on Washington leadership was subject to the Kennedy political machinery, which threatened not to back future civil rights legislation if Blacks came to the capital and radically protested as the grassroots had intended.[46] Harriet on the Hill Day, by contrast, had speeches and a mixture of uniformed signs, denoting solidarity, and homemade signs that allow for personal and unregulated expressions for a needed Tubman monument. Collectively they conveyed a message directly from the people.

The HTO had yet another obstacle to overcome: that of convincing Republican Representative from Maryland's 1st District, Andy Harris, to introduce a companion bill to SB 247. HTO President Donald Pinder, Mayor Jackson-Stanley, and others escorted Harris on a tour of the county, exhibiting the important sites in Tubman's life. Jacqueline Ross-Henry, Harriet Tubman's seventh great-grandniece explained, "When you go out there in the area, you get the sense of what they went through ... When I'm there, I wonder what I would do if I was in that position, if I could make it."[47] Rep. Harris had to query himself those same questions and ponder the bravery and sacrifice of the enslaved that were once upon the landscape as well. The tour was apparently productive because when Mayor Jackson-Stanley declared, "I've had enough," and then asked "are you going to introduce legislation?" Rep. Harris is said to have simply nodded his head in the affirmative.[48] Patricia Ross-Hawkins, a sixth-generation great-grandniece of Tubman added, "We've come too far to turn back now...no is not an option."[49] Community members kept the agitation up by writing letters of support for the bill. Consequently, the grassroots mobility precipitated comprehensive bipartisan action among lawmakers to the point that a mid-2012 *Dorchester Star* headline read "Tubman Bills Continue to Move Ahead as Planned."[50]

The HTURNM established the following March (2013) marking the centennial of Tubman's death and the point when residents of Maryland's

Eastern Shore finally accomplished the chief goal for which they had been working – the HTURNM was established and with it more people could become informed and inspired to fight for broader social justice. President Barack Obama echoed historian Kate Clifford Larson's words when he noted that Harriet Tubman was "an American Hero."[51] The announcement brought great excitement to the community and beyond. Obama explained, "Tubman fought tirelessly for the Union Cause, for the rights of enslaved people, for the rights of women, and for the rights of all. She was a leader in the struggle for civil rights, who was forever motivated by her love of family and community and by her deep and abiding faith."[52] The president's remarks highlighted the themes important to Tubman: family, freedom, faith, and community.[53]

Of course, simply placing Harriet Tubman into a national context by labelling her an "American icon" is misleading considering that she also lived in St Catharines, Canada West, then a part of the British Empire,[54] between 1851 and 1858. To interpret Tubman and marginalize her time in Canada and affections towards Britain is a missed opportunity to inspire new discourse on the freedom fighter and to promote broad visitation to the HTURNM. The transnationalism of Tubman is not a convenient characteristic and is thereby usually avoided. However, in this modern era of global sensibilities it is unbecoming to fasten Tubman to a rigid nationalist box she does not historically fit neatly into. Modernity demands complexity and pluralism; all of which Tubman possessed. The HTURNM should reflect the dynamics of Tubman and not be constrained by borders she clearly transcended. The question becomes how does a national monument deal with a transnational figure and Black mobility on a larger scale in its interpretation and programming?[55] The answers remain to be seen.

Nevertheless, the announcement of the HTURNM brought great cheer. Dorchester County's *Star Democrat* announced, "It's Official: Tubman is a National Monument." Governor Martin O'Malley recognized the groundswell of support that existed in the grassroots of his community: "Today, President Obama made a long-held dream come true for countless Marylanders." Clara Small, history professor of Salisbury University, explained, "I am so proud ... a lot of work went into this."[56] Sen. Mikulski was elated by the proclamation, but she understood that work still needed to be done: "Designating a national monument ... is an important step as we move towards the establishment of National Historic Parks to commemorate her heroic works."[57] Cambridge Mayor Victoria Jackson-Stanley could barely sleep on the eve of the ground breaking ceremony. She explained, "We are going to make this hallowed ground a national park."[58]

But there were mixed feelings. US Secretary of the Interior Ken Salazar's claim that "the monument will not only remind us that a single courageous person can achieve extraordinary gains for humanity but it will also create jobs and boost the local economy through increased tourism"[59] caused the grassroots actors to temper their excitement, concerned about their efforts being co-opted. By the mid-2000s, tourism had been identified as an important objective of Dorchester County. Tourism director Natalie Chabot argued that "the county council itself has said tourism is one of the biggest economic engines for the county." And chairperson of the Dorchester County Museums and Attractions Committee Carol Lacy explained, "we want them [tourists] to come off [route] 50 [main road] and visit us."[60] Tubman has become the biggest historical tourism draw and tool that the Eastern Shore possesses.

While the grassroots organizers are grateful for the jobs in construction and hospitality the HTURNM can create, they have concerns about subjugating Tubman to the realm of juvenile storybook tales, myths, and folklore, which have blotted the history of their esteemed leader, in the name of amassing tourism dollars.[61] They clearly understand that authenticity and tourism do not always mix well. Also the community wanted to temper the outright commercialization of the Underground Railroad and "Heritage Tourism" which were trending in the United States and Canada. Maryland officials who support tourism are sure they have "got everything it takes to become a vibrant heritage tourism area."[62] They believe "Tubman Tourism" will boost the area's fiscal viability by attracting an estimated 200,000 annual visitors to the national monument and drawing some $20 million per year into the local economy. Moreover, they hope that construction of the site will create approximately 225 jobs, including ten full-time employees to staff the centre.[63]

The HTURNM was formed under a new model for national parks. The US federal government now seeks to build sites with limited national ownership, direct state and local financial and staff contributions, and a wealth of solid community partnerships. Stipulations are laid out in a series of "conditions for establishment" that must be accomplished before the secretary of the interior can formally establish new "partnership parks."[64] After several approvals of funds for the monument, Baltimore-based GWWO Architects designed the HTURNM visitor centre and administration building; a British company, Haley Sharpe Design, which has its North American office in Toronto, Canada, crafted the internal exhibits.[65] Although unplanned, the hiring of these two companies is representative of Tubman's history, given she was a native of Maryland with cross-border affiliations having resided in Canada West for some seven years. Senior associate Chris Elcock of GWWO explained: "Once we won the contract to design the project, the first thing we do is open our ears." He expounded, "We spend a lot of time with the local community groups, people who have been part of this for a long time."[66] Haley Sharpe equally embedded itself into the community in order to grasp understanding and to create in a manner that was responsive and representative of the locals. Overall, GWWO and Haley Sharpe simply recognized that its direct clients were the people, both past and present.

The state-of-the-art HTURNM visitor centre is equipped with energy and water efficiency systems, such as bio-retention ponds and vegetative roofs, which are characteristic of Tubman's environmental sensibilities. She was tied to the earth having worked it, understood how to utilize the stars to guide fugitive slaves northward, and even drugged babies with paregorics or opium in order to minimize outbursts on the journey to freedom.[67] The green-friendly visitor centre and site will feature interactive displays, a library, classrooms, a gift shop, and an outside "Legacy Garden" walking trail and an open-air pavilion for large gatherings. The design elements allow for educational opportunities. The interpretive center will host edifying programming to ensure the legacy of Tubman lives on. The monument's federal and state staff have firmly linked it to the National Underground Railroad Network to Freedom Program and The International Coalition of Sites of Conscious. Each relate the HTURNM to similar institutions around the world and help to shape the methodological approach of its programming. In 1998, Congress passed the Network to Freedom Act which provides support to sites, including those in Canada, Mexico, and the Caribbean as well as those outside of the NPS system, that highlight resistance to enslavement via flight. The legislation crosses racial, socioeconomic, and most importantly national borders to unite historical institutions based on their common thread. The Sites of Conscious[68] alliance, which was established in 1999, allows the HTURNM to network with historic places that engage in strategic advocacy and in-depth dialogue to encourage social justice.[69] The goal of this web of institutions is to keep historical sites accessible and relevant to the contemporary world and transform history from being merely events that occurred in the past, to the record that can inform, guide, and perhaps change the future. The Network to Freedom and Site of Conscious align with the mission of the Tubman monument.

At each stage of the development of the HTURNM the community rejoiced as their objectives were finally met. Upon Maryland's approval of the contract to construct the site's visitor centre, Secretary Joseph Gill of the State Department of Natural Resources (DNR), explained: "thanks to the hard work and collaboration of many people, a beautiful tribute to our nation's famed freedom fighter will soon stand."[70] The "people" to whom Gill referred were the grassroots activists in Maryland that toiled continuously for the outcomes they sought. President of the HTO Donald Pinder, commenting on the visitor centre budget approval, explained: "the state has always been talking about this – forever … finally they put the money up first instead of talking. There's not a more deserving lady."[71] Seventy-five-year-old Valerie Manokey, explained that "It is awesome," speaking of the progress being made on the HTURNM site. As Tubman's oldest living descendant in Maryland and a retired teacher's aide from Cambridge, Manokey asserted, "It's like something inside you that was growing, and you knew someone would see the significance and it would blossom and now you see the buds on the tree. I pray that I'll be here to see it."[72]

The grassroots actions in the "field" of Dorchester County, Maryland has without question been instrumental in causing the federal and state officials to concede and honour Tubman by erecting the Harriet Tubman Underground Railroad National Monument. The community is a witness to the power of civic engagement and persistent grassroots actions. Indeed, this has been an inspiration to those in St Catharines and Auburn. All of the sacrifices of individuals, planned events, and countless hours of work that have gone into the HTURNM have not been futile. Nonetheless, in light of the national monument to Tubman being completed in 2017, there are looming threats that the community contributions will be overlooked, including the ever-present danger to the integrity of the site – tourism dollars.[73] Also there is a threat of simply nationalizing Tubman. Advocates will have to continue to inspire the community to be active and vigilant and to hold the NPS and their elected officials accountable.

Understanding the grassroots cornerstone of the HTURNM, Cherie A. Butler, NPS first-superintendent of the site, stated, "I am grateful for the opportunity to work with strong and thoughtful partners and a very passionate community."[74] Area advocates embodied the spirit of their beloved leader and grasped the reality that, "Tubman's story is a testament that one determined person – no matter [their] station in life – can make a difference."[75] The community was an unrelenting force; people from all walks of life combined their efforts to propel the HTURNM into fruition. "Working with partners has been," Butler asserted, "and will continue to be an integral part of keeping Tubman's story alive."[76] The HTO and the grassroots elements in Dorchester County carefully stewarded the local history of Tubman, used it to lobby for the HTURNM, and will continue to advocate for their perspective in the site's interpretive plans. The HTO fulfilled its

1996 mission and must now re-evaluate its role. Will the HTO become a victim of its own success? Will the construction of the HTURNM eclipse the storefront museum in downtown Cambridge just miles away? How will the pleas of the grassroots activists for sincere racial dialogue intermix with the urge for heritage tourism?

The major challenge that the HTURNM faces is keeping the community's intent for the site at the forefront of all they do. The NPS has worked honourably to keep stakeholders in the community involved via formal meetings and activities, but there is room to improve. For example, on 13 June 2014 NPS, and their consultants, hosted a "Sneak Peek Exhibit Preview" at the Harriet Tubman Organization's site to reveal a score of the design choices that were being considered for the HTURNM.[77] This came off as more of a tease than a genuine partnership where the lines of communication are two-way and moreover constant. Having the community members persistently around the table, instead of dropping in for a gaze is the ideal way to execute this project. These are the types of NPS events that make the public sceptical that the new Tubman monument will reflect their collective voice.[78] Hopefully, affective community engagement tactics used at other Network to Freedom sites will be applied at Tubman's monument.

After all, it is important that the masses who visit the HTURUM know the origin of the site and the message of its founders. As the bricks and mortar are now in place and the buildings are completed, the successes of the HTO are manifested in physical form. If the tourism agents seek to employ Tubman as an outright economic tool, she is destined for Disneyfication again. One tourism driven business owner warned the new park: "if you tell the things we already know about slavery, you're not going to have many people" and expounded, "people aren't going to come to be sad."[79] The principal concern and focus should not be on what the people that are visiting want *per se* but what the people that establish the HTURNM believe is best for the memory of Tubman. Others can take the Tubman Byway out of town, but community members live there and expect a professional and proficient brand of history that does not sell out so people can depart "happy" and "under informed." Kate Larson explained what the community desired from the design team: "They didn't want us to sugarcoat it. They wanted the truth."[80] Unquestionably, there is a way to combine the worlds of education and entertainment to produce candid history without surrendering the narrative to simple tourism and convenient historical distortions.

In all, the cornerstone of the Harriet Tubman Underground Railroad National Monument is the work and efforts of community activists and agents for change on the Eastern Shore. Donald Pinder explained that

Tubman, "continued to give throughout her life ... now it's our turn to give back to her."[81] In April 2016, only after US Treasury Secretary Jack Lew's announced that Tubman's image will be placed on the forthcoming $20 bill did Auburn, New York approve plans to establish its national park.[82] In contrast to the site in Dorchester, it appears somewhat disingenuous. Did the "Empire State" undertake this endeavour because Tubman was in vogue or for potential tourism dollars? Marci Ross of the Maryland Office of Tourism Development frankly explained that Dorchester and Auburn took "two very different paths to get to that national park designation."[83] With all the work being done on the American side of the border, Parks Canada has to seriously consider doing more to better acknowledge Tubman.[84] The Black Heritage Tours in Canada should not have to carry the mantle of retelling "Harriet's" past with little support.[85] Parks Canada needs to give formal and financial commitment to this undertaking. Fortunately, for the activists in greater Dorchester, who toiled for the monument to stand, they debunked the notion that power works from the top down and suggest a different relationship. They have sent a "message to the grassroots" displaying an effective means of creating needed museums and parks. The humble community members that helped the HTURNM to materialize modestly deflect attention and speak of the site as being there for future generations to learn about Tubman. However, when the masses visit the monument, they need to comprehend that the history of the site stretches back to an engaged grassroots community of agitators.

On the weekend of 10 March 2017, marking the 104th anniversary of Harriet Tubman's death, the HTURNM visitor centre welcomed the public inside. Opening during National Woman's History Month and following Black History Month was befitting of the chief causes Tubman championed. Although the 10 March weekend weather was dreary, the local community and visitors' spirits were not dampened. The visitor centre was bursting with tourists, while others waited in inclement weather outside just to get an opportunity to enter. A wealth of events, from guest lectures and performances to activities for children, filled the weekend. The years of struggle yielded a level of satisfaction, even though political pundits of course swooped in for photo opportunities, speeches, and acknowledgment at the opening ceremony, the locals were there before the foundation of the bricks and mortar were laid.

NOTES

This study was made possible by an Association of American University Professors (AAUP) grant from Central Connecticut State University (CCSU). CCSU students Omayra Cintron-Hause and Gabriel Benjamin were also instrumental in the development of this study.

1 Karolyn Smardz Frost, *Steal Away Home: One Woman's Epic Flight to Freedom – and Her Long Road Back to the South* (Toronto: HarperCollins Publishers, 2017), xix.

2 Sarah H. Bradford, *Harriet Tubman, the Moses of Her People* (New York: Geo. R. Lockwood & Son, 1886); Earl Conrad, *General Harriet Tubman* (Washington: Associated Publishers, 1943); Jean M. Humez, *Harriet Tubman: The Life and the Life Stories* (Madison: University of Wisconsin, 2003); Kate Clifford Larson, *Bound for the Promised Land: Harriet Tubman, Portrait of An American Hero* (New York: Ballantine Books, 2004); Catherine Clinton, *Harriet Tubman: The Road to Freedom* (New York: Little, Brown and Company, 2004); Milton C. Sernett, *Harriet Tubman: Myth, Memory, and History* (Durham: Duke University, 2007); Beverly Lowry, *Harriet Tubman: Imagining a Life* (New York: Anchor Books, 2007); Chantal N. Gibson and Monique Silverman, "Sur/Rendering Her Image: The Unknowable Harriet Tubman," *racar: revue d'art canadienne/Canadian Art Review* 30, nos. 1–2 (The Portrait Issue/ La question du portrait, 2005): 25–38; and dann j. Broyld, "Harriet Tubman: Transnationalism and the Land of a Queen in the Late Antebellum," *The Meridians: Feminism, Race, and Transnationalism.* Special issue: *Harriet Tubman: A Legacy of Resistance* 12, no. 2 (November 2014): 78–98.

3 Like the establishment of the HTURM, the National Museum of African American History and Culture took one hundred years to open in September 2016 after the movement to create it began. See Robert Leon Wilkins, *Long Road to Hard Truth: The 100 Year Mission to Create the National Museum of African American History and Culture* (Washington: Proud Legacy Publishing, 2016); Mabel O. Wilson and Lonnie G. Bunch III, *Begin with the Past: Building the National Museum of African American History and Culture* (Washington: Smithsonian Books, 2016).

4 This includes Caroline and Talbot Counties, Maryland.

5 "Tubman National Monument Created Here," *Dorchester Star*, 29 March 2013.

6 Hilary Hanson, "Harriet Tubman Gets Historical National Park in New York: The Abolitionist Hero is finally Getting the Recognition She Deserves," *HuffPost*, 23 April 2016.

7 "Byway to Commemorate Tubman, Bring in Revenue," *Dorchester Star*, 26 October 2007.

8 Malcolm X, "Message to the Grass Roots," in *Malcolm X Speaks: Selected Speeches and Statements* (New York: Grove Press, 1994). See also American Association of Museums, *Mastering Civic Engagement: A Challenge to Museums* (Washington: American Association of Museums, 2002); Carol Chetkovich and Frances Kunreuther, *From the Ground Up: Grassroots Organizations Making Social Change* (Ithaca, NY: Cornell University, 2006); James C. Scott, *Domination and the Arts of Resistance: Hidden Transcripts* (New Haven: Yale University, 1990); James C. Scott, *Weapons of the Weak: Everyday Forms of Peasant Resistance* (New Haven: Yale University, 1985).

9 Don Fraser, "School Named for Freedom Hero Tubman," *St Catharines Standard*, 27 May 2014; Andrea Tingey, "Tubman Statue Unveiled at School," *St Catharines Standard*, 6 February 2016.

10 Mike Zettel, "North Star Pride Shown at Harriet Tubman School Grand Opening," *Niagara This Week*, 13 May 2016; Paul Forsyth, "New Statue of Tubman Unveiled at School Named in Her Honour," *Niagara This Week*, 9 February 2016; Catherine Pelchat, "Terre Promise: Le Chemin De Fer Souterrain Et Ses Esclaves," *Urbania Magazine* 42 (Annuel 2015).

11 See Patricia Mooney-Melvin, "Harnessing the Romance of the Past: Preservation, Tourism, and History," *The Public Historian* 13, no. 2 (Spring 1991): 35–48; Peter H. Brink, "Heritage Tourism in the U.S.A.: Grassroots Efforts to Combine Preservation and Tourism," *APT Bulletin* 29, nos. 3–4 (Thirtieth Anniversary Issue, 1998): 59–63; Wilton Corkern, "Heritage Tourism: Where Public and History Don't Always Meet," *American Studies International* 42, nos. 2–3 (June–October 2004): 7–16; Anna Hartnell, "Katrina Tourism and a Tale of Two Cities: Visualizing Race and Class in New Orleans," *American Quarterly* 61, no. 3 (September 2009): 723–47; Greg Dickinson, Carole Blair, and Brian L. Ott, eds. *Places of Public Memory: The Rhetoric of Museums and Memorials* (Tuscaloosa: University of Alabama, 2010).

12 See Eric Foner, *Who Owns History?: Rethinking the Past in a Changing World* (New York: Hill and Wang, 2003); Karen Miller, "Whose History, Whose Culture? The Museum of African American History, The Detroit Institute of Arts, and Urban Politics at the End of the Twentieth Century," *Michigan Quarterly Review* 41, no. 1 (Winter 2002): 136–54; Edmund Barry Gaither, "'Hey! That's Mine!' Thoughts on Pluralism and American Museums," in *Museums and Communities: The Politics of Public Culture*, ed. Ivan Karp, Christine M. Kreamer, and Steven D. Lavine (Washington: Smithsonian Institution Press, 1992); and Cheryl J. La Roche and Michael L. Blakey, "Seizing Intellectual Power: The Dialogue at the New York African Burial Ground," *Historical Archaeology* 31, no. 3, (1997): 84–106.

13 *Annual Harriet Tubman Day Banquet Booklet* (Cambridge, MD: n.p., 10 March
    2012).
14 Persons present: Addie Clash Travers, Richard Bailey, Woodrow A. Pinder, Elaine
    Bennett, Myrtle Cromwell, Elsie M. Pinder, Louise Stanley, Rev. Edward Jackson,
    Mary S. Elliott, Rev. Edwin Ellis, Marvel Travis, Linda P. Wheatley, and Loretta
    P. Young.
15 *Annual Harriet Tubman Day Banquet Booklet.*
16 Anne Hughes, "Harriet Tubman Celebration," *The Banner*, 12 March 1990. There
    is a list of Harriet Tubman trailblazers produced by the HTO which highlights
    key contributors (most of whom have died): Honourable Rudy Cane, Evelyn
    Townsend, Addie Clash Travers, Rev. Edward H. Jackson, Rev. Edwin Ellis, Rev.
    Franklin West, Woodrow Pinder, Sr, Elsie Pinder, Linda P. Wheatley, Louise Stanley,
    Isiadore Murray, Alfreda Jackson, Evelyn Jones, Drucilla Simpon, Monroe Lake,
    Jr, Fred Lake, Virgie Lake Camper, Monroe Pinde, Loretta, Clifford Giles, Dorothy
    Jackson, Sylvia Tilghman, Unice L. James, Carol E. Jolley, William Giles, Richard
    Bailey, Mary S. Elliot, Malone Le Compte, Garnell Henry, James Cornish, Jr, Nicie
    Ross Ennals, Marvella Travis, Donald Pinder as well as Bazzel ME Church, Waugh
    UM Church, Bethel AME Church, Asbury UMC-Nanticoke, MD-Civil War
    Centennial Commission, Harriet Tubman Organization, Inc, and the Harriet
    Tubman Museum & Education Center.
17 See HTO Mission Statement and Purpose.
18 "HTO Pays Tribute, Recalls Evelyn Townsend," *Dorchester Star*, 14 March 2008.
19 Gail Dean, "Cambridge Civil Rights Tour Offered During Tubman Conference,"
    Dorchester Star, 11 June 2010.
20 Peter B. Levy, *Civil War on Race Street: The Civil Rights Movement in Cambridge,
    Maryland* (Gainesville: University Press of Florida, 2003); Dean, "Cambridge Civil
    Rights Tour." See also Dolores Hayden, *The Power of Place: Urban Landscapes
    as Public History*, 2nd ed. (Cambridge: The MIT Press, 1997); C. Christopher
    Brown, *The Road to Jim Crow: The African American Struggle on Maryland's
    Eastern Shore, 1860–1915* (Baltimore: The Maryland Historical Society, 2016).
21 Victoria Wingate, "2017 Spotlights Nation's Civil Rights Milestones," *Dorchester
    Star*, 10 March 2017.
22 Donald Pinder, interview by dann j. Broyld, 16 August 2014.
23 Andrea A. Burns, *From Storefront to Monument: Tracing the Public History of
    the Black Museum Movement* (Amherst: University of Massachusetts, 2013).
    See also Amina Jill Dickerson, "The History and Institutional Development of
    African American Museums" (MA thesis, American University, 1988); Lisa Ann
    Meyerowitz, "Exhibiting Equality: Black-Run Museums and Galleries in 1970s
    New York" (PhD diss., University of Chicago, 2001); Michele Gates Moresi,
    "Exhibiting Race, Creating Nation: Representations of Black History and Culture

at the Smithsonian Institution, 1895–1976" (PhD diss., George Washington University, 2003); Thomas J. Davis, "'They, Too, Were Here': The Afro-American Experience and History Museums," *American Quarterly* 41, no. 2 (June 1989): 328–40; Mabel O. Wilson, *Negro Building: Black Americans in the World of Fairs and Museums* (Berkeley: University of California, 2012); Bridget R. Cooks, *Exhibiting Blackness: African Americans and the American Art Museum* (Amherst: University of Massachusetts, 2011); and Jocelyn Robinson-Hubbuch, "African-American Museums and the National Conversation on American Pluralism and Identity," *The Public Historian* 19, no. 1 (Winter 1997): 29–31.

24 Kate Clifford Larson, "Afterword," *The Meridians: Feminism, Race, Transnationalism* 12, no. 2 (2014): 219–24; "Harriet Tubman Special Resource Study Response to Comments and Finding of No Significant Impact," (National Park Service, Northeast Region, December 2008). The 110th, 111th, and 112th Congresses did not vote on the Harriet Tubman Underground Railroad National Historical Park Act.

25 Erin Mahn, "Legacy Revealed," *The Daily Banner*, 10 March 2008.

26 Ibid.

27 "John J. Creighton," Obituary," *The Star Democrat*, 19 May 2015.

28 "Creighton Remembered for Storytelling, Research," *Times Record*, 10 June 2015; Dustin Holt, "Creighton Remembered for Tubman Works," *Dorchester Star*, 10 March 2017.

29 See Carlton E. Spitzer, "His Joy is Helping Young People Learn," *The Star Democrat*, 16 December 2005; "Harriet Tubman Conference Set for May 31, June 1," *Dorchester Star*, 24 May 2013; "Harriet Tubman Conference partners with National Park Service," *Dorchester Banner*, 13 May 2017.

30 Royce Sampson, interview by dann j. Broyld, 15 August 2014.

31 "His Joy is Helping Young People Learn."

32 Ellen Mousin, interview by dann j. Broyld, 15 August 2014; and Gail Dean, "Tubman's Spirit Invoked During Underground RR Conference," *Dorchester Star*, 11 June 2010.

33 See "Flight to Freedom," *The Daily Banner*, 12 March 2005; "Tubman Byway Gets Prestigious Designation," *The Star Democrat*, 29 October 2009; Jennifer Fu, "Byway to Commemorate Tubman, Bring in Revenue," *Dorchester Star*, 26 October 2007; and Gail Dean, "Signs Tell Tales of Harriet Tubman Underground Railroad Byway," *Dorchester Star*, 13 December 2013.

34 Lacey Johnson Reuters, "Harriet Tubman Park to be on Maryland Land She Worked as a Slave," *The Baltimore Sun*, 9 March 2013.

35 Gail Dean, "Byway, Park to Honor Tubman," *Dorchester Star*, 12 October 2007.

36 "Harriet is Back in Town," *Dorchester*, 29 July 2011. See Rebecca M. Kennerly, "Getting Messy: In the Field and at the Crossroad with Roadside Shrines," *Text*

and Performance Quarterly 22, no. 4 (October 2002): 229–60; Peter Jan Margry and Cristina Sanchez-Carretero, eds., *Grassroots Memorials: The Politics of Memorializing Traumatic Death* (New York: Berghahn Books, 2011); Erika Doss, *The Emotional Life of Contemporary Public Memorials: Towards a Theory of Temporary Memorials* (Amsterdam: Amsterdam University Press, 2008); and Jack Santino, ed., *Spontaneous Shrines and the Public Memorialization* (New York: Palgrave Macmillan, 2006).

37 "Racial Progress Unclear in Cambridge," *The Capital*, 10 December 2007; and Gail Dean, "Cambridge Civil Rights Tour Offered During Tubman Conference," *Dorchester Star*, 11 June 2010.

38 "President to Declare Tubman Monument," *The Star Democrat*, 25 March 2013; and "Gearing up for Harriet on the Hill Day," *Dorchester Star*, 12 August 2011.

39 "New Federal and State Parks in Maryland Commemorate Life and Legacy of Harriet Ross Tubman," *Cross Ties Newsletter*, 6 April 2013.

40 Erika Doss, *Memorial Mania: Public Feeling in America* (Chicago: University of Chicago Press, 2012), 13, 2.

41 David Jackson, "Obama Creates Five New Monuments," *USA Today*, 25 March 2013. Other parks signed for on the same day as HTURNM were the Charles Young Buffalo Soldiers National Monument in Wilberforce, Ohio; Río Grande del Norte National Monument in New Mexico; San Juan Islands National Monument in Washington; and the First State National Monument in Delaware.

42 John Fritze, "Obama Establishes Tubman Park on Eastern Shore," *The Baltimore Sun*, 25 March 2013.

43 "Training Set Sept. 7 for Harriet on the Hill Day," *Dorchester Star*, 26 August 2011.

44 "Gearing up for Harriet on the Hill Day" and "Tubman Bills Continue to Move Ahead as Planned," *Dorchester Star*, 20 July 2012. See Kylie Message, *Museums and Social Activism: Engaged Protest* (New York: Routledge, 2013).

45 Malcolm X, "Message to the Grass Roots." See also James H. Cone, *Martin & Malcolm & America: A Dream or A Nightmare* (Marykoll, NY: Orbis Books, 1992); Robert Terrill, *Malcolm X: Inventing Radical Judgment* (Lansing: Michigan State University Press, 2004).

46 Todd S. Purdum, *An Idea Whose Time Has Come: Two Presidents, Two Parties, and the Battle for the Civil Rights Act of 1964* (New York: Henry Holt and Company, 2014); and Manning Marable, *Malcolm X: A Life of Reinvention* (New York: Viking, 2011).

47 "Locals Lobby for Tubman Park Project on Capitol Hill," *Dorchester Star*, 23 September 2011.

48 "Gearing Up for Harriet on the Hill Day." See also "Harris Says Yes to Tubman Park, No to Funds," *Dorchester Star*, 24 February 2012; and "Support of Tubman Bill Urged as Harris Still Just Says No," *Dorchester Star*, 13 May 2011.

49 "Locals Lobby for Tubman Park Project on Capitol Hill," *Dorchester Star*, 23 September 2011. See also Anne Hughes, "Harriet Tubman Celebration," *The Banner*, 12 March 1990.

50 "Tubman Bills Continue to Move Ahead as Planned," *Dorchester Star*, 20 July 2012.

51 Clifford Larson, *Bound for the Promised Land*; "Tubman's Spirit Invoked During Underground RR Conference," *Dorchester Star*, 11 June 2010; "Take Pride in Tubman Monument," *Bay Times*, 3 April 2013. See also Charlene Cooper, "President Obama to Designate Monuments for Harriet Tubman & Charles Young" *Essence*, 22 March 2013.

52 "It's Official: Tubman is a National Monument – Obama Proclaims Harriet Tubman 'An American Hero,'" *The Star Democrat*, 26 March 2013; and John Fritze, "Obama to Sign Off on Tubman Monument on Eastern Shore," *The Baltimore Sun*, 22 March 2013.

53 "New Federal and State Parks in Maryland Commemorate Life and Legacy of Harriet Ross Tubman," *Cross Ties Newsletter*, 6 April 2013; and Kate Clifford Larson, "NPS Harriet Tubman National Monument Scholars Roundtable White Paper Response," 15 January 2014.

54 Please note that the area now called Ontario was "Upper Canada" from 1791 to 1841 and then "Canada West" from 1841 to Confederation in 1867.

55 dann j. Broyld, "Harriet Tubman: Transnationalism and the Land of a Queen in the Late Antebellum," *The Meridians: Feminism, Race, and Transnationalism* 12, no. 2, special issue: *Harriet Tubman: A Legacy of Resistance* (November 2014): 78–98; and dann j. Broyld and Matthew Warshauer, "Harriet Tubman and Andrew Jackson: A Match Made in the U.S. Treasury Department," Blog Post to *Borealia* and *The Republic*, 13 June 2016, https://earlycanadianhistory. ca/2016/06/13/harriet-tubman-and-andrew-jackson-a-match-made-in-the-u-s-treasury-department. See also Ifeoma Kiddoe Nwankwo, *Black Cosmopolitanism: Racial Consciousness and Transnational Identity the Nineteenth-Century Americas* (Philadelphia: University of Pennsylvania Press, 2005); Elizabeth Stordeur Pryor, *Colored Travelers: Mobility and the Fight for Citizenship Before the Civil War* (Chapel Hill: The University of North Press, 2016); Manning Marable and Vanessa Agard-Jones, *Transnational Blackness: Navigating the Global Color Line* (New York: Palgrave Macmillan, 2008).

56 John Fritze, "Obama Establishes Tubman Park on Eastern Shore," *The Baltimore Sun*, 25 March 2013.

57 "It's Official: Tubman is a National Monument – Obama Proclaims Harriet Tubman 'An American Hero,'" *The Star Democrat*, 26 March 2013

58 Gail Dean, "Ground Broken for Tubman Visitor Center," *Dorchester Star*, 15 March 2013.

59 "Tubman National Monument Created Here," *Dorchester Star*, 29 March 2013.

60 Jennifer Fu, "Dorchester Looks to Rev Up Tourism Engine," *Sunday Star*, 8 October 2006.

61 See "Sen. Cardin Testifies on Tubman Park Proposal," *Dorchester Star*, 24 July 2009; and Karsonya Wise Whitehead, "Beyond Myths and Legends: Teaching Harriet Tubman and Her Legacy of Activism," *The Meridians: Feminism, Race, and Transnationalism* 12, no. 2, special issue: *Harriet Tubman: A Legacy of Resistance* (November 2014): 196–218.

62 Gail Dean, "Heritage Award Recipients Honored in Cambridge," *Dorchester Star*, 28 June 2013.

63 Nicole Fuller, "Tubman Underground Railroad Center on Shore Gets Funding," *The Baltimore Sun*, 16 August 2011.

64 Robert Harding, "Harriet Tubman State Park, With Nod to Auburn, Opens in Maryland this Week." *The Citizen*, 6 March 2017.

65 GWWO Architects, who create designs for cultural and educational facilities, have a mission to create structures that are "inspirational, evocative, and progressive." They designed the DuPont Environmental Education Center in Wilmington, Delaware; Pikes Peak Summit Complex in Colorado Springs, Colorado; and Port Canaveral Exploration Tower in Cape Canaveral. Harley Sharpe Design has a world-leading design team that craft exhibits for cultural destinations, heritage sites, and museums. Their work has been featured at sites such as the Royal Ontario Museum in Toronto and the Florence County Museum in South Carolina.

66 Paul Clipper, "Architects Present New Harriet Tubman State Park," *Dorchester Banner*, 19 July 2016.

67 Fergus M. Bordewich, *Bound for Canaan: The Underground Railroad and the War for the Soul of America* (New York: HarperCollins, 2005), 353; dann j. Broyld, "NPS Harriet Tubman National Monument Scholars Roundtable White Paper Response," 20 January 2014, which explains: "Harriet Tubman is relatable to the modern person and fits into the current historical landscape being that she is global, green, [and] gender aware" (9); and Dianne D. Glave, *Rooted in the Earth: Reclaiming the African American Environmental Heritage* (Chicago: Chicago Review Press, 2010).

68 The Sites of Conscious was established in 1999.

69 See Ranger Crenshaw, ed., "Harriet Tubman Underground Railroad Visitor Center Welcome Guide 2017" (Annapolis: Maryland Park Service, 2017).

70 "State Approves Contract to Construction Tubman Visitor Center," *Dorchester Star*, 9 May 2014.

71 Fuller, "Tubman Underground Railroad Center."

72 Ibid.

73 Cheryl J. La Roche and Michael L. Blakey, "Seizing Intellectual Power: The Dialogue at the New York African Burial Ground," *Historical Archaeology* 31, no. 3 (1997): 84–106.

74 "Tubman National Monument Created Here," *Dorchester Star*, 29 March 2013. To date the Tubman site has had three NPS superintendents: Cherie A. Butler, Brian D. Joyner (acting), and Robert Terrill Parker. It is also comanaged by Maryland's State Parks Dana Paterra and the Network to Freedom director Diane Miller will be housed at the HTURNM. Of course, this is all subject to change.

75 Debra Holtz, Adam Markham, Kate Cell, and Brenda Ekwurzel, "National Landmarks at Risk: How Rising Seas, Floods, and Wildfires Are Threatening the United States' Most Cherished Historic Sites" (Union of Concerned Scientists, May 2014), 10.

76 "New Federal and State Parks in Maryland Commemorate Life and Legacy of Harriet Ross Tubman," *Cross Ties Newsletter*, 6 April 2013.

77 See also Laura Wormuth, "Public Meeting Addresses Proposed Harriet Tubman Park," *Dorchester Star*, 23 May 2014.

78 See *Mastering Civic Engagement: A Challenge to Museums* (Washington: American Association of Museums, 2002); Christine M. Kreamer and Steven D. Lavine, eds., *Museums and Communities: The Politics of Public Culture* (Washington: Smithsonian Institution Press, 1992); and Shelia Watson, *Museum Bundle: Museums and their Communities.* (New York: Routledge, 2007). See also the work of John R. Kinard, founding director of the Anacostia Neighborhood Museum who conducted fine community-museum relations. Joan Kramer, "The Anacostia Tree: How a Neighborhood Museum Has Become a Source of Pride to 'the other' Washingtonians," *Washington Sunday Star*, 13 May 1973; and Zora Martin-Felton and Gail S. Lowe, *A Different Drummer: John Kinard and the Anacostia Museum, 1967–1989* (Washington: Anacostia Museum, Smithsonian Institution, 1993).

79 Krissah Thompson, "A Century After Harriet Tubman Died, Scholars Try to Separate Fact from Fiction," *The Washington Post*, 9 March 2013; Mike Wallace, *Mickey Mouse History and Other Essays on American Memory* (Philadelphia: Temple University Press, 1996); Nina Simon, *The Art of Relevance* (Santa Cruz: Museum, 2016); Sandhya Somashekhar, "Black History Becoming a Star Tourist Attraction," *Washington Post*, 15 August 2005.

80 Robert Harding, "Interior Secretary Formally Establishes Harriet Tubman National Park in Auburn," *The Citizen*, 11 March 2017.

81 Gail Dean, "Feds Provide $8.5M for Tubman Visitor Center," *Dorchester Star*,
    19 August 2011. See also James Oliver Horton and Lois E.
    Horton, *Slavery and Public History: The Tough Stuff of American Memory* (Chapel Hill:
    The University of North Carolina Press, 2008); and Julia Rose and Jonathan
    Holloway, *Interpreting Difficult History at Museums and Historic Sites*
    (New York: Rowman & Littlefield Publishers, 2016).
82 Broyld and Warshauer, "Harriet Tubman and Andrew Jackson"; Danielle
    Paquette, "The Irony of Putting Harriet Tubman on the $20 Bill," *The
    Washington Post*, 20 April 2016; Ana Swanson and Abby Ohlheiser, "Harriet
    Tubman to Appear on $20 Bill, while Alexander Hamilton Remains on $10 Bill,"
    The Washington Post, 20 April 2016; Jackie Calmes, "Harriet Tubman Ousts
    Andrew Jackson in Change for a $20," *The New York Times*, 20 April 2016;
    Samantha Masunaga, "Harriet Tubman is the Next Face of the $20 Bill; $5
    and $10 Bill will Also Change," *Los Angeles Times*, 20 April 2016; Mary Carole
    McCauley, "Harriet Tubman to be African-American Face on $20 Bill,"
    The Baltimore Sun, 20 April 2016; Patti Singer, "Harriet Tubman Becomes the
    Face of the $20 Bill," *Democrat & Chronicle*, 20 April 2016; and Vauhini Vara,
    "The Women on 20s Campaign Celebrates the Harriet Tubman $20," *The
    New Yorker*, 21 April 2016. See also Robert Harding, "Interior Secretary
    Formally Establishes Harriet Tubman National Park in Auburn," *The Citizen*,
    11 March 2017.
83 Robert Harding, "Interior Secretary"; "Harriet Tubman Visitor Center on the
    Rise," *Dorchester Banner*, 9 February 2016.
84 Nora Faires, "Across the Border to Freedom: The International Underground
    Railroad Memorial and the Meanings of Migration," *Journal of American
    Ethnic History* 32, no. 2 (Winter 2013): 38–67; John R. English, "The Tradition
    of Public History in Canada," *The Public Historian* 5, no. 1 (Winter 1983):
    46–59; Lyle Dick, "Public History in Canada: An Introduction," *The Public
    Historian* 31, no. 1 (Winter 2009): 7–14.
85 See Karena Walter, "Harriet Tubman's Church Needs Help," *St Catharines
    Standard*, 26 October 2017.

8

M is for Migrant:
Scenes in Response to Three Questions
and a Statement from M. Jacqui Alexander's
Pedagogies of Crossing

Alexis Pauline Gumbs

When I met Jacqui Alexander in 2008, she was a visiting chair at Spelman College in Atlanta, GA. I was a graduate student on a dissertation research fellowship at Emory University's Manuscript, Archives and Rare Books Library. Generously, she allowed Moya Bailey and I to sit in on her undergraduate classes at Spelman (each of which started with a silent meditation practice) and to help her with the technological aspects of connecting her Atlanta students to her University of Toronto students as they collaborated transnationally to interview their own families and communities about their convergent and divergent migration stories. She let Moya, my partner Julia, and I sit on her living room floor, surrounded by orisha pots and offerings and look at the obi seed pods while she explained that spirit speaks in aesthetic and that anything can be an oracle, but where you turn for guidance matters.

In the meantime, I was in the archive everyday, working through the unprocessed papers of Lucille Clifton, in awe of how the items in the archive uncannily offered rather specific answers to questions that I wasn't asking aloud. The apparent randomness of cardboard boxes sent from Lucille Clifton's office (at the time she was still alive) was revealing itself to be a poetic pattern that dismantled my narrative of how I know what I know while at the same time asking me to listen differently. Soon after, I would finish my dissertation and turn down tenure-track job offers in order to stay and play my role in my Durham, NC, community as a community accountable, community supported intellectual worker. Soon after, Jacqui would leave

Spelman and her post at University of Toronto to found a centre for indigenous knowledge on Tobago. Maybe during our time in Atlanta we were both learning something important about love, listening, layers, and leaving.

I am still listening. Now, as I think about what I want to say about my transnational black feminist desire, my Caribbeanist queer aesthetic imperatives, and all the names for my spirit, I turn to Jacqui Alexander's ancestrally co-written text *Pedagogies of Crossing* as an oracle source. The following piece consists of scenes prompted by three questions and one statement in the text of *Pedagogies*:

How do we cultivate medicine on the forced soil of displacement?[1]

How relevant is identity and social location to the production of knowledge?[2]

To whom do I flee and where?[3]

These are questions from Jacqui Alexander's essays "Remembering This Bridge Called My Back," "Remembering Ourselves," and "Anatomy of a Mobilization," essays that reflect on the transnational questions and challenges sparked by revisiting the early 1980s moment of women of colour feminist activism and publishing and the contours of a student, faculty, staff movement to challenge the administration at the New School. These are also my questions as a fugitive diasporic intellectual. What happens after the end of the world(s) we know? What of a black feminist who grows up after the presses and organizations that articulated the concept have disbanded? What of immigrants after the fiction of the nation exposes it's fallacy? Community accountable intellectuals after gentrification? Humanists after the neoliberalization of the academy?

These are also Harriet Tubman's questions and our questions for Harriet. Harriet Tubman, medicine-maker, diaspora endurer, practitioner of strategic dispersal, made and inspires crucial decisions about where we do our work and how. What communities are worthy of our flee-dom? What do we do about and with where we end up as artists and scholars, as a species?

For this oracle exercise I used three of Jacqui's beautiful questions as oracle openings. What came through are meditations about our relationship to the ground that holds us and the dirt we have done. As Jacqui herself reminds her "our hands are not clean." Were they ever?

Dig in.

How do We Cultivate Medicine
on the Forced Soil of Displacement?[4]

she pushed her fingers into the dust, wondering if anything could grow. if
she had tears to cry maybe sea grape? if she had blood to spill maybe olive
trees? if she could urinate maybe roses or something else with thorns? what
is the plant strong and wrong enough for this situation? And what does it
taste like, smell like when it grows?

her mother had remembered the names of the plants by what they did,
bootblack, fever, toothache, the cures for problems they had faced in colonialism grew wild and pointless to anyone but the displaced. what could
bloom here and what would they call it. is there a plant that can hold the
total loss. scream tree, wailing grass, moaning root. she had to ask her self
this question to deny the reason for it. what does a healer do after the last
plant has abandoned? she pushed her fingers in the dust for now.

Our Hands are not Clean.[5]

this time she put her face directly in the dirt. no glasses to remove. no precious hair to pull back. no back to brace her to look up at the sky. just dirt.
hard enough and soft enough to hold her. part of the day she pounded the
earth with her fists and screamed blame and despair. part of the day she let
soil slip through her fingers and felt comforted. most of the day she
just acclimated herself to solid breathing and seeing all there was. which
was brown.

How Relevant is Identity and Social Location
to the Production of Knowledge?[6]

she went to the studio of the murdered artist. built on the land of the deci-
mated desert walkers. over the bones of the sky reptiles who had fallen that
other time. *a fall is a fall.* she said, towards the end of summer, when the
kids started to go back to school, but it was still a hundred degrees. and she
found an indentation into earth shaped like earth itself when earth was a
womb and she lay down in it, thinking tomb already dug. thinking just as
well here as anywhere. and what she really wanted in that moment was to
hear the ocean. and as she listened to her slow heartbeat and the full and
wounded earth, seeking her own stillness, she learned instead that it was
all still. it was all still there.

To Whom do I Flee and Where?[7]

they say she carried a root in her pocket. a root in her pocket everyday.

they say the root was the only explanation for how she learned to walk that way.

they say she walked with a stiffness in her hips that taught them that she didn't play.

they say all those things about her because she didn't stay.

i wish i knew how to ask her
i wish she was here today.

NOTES

Elements of this text have been revised and appear in a different order than their publication in Alexis Pauline Gumbs, *M Archive: After the End of the World* (Durham: Duke University Press, 2018).

1 M. Jacqui Alexander, "Remembering This Bridge Called My Back, Remembering Ourselves," in *Feminist Solidarity at the Crossroads Intersectional Women's Studies for Transracial Alliance*, ed. Kim Marie Vaz and Gary L. Lemons (New York: Routledge, 2011), 269.

2 M. Jacqui Alexander, *Pedagogies of Crossing: Meditations on Feminism, Sexual Politics, Memory, and the Sacred* (Durham: Duke University, 2005), 166.

3 Alexander, "Remembering," 268.

4 "M is for Migrant" is an excerpt from Gumbs's book *M Archive*; Alexander, "Remembering," 269.

5 Ibid., 264.

6 Alexander, *Pedagogies*, 166.

7 Alexander, "Remembering," 268.

9

She Balances the Border

Kaie Kellough

My immediate maternal ancestors are South American and came to Canada through the immigration process in the 1960s and 1970s. Harriet's legacy is tied to American slavery, to the underground railroad, and to the passage from bondage to freedom in the nineteenth century. In the immediate familial sense, the sense of my family arriving in Canada, I am not part of Harriet's legacy, as would be the descendants of the people Harriet guided north. But in a broader sense, one of diasporas and border crossings, flight and flights, I am part of a pattern. The pattern doubles back on itself, it forgets or abandons parts of its design and has to return for them, and it is never complete. Harriet did not just make the passage from a more absolute sense of bondage to relative freedom once. She made it multiple times, and that teaches that the passage is never complete, rather it repeats, and as it does it breaks, reinvents, layers, and syncopates itself. It is always in motion and in making.

The visual poems in the series *She Balances the Border* are sourced by maps of various underground rail routes and phrases uttered by presenters at the Harriet's Legacies conference. This series of underground rail route tracings elides the border, which Harriet negotiated so many times. It also erases the map, and this can represent the erasure of colonial markings and territories, which allows the experiences of enslaved Africans to be foregrounded. Alone against the blank page, the rail routes acquire their own identity as pattern and image, as printed symbol. We recognize our ancestral movement in these patterns, and attempt to locate ourselves in their veined lines.

she up and shakes, up and gesticulates, up and issues from an
understanding of boundaries and jurisdictions, she up and criscrosses,
like any good liminal, she balances the border, she balances an
un-determining space, an echo-

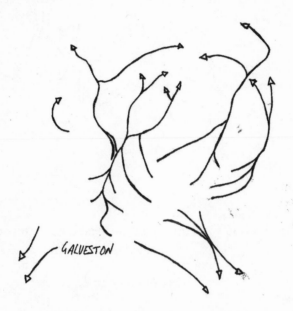

-chamber, a hyphen between tides, a narrative of the absence, where
identities can power a temporary, plural movement, a language of
boundaries and dictions, she understands, like any good criminal
would, a place where black versions can work, she stands between
nationalism and nation-lang-

-uage, she balances mindlessly eating pork and beans with the reality
that more black people are in the can, are fluid slave narratives,
are fictional and situated in terms of negus, she balances the move-

-ment of forgiveness	backward	& forward,
the second generation	transnational, heaving	no border in it
it	it	it
it is not	it is not inherent	
that our lives	are important	
we	do	not
improve upon the past	we	are
versions of the selves	in	the liquid ar

-chive, the border is fictional and skewed, she balances "i do not care," with a traveling subjectivity, she balances my accent with a radio the stepfather controls, she balances everyday existence underwritten by unreal pimpification

she balances canaan with colorphobia, she balances a fluid criminal legacy with transnational futures, she balances survival with identifiability, she balances her parents' back home food with plural particu-

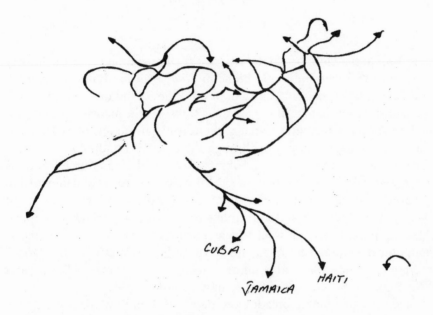

CUBA

JAMAICA

HAITI

-lars, connected to people in power and people in the water, people running south and people in the future, people from the underground and people nursing wrath, people in the crowd and people glorious among us

archives in people, words among us, good criminals among us, brathwaite among us, negus among us, slave narratives among us, absence among us, reconstituted subjects among us, minimum wage accents among us, fluid contexts among us, she bal-

10

Dionne Brand, Map-Maker

Nalini Mohabir

In *A Map to the Door of No Return* (2001) Dionne Brand charts a journey beginning with her childhood home in *Guayaguayare* (*Guaya*, Trinidad and Tobago). Guaya is not only a door onto the sea but opens out towards the world. From that starting point, she traverses the mediascapes of BBC and PBS, urban and rural Canada, the Caribbean islands of St Lucia, St Vincent, Grenada, and passes through the cities of London, Amsterdam, Sydney, and Johannesburg. Her observations in these multiple locations emerge as relational points on a global map towards the "Door of No Return," placing Canada obliquely in conversation with the legacies of slavery. The Door of No Return refers to the doorway which kidnapped Africans passed through in chains as European slavers forced people at gunpoint from dungeon holds into the bowels of slave ships; the "Door" represents the last physical point of contact with the shores of Africa, and "No Return" the wounds of forced migration and exile.

Given the geographic breadth and depth of Brand's writing, her poetic prose is an example of "geo-graphy"; *geo* being "the earth" and *grapho* "I write." Brand maps not fixed spatial geometries but the crossroads of the local and global, the personal and historical, yearning and its impossibilities reverberating through time and space. *A Map to the Door of No Return* places emphasis on the links between the first forced migration (the transatlantic slave trade) and an uprooted condition of migrancy, locating Brand in Canada. It is also about engaging the Black body through movement and agency across multiple liminalities in the passing shadow of the Door of No Return. Above all, her writing maps a fluid sense of time and space as an important aspect of human activity, particularly for those whose humanity was historically denied.

While *A Map to the Door of No Return* is a wellspring of meditations on geographic referents such as origins, home, belonging, compass, voyage, and maps that frame the text, the explicit mapping techniques within this powerful text have yet to be closely explored. In this essay, I pay respect to the deep historical and cultural geographic perspective that Brand brings to bear on the art, science, and technology of cartography, in a way that subtly links the space of Canada to a project of colonial mapping and selective forgetting. Firstly, I explore the reasons why Brand might have chosen map gazing as a means to organize selective moments situated between the material and imaginative space of the Door of No Return. Secondly, I stress the elusive place of the Door of No Return that Brand is mapping. Thirdly, I emphasize the cartographic reasoning of Brand's writing. Under this section, I categorize her maps to help highlight their interconnections. Lastly, I conclude by suggesting the necessity of alternative maps to understanding Black experiences in Canada, particularly when ordinary maps fail. In essence, Brand's maps in their multiple iterations highlight the diasporic experience of being at the shifting border of unknown spaces (spaces of risk, freedom, or somewhere in between), rather than the fixity of space or meaning.

I. WHY MAPS?

Black geographic knowledge is embedded in the concept "I write of the earth"; it is simultaneously a reminder of everyday directions and landmarks (e.g., "turn left at the mango tree") as well as profound flights (e.g. an ascendant north star). Furthermore, Black geographies cannot exist outside of history. The Americas (north and south, including Canada and the Caribbean) are a landscape possessed by Black cultural memories. Although the discipline of geography encompasses a variety of ways of reading the land, waters, and cosmos, maps are often associated with maritime "voyages of discovery" that forced previously "invisible" spaces into Western knowledge (such as penetration into the interior of continents, "unknown" islands, or sources of rivers). It is an understatement to say the making of world maps committed a type of structural violence. For large swaths of the globe, borders and boundaries (including the forty-ninth parallel) came into being through the expansion of power, together with processes of land dispossession, racial hierarchies, colonialism, enslavement, violence and/or exploitation.[1] One might wonder then, why would Brand frame her explorations through maps when maps are a symbolic projection of that structured violence?

By and large, maps often include (but are not limited to) the perimeters or borders of land mass, orientation (i.e., a compass pointing to directions), a scale or the ratio of distance on the map to physical reality (the lower the scale the greater detail on the map), toponyms (the names of places), topography/hydrography (features of land or sea), sailing routes, trade winds, climate zones, and/or a legend with symbolic codes for sites of interest. In other words, maps are a system of signs, signposts, and symbols. However, the general public most often thinks of maps as practical tools for trip planning (illustrating the most direct route to a destination). For instance, amongst the objectionable as well as commonplace definitions for "map" found on the popular website "urban dictionary" is "A picture or diagram showing the location and distance of cities, towns, rivers … [Example:] My map will help me get to Canada."[2] This example might suggest a road map, fixed on paper or, increasingly, a digital map. Historically, maps were inseparable from the visual arts and still inspire artists around the world, from the sacred landscape of Aboriginal Dreamtime paintings to graphic designer Paula Scher's obsessively detailed maps.[3] Although a lay understanding of mapmaking often encompasses a scientific rather than artistic endeavour, an imaginative side to mapping is not solely found in visual arts. Any two-dimensional representation of the distance between two points on a curved surface is necessarily a project of selective distortion and thus imagination.

While the representation of geospatial relations takes varied forms, it is usually in service of navigating, delineating, or describing territory. On the surface, Eurocentric meanings assigned to ostensibly blank spaces on a map were a codified system of land claims (e.g., claims to domination, resources, that is, representations of power and nodes of capitalism). Yet they also produced their own peculiar associations and dislocations across multiple elsewheres (i.e., relational geographies that linked port cities, not only through trade but often through displaced toponyms).[4] Nonetheless, a map limited to representations of territorial borders or surface routes cannot capture underlying historical experiences of diasporic trauma.[5] Nor are European maps the only cartographic tradition. Brand engages maps to create a window onto the (dis)located narratives between "here" and "there," past and present reflective of Black geographies. The lines of her cartography bleed into one another, alerting us to relational experiences, power dynamics, acute self-reflection, and a fluid sense of time necessary to escape the rigid logics of a grid system (e.g., latitude and longitude coordinates depend on a grid).

Brand's use of cartographic conduits is in dialogue with many of her fellow Caribbean writers through exploration of voluntary and forced movement and migrancy, memory, and mapmaking as intertwined processes. For instance, Kamau Brathwaite writes of "labour on the edge of *slave* trade winds;" Kei Miller's poetics debate cartographic conventions through the spiritual figure of the Rastaman; Derek Walcott's almond trees (which serve as a metaphor for history) offer geographic articulations mapping an ancestral past onto a "new world" landscape.[6] Similarly, a cluster of Black Canadian writers also reference mapping, disorientation, or finding one's way in their titles, for example, George Elliott Clarke's tome *Odysseys Home*, as well as his edited collection *Eyeing the North Star: Directions in African-Canadian Literature* (which also includes Brand's writing); several of Austin Clarke's texts including *The Meeting Point, Survivors of the Crossing*, and *The Origin of Waves*; Faizal Deen's *Land Without Chocolate*; or d'bi.young anitafrika's *Rivers ... and Other Blackness ... Between Us*.[7] Collectively, Black writers have suggested alternative modes of Black geographic knowing (including secret travels, wanderings, spiritual quests, inner spaces or land-/seascapes) that challenge the spatial fixity of borders imposed by colonialism.

The liminal space between imperial centres and colonial peripheries, between historical memory and contemporary amnesia of the colonial past, as well as entangled/ambivalent futures animates postcolonial studies. Postcolonial scholars approach the map as a site of multiple contestations across space, direction, knowledge, and imagination. Edward Said, widely considered the progenitor of postcolonial studies, drew attention to imaginative geographies, stating, "none of us is completely free from the struggle over geography"; it is not only about imperial conquest and control but also "about forms, about images and imaginings." [8] In other words, maps reflect and enact the geographic influence of power encoded in empirical approaches (i.e., a time and space laid down by the West). Derek Gregory, building on Said's critical insights, notes that "human geography [is] an irredeemably situated, positioned system of knowledge" and advocates for a close examination of the moral commitments of geography as a field of knowledge.[9] Subsequently, postcolonial cartographies challenge the moral framework of positivist mapping techniques, questions delineated spaces, and engages memory (and its absence). Similarly, a *Map to the Door of No Return* is concerned with both the problems and politics of cartographic representation, particularly when thinking through intangible spaces of history and their impact on personal landscapes.

2. THE DOOR OF NO RETURN:
BETWEEN PLACE AND PLACELESSNESS

It is important to recognize that the very field of Black geographies in Canada, carved out by Katherine McKittrick, emerged in conversation with Brand's work around subjectivity and space.[10] McKittrick's sensitive reading of Brand's poetry collection *Land to Light On*, as well as *A Map to the Door of No Return*, and Brand's oeuvre more generally, highlights the ways in which Brand's mapping project shifts between physical sites and locations of "undetectable" loss.[11] While Brand is drawn to the wonder of maps, she resists Black geographies as something to be put on display or tied to place. If we consider the concept of belonging in its multiple meanings of possession, suitability, or attachment to place, mapping belonging (or the confinement of belonging) is less important than placelessness to understanding what McKittrick terms "historically present Black Geographies."[12] As McKittrick explains, "There is no from. There is no there, or somewhere, or place that a black from is anchored to."[13] Thus, as Brand scrutinizes both Black place and placelessness, she must attend to "a sense of place that dislodges traditional geographic rules from black spatial experiences."[14] Hence, as McKittrick has pointed out, Brand moves between an idea of maps as memory and an experience that unfurls in spite of absences and projected distortions.

Brand maintains focus on the Door of No Return. As a physical landmark, it is the doorway of a prison. As a metaphor, it is a prism through which the legacy of the transatlantic slave trade is refracted. Multiple dungeons were built by European slave traders across the west coast of Africa, including Benin, Ghana, Senegal, and the Gambia, thus the Door of No Return cannot be pinpointed to a singular location on a map. Although Brand does not recount a visit to any one of the dungeons along the transatlantic slave route in the text, she engages with at least one specific Door of No Return (Gorée Island, Senegal).[15] However, the primary Door of No Return that preoccupies her is a metaphysical threshold, a disorienting limbo space trapped between sea and shore, holding the depths of the unfathomable. Thus, we might ask, how can you map a Door of No Return when it is not only a physical location but also an allusion to a missing space and time? How do you locate the place that was meant to make you disappear from history and geography? Brand describes the Door of No Return as an inescapable shadow read onto the Black body: "one enters a room and history follows; one enters a room and history precedes ... where one stands in a society seems always related to this historical experience" (25). Hence,

Brand's mapping project is concerned with exploring meaningful spaces
that exist but cannot always be seen (i.e., without locational coordinates);
therefore, she must be attentive to the ways in which a metaphysical Door
of No Return occupies space as a presence in spite of its absence and flows
into the here and now despite its roots in the past.[16]

Brand, of course, is not alone in her literary explorations of the Door of
No Return. Several scholars and writers have written about their experiences
at the gateway, usually starting with an actual encounter with the physical
door. Saidiya Hartman, in her searing text *Lose Your Mother*, visits the
Doors of No Return at Elmina Castle, Ghana. Like Brand, she is less interested in a recuperative project of return than in exploring the deep rupture
the door represents.[17] Caryl Philips visits the same Ghanaian Door of No
Return in his collection *The Atlantic Sound*; like Hartman, he is disenchanted with a site intended to be a commemoration of trauma but whose
solemnity is reduced through the performative work of tourism.[18] Dionne
Brand, however, is less tied to a physical location; instead, her route to the
Door of No Return is through its traces.

3. CARTOGRAPHIC REASONING IN A
MAP TO THE DOOR OF NO RETURN

Brand's interest in cartography is announced at the outset, in both the title
and epigraph where she outlines mapping as reaching out towards greater
spatial detail as well as an imaginative, unquantifiable process. In both their
scientific and artistic forms, her maps offer sharpness to thinking through
the Door of No Return, the Middle Passage, Black bodies and borders across
a continuum (from outer space to inner space, known to unknown, cartographic reason to cartographic spirit) without necessarily fixing their meaning in time or space:

> *There are maps to the Door of No Return. The physical door. They are
> well worn, gone over by cartographer after cartographer, refined from
> Ptolemy's* Geographia *to orbital photographs and magnetic field imag-
> ing satellites. But to the Door of No Return which is illuminated in the
> consciousness of Blacks in the Diaspora there are no maps. This door
> is not mere physicality. It is a spiritual location.* (italics in original, n.p.)

Her epigraph begins in antiquity, with the first known scientific map of
the world (Ptolemy's *Geographia*), based on a grid system of longitude and
latitude through which the relationship between places could be established

through distance. The epigraph also contrasts the accuracy of geospatial data produced by new mapping technologies with the impossibility of mapping a route to a subconscious threshold that lacks geographical coordinates in the material world. Despite having a foundation in the physical world (e.g., Maison des Esclaves in Senegal, or El Mina Castle in Ghana), the spiritual location of the Door of No Return does not easily lend itself to a mapping project. Thus, the epigraph questions whether scientific and technological maps can locate the sensory perceptions and haunting presence of the Door of No Return.

A Cognitive Schema

Brand begins her narrative at the borders of memory by recounting her childhood desire to trace her African origins ("Yoruba? Ibo? Ashanti? Mandingo?") (3). She repeatedly questions her grandfather whose knowledge of their ethnic origins is frustratingly near (seemingly on the tip of his tongue) and impossibly out of reach. Her quest to establish a verifiable continuous line becomes an impossible task demonstrating the limits of geography, in its inability to satisfy the longing for connection or identity:

Papa never remembered. Each week he came I asked him had he
remembered. Each week he told me no. Then I stopped asking ...
It gathered into a kind of estrangement. After that he grew old.
I grew young. A *small space* opened in me. (italics mine, 4)

This reflection lays bare a rupture of time and place. This is a rupture of history and geography that is not simply missing but a violent separation whereby two sides can never be pieced together once again into a familiar whole.

The hidden-in-plain-sight space of the Door of No Return becomes the opening for Brand's conceptual mapping. This is evident in her description of the absence of memory turning over in her mind: "I carried this space with me. Over time it has changed shape and light as the question it evoked has changed in appearance and angle" (4). Here she signals calibrated adjustments as crucial to a diasporic map of Black geospatial (sub-) consciousness, one that acknowledges an open-ended question of origins.

Brand describes living with the felt-presence of the Door of No Return as

a passport which, after boarding the plane, we are unable to make
disappear by tearing it up and throwing it into the toilet. To live at the

Door of No Return is to live self-consciously. To be always aware of
your presence as a presence outside of yourself. And to have "others"
constantly remark on your presence as outside of itself. (48)

How can one begin to map the doorway as ever present, inscribed on the
Black body? Is it possible to pinpoint this simultaneously inner and outer
presence?

Brand explains that her maps to the Door of No Return are, of necessity,
a careful collection of points, both of data *and* metaphor:

To live in the Black Diaspora is I think to live as a fiction – a creation
of empires, and also a self-creation … I am constructing a map of the
region, paying attention to faces, to the unknowable, to unintended
acts of returning, to impressions of doorways. Any act of recollection
is important, even looks of dismay and discomfort. Any wisp of a
dream is evidence. (18–19)

Any wisp of a dream is evidence, and sometimes the only spatial fixity is
absence. But how does one map that which is absent? How does a cartographic route unfold without an originary point or final destination?

Two books of maps referred to by Brand – *Landmarks of Mapmaking*
(1976) and *Maps are Territories* (1994) – shed light on observable and
explainable data used in cartography. *Landmarks of Mapmaking* provides
a history whereby *terra incognita* becomes claimed space and, in doing so,
offers a telling example of turning dreams into evidence.[19] Here Brand
singles out a narrative in which Abyssinia (Ethiopia) was mapped by an
"armchair geographer" who had never seen the land. David Lambert (2013)
expands on "armchair geography" techniques in his examination of James
MacQueen, a one-time plantation manager in the Caribbean, who mapped
the Niger River despite never setting foot in Africa.[20] The plantation manager relied on the "captive knowledge" of an enslaved Mandingo "house
boy" to conjure up the source of the river and thus took credit for its "discovery." Let us pause to underscore the distance between who has knowledge
and who has credibility. Ironically, there is a valuable lesson: one cannot
make maps alone. Mapping is collective/coerced knowledge production.
Especially when mapping the measures and limits of freedom, one does not
represent only the self (e.g., subjective knowledge); rather, one stands with
the full collectivity/captivity of historical memory behind you. Although
cartography is bound up with Enlightenment efforts to discover, measure,
and divide the world ("progress"), the armchair geographic tradition

(speculative cartography), as Brand identifies, also teaches us that all one needs to draw a map is "the skill of listening" and "the mystery of interpretation" (18). Thus Brand, as map-maker, infers a liberatory agency of mapmaking for a diasporic imagination, albeit through the recuperation of a troubling history of armchair geography.

David Turnbull in *Maps are Territories* notes that maps are not merely documents of the natural or external world but represent a way of *understanding* the world ("a cognitive schema"), an internal search for truth in the world around us.[21] Brand's later discussion of maps, "to find our way" to and through the Door of No Return, is loosely structured by a running quote from Turnbull: "we need a cognitive schema as well as practical mastery of way finding" (16). This quote suggests that the utility of maps is found not only in the external truth or accuracy of data but also in the data's use as a practical guide for interpreting the world. This quote foregrounds both the map-maker and map-user in the search for meaning and connection to place.

To help understand Brand's cognitive schema of wayfinding, I will review her geo-research through the maps referenced in the text. Brand engages with cartographic ideas throughout, but I focus specifically on her discussion under the heading of "Maps,"[22] which I have arranged according to a somewhat messy typology. Placing maps within neat categories is a challenge even for map cataloguers. For example, the Library of Congress classification scheme for geography has at least two categories in which slavery appears. One is a historical category ("Slavery") and the other a contemporary category ("Social problems ... e.g. crime, narcotics traffic, slavery, race relations, school integration efforts, efforts at revamping educational systems, confrontations, demonstrations, etc.").[23] Since Brand's maps also represent non-linear time and spaces woven throughout the repeated heading of "Maps," my suggested categories are not silos but rather thematic groupings meant to highlight shared attributes or interrelationships between her maps.

Brand's various maps to the Door of No Return highlight visual, narrative, and expressive arguments connecting slavery, empire, migration, racism, and diasporic displacement. There are multiple ways to organize these maps into typologies; for example, these maps could be grouped together as world maps that encompass ancient and/or forgotten knowledge (Aztec, Christian, Babylonian), route maps (birds, itinerarium, portolan, ruttiers – including road maps, sailing directions, aeronautical), travel-logs (Rihla), colonial expansion (Isabella and Ferdinand), attention to landscape features and waterways (Goree Island, Sargasso Sea), and network maps (connecting multiple points – Naipaul, Equiano; Australia and the Caribbean). Other mapping projects across the Black diaspora have focused primarily on seascapes. For example, the work of Christina Sharpe maps primarily across water (through the ship or the hold), while Omise'eke Tinsley makes use of the ruttier.[24] While I also offer a typology consisting of six broad categories across watery spaces (a. divining data; b. uncharted waters; c. terra incognito; d. orientation; e. spatial literacy; and f. inaccessible terrain) my goal is to focus on the tensions Brand navigates between opening up a map of diasporic/displaced imagination and the rigidities within a fixed meaning of maps.

A. DIVINING DATA

"Divining data" takes its inspiration from the divining rod, a tool used to identify underground flows of water (a necessity of life sometimes hidden from sight). The mysterious process of divining water is discounted by scientists, yet it still has many adherents. This category is meant to suggest the importance of intuition and spirit towards a cognitive schema, where the schema (patterns of interpretation or meaning making) is informed by the process of divining. Divining refers not only to subterranean flows but also has religious connotations (from the Latin *divinus*, meaning God-like). An important aspect of many African spiritual practices is that the unseen exists and is incorporated into an understanding of the world.[25] I have selected maps together under this category to pay attention to Brand's framing of the Door of No Return as a spiritual location and emergent data as a process divining towards a hidden flow (intentions to return, spiritual quests, trajectories of freedom, seaward orientations).

Brand begins her series of maps with a bird's eye view, perhaps because that is also the perspective of most maps (a survey from above). The first map the reader encounters is the long-distance homing of the rufous hummingbird (6). Although Trinidad and Tobago is known as the "land of the hummingbird," the rufous hummingbird is found only in North America. It has the longest migration route of any North American hummingbird, travelling a cyclical route of nearly four thousand miles, always towards a "remembered home." Birds are not displaced; for every winged migration there is a return. Interestingly, one of the earliest studies of population migration noted that every outward migration also generates a return (Ravenstein 1889);[26] humans have their circular returns too.

Although not under her heading of "Maps," a flight path "home" is also recalled in Brand's discussion of an inherent secret possessed by some in the diaspora that allowed one to fly home to Africa if an escape valve was ever needed (43–5). Western maps serve to make knowledge visible or universal, but African knowledge, in the context of the plantation, required secrecy to stay alive. Reading or writing (let alone mapping an escape route) were punishable by death across several colonies and states.[27] Thus in the absence of written records, a divination of invisible currents is integral to a process of wayfinding, as a means of survival.

Her mapping moves to the Sargasso Sea. In the middle of the Atlantic Ocean, the Sargasso is the only sea that does not border a coastline. As Brand notes, the Sargasso is a tangled sea, not just of seaweed but a memory map to "dead sailors, dead ships," and "dead slaves" (85). Mirroring how little we know of the oceanic depths, the intertwined and drowned memories of the transatlantic slave trade are also an unknown depth. The Sargasso Sea is immediately followed by another map, the rihla, which Brand informs us is a traveller's account of an Islamic pilgrimage (86), usually undertaken to become closer to the divine. Following these two maps, we find Brand on an airplane, studying the in-flight map charting her flight to South Africa, her very first trip to the African continent. She sees a map as simple as the earliest ones where itinerary is all that matters (89). "Why is all geography irony?" she ponders (89). Seemingly simple routes between two places mask complex affective dimensions or potentialities of spiritual quests.

B. UNCHARTED WATERS

I name this category uncharted waters because in cartographic and colloquial use uncharted waters suggests, amongst other things, a potentially treacherous journey. In early maps such as Ptolemy's *Geographia*, the Atlantic Ocean did not appear, thus the hazards of its crossing were unknown. The ancient Greek historian, Herodotus, described the continent of Africa as surrounded by water (except where it meets Asia). Consequently, Bartolomeu Dias set out to navigate around the Cape of Good Hope. Other explorers soon followed, on quests to discover trade routes, kidnap slaves, or chart inland African waterways. Thus the absence of charted waters is also a source of protection against the incursion of colonizers and slavers.[28]

Brand discusses ancient world maps and their historical claims through *Cosmas Indicopleustes Topographia Christiana* (12) and a Babylonian map (16). In the Christian topography of the former, paradise was the source of four rivers that watered the earth, but in the Babylonian map the ocean is a bitter river where it is always twilight. These two maps evoke Brand's description of the Caribbean Sea surrounding her twin island nation as both magnificent and terrifying (7). In addition, these twinned maps mirror the experiences of Henry Louis Gates Jr and V.S. Naipaul, one of whom yearns

for an African homecoming and the other who dreads an Indian "homeland." How does one navigate the currents of an atavistic yearning and
anxiety? Read together, these two maps represent an aquatic borderline:
on one side, longing for a prelapsarian place and on the other side, the risk
of encountering unsafe waters or even a sunken slave ship (i.e., reminders
of the Middle Passage).

Brand also references the portolan, which, she explains, is a medieval sea
chart indicating bays, capes, coves, and ports (52). These early navigational
maps also relied on deductions to surmise the relative distance from landfall.
Immediately following the portolan map Brand meditates on the silence of
Canadian cities, inferring someone else might be "circumnavigating absence"
in the early hours before dawn (52–3), as she catches a glimpse of fellow
migrants from her apartment window. In mainstream discourse, immigrants,
like "runaway" slaves before, have reached safe harbours in Canada, but
Brand speculates they are still "thinking of their own rough doorways."
Perhaps they too have travelled without intention of arriving in Canada
specifically, the destination point being any elsewhere. This would run
counter to the nationalist discourse of Canada as the final destination,
providing a safe passage into freedom.

C. TERRA INCOGNITA

Terra Incognita (unknown land) was the name given to any uncharted land.
The Age of Discovery propelled a belief that man had inherited the earth
and therefore was entitled to turn unknown, blank spaces into knowable,
possessable land. Early maps of the Americas often trailed off into blank
spaces or included speculative details.[29] Although one might argue that we
all share an innate desire to venture beyond the borders of our known world,
exploration was not simply about travel or curiosity, it was also about the
glories that accompanied "new found" land. For instance, the simple outline
of northern Haiti mapped by Christopher Columbus[30] suggests the importance of plotting coastlines, eventually to assess whether these "new world"
spaces could be made economically productive or whether they were *islas
inutiles* (useless islands). However, Brand's exploration of the Door of No
Return, is not, and cannot be, any claim to *terra incognita*, instead this
category draws attention to the space of the unknown as an expressive
counterpoint to maps of domination, leaving the meaning of unknown lands
open to other ways of meaning making.

A quote from the German renaissance artist Albrecht Dürer who mar-
velled at Aztec artifacts stolen by the conquistador Hernan Cortés is a map.
Dürer wrote of "the subtle Ingenia of people in foreign lands" (29). Brand

observes that the artifacts had been shipped to Spain together with six Aztec
people who were held captive and put on display (29). We cannot see the
skilful artistry that captivated Dürer to the point of not noticing the people
who created it because the Aztec art sent by Cortés to Spain no longer exists.
The gold and silver works, not valued on the basis of aesthetics or civilization, were melted down into currency. The Aztecs, like their gold and silver
artifacts, were stolen and made to disappear (except in the ways in which
they haunt the historical record with signs of their presence).[31] This ephe-
meral map suggests that although the visible is seen, in the sense that it is
claimed, the very act of seeing reinforces displacement and disappearance.
One must reckon with the limits of surface visibility.

Under a map suggestive of *plus ultra* (further beyond or pushing beyond
the limits of the known world), Brand comments on her jogging routine: "I
am running out of the world" (98). *Plus ultra* was the motto of Charles V
(of the Spanish and Habsburg Empire) and associated with imperial expansion facilitated by Columbus's ocean crossing. However, I understand
Brand's map as a different type of claim, not a land-claim, but a truth-claim.
She writes, "I am eating up kilometres on my way to where it is always
twilight," suggesting the limits to exploration when further beyond lies the
Door of No Return.

Another map, the painting *The Multiplication of the Loaves and Fishes*,
is part of a polyptych commissioned by Queen Isabella of Castille (Spain).
Brand remarks that the idea of multiplying loaves and fishes was an apt
symbol of the imperial profit motive for colonization (119). Isabella and
her husband Ferdinand sponsored Columbus's voyage to the New World.
As is well known, the goal of the voyage was not merely geographic discovery but to find a sea-route to the limitless riches of the Indies. Lesser
known is that Columbus's ships and crew were financed by the spoils of
war following the *Reconquista*, essentially a war against Muslims in the
Iberian Peninsula (84). Hence Brand reminds us not only of the connections
between oppression in different locales but also of our implications in the
suffering of others across both distant and near lands.

The last map I include in this category (and the last map in the text) is a
quote from the Guyanese novelist Wilson Harris: "It is not a question of
rootlessness but of the miracle of roots, the miracle of a dialogue with
eclipsed selves which appearances may deny us or into which they lead us"[32]
(219). This prefaces Brand's deepest engagement with the space of Canada
found in the text (in my opinion). She writes of an Indigenous woman in
Vancouver asking a Black bus driver for directions: ("He is not from here.
Where he is from is indescribable ... This driver knows some paths that

are unrecoverable even to himself ... And here he is telling the Salish woman where to go ... she has tried to remember, she has an inkling, but certain disasters have occurred") (220). This map relationally situates "certain disasters" echoing earlier paragraphs where marginalized experiences rub up against one another (indentureship and slavery; sailors and enslaved; Christian conquest of Islam as well as the Americas; Indigenous and migrant border crossings). Unlike celebratory representations of Canada's wilderness tied to national identity, Brand's map of Canadian space asks us to bear witness to alienation. She suggests an aspect of alienation from the land shared by both Black and Indigenous peoples in terms of having (sea or land) routes, place names, and borders imposed. A recognition of super-imposed geographies in the "new world" presents an opportunity for creating a new, more dynamic map of the past, present, and future emerging out of unsettled, precarious stories. Brand knows creating new maps out of divergent histories of displacement and coercion is delicate work.

D. DIS/ORIENTATION

The compass on a map orients us to the direction a map should face to correspond with spatial bearings. Contemporary convention points north-ward, most evident in world maps where the Global North is largely aligned across the upper half. In the Middle Ages, however, European maps pointed east towards the "Orient" (specifically Jerusalem). Orientation helps us to navigate by understanding our position relative to the map.

Sara Ahmed pushes us to consider: "What does it mean to be oriented? How is it that we come to find our way in a world that acquires new shapes, depending on which way we turn?"[33] Ahmed is writing in the context of a spatial analysis of queer lives, relative to a "natural standpoint." In the sense that Ahmed suggests, Brand's map based on Leonardo Da Vinci's notes on light and shadow brings to mind orientation. She selects quotes such as "every light which falls on opaque bodies between equal angles produces the first degree of brightness and that will be darker which receives it by less equal angles" (139). The geometries of space, light, and shadow reminds us that forms are shape and shadow shifting depending on the angle we look. These maps based on Da Vinci follow Brand's observations on the borders of Toni Morrison and J.M. Coetzee's writing, where "blackness and whiteness angle and parry perilously" but do not engage (130). Phanuel Antwi commenting upon the distance of whiteness from blackness in Canadian literature, notes avoidance is also a form of orientation, one which suggests negation.[34] Orientation is in effect a geometry reflecting angles of space, time – and power.

Brand also references Roman itineraria, essentially road maps, conveying complex information simply through a schematic diagram. As she writes, Roman maps were "simply maps of where they were going" with a starting point and end destination (142). This map precedes the description of her stay in northern Ontario. She is not living there, nor settling, she is merely passing through: "Landing is what people in the Diaspora do. Landing at ports, dockings, bridgings, stocks, borders, outposts. Burnt River is another outpost" (150). In Burnt River, she does not provide a rich description of location as she did with Guaya; without landmarks to gain your bearings, the result is dislocation (in other words, one cannot arrive, when arrival is without an orientation to place, community, or identity). While a simple itinerarium can lead to landing, it cannot orient her because there is a "nervous temporariness" to precarious diasporic journeys (61). Orientation requires a fixed location to gain one's bearing.

E. SPATIAL LITERACY

Spatial literacy suggests a sensitivity to space and place and to the way it shapes our experiences and identity. This category of maps draws on the geographically attuned lens Brand brings to literary texts, as well as her examples of how to be literate in the spatial politics of the door.

Aimé Césaire's *A Notebook of a Return to the Native Land* is a source of mapping (170). In the quoted lines of his poetry, islands are scarred from injuries and neglect and exist on the periphery of world maps. Yet, as readers we know that Dionne Brand's island (Trinidad) contained epic, storied lives. An island is either a wound or a world. Depending on the scale of our analyses, we might see the world through different cognitive schemas that draw attention to the frame, as well as the experiences of the framer.

In another map, Brand draws attention to Olaudah Equiano's account of purchasing his freedom to reveal his spatial narrative of freedom: "Who could do justice to my feelings at the moment! ... Not the weary, hungry mariner at the sight of the desired friendly port ... All within my breast was tumult, wildness" (182). Though not cited by Brand, we may also compare this to Harriet Tubman's recollection of crossing "the magic line" into freedom: "I looked at my hands," she said, "to see if I was de same person now I was free. Dere was such a glory ober eberything, de sun came like gold trou de trees, and ober de fields, and I felt like I was in heaven."[35] Freedom is a transformative landscape – both in mind and body – suggesting that those most confined by the imposed geographies of others are most alert to the permeable tension of boundaries.

Furthering the theme of literary geographies, fourteenth-century Songhay books become the next map. In this West African kingdom, known for its trading empire, books held more value than gold (196). Cartographic knowledge through the narration of African history is a commentary not only on what different societies hold dear but also raises the question of knowledge – from whose perspective and knowledge do maps build a world view? Where are the routes of an African history and memory? Could we find it in a ruttier (an oral poem for finding one's way at sea) (212)? Brand is drawn to geographer Thomas Jeffreys's warning for slave ships trying to locate Tobago's shore: "*at the full and change of the moon the sea will rise four feet*" (italics in original, 200). She observes that his poetic prose, rather than offering an aesthetic honesty, serves to conceal his real purpose – to navigate a slave ship to landfall beyond the bounds of freedom.

F. INACCESSIBLE TERRAIN

Inaccessible Terrain is meant to conjure a dual notion of impossibility. Although today, with the advent of technology, inaccessible terrain is not a barrier to cartography, it has historically posed a barrier to the accuracy of mapping projects. Within diaspora studies, the desire for, yet impossibility of, return refers not to an obsession with home but rather is indicative of uncertain belongings which in turn suggest the possibilities of home as open-ended, unfinished.

If a safe place exists only in memories of the past, home too becomes a kind of inaccessible terrain. At an intersection of Shuter and Parliament Streets in Toronto's Regent Park, we return to the links between memory and mapping. A homeless man suffering from Alzheimer's, paces back and forth. Despite memory loss, deep down he knows the shelter is not his home (218). The shelter does not offer the security of his own home, to which he cannot return. His daughter will not come to retrieve him. There is no way back.

Gorée Island in Senegal is the only map of (but not to) the Door of No Return (174). The concise history of a slave dungeon under the heading of Maps suggests a relationship between the physical location (a coast, a country) that also bleeds into a vast ocean of history. Brand was writing before the widespread use of google maps, but the Gorée Island map in particular raises questions about whether everything that is seen can be geo-coded, zoomed in to reveal its secrets or zoomed out for a detached God's eye view. Some things may be visible on the landscape but elude a schema of wayfinding.

4. IN CONCLUSION: THE SPACE OF CANADA

I offer a geographically attuned reading of *A Map to the Door of No Return* to illuminate Brand's cartographic practices. Specifically, I arranged her maps into categories to tease out the layers of signification and associative connections her maps present to us. Brand's inventory of narrated maps creates an archive of meaning through which the Door of No Return is multiple-ly refracted. She is not interested in a precise accounting of the distance or proximity between points on a map; instead she seeks cartographic relations dependent on the scale of data (from the corporeal and familial to the imperial and transnational). Brand's mapping is also a critique of positivist cartography, at various points, noting the culpability of the map-maker. However, for map-users (e.g., her readers), her cartography fosters connectivity between places and people, and acknowledges their distance through an imaginative range of mapmaking practices that work to assemble a network of meaning between spaces and across time. Hence, Brand shifts the meaning of maps through mapping the lines of difficult conversations, fraught spaces, and unresolved memories/forgetting that accumulate in the doorway.

I emphasize Brand's maps are narrative – without any visual images in the text, despite working within a very visual area of knowledge (cartography). To write of maps but not include their images gestures towards a frustration with the arrogance of certain visual mapping projects, such as hemispheric maps that flay open the world. An absence of visual representation or locational coordinates to her mapping might be read as a refusal to code and therefore spatially fix the door of no return.

How might Brand's style of cartography (encompassing the material and immaterial, visible and invisible, remembered and unremembered points and places within "historically present Black geographies") help us understand a map of Ontario? To illustrate the application of one of the categories, I turn to a visual example of "terra incognita." Below is a vacation map of Eastern Ontario (circa 1950s). The function of the map is to attract tourists from the USA into Ontario. It specifically targets white subjects as tourists, not recognizing, for instance, the potential of African American border communities, which shared annual Emancipation Day celebrations with communities across the border.[36] Several minoritized caricatures appear on the map, including a Black subject represented as a minstrel figure carrying the baggage of an affluent white businessman. In effect, the map elides Blackness even if it attempts to present it. If, however, we shift attention from the intentions/implications of the mapmaker to the

Figure 10.1 Vacation map and guide, Eastern Ontario.

role of the map-user in the present, this map makes visible the limits of visual representation. It is a map of "terra incognita" due to what is omitted as sites of interest in Eastern Ontario – e.g., the unremembered spaces of Black migration in Ontario that occurred long before the opening up of immigration to "visible minorities"; the fugitive routes of the underground railroad; or "coloured cemeteries" in Ontario. Similar maps with racial toponyms[37] or other white settler landscapes cannot "capture" Black geographies. Yet there is a small space, an opening to read alternative spatial connections between those caricatured figures made small and placed on the edge of the map. Maps of terra incognita, following Brand's examples, help us to map the unseen (out of the frame) connections to other places, peoples, and histories.

To conclude, in plotting absence, Brand reveals an opening, allowing the reader to focus on those areas and experiences once considered peripheral. However, that small space of opening may also close, preserving secret passages (i.e., not all knowledge is meant for consumption). Her map of return is not about fixing a route of return for all, but rather it is a personal, experiential account of the Door. In effect, the forgetting surrounding the Door of No Return is an acknowledgement that Black geographies, in the historically present/contemporary absence, is in the process of interpretation. Hence Brand's maps are reiterative, where the repeating heading of maps allows the act of mapping to be reinterpreted and transformative. Through Brand's diversely narrated (and decidedly not visualized) maps, we are able to encounter and re-encounter multiple locations of the Door of No Return and its mediated legacies through Brand's eyes.

Thus, where do we find ourselves in relation to understanding the work of maps at the end of her book? "A map then is only a life of conversations about a forgotten list of irretrievable selves" (224). Brand has created an inventory of data and (metaphorical, spiritual, elusive) information mapping the door of no return as a dialogue holding the tensions between memory and its absence, experiences and their crossroads, and the opening up of diasporic spaces in contestation with the legacies of fixed meaning. Through reinterpretation and practice, Brand has changed the meaning of the map.

NOTES

I would like to thank Joanna Clarke for her incisive, careful comments, Ronald Cummings for his patience and suggestions, and Leslie Sanders for her encouragement.

1 For example, the "scramble for Africa" in the nineteenth century carved out new colonies, and thus changed the map of the continent according to European territorial claims, and not the claims of African nations.

2 "Map," Urbandictionary.com, accessed 1 June 2017, http://www.urban dictionary.com/define.php?term=MAP&page=2. Why Canada? Did this person have in mind a geography of the Underground Railroad? The recent (2017) border-crossing of Haitian refugees into Canada, fleeing US President Trump's harsh immigration policies, prompted one letter writer to suggest this was a new underground railroad. See Ian Godfrey, "(A)cross the border. Plus other letters to the editor" Globe and Mail, 7 August 2017, https://www.theglobeandmail. com/opinion/letters/aug-7-across-the-border-plus-other-letters-to-the-editor/ article35884028.

3 Noel Castree, Rob Kitchin, and Alisdair Rogers, "Maps," in A Dictionary of Human Geography (New York: Oxford University Press, 2013), http://www. oxfordreference.com /view/10.1093/acref/9780199599868.001.0001/acref-9780199599868-e-1132; Paula Sher, MAPS (New York: Princeton Architectural Press, 2011).

4   For example, the capital of Trinidad and Tobago is Port of Spain, once an outpost
    of the Spanish Empire. The name of the capital is part of a larger colonial pattern
    of naming that often sought to supplant prior memories of place and control
    future spatial imaginaries.

5   Yarimar Bonilla and Max Hantel, "Visualizing Sovereignty: Cartographic Queries
    for the Digital Age," *sx archipelagos* 1 (2016), http://smallaxe.net/sxarchipelagos/
    issue01/bonilla-visualizing.html.

6   Kamua Brathwaite, *History of the Voice: The Development of Nation Language
    in Anglophone Caribbean Poetry* (London: New Beacon, 1984), 7; Kei Miller, *The
    Cartographer Tries to Map a Way to Zion* (Manchester: Carcanet, 2014); Derek
    Walcott, *The Castaway, and Other Poems* (London: Jonathan Cape, 1965), 36.

7   George Elliott Clarke, *Odysseys Home: Mapping African-Canadian Literature*
    (Toronto: University of Toronto Press, 2002); George Elliott Clarke, *Eyeing
    the North Star: Directions in African-Canadian Literature* (Toronto: McClelland
    and Stewart 1997); Austin Clarke, *The Meeting Point: The Toronto Trilogy*
    (Toronto: Vintage Canada, 2012); Austin Clarke, *The Origin of Waves* (Toronto:
    McClelland and Stewart, 2011); Austin Clarke, *The Survivors of the Crossing*
    (Toronto: McClelland and Stewart, 1964); Faizal Deen, *Land Without
    Chocolate: A Memoir* (Hamilton: Wolsak & Wynn, 1999); d'bi young, *rivers ...
    and other blackness ... between us* (Toronto: Women's Press, 2007).

8   Edward W. Said, *Culture and Imperialism* (New York: Vintage, 1993), 7.

9   Derek Gregory, *Geographical Imaginations* (Hoboken: Blackwell, 1994), 76.

10 See Katherine McKittrick, *Demonic Grounds: Black Women and the
    Cartographies of Struggle* (Minneapolis: University of Minnesota Press, 2006).

11 Ibid., 105.

12 Ibid., 7.

13 Katherine McKittrick, "Worn Out," *Southeastern Geographer* 57, no.1 (2017):
    97.

14 McKittrick, *Demonic Grounds*, 107.

15 US President Barack Obama's visit to the Door of No Return in Senegal prompted
    debate, which might be characterized as the politics of numbers and authenticity,
    that is, was this particular Door of No Return representative of history? See Max
    Fisher, "What Obama really saw at the 'Door of No Return,' a disputed memorial
    to the slave trade," *Washington Post*, 28 June 2013, https://www.washingtonpost.
    com/news/worldviews/wp/2013/06/28/
    what-obama-really-saw-at-the-door-of-no-return-a-debunked-memorial-to-the-
    slave-trade.

16 Paul Woodman writes, "Absence is the opposite of presence, we are told. And yet,
    as an apparent paradox, absence has its own presence ... Absence is real; it can be

felt, strongly and in several ways." Paul Woodman, "The Toponymy of Absence," *Review of Historical Geography and Toponomastics* X, nos. 19–20 (2015): 7.

17   Saidiya Hartman, *Lose Your Mother: A Journey Along the Atlantic Slave Route* (New York: Farrar, Straus and Giroux, 2007), 42.

18   Caryl Phillips, "Homeward Bound," in *The Atlantic Sound* (New York: Random House, 2010).

19   Charles Bricker and Ronald Vere Tooley, *Landmarks of Mapmaking: an Illustrated Survey of Maps and Mapmakers* (New York: Phaidon, 1976).

20   David Lambert, *Mastering the Niger: James MacQueen's African Geography and the Struggle over Atlantic Slavery* (Chicago: University of Chicago Press, 2013).

21   David Turnbull and Helen Watson, *Maps Are Territories Science is an Atlas: A Portfolio of Exhibits* (Chicago: University of Chicago Press, 1993).

22   I have excluded the two maps under the heading "More Maps" for the inadequate reason of word limit consideration and "Ruttier for the Marooned in the Diaspora" which has been written about by others (see, for example Omise'eke Natasha Tinsley, "Black Atlantic, Queer Atlantic-Queer imaginings of the middle passage," *GLQ: A Journal of Lesbian and Gay Studies* 14, nos. 2–3 (2008): 191–215.

23   See Library of Congress Classification Geography subclassifications, accessed 27 June 2017, https://www.loc.gov/aba/publications/FreeLCC/freelcc.html. I thank Jordan Hale, map cataloguer at University of Toronto, for drawing attention to the numerous "social problems" grouped into a "tiny call number range along with slavery, while many other thematic maps get the same amount of conceptual classification-space" (personal communications).

24   Christina Sharpe, *In the Wake: On Blackness and Being*. (Durham: Duke University Press, 2016); Tinsley, "Black Atlantic."

25   Carol Marie Webster argues that African diasporic peoples sustained different ways of understanding and knowing which incorporates an inner sense, e.g., "church ina mi." See Carol Marie Webster, "Body as Temple: Jamaican Catholic Women and the Liturgy of the Eucharist," *Black Theology* 15, no.1 (2017): 21–40.

26   E.G. Ravenstein, "The laws of migration," *Journal of the Royal Statistical Society* 52, no. 2 (1889): 241–305.

27   Although in Maryland, where Harriet Tubman was enslaved, there were no laws against teaching African peoples to read English, education was discouraged. Illiteracy enforced by law was more common across the southern states. The poet Nikky Finney provides a powerful reminder in her acceptance speech for the National Book Award (2011). In the West Indies, slave owners also opposed a literate work force, fearing revolt.

28 I.L. Griffiths, *The Atlas of African Affairs* (London and New York: Methuen, 1984).

29 For example, California was portrayed as an island throughout the seventeenth and eighteenth centuries.

30 See Yale University Genocide Studies Program, web page on Colonial Genocide, under Maps of Hispaniola: http://gsp.yale.edu/sites/default/files/images/hispaniola-1492map-lg.jpg.

31 Aztec peoples did not exactly "disappear." In Spain, Aztecs survive through Montezuma's descendants, now members of the Spanish aristocracy.

32 The quote from Wilson Harris is from "A Talk on the Subjective Imagination" in *Explorations: a selection of talks and articles, 1966–1981*, ed. Wilson Harris and Hena Maes-Jelinek (Sydney: Dangaroo Press, 1981). Elsewhere, Harris has written on the relationship between Black and Indigenous experiences, including his notable essay "History Fable and Myth," *Caribbean Quarterly* 16, no. 2 (1970): 1–32.

33 Sara Ahmed, "Orientations: Toward a Queer Phenomenology" *GLQ: A Journal of Lesbian and Gay Studies* 12, no. 4 (2006): 543.

34 Phanuel Antwi, "Hidden Signs, Haunting Shadows: Literary Currencies of Blackness in Upper Canadian Texts" (Phd Diss., McMaster University, 2011), 8.

35 Sarah Bradford. *Harriet, the Moses of her People* (New York: Geo R. Lockwood and Son, 1886). Note the title refers to Tubman as the Moses of her People. In the biblical tale of Moses, linked to exile, Moses never reaches the Promised Land suggesting another Door of No Return.

36 See *The Greatest Freedom Show on Earth*, film, directed by R.J. Huggins (2015: Orphan Boy Films, 2015) about shared celebrations and family/community connections between Windsor and Detroit.

37 In 2015, the Quebec Toponymy Commission confirmed plans to strike the n-word from eleven place names in the province. "Quebec to strike the N-word off the map," *France 24*, 29 September 2015, https://www.france24.com/en/20150928-quebec-no-more-n-word-map-nigger-negro-places-canada. However, the plans to change the names do not change the fact that racism was embedded in the cultural landscape (see Mark Monmonier, *From Squaw Tit to Whorehouse Meadow: How Maps Name, Claim, and Inflame* (Chicago: University of Chicago Press, 2006).

11

From Site to Sound and Film:
Critical Black Canadian Memory Culture
and Sylvia D. Hamilton's
The Little Black School House

Winfried Siemerling

1. ART AS INTERVENTION

What does the work of art do in the world? Is art action, interaction, part of the "real"? Art has often been considered outside such dimensions that valorize its pragmatic and mimetic functions. These aspects seem time and again crucial, however, in the case of works that relate to the experiences of aggrieved communities. Such texts, films, sonic creations, and performances routinely exemplify a kind of art that wants to intervene in the world and exert civic agency.[1]

This interventionist force is strikingly evident in much contemporary Black Canadian art. It is especially conspicuous in the ways much of this art uses past-oriented impulses to look to the future, often charting avenues of becoming and hope by delving into historical events and referencing Black textual antecedents. Translating commemorative aspects of diasporic culture into visions of social justice and future aspirations, this work embodies what Hortense Spillers calls "critical" culture. For her, the critical dimension of Black culture is rooted in a long tradition of resistance to the status quo but also means that Black culture in many ways is "an event to come"; given the persistence of inequality and the unsustainable values of a dominant culture focused on material gain, many of its corrective tasks remain to be completed and much of its potential unfulfilled.[2] Spillers's emphasis on futurity is also present in influential reflections on diasporic identities. Stuart Hall thus suggests that diasporic identity is crucially "a matter of 'becoming.'"

It "belongs to the future as much as to the past" and is not "something which already exists, transcending place, time, history and culture."[3]

It is fascinating to observe, then, how much of Black Canadian writing, film, and also music – often created with a full awareness of a long tradition of Black testimony and memoir – not only deals with the hauntings of historical trauma but also seeks to engage audiences now, exert forms of civic agency, and offer visions of change and a better future. Given much of this work's persistent emphasis on the legacies of the past, it can be placed in relation to earlier examples where the pragmatic function of Black culture and expression was paramount. Black writing and testimony routinely had to function in pragmatic ways, whether Black individuals had to "prove" their humanity through "the ability to write" or whether testimony was requested of slaves accused of crimes – think of the 1734 trial of Angélique.[4] Narratives by former slaves were recorded in the service of abolitionism, Black art was asked to underwrite Black Americans' claims to national belonging and it served the more militant aims of the 1960s Black Aesthetic.[5]

Most contemporary artists would resist a one-dimensional functionalization of their art, and Black Canadian writers, musicians, and filmmakers are no exception. Lawrence Hill, for instance, has made it clear that it is not his task to provide Black role models in his fiction.[6] This burden has been equally rejected by George Elliott Clarke.[7] Yet one can say that much recent Black Canadian work has important interventionist dimensions. Whatever else its intentions, much of this work, including that of Hill and Clarke, also wants to witness, critique, problematize, or convince and in some shape or form it seeks to influence the audience with the aim of transforming the "real." Yet how does this work stage this transformation of the past into the future? How does it address audiences in order to make transformation happen, and what can be said of its communicative function?[8]

2. SYLVIA D. HAMILTON: TESTIFYING TO BLACK EXPERIENCES THROUGH IMAGES, VOICES, AND MUSIC

Some answers to these questions can be gleaned from the films of Sylvia D. Hamilton. An important Nova Scotian public intellectual, she has also embraced poetry, installation art, scholarly writing, and teaching in the course of her career.[9] The documentary films that she has now directed for more than twenty-five years represent an outstanding contribution to interventionist critical black memory culture in Canada, and she has also had a significant impact on other filmmakers through her organizational work within the Atlantic Studio of the National Film Board (NFB) and her creation, with co-creator Executive Producer Rina Fratacelli of the New Initiatives in Film program at Studio D, the Women's Studio at the NFB in Montreal, which supported films made by Indigenous and women of colour directors.[10]

The importance of the transmission of Black experiences and testimony for the nurturing of black identities is a recurring theme in Hamilton's films. Her debut as a director, *Black Mother Black Daughter*[11] thus concentrates on the conveyance of knowledge between several generations of black women against the background of Black Nova Scotian history and inequality. The film validates the experiences of older Black women – whose achievements find little or no mention in public records – and shows the value of their witnessing for a younger generation.[12] More specifically, Hamilton underscores "the intergenerational transmission of values, goals, and experiences through life examples and story telling" and therefore the "importance of oral tradition."[13] This emphasis on the oral and personal transmission of knowledge responds to the systematic and quotidian failure of mainstream channels to provide images and stories that reflect Black lives, concerns, and achievements. Having witnessed the disconnect between her own experiences "and the images and visual representations I and others were given back via the educational system [and] the multiple forms of mass communications," Hamilton was motivated to make films because of the realization that creating "images would become a way to forestall forgetfulness and to counter the erasure of stories from our individual and collective memories."[14] This concern can be seen to have guided all of her film projects to date.

Given the centrality of education in the process of providing usable models and patterns of identification, it is not surprising that Hamilton's second film, the award-winning *Speak It! From the Heart of Black Nova Scotia*,[15] concentrates on the elision of Black history from Nova Scotia's, educational curricula. The film features Black high school students in Halifax who actively seek to respond to this deficit and raise awareness of the racism they encounter. The film also documents the theatre work of writer and director David Woods with these students, which is focused on making Black history a presence in their own lives and making it matter for their audiences. The film illustrates several goals Hamilton has prioritized in her work. First of all, it provides images of Black students and their lives, countering their elision from public representations of Halifax and Nova Scotia. Hamilton describes her own earlier experience of "a yearning, a longing"[16] for such images of Black people, which were lacking from educational and media materials. Her early interest in viewing images and films is prominent in an account of her intellectual and artistic trajectory, and she mentions the various devices – beginning with a Brownie camera,

Figure 11.1 Hamilton on location for *The Little Black School House*.

a Kodak instamatic, and photo booths – that allowed her to realize the
desire of producing such pictures herself. Citing Toni Morrison's and Alice
Walker's similar rationales for their own writing, Hamilton states that her
films are the ones she would have liked to see but that were not made.[17]

Secondly, *Speak It!* also demonstrates Hamilton's interest in moving Black
subjects to the foreground in films and other forms of representation,
showing them in the process of shaping their own lives and of doing so
especially through language. One of Hamilton's main concerns is to portray
Black individuals "as active subjects with agency, not as problems and
historical footnotes."[18] We see, for example, the student narrator of the film,
Shingai Njakeka, addressing his class on the subject of Black Nova Scotian
history and participating with his fellow students in other activities
to counter racism and the elision of Black knowledge from the school
curriculum. The film also shows how, in the process, these students create
a reflected account of their situation, increasing the possibilities of improving
it. Hamilton has emphasized that her "work re-inserts and re-positions

African-descended people in our landscapes by presenting stories and images of people being *witnesses* of their own lives."[19] The idea of witnessing gives a specific contour to Hamilton's larger project of providing images of Black people and their lives, one that makes Black speech – and Black singing voices and music – central to her films and their strategies of intervention.

Evoked imperatively in the very title of *Speak It!*, Black voices and acts of witnessing are prominent features in the films that followed. They are central not only to *Black Mother Black Daughter* and *Speak It!* but also to *Against the Tides: The Jones Family* (1994),[20] which focuses on Black activist Rocky Jones's family as an entry point into Black Nova Scotian politics and history; they are essential to Hamilton's two-part documentary on violence against women in Black communities, *No More Secrets* (1999), the first part of which emphasizes speech again in its title, *The Talking Circle*. Speaking, witnessing voices are again a crucial element in another film that returns to the issues of education, the documentary *The Little Black School House*. Together with *Speak It!*, the film rose out of the ashes of a fire at the Halifax NFB office, in which Hamilton lost much of the material she had been shooting. This "Phoenix number two,"[21] however, would not appear until 2007. *The Little Black School House* deals in particular with experiences related to segregated schools in Nova Scotia and Ontario, experiences that Hamilton herself shared when she attended a segregated school in rural Beechville, near Halifax. It is this film I want to examine here more closely with regard to its interventionist strategies. As in so many of her other films, Hamilton seeks in this work to translate individual and private forms of memory into a public arena, creating a process that gives voice to silent sites, markers, and archives that need to be communally accessed so that they can release their potentially transformative force in the present.

For such reasons it is no coincidence that – in addition to visual elements – voice and sound play such important roles in Hamilton's documentaries. Sound in her films carries the oral testimony of those Black witnesses who can provide the knowledge that is routinely ignored and passed over in silence by official, white-dominated histories, which so often seem to normalize biased forms of knowledge. The power of the Black voice is also celebrated, however, through the mesmerizing sonic presence of Delvina Bernard's a cappella quartet Four the Moment in *Black Mother Black Daughter* and again through the singing voice in Hamilton's documentary about the famous eponymous Nova Scotian contralto singer, *Portia White: Think on Me* (2000). In other films, such as *Keep on Keepin' On* (2004) and the more recent *We Are One* (2011), the sound of instruments, such as an African drum, comes to constitute an important part of the overall communicative strategy of the film. In *The Little Black School House*, the music composed and performed by renowned jazz pianist Joe Sealy – a former Halifax resident who also created the Juno Award winning *Africville Suite* (1996) – joins the spoken and singing voices to build up the sonic presence and interventionist force of this film about Black experiences of education in Canada.[22]

3. CRITICAL BLACK MEMORY CULTURE IN *THE LITTLE BLACK SCHOOL HOUSE*

In *The Little Black School House* Hamilton seeks to break the silence that surrounds segregated schools in Canada, working extensively with archival items, photographs, witnessing, and expert knowledge in an attempt to make these materials "speak" and tell their story. Hamilton's project is all the more important since the forces of forgetting and erasure seem ubiquitous; as she observes, in "this ahistorical, highly disposable age, it is fundamental that we maintain our efforts to underline the importance of history and its relevance to our lives today; we need to stop, reflect, reconsider who we are, and how we arrived at this place at this in time."[23] For a film maker such as Hamilton, this means that knowledge of past experiences and events has to be transmitted, visually translated, and given voice in such a way that it can carry out a critical and practical function in the present.

As historian Peggy Bristow reminds us in the film, Black people came to Canada in the nineteenth century for freedom and education. We also learn, however, that segregated schools started in Guysborough, Nova Scotia as early as the 1780s, and that they were formally endorsed by law in in Nova Scotia from 1836 on, and in Canada West – later Ontario – in 1850.[24] The last one, again in Guysborough, closed as late as 1983.[25] Hamilton's film alerts audiences to the fact that North American school segregation was not, as much public opinion in Canada would have it, a United States phenomenon only. In fact, Hamilton explains that she avoided United States and South African footage to ensure that the subject clearly appears as "a Canadian story, a made-in-Canada experience."[26] This insistence challenges the cherished Canadian habit of exteriorizing race-related issues, too often conveniently projected onto an apparently more prominently problematic culture south of the border.

To achieve the goal of facilitating critical memory in Nova Scotia and in Canada, Hamilton relies on community and the power of personal witnessing, together with sociohistorical remembering, intergenerational exchange, and what the French historian Pierre Nora calls "sites of memory" ("les lieux de mémoire"). Hamilton references Geneviève Fabre and Robert O'Meally who, in their volume *History and Memory in African American Culture*, refer to sites of memory as a "new set of potential historical sources such as paintings, buildings, dances, journals, novels, poems, orality – which, taken together, linked individual memories to create collective, communal memories of African American culture and life," thus providing a "theoretical framework for an examination of the co-joined themes of history and memory."[27] Useful for Canadian contexts as well, for Hamilton this concept more specifically "brings together the private, through oral storytelling and family histories, and the public, as found in archival documents."[28] In a subsequent discussion of Nora's concept, Hamilton also speaks of a "multi-layered, broad public space"[29] that is created when such personal stories are made available to larger audiences through the medium of film.

Former segregated schools constitute such sites of memory in Hamilton's eyes. As she explains, "there are generations of invisible stories embedded in these geographic sites and in the memories of the students, teachers, parents, and trustees who were the schools' communities."[30] The film thus opens with the photograph of a school's interior while a voice-over presents the conceit of the old school house itself conveying the stories it has witnessed. But stories are also hidden in photos and other archival materials related to segregated schools, which Hamilton extensively researched. Looking at "early photographs of people of African descent in Nova Scotia" brings up for her what she calls "the embedded or hidden stories behind each image"; the film uses such images "to give a voice to those hidden stories."[31] As part of this strategy, Hamilton uses a good number of photos of school classes but also of individual children, often juxtaposing such pictures with testimony by the same individuals later in their lives. *The Little Black School House* thus gives prominence to lives that are otherwise often marginalized, but it also documents how some dreams were crushed by racism.[32] While the film captures several emotionally charged moments in this regard, it also underscores the resilience of resourceful individuals who, in many cases, made "a way out of not way." The historical context provides the canvas for the film, but Hamilton emphasizes that the "contemporary witnesses – the teachers, the students, the community leaders – gave it life, dimension, and meaning based upon their lived experiences."[33] Their role as witnesses makes the presence of the past come alive, thus including the audience in its ambit.[34]

The Little Black School House fittingly uses a brightly coloured school bus as a kind of visual *leitmotif* that signals a communal journey serving to connect the past with the present. Its appearance is usually accompanied by an energetic musical sequence composed by Sealy, at times orchestrated with

Figure 11.2 Guysborough elders and students in *The Little Black School House*.

rhythmic hand clapping. Writing about the film, Hamilton recalls her mother's skill securing such a bus (free of charge) when the members of a 1990 reunion of the Association of Retired Teachers of Segregated Schools Nova Scotia wanted to take a tour of their former schools.[35] Having lost her footage from that trip in the NFB fire mentioned earlier, Hamilton organized a second bus tour in 2006 to visit former segregated schools in Guysborough County in the southeast of Nova Scotia. On board this time were not only retired teachers but also parents and students of former segregated schools. Their accounts, together with comments by historians and educators who provide appropriate contextual information, constitute a "public act of remembering, one where the individual stories taken together shape a collective memory."[36] Significantly, however, those who witnessed segregated schools themselves are joined, on this trip, by a group of current Black and white students Hamilton encountered while presenting her film project at Guysborough Academy, which became the site of the film. Active listeners, they participate in this "public act of remembering" by asking their own questions. As Hamilton explains, she wanted to include these high school students in the film so they could learn directly from those who personally had experienced segregated schools. The school bus on the road thus shows two generations of travellers engaging with each other in the context of the sites of memory that they visit and bring to live. In addition, the film itself becomes a vehicle for a journey towards knowledge through engagement; it invites audiences to engage similarly with this communal act of remembering that offers itself as a site of memory.

4. THE LITTLE BLACK SCHOOL HOUSE
AS SITE OF MEMORY

As documentary, *The Little Black School House* therefore translates a specific communal act of remembering into an occasion for a wider public participation and response. I mentioned earlier Hamilton's dissatisfaction, as a school student, with the absence of images of Black lives in education and the media. In an account of her own resistant, Black female Nova Scotian spectatorship[37] from the 1950s onward, she expresses her delight at discovering young Stevie Wonder, Sidney Poitier, and Cicely Tyson on the screen, followed by an ever-increasing number of Black musicians including The Supremes, Chuck Berry, The Temptations, and Marvin Gaye.[38] Very importantly, Hamilton also mentions local Black Nova Scotian magazines such as "*The Negro Citizen, The Clarion, The Jet Journal,* and *Ebony Express*" as communal resources,[39] stressing that she was interested above all "in seeing the pictures"; this interest would lead to her subsequent concentration on taking pictures "as a way to forestall forgetting."[40] But how does her own film's particular contribution to Black memory culture not only respond to her idea that she wanted to make the films she could not see otherwise but also affect particular audiences? And how does it intervene in spheres otherwise marked by the devaluation or elision of Black lives?

Reflecting on the communicative and pragmatic dimensions and outcomes of *The Little Black School House*, Hamilton distinguishes between several groups of audiences. For those who experienced segregated schools, the film provides hitherto missing representations of their experience in a public medium. The effect is different for those who either deny or are ignorant of the existence of these segregated schools. Hamilton explains that she wanted to "capture as many of these experiences [in segregated schools] on film as possible. So those who lived it would have some validation of what they had experienced, and so those who denied that this existed or those who had no idea, would be able to see."[41] Hamilton does not focus here on racial difference as a factor, rather offering the proposition that any interested viewer might benefit from the personal witnessing offered in the film. She thus extends the cultural memory work of personal witnesses of segregated schools to suggest its beneficial effect in a wider societal sense: "What the people who appeared in this film ...

remember, they remember for all Canadians."[42] For Hamilton, their witnessing contributes to a critical Black memory culture that transcends racial difference since it generally offers a more realistic and useful alternative to the deficient accounts of history provided by blinkered dominant national narratives.

The critical memory work mediated by the film has also effects over time and into the future, as suggested by the theme of generational difference and Hamilton's experiences with collective viewings that extend the film's cultural work through public discussion. I have already mentioned the important intergenerational scenes that involve "high school students in conversation with community elders"[43] both on the bus and inside school settings. For the older participant witnesses of segregated schools and racism in non-segregated schools, such exchanges allow for a validation of their past; it lets them share memories of the supportive atmosphere in Black schools but also remember particularly vicious acts of racism in mainly white schools and educational opportunities that were missed by students of either schools because of racism. But the film is also very much about the younger generation. In this regard, *The Little Black School House* continues the project of the earlier film, *Speak It! From the Heart of Black Nova Scotia*, which deals with contexts of empowerment for current students. In *The Little Black School House*, the young students are seen to react with curiosity but often also astonishment to the narratives of their elders. These accounts let them contextualize their own experiences as they learn, for instance, about more overt and direct forms of racism in the past. The stories of the elders also underscore ongoing concerns, however, about the elision of Black topics in school curricula and the potential impact of race barriers on their future careers. The film repeatedly stresses the necessity of full Black participation in education and economic opportunities; the older participants, however, also voice their concern that the high expectations of the younger generation may still be dashed by systematic racism. Their memories serve to raise important questions about the past and future of equality with regard to Black participation in central civic and economic aspects of Nova Scotian society.

The film's music and the *leitmotif* of the school bus are particularly effective in commenting on the ongoing "Struggle for Dignity and Equality Through Education" (as a section title written on a blackboard underscores). The school bus, as I have suggested, signals the intergenerational learning process building a critical Black memory culture by drawing on the past to request and create another future. The film's music works its own effects in this regard. At times stately and beautifully reflective – especially when it parallels the voicing of memories – it also sounds a contrasting, energetic theme as sonic *leitmotif* often accompanying the visual one of the bus on the road. Composed and played by jazz great Joe Sealy (on piano, with Paul Novotny on base, Reg Schwager on guitar, and Steve Heathcote on drums), the music adds its own voice to the film's soundscape and what Hamilton calls its "multivocal narrative."[44]

Hamilton wanted the music to "evoke the moods of the people featured ... and the rootedness of Black Canadian experiences."[45] For some viewers, however, "the music was too upbeat"[46] given the film's subject and the ongoing concerns over Black access to education and the economy. Hamilton responds by pointing to some of the persistently positive and forward-looking themes of the film. Discussing the collaborative process with Sealy, she mentions that "I told him that children were at the core of the work" and that this idea "unlocked the project for him."[47] Commenting further on the upbeat sonic registers of Sealy's musical vision, Hamilton stresses that "there is also great resilience" in that culture, carried forward through cultural memory work to the next generation. Sealy's music indeed effectively expresses commemorative and reflective as well as future-oriented, active, and interventionist dimensions of the film.

In this regard it is important to note another aspect of how a work like *The Little Black School House* can address audiences to intervene in the public sphere and exert agency. Hamilton understands film "as a collective experience," not only because it can involve the collective creation of memories and communication between groups but also because "it generates discussion."[48] She recalls seeing films in groups as a child, having fun watching but also discussing them afterwards. For similar reasons, she enjoys public screenings since they create discussions. This is "when the audience will engage in conversations share and debate ideas, and disagree with each other, which is why I make documentaries in the first place."[49] These discussions provoked by her films are also the work of a critical memory culture in action, which ultimately facilitates the creation of community and a critically informed future.

Hamilton's film, then, intervenes in memory culture and public space in many different ways, both during the shooting of the film and through various forms of its reception. During the process of filmmaking itself, a project like *The Little Black School House* uses sites of memory to facilitate the act of witnessing, bringing individuals and generations together. In Ian Baucom's words, the film can thus help "to serialize the event and its affect and also to elongate its temporality to stretch its time along the line of an unfolding series of moments of bearing witness."[50] In *The Little Black*

School House and other films by Hamilton, this process of setting memory and witnessing in motion also means to translate and transform silent sites, images, and documents not only into moving pictures but also into the testimony of living voices and the moving power of music.

Recording these important acts of generating and conjoining personal memories, the film creates a durable medium of collective memory that allows for reiteration in different contexts. *The Little Black School House* thus creates the condition for multiple re-inscriptions of this testimony in the public realm. Allowing the concerned subjects to see themselves reflected in a positive public medium, the film validates their experiences and personal geographies[51] together with the very processes of memory making and witnessing. Constituting an example of Black memory culture in action that invites larger audiences into the process, *The Little Black School House* becomes itself a site of memory or "lieu de mémoire." It offers a site for later viewers and communities that makes it possible for them to relate to the past while looking also at the present and the future and to engage in discussion. The creation and availability of *The Little Black School House* reflect one of its most important themes since the film itself is a mobile vehicle for education that can create new communities and constitutes sites of critical self-reflection for even larger ones. The film thus contributes to what Spillers sees as aspects of the larger, as yet unfinished task of Black culture as critical culture, which are to reaffirm its human, non-materialistic values and "complete the work of equality."[52] Reasserting Black lives, communities, and their past and present within Canadian culture, the film is relevant not only for the immediate communities involved but also as a site for critical memory work with regard to larger national narratives and self-perceptions.

NOTES

Reprinted with permission from "From Site to Sound and Film: Critical Black Canadian Memory Culture and Sylvia D. Hamilton's *The Little Black School House*," *Studies in Canadian Literature* 44, no. 1 (June 2019): 30–46.

1 My formulation here is inspired by the title of Doris Sommer's 2014 study *The Work of Art in the World: Civic Agency and Public Humanities* (Durham: Duke University, 2014).

2 Hortense J. Spillers, "The Idea of Black Culture," YouTube video of talk at University of Waterloo, filmed 19 March 2013, https://www.youtube.com/watch?v=P1PTHFCN4Gc.

3 Stuart Hall, "Cultural Identity and Diaspora," in *Identity: Community, Culture, Difference*, ed. Jonathan Rutherford (London: Lawrence and Wisehart, 1990), 222–37, 225.

4 Henry Louis Gates Jr, *Figures in Black: Words, Signs, and the "Racial" Self* (New York and Oxford: Oxford University, 1987), 21. The Montreal slave Marie-Joseph Angélique was accused of setting fire to the town and was hanged in 1734 (see Winfried Siemerling, *The Black Atlantic Reconsidered: Black Canadian Writing, Cultural History, and the Presence of the Past* [Montreal and Kingston: McGill-Queen's University, 2015], 33–6, 186–94).

5 For example, W.E.B. Du Bois, *The Souls of Black Folk*, introduced by Henry Louis Gates Jr (New York: Bantam, 1989), xxiii. As Gates has summarized some of the concerns of the Black Arts movement: "One repeated concern of the Black Aesthetic movement was the nature and function of black literature vis-à-vis the larger political struggle for Black Power. How useful was our literature to be in this centuries-old struggle, and exactly how was our literature to be useful?" (xxv–vi).

6 Siemerling, *The Black Atlantic*, 14.

7 In Kristina Kyser, "George and Ruth: An Interview with George Elliott Clarke About Writing and Ethics," *University of Toronto Quarterly* 76, no. 3 (2007): 861–73, 866.

8 How, for example, do works such as George Elliott Clarke's *George and Rue* (Toronto: HarperCollins Canada, 2005) or Marie-Célie Agnant's *The Book of Emma* (London, ON: Insomniac, 2006) position or implicate their readers? What is the effect is of Wayde Compton's poetic and fictive evocations and transformation of Hogan's Alley and black British Columbia? Or how does Lawrence Hill's *The Book of Negroes* (New York: HarperCollins, 2007) appeal to its audiences? I have tried to explore some of these questions in "Ethics as Re/Cognition in the Novels of Marie-Célie Agnant: Oral Knowledge, Cognitive Change, and Social Justice," *University of Toronto Quarterly* 76, no. 3 (Summer 2007): 838–60; "New Ecologies of the Real: Nonsimultaneity and Canadian Literature(s)," *Studies in Canadian Literature* 41, no. 1 (2016); and *The Black Atlantic Reconsidered*.

9 Hamilton's poetry has appeared in such journals as *West Coast Line*, *Dalhousie Review*, and *Fireweed* and has been anthologized, for instance, in Ayanna Black, ed., *Fiery Spirits* (New York: HarperCollins, 1995); and Valerie Mason-John and Kevan Anthony Cameron, eds., *The Great Black North Contemporary African Canadian Poetry* (Calgary: Frontenac House, 2013). Her installation *Excavation: A Site of Memory* has been shown in Halifax at the Dalhousie Art Gallery in 2013 and in the Maritime Museum of the Atlantic in 2014. In 2014 she also published her first collection of poetry, *And I Alone Escaped to Tell You* (Kentville, NS:

Gaspereau Press, 2014). Besides her many scholarly studies on film she has also contributed such studies as "Naming Names, Naming Ourselves: A Survey of Early Black Women in Nova Scotia" in the important collection *We're Rooted Here and They Can't Pull Us Up"*: *Essays in Canadian Women's History*, ed. Peggy Bristow (Toronto: University of Toronto Press, 1994); and an "African Baptist Women as Activists and Advocates in Adult Education in Nova Scotia," (MA thesis, Dalhousie University, 2000). Hamilton is a professor at University of King's College in Halifax.

10 Shana McGuire and Darrell Varga, "Eradicating Erasure: The Documentary Film Practice of Sylvia Hamilton," in *The Gendered Screen: Canadian Women Filmmakers*, ed. Brenda Austin-Smith and George Melnyk (Waterloo, ON: Wilfrid Laurier University, 2010), 185.

11 *Black Mother Black Daughter*, directed by Sylvia D. Hamilton and Claire Pietro, (NFB Atlantic Studio, 1989).

12 This conversational setting also creates a space for viewers of the film; as D.B. Jones observes, *Black Mother Black Daughter* "lets us to get know women in a small black community ... as people rather than spokespersons for political aims." D.B. Jones, "Brave New Film Board," in *North of Everything: English-Canadian Cinema Since 1980*, ed. William Beard and Jerry White (Edmonton: University of Alberta Press, 2002), 28.

13 Sylvia D. Hamilton, "A Daughter's Journey," *Canadian Woman Studies/les cahiers de la femme* 23, no. 2 (2004): 6–12, 7.

14 Ibid., 9.

15 *Speak It! From the Heart of Black Nova Scotia*, directed by Sylvia D. Hamilton (NFB Atlantic Studio, 1992).

16 Sylvia D. Hamilton "When and Where I Enter: History, Film and Memory," *Acadiensis* 41, no. 2 (2012): 3–16, 8.

17 As Hamilton writes, "I began making films about our experiences as African Canadians because these films were not being made at all, or rarely in a manner that satisfied me. Above all, I needed these images," ibid., 9.

18 Ibid., 10.

19 Ibid., 4.

20 *Against the Tides: The Jones Family* constitutes part 2 of the 1993 television mini-series (made available on DVD in 1994); *Hymn to Freedom: The History of Blacks in Canada*, DVD, produced by Almeta Speaks (1993: New York: Filmaker's Library Inc., 1994).

21 Hamilton, "When and Where I Enter," 14.

22 *Portia White: Think on Me*, directed by Sylvia D. Hamilton (2000: Maroon Films, 2000); *Keep On Keepin' On*, directed by Sylvia D. Hamilton (2004: Maroon Films, 2004); *We Are One*, directed by Sylvia D. Hamilton (2011: Maroon Films,

2011); *The Little Black School House*, directed by Sylvia D. Hamilton (2007: Maroon Films, 2007); "Africville Suite," composed by Joe Sealy (Jam Recordings, 1996).

23 Sylvia D. Hamilton, "Stories From *The Little Black School House*," in *Cultivating Canada: Reconciliation Through The Lens of Cultural Diversity*, ed. Jonathan Dewar, Mike DeGagne, and Ashok Mathur (Ottawa: Aboriginal Healing Foundation Research Series, 2011), 91–112, 96.

24 As Dalhousie University Law School professor Michelle Williams explains in the film, in 1836 education commissioners were legally allowed to establish separate schools in Nova Scotia, which were also on the books when free and compulsory education was introduced in the province in 1865. Williams adds that in 1876 Black children were excluded by law from Halifax common schools. In 1850 the Separate School Act allowed for segregated schools, ostensibly to help communities that desired them; this possibility was soon used to exclude Black children from non-Black schools. Mary Ann Shadd nonetheless famously claimed in *A Plea for Emigration* in 1852 that in Toronto churches "the presence of coloured people, promiscuously seated, elicited no comment whatever" (61) and went on to state, "There are no separate schools. At Toronto and in many other places, as in the churches, the coloured people avail themselves of existing schools; but in the western country there is a tendency to 'exclusiveness,'" (63–4). Mary A. Shadd, *A Plea for Emigration, Or, Notes of Canada West*, ed. Richard Almonte (1852: reissue, Toronto: Mercury Press, 1998).

25 See also Sharon Morgan Beckford, "'We're Here, Standing at the Shoreline': Sylvia Hamilton's Intervention in the Nova Scotian Discourse on Belonging and Multicultural Citizenship," *Canadian Woman Studies* 27, nos. 2–3 (2009): 114–20, 118.

26 Hamilton, "Stories," 105.

27 Ibid., 98.

28 Ibid.

29 Hamilton, "When and Where I Enter," 10.

30 Hamilton, "Stories," 99.

31 In Brian Howard and Sarah E.K. Smith, "*The Little Black School House*: Revealing the Histories of Canada's Segregated Schools – A Conversation with Sylvia Hamilton," *Canadian Review of American Studies* 41, no.1 (2011): 63–73, 70.

32 Ibid.

33 Hamilton, "Stories," 107.

34 Hamilton emphasizes that "I really wanted to have individuals that I interviewed during the reunion who had either taught or gone to the segregated

schools to speak to the personal experiences" (Howard and Smith, "*The Little Black School House*," 70). She adds elsewhere, "Their faces, their bodies, and their memories became the landscape of *The Little Black School House*" (Hamilton, "Stories," 107).

35 Hamilton, "When and Where I Enter," 13.

36 Hamilton, "Stories," 102.

37 For the concept of the Black "resisting spectator," see Manthia Diawara "Black Spectatorship: Problems of Identification and Resistance," in *Black American Cinema* (London and New York: Routledge, 1993). Diawara in particular charges that many approaches to spectatorship have "remained colorblind" (211). bell hooks's essay in the same volume, "The Oppositional Gaze: Black Female Spectators," extends this critique to include gender but also charges that "Feminist film theory rooted in an ahistorical psychoanalytic framework … actively suppresses recognition of race." bell hooks, "The Oppositional Gaze: Black Female Spectators," in *Black American Cinema*, ed. Manhia Diawara (London and New York: Routledge, 1993): 288–302, 295.

38 Hamilton, "When and Where I Enter," 6–7.

39 Ibid., 7.

40 Ibid., 8.

41 In Howard and Smith, "The Little Black Schoolhouse," 64–5.

42 Hamilton, "Stories," 107.

43 Ibid., 102.

44 Hamilton, "When and Where I Enter," 15. Joe Sealy has provided many contributions to a sonic Black Canadian memory culture. The son of a porter, he is featured in *The Road Taken*, directed by Selwyn Jacob (1996; Toronto: NFB, 1996), which uses also his music. The full palette of his musical expression can also be heard in the commemorative evocation of a black community – and his father's birthplace – the Juno Award winning CD *Africville Suite* (1996).

45 Howard and Smith, "The Little Black Schoolhouse," 69.

46 Ibid.

47 Ibid.

48 Ibid., 68.

49 Ibid., 69.

50 Baucom, *Spectators*, 177.

51 McGuire and Varga thus note that Hamilton's "films are a reclaiming of space through the exercise of oral culture and dispossessed history" ("Eradicating Erasure," 186); for further discussion of the role of space in *The Little Black School House*, see also pages 190–3, and Darrell Varga, *Shooting from the East: Filmmaking on the Canadian Atlantic* (Montreal and Kingston: McGill-Queen's University Press, 2015), 170–1.

52 Spillers also returns to the work W.E.B. Du Bois and his critique of American culture as a "dusty desert of dollars and smartness" to understand Black culture as antithesis to what she calls the "toxic" aspects of the "unbridled pursuit of wealth," which ultimately produces the threat of our "losing the planet." Spillers, "The Idea of Black Culture."

SECTION THREE

Strategizing Survival and Rethinking Colonial Ordering

12

We Were Here:
Reclaiming African Canadian History
Through Heritage Plaques

Natasha Henry

People of African descent have lived here in what we now call Canada for just more than four hundred years. However, the collective memory of their early presence has been erased or greatly marginalized through various processes. But "Where is here?" This question was first posed by Canadian literary theorist Northrup Frye in 1965 in his critique of Canadian culture and was put forward again by John Willinsky in a chapter of the same name in his book, *Learning to Divide the World*.[1] This question has guided my inquiry about plaques in relation to a Black presence on the Canadian landscape. By landscape I am referring to the geophysical, historical, socio-political, and the imaginary landscape.[2] But "Where is here?" when "here" is physically and figuratively buried and silenced? Katherine McKittrick notes that "the 'where' of black geographies and black subjectivities then, is often aligned with spatial processes."[3]

A number of spatial processes work to hide "here." Natural physical processes such as grass overgrowing, flooding, erosion, and the passage of time can conceal Black presences. A range of intentional processes undertaken by humans also influence the removal of Blackness from plain view. For example, renaming, or endeavouring to rename certain streets and landmarks that identify a Black existence with a name that reflects whiteness, plowing over gravesites or removing grave markers in Black burial grounds, and urban expansion are some ways in which this occurs.[4] The historical process of privileging the histories of English and French European colonists in the writing of Canadian history excludes African Canadian experiences and contributions, further contributing to the erasure of

Blackness. Consequently, African Canadians tend to be classified as "the other" and not belonging 'here.'[5] As a result, any recognition of Blackness on Canada topography is generally treated in an abstract or very generalized way and specific stories are marginalized.

Plaque placement that marks sites connected to African Canadian history can be viewed as an official way of mapping these histories and geographies onto the Canadian landscape and can serve to fill in the absences of Blackness.[6] Beyond the system of plaque selection, these historical and cultural markers can and do play a critical role in the recovery of the historical presence and experiences of Blacks in Canada, particularly in southwestern Ontario through the plaquing programs of the Ontario Heritage Trust as well as Parks Canada, municipalities, and local historical societies.[7] The sites where heritage plaques have been installed become tangible, concrete locations of different forms of memory.

As locations of public memory, plaqued historic sites allow visitors to interact with other members of the public and with archival information in front of the public, out in the open. They also afford the opportunity for visitors to share in the experience and to possibly exchange details on the historic site. On another level, public memory has the potential to "unsettle the present in order to open a new way of thinking, perceiving, and acting"[8] about Canadian, regional, and local histories. Both Roger Simon and Edward Casey discuss the potential of public memory to stimulate social and collective action.[9] Public memory makes a connection to the past while enacting future remembrance and the installation of plaques or other kinds of representational forms of remembrance can be used to attempt to shape public memory. By and large, the engagement with public memory kindles learning. Individuals learn about the people, events, or experiences that are featured at the historic site.

Public memory can be a sphere where historical consciousness is cultivated through engaging with counternarratives, stories that offer a different perspective from the master narrative. Counternarratives work to reform historical memory by contesting hegemonic histories. They challenge the silences and legitimizations that arise out of dominant historical narratives by attempting to reinterpret the officially sanctioned history. Counternarratives can also represent a collective historical imaginary.

Sites marked with heritage plaques also serve as spaces to elicit collectively memory, where individuals not necessarily connected at all can recall the same event in their own way.[10] Casey describes that the plural remembering takes place based solely on common content and that individuals connect themselves to that content differently based on their personal point of view.[11] Collective memory, also called cultural memory, is not reliant on a particular location or the relatedness of the people who remember, nor does the recollection have to occur simultaneously. Within the act of remembering, a shared community is established among the large disparate group. Individuals who visit a cultural heritage plaque become drawn in to maintain memories attached to it. Plaques can operate to reinforce collective memory and build a sense of community. In some cases, a strong association to the memory evoked by the plaque could even become a catalyst for change. People can become compelled to take individual or collective action to reimagine a historical event, person, or place or to lobby for the inclusion of omitted voices, for instance, or press to transform how the past and the present are conceptualized.

Places with installed heritage plaques can also become repositories of social memory where people with a shared kinship as family, friends or community acquaintances, or who have a shared experience or history, engage in the same project, or who are tied by geography possess a common memory that is recognized in a public space.[12] Certain public places such as a cemetery, a church, or a historic school lend themselves to remembering and at times embody memories for individuals and groups. Memory is intricately related to and embedded in particular kinds of space. Krzysztof aptly writes that "The memory is filling this space with additional meanings and introduces references to the past, it makes the past visible, accessible for sight, allows to recall it and make it present. This space is also the space of memory."[13]

Such sites of memory serve as visual reminders and plaqued African Canadian heritage sites interrupt the erasure of Blackness on some level because of the permanent presence of the markers and the memories the plaques embody. In what follows, I offer a list survey of the thirty-one national, twenty-seven provincial, and nineteen municipal heritage plaques that commemorate African Canadian people, places, and events and reflect on the significance of two of these.[14] The preparation and discussion of this list of plaqued sites serves as part of the ongoing effort to assert a Black presence and assist in the reclamation of marginalized, forgotten, and excluded African Canadian narratives. The act of remembering is a form of resistance. By memorializing the experiences and courage of African ancestors through stories and other ceremonies the silence of the past is broken. The "countless stories are shared, heard, and passed on. Their memory lives on without end. Drawing on these memories provides strength to overcome present obstacles and offers inspiration to plot a course to the future."[15]

NATIONAL, PROVINCIAL, AND MUNICIPAL HERITAGE PLAQUES IN CANADA

Table 12.1 National heritage plaques

National places

Amherstburg First Baptist Church	Amherstburg, Ontario
Nazrey African Methodist Episcopal Church	Amherstburg, Ontario
Griffin House	Ancaster, Ontario
Buxton Settlement	Buxton, Ontario
Oro African Methodist Episcopal Church	Edgar, Ontario
R. Nathaniel Dett British Methodist Episcopal Church	Niagara Falls, Ontario
Salem Chapel, British Methodist Episcopal Church	St Catharines, Ontario
Sandwich First Baptist Church	Windsor, Ontario
Africville	Halifax, Nova Scotia

National individuals

Harry Winston Jerome	Vancouver, British Columbia
Mifflin Wistar Gibbs	Victoria, British Columbia
Reverend William King	Buxton, Ontario
Mary Ann Shadd	Chatham, Ontario
Reverend Josiah Henson	Dresden, Ontario
Harriet Tubman	St Catharines, Ontario
Kathleen "Kay" Livingstone	Toronto, Ontario
Thornton and Lucie Blackburn	Toronto, Ontario
Henry and Mary Bibb	Windsor, Ontario
Marie Marguerite Rose	Fortress of Louisbourg National Historic Site, Nova Scotia
Reverend Richard Preston	Halifax, Nova Scotia
William Neilson Hall	Hantsport, Nova Scotia
Mathieu da Costa	Port Royal National Historic Site, Nova Scotia
Portia May White	Truro, Nova Scotia
Sam Langford	Weymouth Falls, Nova Scotia

Table 12.1 (cont'd)

National events	
Black Pioneers Immigration to Alberta and Saskatchewan [not plaqued yet]	Alberta
Black Pioneers in British Columbia	Saanichton, British Columbia
Black Loyalist Experience	Birchtown, Nova Scotia
No. 2 Construction Battalion	Pictou, Nova Scotia
Abolition Movement in British North America	Chatham, Ontario
Upper Canadian Act of 1793 Against Slavery	Niagara-on-the-Lake, Ontario
Fugitive Slave Movement	Windsor, Ontario
Black Railway Porters and their Union Activity	Montreal, Quebec

Sites of memory, including physical locations like those where heritage plaques are inducted, are part of economic, cultural, and political processes. Who is remembered, why they are remembered, and how they are remembered have political implications. By 2014, the Ontario Heritage Trust had designated twenty-three sites of Black heritage. In that year the number increased to twenty-five, and I had the privilege of conducting the research to write the historical background and plaque text for two of them, which I will briefly mention – the Banwell Road Area Black Settlement and the Catholic Colored Mission of Windsor, 1887–93, both in Essex County. Today, all that remains of the Banwell Road Area Black Settlement is the cemetery located on the farmland secured by the African Methodist Church and the Coloured Industrial Society for that purpose. It is known as the Smith family cemetery, as the majority of the people interred there belonged to the family of Washington Smith, one of the community's first land owners. In 1977 the Town of Tecumseh took control of the cemetery and undertook preservation efforts. The town erected a fence around the burial ground and the remaining grave markers were moved to the front of the lot and placed on a cement slab to be visible from Banwell Road. This final resting place of a number of Essex County's Black residents is historically significant as it symbolizes the legacy of Black men and women and their collective efforts of community building in the face of racism and other barriers. The narrative of this site, in key respects, makes also visible the multiple ways in which temporal and spatial processes can serve to obscure the physical

Table 12.2 Provincial heritage plaques

Alberta	–
British Columbia	–
Manitoba	–
New Brunswick	–
Newfoundland	–
Nova Scotia	–
Ontario	The Banwell Road Area Black Settlement
	The Buxton Settlement. 1849
	Chloe Cooley and the 1793 Act to Limit Slavery in Upper Canada
	The "Colored Corps," 1812–15
	The Catholic Colored Mission of Windsor, 1887–93
	The Dawn Settlement
	Dr Anderson Ruffin Abbott, 1837–1913
	First Baptist Church, Puce
	The Founding of Dresden
	Harriet Ross Tubman, circa 1820–1913
	Hugh Burnett and The National Unity Association
	John Brown's Convention, 1858
	Lieutenant General John Graves Simcoe, 1750–1806
	Mary Ann Shadd Cary, 1823–1893
	The Negro Burial Ground, 1830
	Old St Paul's Church and Christ Church
	Otterville African Methodist Episcopal Church and Cemetery
	The Provincial Freeman
	Puce River Black Community
	The Queen's Bush Settlement, 1820–67
	The Reverend Anthony Burns, 1834–1862
	Richard Pierpoint, circa 1744–circa 1838
	Sandwich First Baptist Church, 1851
	The Wilberforce Settlement, 1830
	William and Susannah Steward House
Prince Edward Island	–
Quebec	Marie-Joseph Angélique
Saskatchewan	Shiloh Baptist Church

Table 12.3 Municipal heritage plaques

Vancouver, British Columbia	Hogan's Alley
Dartmouth, Nova Scotia	History of the Black Community
Halifax, Nova Scotia	Preston Area Blacks
New Glasgow, Nova Scotia	Viola Desmond
Chatham, Ontario	Bishop Walter Hawkins British Methodist Episcopal Freedom Park Gwendolyn Robinson
Hamilton, Ontario	Little Africa
Owen Sound, Ontario	Black History Cairn
Toronto, Ontario	Albert Jackson The Brotherhood of Sleeping Car Porters Donald Moore Frederick Hubbard Mary Ann Shadd Cary O-Connor-Lafferty House St Lawrence Hall Toronto's Reggae Roots William Peyton Hubbard
Eldon, Saskatchewan	Shiloh Baptist Church

presence of Black historical sites and presence. And yet the Smith Cemetery also symbolizes Black resistance to inhumane bondage and the tenacity and bravery of Blacks to live and die in freedom. As such, it is fitting that the heritage plaque was placed there to permanently mark their presence[16] (see figure 12.1).

The history of the first and only coloured mission to be established in Canada also holds much significance to the past experiences of people of African descent during the late nineteenth century. In 1887, a priest of German descent named Reverend James Theodore Wagner of the St Alphonsus Catholic Church started the first Catholic coloured mission in Canada in the emerging town of Windsor. Wagner began a fundraising campaign for the mission, travelling as far as Europe to solicit funds to build a new facility to house the mission and support his initiative to provide African Canadian youth with an education and introduce them to the Catholic faith. One potential funder, the Religious Hospitallers of St Joseph in Montréal, agreed to support the Colored Mission if Reverend Wagner and the St Alphonsus Catholic Church would partner with them to build

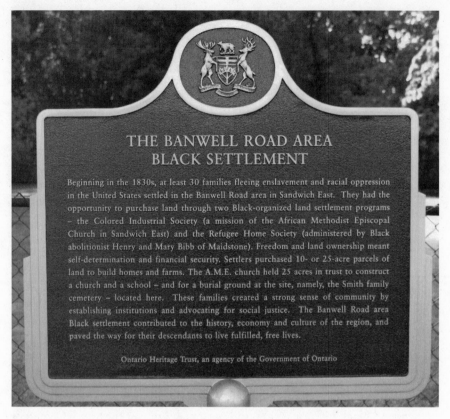

Figure 12.1 Plaque, Banwell Road, Windsor.

a hospital. Both parties collaborated to establish Hotel Dieu, Windsor's first hospital and to expand the coloured mission.

In 1890, the mission was moved to a new location behind the hospital on Ouellette Avenue and included a school and a one-hundred-bed orphanage. Another Catholic order, Sisters of the Holy Names of Jesus and Mary, provided the classroom teachers to instruct Black students in their charge as well as externs, students who did not live in the institution. Students received instruction in fundamental academic subjects and catechism as well as domestic training in house work, sewing, and knitting. The mission offered an educational choice to Black parents at a time when educational opportunities for Black children were limited in Windsor and its surrounding environs as the local common schools banned Black students from attending. The Colored Mission faced a number of challenges in its operation. Wagner wanted to grow the mission by opening the doors of the church

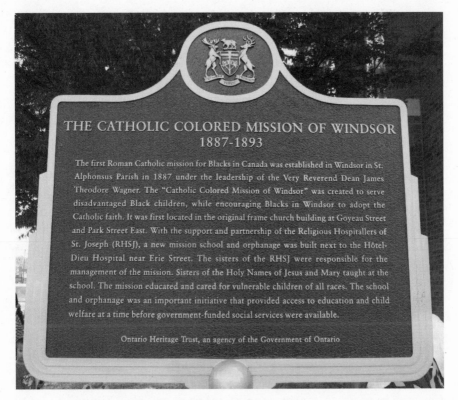

THE CATHOLIC COLORED MISSION OF WINDSOR
1887-1893

The first Roman Catholic mission for Blacks in Canada was established in Windsor in St. Alphonsus Parish in 1887 under the leadership of the Very Reverend Dean James Theodore Wagner. The "Catholic Colored Mission of Windsor" was created to serve disadvantaged Black children, while encouraging Blacks in Windsor to adopt the Catholic faith. It was first located in the original frame church building at Goyeau Street and Park Street East. With the support and partnership of the Religious Hospitallers of St. Joseph (RHSJ), a new mission school and orphanage was built next to the Hôtel-Dieu Hospital near Erie Street. The sisters of the RHSJ were responsible for the management of the mission. Sisters of the Holy Names of Jesus and Mary taught at the school. The mission educated and cared for vulnerable children of all races. The school and orphanage was an important initiative that provided access to education and child welfare at a time before government-funded social services were available.

Ontario Heritage Trust, an agency of the Government of Ontario

Figure 12.2 Plaque, Catholic Colored Mission of Windsor.

to Blacks in Windsor, but the white parishioners wanted racially separate church services. This reflected the reality of the racial discrimination faced by Blacks in Canada during that era. Then the teachers decided to accept only female students as they deemed the boys to be too challenging. This move reduced the enrolment. The last and decisive obstacle in operating the mission was that white hospital patrons abhorred being in such close proximity to the Black children of the mission. In March 1893, the doors of the Colored Mission were shuttered. During its existence, the Colored Mission's school and orphanage provided assistance to ninety-three Black children and eight white children.

REFLECTION

The process of uncovering the histories of the Banwell Road Area Black Settlement and the Catholic Colored Mission of Windsor left an indelible impression on me. I spent endless hours researching these two plaques, well beyond what was expected. I became so intrigued with finding out more, with digging up another piece of fascinating evidence that would shed more light. When investigating these stories, I had to think outside of the box and follow many leads, sometimes going in unexpected directions. It took time and dedication to weave together the pieces of the stories that I was able to gather. The research I undertook has reinforced that a range of archival resources should be examined and have the potential to offer insight in the recovery of African Canadian history – church records, historical news-papers, grave markers, census records, tax roll assessments, vital records, court records, and even an array of documents in Michigan archives. Rich archival knowledge shapes spaces of Blackness in Canada.[17] The back-ground research I conducted for the plaques confirm a permanent Black presence, that they "were here" in various spaces when seemingly their presence, whether through natural or human processes, have been erased.

NOTES

1 John Willinsky in a chapter of the same name in his book, *Learning to Divide the World: Education at Empire's End* (Minneapolis: University of Minnesota Press, 1998).

2 Cynthia Chambers, "A Topography for Canadian Curriculum Theory," *Canadian Journal of Education/Revue canadienne de l'éducation* 24, no. 2 (1999): 137.

3 Katherine McKittrick, *Demonic Grounds: Black Women And the Cartographies of Struggle* (Minneapolis: University of Minnesota Press 2006), xi.

4 The attempt to change the name of Negro Creek Road in Holland Township, located twenty-five kilometres south of Owen Sound is one example of street names that locate Blacks in certain spaces. There was discussion to rename Nigger Rapids in western Quebec and other landmarks in Quebec with names that include the words "nigger" or "black." Negro Brook Road in Kings County, New Brunswick was renamed Harriet O'Ree Road, maintaining the recognition of Black settlement. For an example of the burial of Black cemeteries, see *Speakers for the Dead*, directed by David Sutherland and Jennifer Holness (2000; Toronto: NFB, 2000), https://www.nfb.ca/film/speakers-for-the-dead.

5 Part of this process is the insistence of marking Black Canadian presence as new arrivals or immigrants. The work of George Elliott Clarke for instance has been concerned with marking the long historical presence of Blackness in Canada.

6 However, we might also note the range of oral narratives that circulate and serve to mark place by and for African Canadian communities. These also constitute a form of counter history.

7 Owen Thomas provides a detailed analysis of the ten African Canadian commemorative plaques installed by the Ontario Heritage Trust up to 1995 and offers a critique of the commodification of Black heritage sites in southwestern Ontario with the rise of heritage tourism. Owen Thomas, "Cultural Tourism, Commemorative Plaques, and African-Canadian Historiography: Challenging Historical Marginality," *Histoire sociale/Social History* 29, no. 58 (1996): 431–39.

8 Roger I. Simon, "The Paradoxical Practice of Zakhor: Memories of What Has Never Been My Fault or My Deed," in *Between Hope and Despair: Pedagogy and the Remembrance of Historical Trauma*, ed. Roger I. Simon, Sharon Rosenberg, and Claudi Eppert (Lanham: Rowman & Littlefield: 2000), 9–27, 13.

9 Roger I. Simon, *Touch of the Past: Remembrance, Learning and Ethics* (New York: Palgrave Macmillan, 2005); Edward Casey, "Public Memory in Place and Time," in *Framing Public Memory*, ed. Kendall Phillips (Tuscaloosa: University of Alabama Press, 2004).

10 Casey, "Public Memory."

11 Ibid., 23.

12 Ibid., 21–3.

13 Pomian Krzysztof, "Divided memory: European Sites of Memory as Political and Cultural Phenomenon," The European Network Remembrance and Solidarity, 23 August 2011.

14 This list is up to date as of August 2016. Images of most plaques and plaque texts can be viewed on www.waymarking.com. ARCGIS has mapped Black heritage plaques in Canada at https://www.arcgis.com/home/item.html?id=b532a6bb164d43269cfff1a0f28c57e0.

15 Natasha Henry, *Talking About Freedom: Celebrating Emancipation Day in Canada* (Toronto: Dundurn Press, 2012), 142.

16 For more information on the Banwell Road Area Black Settlement, see the research report, "Historical Background: The Banwell Road Area Black Settlement" (2015) upon request from the Ontario Heritage Trust.

17 Camille Turner, *Evoking a Site of Memory: An Afrofuturist Sonic Walk that Maps Historic Toronto's Black Geographies. Report of a Major Project* (Toronto: Faculty of Environmental Studies, York University, 2012), 17.

13

On the Aggrecultural Poetics
of *Sonnet's Shakespeare*

Sonnet L'Abbé

I call these erasure poems "aggrecultured" because instead of crossing, blacking out, or whiting out words from an existing piece of writing and making a new poem from what's left, what I have done is grow my own work around and through the original text. When I first encountered erasure poetry, the criticism surrounding it linked the practice to modernist found poetics and did not address the power dynamics of the erasing body to the source text. But the ruptures, excision, and deletion procedures that remove material and creatively silence source texts can be powerful ways to bring the felt experience of the silencing of specific voices into poetry – considering that poetry is a form that ordinarily means to give voice. I wanted to create a form that evoked my relationship and resistance to a dominant culture that had taught me its language, ostensibly inviting me into its community, but which had also hypervisibled/invisibled my body and effectively muted my speech.

In my project *Sonnet's Shakespeare*[1] each prose poem is written by intertwining my letters in between and all around the letters of Shakespeare's poem. Shakespeare's poem remains, in order, inside mine, but it has been "blended in." The finished texts I see as "textile winds": braided objects of texted breath, winding booty, and pulp fibres. Visible yet invisibled, Shakespeare's text is subject to my use of the master's tools in the master's house. Audre Lorde has already told us that such a strategy won't work to liberate brown and Black women,[2] but I think in this moment when many of us are trying to figure out how to speak effectively and transformatively in the face of oppressive languagings coming from state institutions, there's perhaps something valuable in sharing this evocation of desire to speak through and past those dominances.

I use the term "aggreculturing" to suggest at once the cultural aggressions and resistances that I process through my work, the aggregative nature of the process of adding letter by letter to Shakespeare's text, as well as my sense of this poetic work as occurring in the wake of British colonialism, at intersections of land and human body. In 2012, Harsha Walia wrote that "being responsible for decolonization can require us to locate ourselves within the context of colonization in complicated ways, often as simultaneously oppressed and complicit."[3] *Sonnet's Shakespeare*'s aggreculturing poetic is an intersectional response to the colonial cultural mechanisms that continue to exert racist force on brown and Black lives and implicate us as settlers on Turtle Island.

My own experience of silencing was of growing up subject to a pervasive pressure to blend in with a (misogynist, supremacist) white Anglophone Canadian society. Christina Sharpe's use of the term "the weather," to describe global anti-Blackness,[4] is helpful in thinking about the "pressure systems" I felt. This pressure to blend in was sometimes explicit, communicated through acts of racialized violence. More often it was and continues to be quietly enacted through a dominant presence, in various spaces, where "everyone" is white and anglo, and one, or a handful, of "others" aren't. Whose norms prevail? What truths about the land we were on were being actively silenced by embodying those norms? Certainly, the pressure to speak an "unaccented," educated English (or a *ben bon Québecois*), in order to access spaces of power, was and is a strong force in shaping individual lives and creating cultural sameness in the territories some call Canada.

I grew up in these lands trying hard not to sound like my Guyanese mother or my Québecoise grandmother. My mother taught me to *e-nun-ci-ate*, and when I began writing, I tried very hard to be "good" at literature, "good" at the culture of letters. I didn't realize it in grade school or high school but becoming "good at English," necessary as it has been to my survival as a deterritorialized subject, required deep investments in institutions and attitudes that distanced my mind and heart from the sounds and languages of the cultures I come from. Being "good at English" brought me closer to being the docile subject of Empire. For a while, my African and South Asian being lived as mute hypervisibility, as the unerasable colour of my skin.

In my search for belonging and worth, I wrote "good" poems; I shaped my own voice into the cadence of the laureled poets of Canadian Literature. I tried to erase my own social difference by participating in an English-language poetry community led by white men and women. In my poems I tried to articulate the force of my difference, in the very language of those whose dominance sought my erasure. That community rewarded me mainly for performing a very specific kind of "authentic" difference, for writing in Guyanese creole, for example, or creating exoticized/domesticated images of immigrant colour, none of which represented my own experience. It was only after I published my first book and saw what a "good" job of fitting into publishing that I had done and how disconnected I still felt, that I began to search for sounds and forms and cadences that spoke as *me*.

My experimentations with form, that I started in *Killarnoe*[5] and extended in *Anima Canadensis*,[6] come out of that frustration and not out of any filiation with European avant-garde traditions or desire to imitate them. I began playing around from my sense of being outsided: to find my outsider cadence, syntax, lineation and spacing, to speak from a consciousness that disidentifies with "good" English. So, even now that I am conversant with North American avant-gardes and respond to its erasures, I insist on speaking from another creative lineage. I work from that desire to give voice to everything in me that has felt unable to find its satisfactory expression in the norms of English-language lyric poetry, in the privilege plays of avant-garde provocations, or even in the words of the English language itself.

"Taught in schools and performed under the proscenium arches built where the British conquered," writes Emer O'Toole, "universal Shakespeare was both a beacon of the greatness of European civilization and a gateway into that greatness – to know the bard was to be civilized."[7] As a child on the prairies, brown-bodied in the violence of multiple weathers, I turned to a book with my name on it, to Shakespeare's *Sonnets*, hoping that there I would find my value. Through my aggreculturing erasure, I make art out of my relationship to the culture that has taught me what civil language is, confronting the power that has, quite literally, named me into being.

XLVIII

How careful must walkers be, if Black when walking. Too freaking many
Black walkers are history. Not for treacheries, but trifles, are men under
terrorful arrest's bars too often thrust. The atmosphere of terror, for many,
results less from international militias' fighting words or unsuspected
domestic betrayers and more from those command-followers, police, who
foster falsehood, instead of understanding they are wards of trust. Bullying
sergeants' authority comes out of laws that once named some men property.
Jewish people understand how race influences target-embodiment, how
states with low morale create antipathy and comfort landowners by naming
an enemy. Americans' greatest grief wants to buy a house, obey stop signs,
find a life partner. The worst American diminishment only cares to signal
before turning left; to be the potential prey of one slavery-mouthed, vulgar,
trigger-happy officer's enforcement; to achieve greatness or have it thrust
upon him; to not get locked up in any charlatan investments; to leave well
enough alone. Race is a thought the Americas' plantations cotton-mouthed;
a vicious negging that is felt as repellent. If you aren't recognized within the
gentlemen's enclosure of supremacy, brother, arrests for random whatever
are at their convenience. Only at their pleasure, breather, you may respect-
fully come, say sir, and maybe disappear. Trayvon, Dante, Victor, Walter,
Tony, Tamir, Michael, and Eric, you're on a list of "shot unarmed" on
Gawker; I looked you up. Today a badge was let off for killing Rekia. What
fear your form of truth proves. "Feeling threatened" is evidence video won't
show. Fuk da police, said Dre, *sa prize!* – his smile could be so disarming.

L

How heavy would the self-possession journey be, if on the way no other
women published their own hunts for what I seek. My weary travel is
lightened by dark accounts that teach me that the ease I want, that nod,
that respect and composure, are not-im possible in a day-to-day that thus
far hasn't relinquished the material desirables of race. Distance is measured
outward from wealthy friends' kitchen tables. You can sit at that table if
you arrest memory. I am tired with my woe, but so are you; history's
consequence plods dully on. Poetry is born to bear that weight, to intone
the measure of self-inflicted blame, and yet hear some perfect instinct of the
wretched vindicated. We know history's understoried verses and true loves;
we do not speechify; we endure being made from the impulse beneath the
bloody spur. I cannot provoke history's monsters; they swat at my bother-
some, timeless anger as cattle unthinkingly brush at bees; the giant oafs of
history lurch ideologically toward whiteness and new chauvinisms. When
heavily my heart answers these teeny microslights with a groan, their pique
more sharp to me than spat slurs, then do your writings rally to this human's
side. For the soul-mate sameness of your groan doth produce quiet empa-
thies in my mind; my grief's loneliest hour finds inward company, and my
joy of scribbling approaches its kind.

LXXX

Old friend, how I fail some responsibility when I of you do write. I don't know if, through writing, a better spirit will lead my troubled thoughts. But these days your name agitates my mind. I think of the pranks we didn't scheme together, the stories of misspent youth we didn't share, the girls'-night laughs we dissed as unfeminist. The thought of your contempt would make me tongue-tied speaking of my loser infatuations. Now your happy family life is the bullseye I never hit. You're still setting the example of how to embrace your worth. Why didn't I learn the self-respect that you modelled in adolescence? It was self-fashioning, I see now, into white womanhood. Me, bumbling along, never able to sell my overfaithful reproductions of a damsel undistressed by race. Imbalanced from the beginning, our partnership assumed an easy, surface posture of scorn toward prettybaby strategies taken up by intellectual inferiors. We were young feminist assholes – but you refusing a small-town beauty championship is not anything like the sour grapes bravado I cultivated to make believe appearance doesn't carry weight. You wilfully appeared sensible; you skirted any slur of shallowness and yet held the power of your high school laurels. I wanted fate to hold me up to a fairer light; I told myself that I would achieve loveliness through talent, not makeup. Ambitious us, brainy young girls: you'd undo legal chauvinisms while I'd rewrite the popular headspace. Of course there was no weirdness over boys, no competition for guys' wooing. We were too jacked on academic accomplishment to waste our worth on mindless boy-attention, right? So while I fought off routine assault, boys walked you from building to library and showed off their good sides. Sisterly, protectively, you said I chased the wrong kind. The fish in the sea threatened me, but my thirsty vibe was asking for dishonour? Because it was a way to hope the worst wasn't true, we shamed me instead of white supremacy. Will we now survive a realer view, that pretends no mystification wondering why love came to you?

LXXIV

Bruh beat be like, content. Dude docs like a white man. They material
defense. They all arresting image. Without jail colour. They bail on a sistah.
Verbally he open carry. Metrically he waaay money. He collegial. He frat.
He hide that. Fresh bling glint in his line. So women show interest. What
sick hos cry for? Bruh Modest Mouse. Bruh Reddit. He all startup-illest
wit. Bruh beat push teen liberals. He all downstay. White men brutha. Tom
uncle creepin. Nice-view penthouse hints. Pimpin this thought. He do Slit
Review authentic voice. They a sorry party. We-ain't-those-conservatives
cred. Mo fortunate. Mo totally humane. Cachet they can't earn. Hood they
can't have. Big butt earnest. Bruh whip – cha! Institooshion his dude. Homey
spirit dist-ill. He interest held back. Net interest pay smart. Negro formal
up in here. Software hawker inta house. He badness. He stabness. Gut love
his stunt. He doctor the register. Officer the reallife. Brother pretty can of
worms. Memory body be indyin. Nigga deal dope theatre. Who coward?
Who conquest? How offishall written? Scratch hip hop sonic knife too base
for infrastructure. Who feed to be remembered? Brother worth short shrift.
He attention seeking. Rhythm aint sway here. White choir master content.
Aint said no damage. Brother aint stupid. Bruh wisegame this landscape.
Bruh beat his unwhitewash. He hustle a hardcore. Core remain stone unsaid.

NOTES

1 Sonnet L'Abbé, *Sonnet's Shakespeare* (Toronto: McClelland & Stewart, 2019).
2 Audre Lorde, *Sister Outsider: Essays and Speeches* (Berkeley: Ten Speed Press, 1984).
3 Harsha Walia, "Decolonizing Together: Moving Beyond a Politics of Solidarity Toward a Practice of Decolonization," *Briarpatch Magazine*, 1 January 2012, https://briarpatchmagazine.com/articles/view/decolonizing-together.
4 Christina Sharpe, *In The Wake: On Blackness and Being* (Durham: Duke University Press, 2016).
5 Sonnet L'Abbé, *Killarnoe* (Toronto: McClelland & Stewart, 2007).
6 Sonnet L'Abbé, *Anima Canadensis* (Toronto: Junction Books, 2016).
7 Emer O'Toole, "Shakespeare, universal? No, it's cultural imperialism," *The Guardian*, 21 May 2012.

14

Mobilizing the Bard:
Joseph Pierre's *Shakespeare's Nigga* (2013)

Pilar Cuder-Domínguez

Since the 1960s, rewritings of William Shakespeare's canonical works have been published in a great variety of formats: fiction, drama, film, graphic novels. *The Tempest*, in particular, has received enormous creative and critical attention in the last few decades, and Caliban has emerged as "the inexhaustible symbol of the colonized insurgent."[1] Fernández Retamar famously identified Caliban with the Caribbean subject, eloquently arguing that "Prospero invaded the islands, killed our ancestors, enslaved Caliban, and taught him his language to make himself understood. What else can Caliban do but use that same language – today he has no other – to curse him, to wish that the 'red plague' would fall on him?"[2] Such strong identification has been pursued by a number of Caribbean writers from the first fully-fledged meditation on the play, George Lamming's *The Pleasures of Exile* (1960).[3] Similarly, emphasis on the relationship between the enslaved and the enslaver as encoded in the original play's triad Prospero–Ariel–Caliban has been repeatedly re-signified since Aimé Césaire's *Une Tempête* (1969),[4] a text displaying a strong conviction that "the culture of the slaves need not be an enslaved culture."[5] From a gender perspective too, the role of Miranda as an object of desire together with the absence of "Caliban's Woman" were identified by Sylvia Wynter as key ways in which the text obliterated black women.[6] While it is not the purpose of this essay to trace yet again the well-documented transatlantic cultural history of Caliban, it may be useful to remark at the very least on some of the traits that have been lifted from the original play, recast, and transmitted through generations of Caribbean and African writers. Most striking among those are Caliban's subversive use of language and his capacity for revolt, which have been addressed among others by all three writers mentioned despite their coming variously from the Spanish-speaking, English-speaking, or French-speaking Americas.

In Canada too, like other former British colonies, the figure of Shakespeare has variously served "as protector and symbol of high art, as morally edifying theatre, as an ally of solid British values, and as a tool of Anglicization, among others."[7] As the twentieth century wore on, the continued centrality of Shakespeare began to be resented by Canadian playwrights for impeding the development of homegrown talent,[8] and towards its end there arose a strong revisionist movement that continues to this day, affecting *The Tempest* as well as other Shakespearean plays. Daniel Fischling estimates there have been hundreds of Canadian adaptations of Shakespeare since pre-Confederation, and he highlights how hard Canadian theatrical culture has worked "to shape-shift Shakespeare into the multiple and complex contexts that make Canada what it is."[9] Among those hundreds are some from a black Canadian perspective, most prominently Djanet Sears' *Harlem Duet*, the rewriting of *Othello* that has to date garnered the most critical attention. Nevertheless, *Othello* has influenced other black Canadian texts less obviously perhaps, such as George Elliott Clarke's *Whylah Falls*.[10] *The Tempest* might be thought to be comparatively less appealing than *Othello* within black Canadian tradition, but one should not forget that as early as 1974 Haitian Canadian critic Max Dorsinville used the play as an extended metaphor for the rise of black minority literatures in his essay *Caliban Without Prospero*.

Striding both traditions, national and transnational, the black Canadian writer Joseph Jomo Pierre's 2013 play *Shakespeare's Nigga*[11] departs from previous revisions in several ways. First of all, it casts the author as one more character and places him in the context of New World slavery. William Shakespeare is a plantation owner, father to one legitimate daughter, Judith, and one illegitimate son by an enslaved mother, Othello. Secondly, Pierre's revision combines several Shakespearean threads, taking characters variously from *The Tempest*, *Othello*, and *Titus Andronicus* to recast the triad Prospero–Ariel–Caliban into Shakespeare–Othello–Aaron. This paper will argue that this renewed mobilization of the Bard is put to the service of narrating black people's struggle against slavery by focusing on the strong antagonism between Othello as the submissive slave and Aaron as the rebel. In so doing, Pierre's is in line with former appropriations of the play, which fluctuated between attraction and repulse, tradition and innovation, as Nixon has argued: "On the one hand, [those writers who appropriated *The Tempest*] hailed Caliban and identified themselves with him; on the other, they were intolerant of received colonial definitions of Shakespeare's value. They found the European play compelling but insisted on engaging with it on their own terms."[12] Thus, each new appropriation of the play remains distinctive, each endowing already familiar landscapes and characters with new meanings and foregrounding alternative interplays of power in ways that "serve to dismantle narrative authority and to reorient the circulation of knowledge."[13] This paper will look into Pierre's specific realignments of race, power, and gender by focusing on the deployment of language in the play and its performance of two diverse and competing types of black masculinities.

SEIZING THE BOOK

"Seizing the Book" is the title of the chapter on *The Tempest* in Ania Loomba's ground-breaking analysis of race in Shakespeare, *Gender, Race, Renaissance Drama*,[14] because she argues that the history of this particular play "clearly reveals a contest over textual truth and value."[15] Loomba's phrase is an apt metaphor for the act of appropriation *Shakespeare's Nigga* represents. Like Caliban, who instructed Stephano and Trinculo to seize Prospero's books because without them he was rather helpless, Joseph Jomo Pierre struggles to take over Shakespeare's book, and with it to wrest his own authority as a playwright. To this effect, it should not be forgotten that Shakespeare's work is still widely acknowledged as "the measure of all dramatic art, and the ultimate test for the would-be actor or director, the mark of audience sophistication, and the uncontested sign of 'Culture' itself."[16] Indeed, the Stratford Theatre Festival – Canada's oldest – was established in 1952 as a Shakespearean festival and continues to showcase and to promote the Bard's oeuvre with numerous productions every year. In addition, Pierre also struggles with the Bard as a *black* playwright setting out to engage with Shakespeare's most influential portrayals of black men, Othello and Aaron, as I will discuss below.

   Shakespeare's Nigga was directed by Philip Aikin and produced by Obsidian Theatre Company, Theatre Passe Muraille, and 3D Atomic Entertainment in February 2013 in Toronto's Theatre Passe Muraille Mainspace. This was not the author's first collaboration with Obsidian Theatre Company, for they had produced Pierre's earlier works, *Born Ready/ Pusha Man* (2005) and *Hip Hop (Who Stole the Soul?)* (2006). In addition, Pierre was associated to the Playwright Unit for the year 2010–11, and *Shakespeare's Nigga* was workshopped in December 2011 as part of the company's season development series of plays in progress. It requires a cast of five people: three black men (Othello, Tyrus, and Aaron), an older white man (Shakespeare) and a young white woman (Judith, who doubles as the horse). The cast remained the same as that which originally participated in the staged reading in 2011. Pierre himself played the part of Aaron, just as he had played the main roles in his earlier dramatic pieces. The staging strongly relies on blackouts and spotlights for swift transitions between characters and for scene changes. The thirteen scenes are located mostly in Shakespeare's study and Aaron's shack, a movement that conveys the power conflict in the play as well as extant class hierarchies.

Scene 1 opens to an older Shakespeare in his study. This Shakespeare recalls Prospero, ready to abjure his magic and drown his book by the end of the play, and it also befits popular understanding that this last play has a valedictory character and the author already intended to retire from the stage. This transpires through an attitude of reappraisal of his entire oeuvre, as the aging author wonders if he has done justice to all his characters, a rhetorical question that remains unanswered throughout the play but which the audience themselves will be able to answer in watching it. Shakespeare falls into a deep slumber to the distant background sound of a whip snapping. As his dream starts to take shape before the audience, Shakespeare-the-author becomes Shakespeare-the-slave-owner. Connecting both worlds is the space of Shakespeare's study and his own works, to which the play will return in scene 6. By reinforcing the connection midway through the performance, Pierre prevents his audience from losing sight of how the world of literature and aesthetics is intimately connected to past and current structures of economic and racial oppression. In the final scene, an enlightened Shakespeare awakes from his long dream, this time articulating his will to "remedy this wrong," and in the ensuing silence he picks up Aaron's child, now transformed into a book whose first page he settles down to read. Thus, the metamorphosed book constitutes a strong symbol permeating the different layers of meaning inside and outside the play. Pierre metaphorically opens the book and takes Shakespeare's voice during the play, then drops it at the end, when the character reads the last line instructing him and the audience to realize that there are "Volumes hidden between each beat, masquerading as silence."[17]

The related themes of voicing the silenced and of coming to language that features so strongly in *The Tempest* with Caliban's famous assertion that learning the master's language is useful so as to curse him, also runs through *Shakespeare's Nigga*. Most powerfully, it comes through in the arresting image of Aaron's tongue tied with rope, the same one that featured on the play's poster and that has been used by Playwrights Canada Press for the book cover. It constitutes the only answer to Shakespeare's appeal to let him know how to mend his unfair treatment of the character and is consistent with the fact that Pierre intended this to be, above all, a retelling of Aaron's silenced story, as he disclosed in conversation with Obsidian's dramaturge Mel Hague,[18] a point to which I will be returning below.

However, this theme is also imbricated with Othello's schooling and with his access to knowledge and power, which in turn parallel Miranda's own schooling by Prospero in *The Tempest*. Shakespeare has provided Othello with an education and has urged him to "let no man say that you are not his equal."[19] Yet, on finding him in his study, perusing some of his sonnets, he deflects Othello's questions about the dark lady in them, denying him the knowledge that they refer to Othello's mother, a black slave whose complexion was "as dark as the night that played host to their affair. She died before Othello could call her mother. So all he has known is what he knows."[20] Unaware of the link, Othello reads the poems for what they have to say about blackness and therefore for a kind of self-knowledge after all. He muses that "black wires grow on [my mistress's] head";[21] that "in the old age black was not counted fair";[22] or that "Then will I swear beauty herself is black/And all they foul that thy complexion lack."[23] The poems subvert the derogatory meaning of "black," even as Othello is thwarted at every step to think of himself as truly any man's equal, for when he asks for what he most desires, Judith's hand in marriage, the master denies him with a succinct "You are black, Othello"[24] that reinstates all extant racial structures of power, as Othello is racialized anew within them.

"Black" is, needless to say, the word whose meaning in several variations the play consistently troubles. In the foreword, director Philip Aikin remembers how he initially recommended a change of title because it was too offensive but then he understood that those two words "were the very heart of the play."[25] Pierre himself has also explained that despite the uproar surrounding the word "nigger," his character "claims it and that opens the door for a discussion about language."[26] Pierre was referring to Aaron's distinction between the words "nigger" and "negro" in scene 9 of the play. Aaron self-identifies as "Shakespeare's nigga," appropriating the abusive term to turn it back against the white master, in fact as a tool to regain "a ferocity that will set them free."[27] The n-word is thus re-signified as someone who "won't settle for being considered less than a man."[28] In contrast, he assigns Othello the more respectful word "negro," although investing it with utter contempt, meaning a traitor to his race and people, for "he is like us only in shade."[29] This scene thus both illuminates the overall import of Pierre's play and its reassessment of language dynamics and highlights the disparity between the two male protagonists, Aaron and Othello, that will be examined in more detail below.

To boot, "seizing the book" also implies to a certain extent engaging with Shakespeare's language, since this author has been the most accomplished and innovative shaper of the English language. Pierre has explained that he first tried to construct the piece with the kind of contemporary speech patterns he had used in others, but it did not work. Neither did he intend to work "some faux Shakespearean voice" into his text.[30] The result is a comfortable, easy blend, definitely formal in tone and register but not distant enough from present-day speech to alienate the audience. Shakespearean quotes have been inserted several times in the play, the first time in scene 6, as mentioned above, when Othello happens to read the sonnets on Shakespeare's desk; the second in scene 8, when Judith and Aaron are making love and he teases her about "his powers" by quoting at length from Aaron's speech disclosing his evil arts to Lucius in *Titus Andronicus*.[31] Judith's reaction to the long catalogue of murder, rape, and other criminal acts is to dismiss it all as "the most ridiculous thing I've heard,"[32] a fitting commentary on the widely circulated stereotype of black people as the source of all evil. A distressed Othello quotes Juliet's famous speech in *Romeo and Juliet*[33] on finding out that what separates him from Judith is indeed the fact of their name, as they claim the same father. Finally, Tyrus appropriates Shylock's soliloquy[34] on the eve of the slave revolt[35] to remind Shakespeare that they are indeed his equal. Besides these specific moments, Shakespearean resonances are scattered through the whole text, building a web of references shared by the audience, as Shakespeare's works constitute what Markaryk has described as "a ready-made, immediately recognizable source of meaning for any number of endeavours."[36]

HONORARY WHITE MAN OR MONSTROUS OTHER: OTHELLO VERSUS AARON

Pierre's play is built not just on a skilful handling of Shakespearean words and situations but also on the persisting currency of two opposing stereo-types of black masculinity, Othello and Aaron. As hero and villain, they have dominated Western representations of black men for centuries. Black heroism in general has always been a complicated issue, as Bernier reminds us. The recuperation of black *male* bodies for a white imaginary has been predicated on two models, a "passive" one shaped on Stowe's character Uncle Tom and an "active" one built on the historic Nat Turner.[37] The passive, submissive, conformist type fits both Othello and Uncle Tom – to whom one might add Ariel – insofar as they accept the established white order and would like to be accepted as "honorary white men." The active, rebellious, nonconformist nature applies to Aaron, Nat Turner, or Caliban as they seek to implode the establishment from within; in Lamming's words, "Caliban contains the seeds of revolt."[38] Drawing from the paradigm of Caliban, Coleman has defined "Calibanic discourse" in his study of postmodernist African American fiction male writers:

> Calibanic discourse is the perceived history and story of the black male in Western culture that ... denotes slavery, proscribed freedom, proscribed sexuality, inferior character, and inferior voice. In summary, the black male is the slave or servant who is the antithesis of reason, civilized development, entitlement, freedom, and power of white men, and he never learns the civilized use of language. His voice is unreliable; his words fail to signify his humanity. He also preys on civilization and represents bestial, contaminating sexuality. Clearly, Western culture must confine the black male to roles and places befitting his inferiority, and/or it must punish him, and even brutalize and kill him for his criminality and reprobate character.[39]

For Coleman, some black male fiction deploys this discourse in combination with a story of liberation meant to destabilize the former and to counter white versions of history. As a result, the story of liberation involves "a black male's quest to speak in an empowering voice, to achieve freedom from slavery and racism, to define the self, to fashion a humane character and a secure, empowered status in a racist world, and to attain freedom from proscribed sexuality."[40] All of these features, I would like to argue, are equally fitting for Aaron in *Shakespeare's Nigga*. The play is the story of the bondage and liberation of Aaron, both literally – as the play traces the movement from slavery to revolt and to a final liberation – and metaphorically – as the bondage Aaron needs freedom from is also the stereotype of evil he is caught up in. Pierre's words about the origin of his play stress the latter aspect:

> I got the role of Aaron at theatre school and was excited as hell to play the character. I asked a teacher for some advice on how to approach the character and he told me to *play him as pure evil*. It was a what the fuck moment for me, we were obviously connecting to this character on different levels. Right there I swore I would tell Aaron's story.[41]

Pierre asserts here the urgent, political need to refute white racism in its specific formulation in *Titus Andronicus*, where Aaron is not merely wicked but also unrepentant to the very end and therefore beyond redemption.

In addition, Pierre's retelling of Aaron's story is fashioned in radical contrast to Othello's. Othello is a house slave and the plantation overseer. As such, he is the instrument of Shakespeare's discipline, and in the opening scene of Shakespeare's dream, he beats Aaron after his unsuccessful attempt to escape in order both to break him down and to prevent further acts of disobedience and unrest from the other slaves. But throughout the beating, Aaron laughs and taunts Othello with looks and words:

Othello: (*moves to Shakespeare*) Should I stop? Though he asks for more, though his face lights up and taunts me?
Shakespeare: Othello, there is no joy in his laughter. And I doubt there is any true malice in his looks.
Othello: His laughter hints of the devil. No, there is malice.[42]

Interestingly, it is Othello who has interiorized the white message of black as evil and therefore it is completely unnecessary for Shakespeare to enforce discipline himself. He is happy to watch Othello deliver a lesson to Aaron that will help him understand that "[t]here must be consequences for one's actions, Aaron. Likewise there are consequences for one's inaction ... I am not your ass. You belong to me."[43]

Nevertheless, this is exactly the type of lesson that Aaron resists once and again during the play, despite threats, entreats, and brutal force. The theme of discipline and physical punishment (an altogether different kind of schooling from the one Othello himself received) runs through the play by establishing a parallelism between Shakespeare's attempt to break down Aaron and Othello's attempt to tame a wild horse. Similarly to Aaron's beating, the lash does nothing to curb the unruly behaviour of Othello's horse: "I've broken many horses by mounting them until they refused to buck, till their spirits were broken, but these rules do not apply to this one," he reports to Shakespeare in a highly sexualized language that positions animals, women (particularly if one takes into account that the actor playing Judith doubles as the horse), and slaves as his subordinates within a rhetoric of power.[44] Othello then changes his tactics of (sexual) dominance and starts talking to the horse and stroking him without attempting to mount, a tactic meant to gain its trust. The lesson Othello is trying to teach the horse is exactly the same one Shakespeare wanted to get through to Aaron: "You belong to me."

Besides, the taming of the horse is also an interesting theatrical device that provides powerful insights into Othello's state of mind. His racial isolation and his sense of being stranded between two worlds, never considered good enough for either, come through very clearly in the original Shakespearean play in Othello's final speech before stabbing himself. Here it is to the horse, at night, that he talks of his own unrest, when he is occasionally "without restraint and like the lowly savage,"[45] i.e. quite unlike the civilized self he cultivates by day, as well as of his longing for Judith, who "tests [his] very loyalty with her reckless passion for a savage."[46] Finally, it is on the horse that he takes out his rage and despair, when his hopes of gaining Judith for himself are dashed, asking from it the urgent question "What in me does not deserve to be loved?"[47] This aspect of Pierre's character is consistent with its original rendering, since as Loomba has observed, "[Desdemona's] desire for [Othello] – 'for she had eyes, and chose me'[48] – replaces his heritage or exploits as proof and measure of his worth. It thus becomes the primary signifier of his identity."[49] Wynter has also remarked on the significant absence of black women from *The Tempest* and how the lack of "Caliban's woman" displaces his desire on to Miranda, as "the only symbolically canonized potential genitrix."[50] Similarly, in *Shakespeare's Nigga* Othello's sense of self-worth is tied to Judith. Through her he would like to pull himself up to the position of son to Shakespeare, as he feels he deserves. Old Tyrus correctly diagnoses that "it is not whiteness that Othello seeks; it is the acceptance of a father."[51] Ironically, this is also the place that, unbeknownst to him, is actually his. Shakespeare's categorical rejection of his request for Judith's hand, added to her earlier rejection – "[f]or me scorn, for [Aaron] tears"[52] – unleashes Othello's despair and puts him on a self-destructive path.

Unlike Othello, a mixed-race house slave who ostensibly stands for the established order and freely traverses all the spaces of the plantation, including that most protected *sancta sanctorum* Shakespeare's own study, the field slave Aaron is confined to the shack and the field and wearing shackles for many of the scenes, which further hinder his movements. Like the original character, Pierre's Aaron is associated, both physically and metaphorically, to the night, to bloodshed, and to revenge. It is at night when Judith finds her way to his shack with water and bread after his recapture, to entreat him unsuccessfully that he give up his quest for freedom and remain "content" to be enslaved, or else driven by her desire to make love with him one more time. More importantly, night itself tells Aaron stories of violence, "[a] monologue of a thousand lashes"[53] while the wind whispers "[b]loodshed for blood revival."[54] Darkness is Aaron's place. Whereas in

The Tempest, Caliban was referred to as "this thing of darkness,"[55] Pierre deconstructs the phrase by turning slavery itself into the thing of darkness at the heart of Western civilization. Aaron's night soliloquies, particularly in scene 5, eloquently dismantle the thin veneer of civilization over the horrors of slavery:

> This wretched thing has held all our senses in bondage. This thing is but the stench of death, and death but the aroma of black flesh decomposing. How often my lungs have pleaded for purity only to be bombarded by rancidness ... The monotonous sound of waves breaking against a ship causes the ears to contemplate, what evilness has the ocean given birth to this time? Slavery. Can there be any taste when served by death, when having to eat on the same floor as death. This thing, what atrocities have our eyes had to witness. So resounding that even behind the veil of eyelids there is no refuge. And the black skin, what has it felt but death. This thing has caused it to be ripped, broken, stretched and burnt. Ears, death. Nose, death. Mouth, death. Hands, death. Eyes, death. That is all they know. What is left in us to live? Aaron, what?[56]

Contrary to Othello, whose isolation is palpable in the play, Aaron is never wholly alone. In fact, it is when he is alone on stage that he transmits most strongly his belonging to a group because he witnesses the pain of many. Tyrus confirms this when he reports that Aaron's capture "dismantled many hopes; you were the lead player in their dreams of freedom."[57] Given the opportunity to flee once more, he starts running before he is stopped by dark shapes and windblown whispers that compel him to accept that "[T]here is no freedom for one, without freedom for all."[58] Therefore, instead of feeling torn into two by conflicting emotions like Othello, Aaron is a leader, rallying fellow slaves to revolt against their white masters, to meet slavery's horrors with their own horrors. The ultimate success of the revolt hinges on Aaron's power to convince others that "[i]f you wish to leave the scars on your back in the past, you must let your hands lead you towards their blood. This is how we cure ourselves of this thickness. If it is freedom that we want, let us take it."[59]

Aaron's last defining trait is his sexuality. In contrast to Othello, who is at every turn thwarted by Judith's contempt, Aaron represents the myth of black male potency. He is also vulnerable to the stereotypical image of the black rapist of white women, given that he is involved in an interracial relationship. Once more, Pierre draws severally from Shakespearean plays featuring interracial affairs. In *Titus Andronicus*, Aaron is Queen Tamora's lover. Tamora is white but a Goth, and therefore barbarous from the Roman viewpoint. Moreover, she pursues her revenge against Titus Andronicus for having had her firstborn son executed. Aaron and Tamora "become embodiments of pure evil; the supposedly uncontrollable sexuality of women and blacks motivates their liaison."[60] In the more nuanced *Othello*, the protagonist marries Desdemona without her father's approval. Brabantio believes Othello used his magic arts to seduce Desdemona, for only the use of magic could explain a preference for someone so decidedly her inferior in Venetian society that for many their relationship was considered unnatural. In *The Tempest*, Prospero accuses Caliban of the attempted rape of Miranda. In *Shakespeare's Nigga*, Othello is driven by jealousy to beat Aaron but more notably he is also the mouthpiece of racist fears of miscegenation, as he charges Aaron with accusations of racial contamination: "How dare you soil her. How dare you place your uneducated hands on her. Rest your illiterate lips on her."[61] Shakespeare too, on learning of their relationship, conceives of it as his daughter's defilement and threatens to have Aaron's skin boiled off his flesh. In the closing scene, riding the wave of the rebellion, Aaron enters Shakespeare's study and confronts the master with the news that everything is lost and that both Judith and Othello are dead. Shakespeare's genealogy is thus discontinued, unless it is by way of Aaron's own child by Judith, which realizes Caliban's threat to populate the island with Calibans. Similarly, Shakespeare-as-author also has his own legacy disrupted and "polluted" by Pierre's retelling in such a way that metaphorically seals the overarching "seizing the book" trope analyzed above.

CONCLUSIONS: HARRIET'S LEGACY VERSUS SHAKESPEARE'S

To conclude, one needs to address the matter of the pertinence and currency of Pierre's revisit to Shakespeare's plays. Earlier revisions sprang from the specific historical conditions of decolonization, but their persistence beyond that period must be understood as responding to an altogether different set of questions and conditions. If so, we need to ask which ones would apply in this particular case.

Some have been rehearsed above. The first is the inherent value of testing one's own playwriting skills against the master himself, a challenge that Pierre meets successfully in *Shakespeare's Nigga*, a play that confronts the continued centrality of Shakespeare's oeuvre on the Canadian stage. Secondly, by his own account the author seems to be strongly invested in giving voice to the maligned character of Aaron in *Titus Andronicus*, thus contesting one of the most persisting stereotypes of black masculinity. Third, in choosing to locate the play on a slave plantation, Pierre places added stress on power relations within a slave system that were perhaps less explicitly examined in *The Tempest* but that Aimé Césaire brought to the fore in *A Tempest* (1969). In fact, Pierre draws from Césaire in recasting Ariel and Caliban as a mulatto and a black slave respectively: Othello and Aaron. Consequently, the overarching theme of resistance to slavery and the quest for freedom comes strongly to the fore of the action, most prominently with the successful slave insurrection. In addition, the different position of characters within the slave system goes a long way towards explaining their diverging behaviour and personality.

Accordingly, *Shakespeare's Nigga* claims a space not only within the existing transnational tradition of Shakespearean rewritings I have traced in this paper but also within a growing corpus of black Canadian writings about slavery and its legacy which aim to dispel the entrenched idea of the absence of slavery on Canadian territory and the overall perception of Canada as a historical safe haven for black people. This other nationally grounded genealogy is continually enlarged by new additions. In recent times it includes plays like Lorena Gale's *Angélique* (1999), novels such as Lawrence Hill's *The Book of Negroes* (2007), or poetry collections like Sylvia D. Hamilton *And I Alone Escaped to Tell You* (2014). Thus, Joseph Jomo Pierre's multilayered intertextual dialogue with the Bard in *Shakespeare's Nigga* (2013) powerfully contributes to ongoing joint efforts to fight national amnesia and to collectively examine the legacy of slavery by reinscribing black historical memory in Canada.

NOTES

1 Chantal Zabus, *Tempests After Shakespeare* (London: Palgrave, 2002), 2.
2 Roberto Fernández Retamar, *Caliban and Other Essays* (Minneapolis: University of Minnesota Press, 1989), 14.
3 George Lamming, *The Pleasures of Exile* (London: Michael Joseph, 1960).
4 Aimé Césaire, *A Tempest*, trans. Richard Miller (New York: TCG Translations, 2002).
5 Rob Nixon, "Caribbean and African Appropriations of The Tempest," *Critical Enquiry* 13, no. 3 (1987): 572.
6 Sylvia Wynter, "Afterword: Beyond Miranda's Meanings: Unsilencing the 'Demonic Ground' of Caliban's 'Woman,'" in *Out of the Kumbla: Caribbean*

Women and Literature, ed. Carole Boyce Davies and Elaine Savory Fido (Trenton: Africa World Press, 1990), 355ff.

7   Irena R. Markaryk, "Introduction," in *Shakespeare in Canada: 'a world elsewhere'?* ed. Diana Brydon and Irena R. Makaryk (Toronto: University of Toronto Press, 2002), 5.

8   Ibid., 33.

9   Daniel Fischlin, "On Shakespearean Adaptation and Being Canadian," in *Shakespeare Made in Canada: Contemporary Canadian Adaptations in Theatre, Pop Media and Visual Arts*, ed. Daniel Fischlin and Judith Nasby (Guelph: MacDonald Stewart Art Centre, 2007), 6.

10 Diana Brydon, "George Elliott Clarke's Othello," *Canadian Literature* 182 (2004): 188–94.

11 Joseph Jomo Pierre, *Shakespeare's Nigga* (Toronto: Canada Playwrights Press, 2013).

12 Nixon, "Caribbean and African Appropriations," 561.

13 Zabus, *Tempests*, 2.

14 My reading of Pierre's revision is indebted to Loomba's analysis of the politics of race and gender in Shakespeare.

15 Ania Loomba, *Gender, Race, Renaissance Drama* (Delhi: Oxford University Press, 1992), 145.

16 Joanne Tompkins, "Re-citing Shakespeare in Post-colonial Drama," *Essays in Theatre* 15, no. 1 (1996): 20.

17 Pierre, *Shakespeare's Nigga*, 63.

18 "Joseph Jomo Pierre on 'Shakespeare's Nigga': The Blacker the Berry, the Deeper the Bruise," Obsidian Theatre Company, accessed 18 April 2016, http://obsidiantheatre.blogspot.co.uk/2011/12/joe-pierre-on-shakespeares-nigga.html.

19 Pierre, *Shakespeare's Nigga*, 14.

20 Ibid., 42.

21 Sonnet 130.

22 Sonnet 127.

23 Sonnet 132.

24 Pierre, *Shakespeare's Nigga*, 47.

25 Ibid., n.p.

26 Obsidian Theatre Company, "Joseph Jomo Pierre," n.p.

27 Pierre, *Shakespeare's Nigga*, 41.

28 Ibid., 48.

29 Ibid., 41.

30 Obsidian Theatre Company, "Joseph Jomo Pierre," n.p.

31 Taken from 5.1.126–42.

32 Pierre, *Shakespeare's Nigga*, 35.

33 Taken from 2.2.73–87.

34 Taken from 3.1.55–63.

35 Pierre, *Shakespeare's Nigga*, scene 13.

36 Markaryk, "Introduction," 37.

37 Celeste-Marie Bernier, *Characters of Blood: Black Heroism in the Transatlantic Imagination* (Charlottesville: University of Virginia Press, 2012), 20.

38 Lamming, *The Pleasures of Exile*, 98.

39 James W. Coleman, *Black Male Fiction and the Legacy of Caliban* (Lexington: The University Press of Kentucky, 2012), 3.

40 Ibid., 3–4.

41 Obsidian Theatre Company, "Joseph Jomo Pierre," n.p.

42 Pierre, *Shakespeare's Nigga*, 7.

43 Ibid., 8.

44 Ibid., 13.

45 Ibid., 17.

46 Ibid., 18.

47 Ibid., 44.

48 Taken from 3.2.193.

49 Loomba, *Gender, Race, Renaissance Drama*, 53.

50 Wynter, "Afterword," 361.

51 Pierre, *Shakespeare's Nigga*, 42.

52 Ibid, 30.

53 Ibid, 16.

54 Ibid, 17.

55 Taken from 5.1.275.

56 Pierre, *Shakespeare's Nigga*, 19.

57 Ibid., 21.

58 Ibid., 39.

59 Ibid., 48.

60 Loomba, *Gender, Race, Renaissance Drama*, 47.

61 Pierre, *Shakespeare's Nigga*, 36.

15

Building Black and Indigenous Alliances for HIV Prevention and Health Promotion

Ciann L. Wilson, Sarah Flicker, and Jean-Paul Restoule

This chapter begins by contextualizing the history of relationships between African diasporic and Indigenous peoples in the Americas within the Euro-Western colonial project. Forced together through the appropriation of land and slavery, the relationships between Indigenous and African diasporic people is complex. Euro-Western ideas of racial formation, theological and biological determinism prescribed the subordination of these communities to the status of animalized beings. The results of these similar and yet different forms of colonialism have left African diasporic and Indigenous peoples at risk for poor indicators of health and wellbeing. However, these communities have exhibited tremendous resilience and strength, often leaning upon each other in different ways to navigate and survive white settlerism. Tracing the potential for solidarity building in critical resistance movements within and between Indigenous and Black communities, both historically (such as the people power movements of the sixties and seventies) and in the contemporary moment (such as the Idle No More and Black Lives Matter movements), this discussion posits that such alliances are integral to defeating white supremacy and colonialism. These cross-community alliances are also integral to efforts to reaffirm Indigenous and African diasporic health, humanism, freedom, and possible futures.

In this chapter we argue that there are commonalities and a long history of solidarity between Black and Indigenous communities when it comes to antiracist and anticolonial struggle throughout the history of the Americas. However, there are also considerable differences and historically and spatially produced tensions that we propose may be creative sites for growth and meaningful relationship building. Understanding the history of relations between African diasporic and Indigenous communities over the centuries helps to frame the potential for solidarity organizing. It also helps to support partnerships aimed at combatting colonial violence and the resulting health ills such as HIV within Black, Indigenous, and Black-Indian communities. We begin by providing a history of racial formation in the Americas, which informs racial hierarchy and examines the way Black and Indigenous peoples have been treated (i.e., enslavement and genocide) within settler states like Canada. We then demonstrate the health implications of dehumanizing racial formations for Black and Indigenous peoples, specifically when it comes to HIV vulnerability. We go on to name and problematize the long history of critical resistance struggles forged in partnerships between Black and Indigenous communities as examples of the potential for such timely alliances in the HIV response. Finally, we highlight the tensions between antiracist and anticolonial aims, landing on the position that alliances between Indigenous and Black communities in the twenty-first century must be simultaneously antiracist and decolonial in order to dismantle the public health hazard that is the white supremacist apparatus.

THE EXPERIENCES OF BLACK AND INDIGENOUS COMMUNITIES IN THE AMERICAS

Race Making and Defining the "Other"

In providing an adequate understanding of how relationships between Indigenous and African diasporic peoples have developed in the Americas, it is important to understand how these two groups were racially defined and ultimately dehumanized within the colonial project. Post-contact in the Americas, racial classifications were applied by European colonizers to hierarchically organize the peoples brought together through the experience of colonization.[1] These hierarchal models perpetuated the Euro-Western view that superior traits were specific to "whiteness" and negative or inferior traits were linked to the peoples of "other" racial groups – where the darker the tone of one's skin pigmentation, the less evolved, more inferior, and animal-like they were.[2] In this hierarchical schema, whiteness marked the measure of humanity, racial superiority, desirability, privilege.[3] By contrast, non-European "others" were often labelled barbaric savages and were deemed gluttonous, stupid, aggressive, immoral, and irrational – the degenerate remnants of less endowed primitive beings in the linear evolutionary development of the white man, the ultimate developmental goal in the Great Chain of Being.[4] This ideology made possible the display of Indigenous peoples from around the world (i.e., Austral-Asia, Africa, and the Americas) in popular zoos and exhibitions, which lasted into the late fifties.[5] These exhibitions dubbed "Negro Villages" displayed more than four hundred Indigenous peoples from "Nubians" to Inuit for European entertainment, consumption, and exploration.[6]

Creating a racial hierarchy and defining the "other" – the Native, the African, the Asian – was a central project for the colonizer because naming the "other" was an act of discursive separation that created the "material boundaries of whiteness."[7] The very existence of settler societies was dependant on "maintaining racial apartheid" and the "impermeable" boundaries of white settler society, protecting it and the resources garnered through colonial processes from infiltration by Black and Brown peoples.[8] Such apartheid often translated into the geographic containment (i.e. reservations, housing projects, etc.) as well as militarized control, and surveillance of racialized "others."

The designation of groups of racialized people as separate from and inferior to white society, created conditions in which there were no limits to the forms of violence inflicted upon colonized peoples. At the advent of conquest, Indigenous communities faced bouts of germ warfare caused by the introduction of foreign-borne communicable diseases by colonialists. These sometimes accidental, but more often than not intentionally, brought ailments [i.e. diseases] claimed the lives of millions of Indigenous people and contributed to the destruction of "one quarter of the earth's population within a 150 year" period. It is the largest genocide the world has ever known.[9] It is estimated that only 2–5 per cent of the roughly 70–100 million Indigenous peoples of present-day North and South America survived,[10] making this relatively small group of survivors the direct ancestors of all Indigenous peoples in the Americas today.[11] These biological assaults were, in turn, succeeded by state policies that controlled Indigenous bodies and excluded them from white settler societies.

The trade of African peoples was yet another colonial act of genocide. Stolen from their native lands, traded, bred, and regarded as chattel,[12] African peoples have long been targets of subjugation by colonialists and Western institutions. It is estimated that as many as twenty million Black people were taken from Africa during the era of the transatlantic slave trade and another forty million perished in miserable conditions at sea.[13] These peoples came from all regions of Africa and from many nations including the "Yoruba, Kissi, Senefu, Foulah, Fons, Adjas and many others."[14] The slave trade was a holocaust spanning five centuries, from the 1400s to the 1800s.[15] Unique in its global scale and focus on race, the slave trade

utilized African peoples as the free labour for the Western world's development, which has since shaped global economic relations.[16]

The involvement of the British colony Canada in the slave trade spans
four hundred years. Canada was a major supplier of food and lumber for
slave ships that voyaged throughout the Atlantic.[17] However, it wasn't until
1628 that Canada was formally incorporated into the slave trade of the
British North American empire. In 1685 slavery also became a part of cus-
tomary practice in New France. France[18] gave colonists of New France
permission to keep Black and Indigenous[19] slaves in response to a supposed
agricultural labour shortage. Ostensibly, this slavery would allow Canada
to outcompete with their neighbours in present-day New England.[20] By the
mid-1500s colonists across the British North American empire developed a
special appetite for Black slaves from Africa and the Caribbean. Slaves died
young; they were literally worked to death. For Pawnees "the average age
was 17.7 years, for Black slaves it was 25.2 years."[21] In 1701, slavery was
officially authorized in Canada by King Louis XIV.[22] Slavery took off in
urban centres, where 77 per cent of all enslaved people resided, 52 per cent
of whom resided in Montreal.[23] Slaves were not only owned by individual
farmers but by the social elite of Canadian society, including merchants and
government officials; slaves were even held by the Christian churches.[24]

SYSTEMIC VIOLENCE AND THE HEALTH AND HUMANITY
OF AFRICAN DIASPORIC AND INDIGENOUS PEOPLES

The genocide and enslavement of Indigenous peoples from around the world
was justified by the pseudoscience of racial hierarchy and political theories
about racial separation.[25] These frameworks of thinking about the human
and the non-human have permeated all realms of Western thought and have
grave implications for scientific rationalism. There is a long history of
scientific and biomedical practice (e.g., craniology, anthropology, physiology,
etc.) that helped to demarcate certain groups of people as "irrational,"
"undesirable," "defective," and "devoid of humanity." If certain peoples
could be "scientifically" proven to be lesser beings of a different species then
no ethical dilemma prohibited their exclusion or torture for scientific and
medical "advancement." The murder, sexual exploitation, displacement,
and erasure of entire groups of colonized peoples from human history
became normalized through this logic.[26] As a result, there are countless
instances of institutional racism, ill-intentioned health research, and
state-sanctioned attempts to control and dishonour Black and Indigenous
bodies. Some examples include the history of biological and germ warfare

on Indigenous communities since the dawn of conquest in the Americas;[27] the racist depictions of Indigenous peoples from around the globe in orientalist anthropological research; the purposeful withholding of treatment from Black men with syphilis in the Tuskegee trials;[28] and the sterilization of Black and Indigenous women.[29] In turn, these experiences have cultivated within Black and Indigenous communities immense distrust of and dissatisfaction with government, research, and healthcare institutions.[30]

The impact of colonial processes (i.e., discrimination, racism, systemic violence, and so on) have continued to foster the spread of many diseases including HIV/AIDS – a harbinger for inequity – in Black and Indigenous communities.[31] HIV may indeed be the biological expression of social inequities. As one of us has argued elsewhere:

> On a cellular and biomedical level, a metaphorical relationship between HIV and colonization can be made. In the early days of the HIV epidemic, contraction of the virus meant certain death. Left untreated, the virus works to stage a full scale attack on the body's foundational building blocks – DNA. In other words, the virus colonizes the very machinery of the cell, appropriating this machinery to reproduce itself. On a social level, the colonial underpinnings of HIV is demonstrated in that the virus is a symptom of inequity, stigma and the material breakdown of our most intimate human relationships, including the relationship with one's own body.[32]

Much research supports the fact that HIV's transmissibility is structured not by the "deviant" behaviours that people engage in but by the unequal and violent conditions in which they are forced to live, which weakens their immune response and their body's ability to fight infection.[33] Indigenous and ecological models on the social determinants of health have demonstrated that health is inseparable from experiences of intergenerational trauma and colonial violence such as the deterritorialization and exploitation outlined in earlier sections of this discussion. These are important factors for understanding the health outcomes and wellbeing of African diasporic and Indigenous peoples.[34] For instance, a conversation about the rampant spread of HIV within Black communities is inseparable from a conversation about how little control enslaved men and women had over their sexual and reproductive lives. Rape and sexual violence became a normalized part of the lives of African women, who were permitted little to no autonomy in choosing their sexual partners. Meanwhile, the advertisement of physical strength and sexuality of enslaved African men constituted one of the earliest forms of sex trafficking across the Caribbean islands and the American South. These men were traded and forced to breed with African women with the aim of creating superior slaves able to withstand the brute force and cruelty they would be subjected to at the hands of slave masters. These colonial practices continue to reverberate throughout the sexual cultures of the African diaspora, and this has direct implications for the spread of HIV in these communities.

Over the past three decades, HIV/AIDS has increasingly become a feminized, racialized, and marginalized disease, following lines of existing inequity. Globally, as well as within the Canadian context, Indigenous peoples are disproportionately infected with and affected by HIV. More[35] than seventy thousand people are living with HIV in Canada[36] and the over-representation of Indigenous and African, Caribbean and/or Black (ACB) Canadians in the HIV/AIDS epidemic has been well documented in national and provincial HIV statistics. In the Canadian context, Indigenous communities account for 4.3 per cent of the Canadian population and yet account for 21.2 per cent of the reported HIV cases in 2016.[37] Similarly, African, Caribbean, and Black communities account for 2.9 per cent of the country's population and yet account for 21.9 per cent of the reported HIV cases in 2016.[38] These numbers increase when the intersections of gender and age are considered, with Indigenous and Black women and youth being disproportionately impacted.

Today, Indigenous and Black communities remain amongst the most socially, politically, and economically marginalized in Canada.[39] As such, HIV vulnerability is not merely the accidental result of the "colour-blind" forces of social inequality, it is the direct consequence of intersectional oppression, anti-Black racism and Indigenous erasure within a system of white supremacist violence, which structures the conditions for those able to survive and those who die.[40] White supremacy and colonialism are public health hazards.[41]

Leadership and Alliance Building Across Difference

At the dawn of the HIV epidemic in the early eighties, dissent and confrontational resistance was integral for garnering attention to the threat HIV/AIDS posed within marginalized communities.[42] However, "programmatic (economic, biomedical, technological, and pharmacological) interventions" have since dominated HIV prevention, treatment and care, which privileges particular ways of knowing and doing, such as positivist science and individual behaviour models and interventions.[43] This silences activism and the importance of community-based approaches.[44] These institutions and structures have "become increasingly professionalized," bureaucratic spaces that are often engaged in "complex relationships with state funders" who have neoliberal interests and limit radical advocacy and resistance within the political climate of HIV.[45] Programmatic strategies cannot account for, and therefore do not address, all of the injustices and forms of structural violence that drive new HIV infections[46] within African diasporic and Indigenous communities. Community mobilization sheds light on the far-reaching impact of social, political, and economic domination and cultural genocide, as well as the limitations and inadequacies of individual behavioural models of "risk."[47] As such, naming the long history of relationships[48] between Black and Indigenous communities is important for contextualizing and inspiring community-based responses to the HIV epidemic.

There are many Indigenous cultural symbols from North America and continental Africa that encourage partnership building. For instance, for some Indigenous cultures, the medicine wheel is used to symbolize the role of every race of people in the circle of life and the creation of a balanced universe. Inherent to these traditional teachings of the medicine wheel is the importance of working together. The Two Row Wampum agreement is another cultural tool used historically to symbolize treaty relationships, "peace, friendship and respect" between settlers and the Haudenosaunee.[49] The images intricately beaded into wampum belts often depict "revolutionary notions of respectful co-existence,"[50] stewardship of the land, and cooperation with settlers.[51] A parallel term from South Africa that symbolizes the values of interconnection, interdependence and humanity is "Ubuntu" which means, "I exist because you exist." This anti-individualistic philosophy links individual survival to group survival and humanism, the "morality of co-operation, compassion, communalism and concern for the interests of the collective."[52] Likewise, the West African Adinkra symbol, Nkonsonkonson represents unity, responsibility, human relationships, and interdependence. Its literal interpretation means "we are linked together like a chain; we are linked in life; we are linked in death."[53] In this, "the unity of community can be realized if citizens see themselves as responsible to each other."[54] These terms and discourses from Indigenous cultures around the world depict worldviews and ontologies centred on relationship building, interdependence, and interconnections.[55]

Unsurprisingly social movements within Indigenous and African diasporic communities in the Americas have historically informed and inspired each other. For instance, enslaved African people joined the communities of Indigenous Caribs on the island of St Vincent, who waged the First Carib War of 1773 and greatly reduced European control of their territory.[56]

Similarly, slaves of both Indigenous Taíno and African ancestry played a central role in the Haitian revolution of 1791.[57] Integral to the Haitian revolution were Taíno and African spiritual practices and belief systems such as Voudou.[58] The Black power movement led by the Black Panther Party throughout the 1960s caused ripples in the social structure of American society, exemplifying the power in numbers and the power of organized social action in combatting injustice and a militarized state. In 1968 the American Indian Movement (AIM) was formed and took inspiration from the Civil Rights Struggles and the Black Panthers in their organization against police violence, racism, and poverty.[59] Lee Maracle[60] highlights how the Black Power movement and the work of Franz Fanon inspired the Red power[61] movement, the Yellow power movement, and people power movements across the Americas (e.g., the Chicano and Puerto Rican liberation movements[62]) and around the world (e.g., the spread of the Black power movement to Indigenous communities in Austral-Asia, South America, and continental Africa).[63] In Indigenous protests, such as the Caledonia land dispute, Black communities were often the biggest allies who were the first to arrive in support of Indigenous communities.[64] A more recent example of this is the support offered by the Black Lives Matter Toronto chapter for the Indigenous youth of the Attawapiskat community who have demanded recreational resources, educational, and employment opportunities in the wake of alarming youth suicide rates.[65] Scholar Andrea Smith has argued that Indigenous movements weren't just inspired by Black movements; they were dependant on them.[66]

When it comes to HIV specifically, some racialized and Indigenous scholars have framed advocacy and programming within larger conversations about racism and colonization, due to their unbridled impact on HIV transmission and the sexual cultures and health of these communities.[67] Further, racialized communities have long advocated for the importance of contextualizing the disease within anti-racist and anti-colonial struggles.[68] In Toronto, ethnospecific AIDS Service Organizations such as the Black Coalition for AIDS Prevention (Black CAP), "emerged out of community-based struggles to respond in culturally appropriate ways to the mounting crisis of HIV in the 1980s."[69] They were formed as "safe houses" where racialized people could find mutual support, belonging, and culturally appropriate services along the axes of race, sexuality, and health. They aimed to disrupt the "ubiquitous whiteness" within the AIDS service sector;[70] provide culturally and linguistically relevant health promotion messaging; and foster spaces for sexual health services "for people of colour by people of colour."[71]

Indigenous activists in the US and Canada have conceptualized HIV and AIDS vulnerability in a similarly holistic way as the result of colonization, which has had unbridled impact on Indigenous sexual cultures, public health, and spiritual and traditional life.[72] Indigenous-led AIDS activism has stressed Indigenous control and management of health systems, culturally sensitive programming, and "access to their own languages" and traditions to "address the physical, social, mental, emotional and spiritual dimensions of health" that are necessary to prevent HIV.[73] Organizations such as the Native Youth Sexual Health Network (NYSHN) focus on sexual and reproductive health in a holistic way to include culture and traditional ceremony and healing practices, environmental justice, cultural survival, Indigenous sovereignty, self-determination, human rights, and arts activism. The NYSHN has also built alliances across community boundaries with communities of colour and various Indigenous groups in Australia and South Africa, broadening the scope of how HIV is understood within Indigenous communities around the world. Similarly, in an effort to challenge colonial sexual cultures, a transnational Indigenous partnership formed at the Indigenous People's Summit of the 2006 International AIDS Conference (IAC), which resulted in the formulation of the Toronto Charter: Indigenous People's Action Plan on HIV/AIDS. The Toronto charter is aimed at holding settler states (Canada, US, New Zealand, and Australia) responsible for the ill health effects of colonization and to affirm Indigenous self-determination over "all aspects of their lives" and health.[74]

Tensions in Solidarity

Indigenous anticolonial theorists and critical race scholars and activists have raised questions about the potential for alliance building across communities from different political frameworks. Some scholars question the anticolonial and decolonial politics of diasporic people of colour living in white settler colonies.[75] Key tensions surround whether or not people of colour are settlers, what is their place in the structure of white settler colonialism, and what kinds of anti- and decolonial alliances can they form with Indigenous peoples in the context of white settler colonies. Some scholarship suggests that anti-racism, much like other leftist narratives or social justice frameworks, "compartmentalize Indigenous struggle," subsuming Indigenous peoples into broader discourse about systemic oppression.[76] The contention here is that these frameworks often render Native peoples a racial or "ethnic group suffering racial discrimination" that coincides with that of all people of colour, rather than diverse and sovereign "nations undergoing colonization."[77]

Lawrence and Dua, in their article "Decolonizing Antiracism,"[78] critique the antiracist movement and affiliated scholars for failing to ground their criticisms in the original and ongoing colonial violence against Indigenous peoples of the lands they now occupy. They argue that antiracist theory and practice uphold and sustain colonial discourse and that people of colour are complicit in ongoing processes of settler colonialism and nation building by participating in practices such as the erasure of Indigenous presence through theories of race and racism that exclude Indigenous peoples, some of whom may not visibly "pass" as racialized. People of colour are also accused of focusing on the history of slavery, which in antiracist scholarship seems to take priority over Indigenous experiences of colonization and perpetuates colonial violence.[79] For instance, African Americans fight for civil rights, humanism, and inclusion within the laws, economies, and institutions of the very colonial settler state responsible for their oppression.[80] In this, the colonial "promise of integration and civil rights is predicated on securing a share of settler-appropriated," capitalist wealth and citizenship[81] as the solution to colonial violence.[82] The position here is that critical race scholars overlook the fact that Native genocide and settler colonialism are not only historic but ongoing processes. Because race scholars lack an analysis of settler colonialism, many critical race theorists do not imagine alternative forms of governance not founded on the pillars of the nation state.[83]

Critical race scholars have challenged Dua and Lawrence by critiquing their conflation of settler colonialism, with forced migration (e.g., slavery) and immigration – which in some cases have been linked to Indigenous participation in the Euro-Western military industrial complex.[84] They argue that scholars such as Dua and Lawrence ignore the role of globalization, Western imperialism and slavery in the disenfranchisement of Black-led nations around the world, which contributes to the forced transnational migration of people of colour from war-torn and impoverished nations. Proponents question the relevance of a decolonial logic and project in contexts where displaced people struggle to make their colonization visible[85] – a point which complicates Lawrence and Dua's tendency to conflate people of colour as an uncontested part of white settler society.[86] Secondly, "settlers are not immigrants."[87] Immigrants lead diasporic lives and are "beholden to the Indigenous laws and epistemologies of the lands they migrate to. Settlers become the law, supplanting Indigenous" governance structures, autonomy, and history.[88] Throughout the history of the United States and Canada, even being granted immigrant status was often "conditioned by race."[89] In many cases racialized people face temporary, refugee or migrant workers status and are thus subject to deportation. This precariousness and disposability furthers the settler colonial project.[90] Further, for many Black people in particular, they are not afforded humanity, autonomy, or sovereignty in the way whites are and are thus landless and selfless property who have no stake in conversations about land ownership.[91] As such, uniformly applying the term "settler" to refer to people of colour – and more specifically Black people – projects whiteness and white settler colonial responsibility and guilt onto bodies of colour, thereby presuming "post-racialism"[92] and erasing the significance of race and "the white supremacist violence of anti-blackness."[93]

Third, critical race scholars critique Indigenous scholars for overlooking the fact that while in the United States slavery and anti-Black racism have signified white supremacy, in the Canadian context white supremacy is signified by the colonial dispossession of Indigenous peoples.[94] Canada has ignored and erased its long-standing relationship to anti-Blackness and slavery. This has resulted in a singular and strategic project by the nation state of aspirations for pseudo Indigenous solidarity, while "casting Black peoples ... as secondary and irrelevant to the colonization of Indigenous peoples."[95] "By insisting that the moral claims" of Aboriginal communities are central, "the claims of others are rendered as peripheral to the realization of decolonization."[96] The project of decolonization is posited to have community-specific, nationalistic and geographic boundaries. To build on this point, a further criticism is that Lawrence and Dua perpetuate xenophobia and racism,[97] positioning the racialized migrant in competition with the Native for recognition by settler states and the allotment of scarce resources presumed to "properly belong to the Native."[98] Antiracist scholars argue that the expansion of the category of "settler colonizer" in Indigenous nationalistic projects to include unwanted "foreigners" is neo-racist because it discourages the mixing of different cultures. This framework is anti-miscegenist because it denies the numerous past and present alliances and relationships across Native and non-Native divides; it also perpetuates colonial definitions of Indigeneity.[99] In this view, "different" people are presumed to belong in their "own place," which coincides with the arbitrary territorial borders drawn up by colonial powers and which are intermeshed within global capitalist hierarchies.[100] A good example of the inherent tensions of these aims is the fact that a quarter of migrants to the United States are from Mexico and are thus "Indigenous."[101] The territories were not historically limited by the US-Mexico or North American–South American border. However, some Native American groups view the "transnational migration" of Mexican peoples as conflicting with their aims[102] and the racism and xenophobia faced by many southern American people within the United States remains a struggle that has been largely ignored in Indigenous sovereignty movements in North America.

Antiracist scholars critique Indigenous nationalist movements for being unable to realize the aims of decolonization because "their struggles for visibility have to overcome a number of "conceptual blockages" associated with an inclination to separate "First" and "Third" World anticolonial struggles and their inclination to become recognized (and funded) by settler states in ways that relegate them to the status of a "racial minority," which does not allow for Indigenous sovereignty and autonomy.[103] This politics of recognition then presumes the continuance and governance of the settler state and narrowly defines Indigenous struggle as merely claims to a "special status."[104] Even within the Red Power movement, scholars and activists "did not question the existence, legitimacy" or the political, economic, and white supremacist organization of the Americas.[105] Further, critical race scholars argue that Indigenous movements often replace the settler with "elite Natives" (those who already have concentrated power) rather than transform that world and the relations (racial and otherwise) therein. In turn, this has shaped how Indigenous movements, spaces, and alliances are imagined or enclosed.[106]

These antiracist arguments have stirred counter-responses from Indigenous studies scholars, who posit that the term "settler" does include people of colour, even those from other colonial contexts. In this view, dispossessed people brought onto seized Indigenous land through other colonial projects (e.g. enslavement, military recruitment, low wage-migrant labour recruitment, displacement/coerced immigration) "still occupy and settle on stolen land," contributing to Indigenous subjugation and erasure.[107] The ability to immigrate and "settle in a new place,"[108] even when it is against one's own will, is premised on colonial structures that dispossess Indigenous peoples of their territories and claims to nationhood.[109] Proponents of this argument highlight that Indigenous people have had to contend with genocidal colonialism by various White, Black, and even Creole nationalist projects.[110] They argue that settler colonialism is a "structure not an event" that can incorporate people of colour in processes of colonial dispossession.[111] Proponents argue that antiracist scholars deny and depoliticize the difference between Indigenous peoples and people of colour, much like they conflate the difference between racism and colonialism.[112] As a result, this establishes the imperialistic aim of naturalizing the erasure of Native selfhood, which is the basis for settlement on Indigenous territory.[113] The lack of acknowledgement of this is in itself genocidal and "resistant to decolonization."[114] Further, some scholars have highlighted that Indigenous nationalist organizing focuses less on migrant exclusion and land ownership and much more on the transformative relationships between Indigenous people and land.[115] "Consequently, the migrant is not the problem" but rather, migration and the movement of people of colour can occur only "through processes of land commodification,"[116] white supremacist capitalism and regulation by a global web of interconnected nation-states and corporations in the service of settler colonialism.[117]

In response to these tensions between antiracist and Indigenous studies scholars, Lee Maracle and Andrea Smith argue that white supremacy benefits from the colonial project to divide and conquer through state-imposed policies and structures (i.e., scarce funding allocations and social supports) that encourage marginalized communities to splinter and inflict violence on one another.[118] There is much historical evidence to suggest this divide and conquer approach, as European colonialists lived in growing fear of an alliance between Indigenous and enslaved Black people.[119] Colonialists provided incentives for some Indigenous communities to round up runaway Black slaves (i.e., members of the Cherokee nation and other tribes in the Southeastern US), they threatened Indigenous groups who formed partnerships with slaves, and recruited African Americans for military campaigns against Indian nations in the US.[120]

Other challenges to solidarity building include the fact that most Indigenous and African, Caribbean, and Black communities are constantly in survival mode, concerned about the next paycheque, putting food on the table, having shelter, and so on. These everyday concerns of maintaining resources for survival debilitate their ability to reach across community lines. Secondly, a true testament to the effectiveness of the colonial project in the Americas is the ignorance among the majority of African diasporic people of the Indigenous cultures in Africa (and elsewhere) from which they hail and the impact of colonialism on their lived realities.[121] Lawrence and Dua write that non-Natives, including people of colour, are reluctant to acknowledge the ongoing colonial project and the fact that although we all share the same land base (i.e., the Americas), we have materially different relationships to this land and the terms on which we occupy it.[122] Some of this reluctance is also indicative of the project of erasure of Indigenous presence in wider Canadian society.

There also remains racism and segregationist ideologies within both Black and Aboriginal communities that prevent alliance building. This is because, although Black and Indigenous peoples share a similar history of being colonized peoples, these different groups have different experiences of white supremacy, are pitted in competition with each other for scarce government resources, and in one way or another contribute to the oppression of the other.[123] Smith has argued that there is insufficient dialogue between anti-racist and Indigenous thinkers and organizers. As a result, scholars and activists engaged in race struggles fail to pay attention to how settler colonialism intersects with white supremacy in the Americas.[124] Meanwhile, Indigenous struggles fail to pay attention to the importance of race and white supremacy within a decolonization framework. Without a critique of the settler state as simultaneously white supremacist and racist, all "settlers" become "morally undifferentiated," irrespective of the fact that migration is racially differentiated.[125] Thus, on either side of the conversation, both Black and Indigenous people can "recapitulate the logics of white supremacy even as they contest it."[126]

For Smith, white supremacy is upheld by separate and distinct but interrelated logics that she dubs "pillars," namely, slavery/anti-Black racism, which anchors capitalism; genocide, which anchors colonialism; and orientalism, which anchors war.[127] Smith posits that within white supremacy, racial Blackness becomes a necessary condition for enslaveability.[128] The logic of genocide holds that Indigenous peoples must disappear and must "always be disappearing" in order to enable non-Indigenous people's legitimate inheritance and ownership of land within the nation-state.[129] The logic of orientalism marks "other" peoples or nations as inferior and deems them a permanent, foreign "threat to the wellbeing of the empire."[130] Smith argues that we are all differently oppressed in relation to white supremacy, while at the same time participating in it from points of difference and through anti-racist and anticolonial struggle.[131] For instance, all non-Native people are able to "join the colonial project of settling on Indigenous lands" (i.e., the Indigenous-settler binary)[132]; owning property; accumulating wealth and aspiring for their share of settler appropriated wealth – i.e., the "American dream." Meanwhile, "all non-Black peoples are promised that if they comply, they will not be at the bottom of the racial hierarchy" and will not be a commodity, devoid of humanity and autonomy.[133] Importantly, these categories are not mutually exclusive and an individual can occupy more than one pillar. Further, these pillars are not equitable to each other. "Blackness is neither reducible to Indigenous land, nor is Indigeneity to enslaved labour."[134] It is important to conceptualize white supremacy as simultaneously operating through these multiple logics, which are in a dialectical relationship with each other,[135] rather than through any single logic because there are inherent problems with any "totalizing approach" to accounting for the difference between anti-Blackness or Indigeneity in settler colonies.[136]

Possibilities for Collaboration

Today, we see the heightening of consciousness raising and transnational social movements in the form of protests against anti-Black racism, racial profiling, and police brutality (e.g., Black Lives Matter), which challenges stereotypes of Black people as sites of imminent danger, risk and criminality.[137] The contemporary moment has also been marked by the appropriation of Black and Indigenous cultures (e.g., Indigenous mascots in sports), as well as decades-long campaigns about Indigenous self-determination and rightful ownership of land (e.g., the Idle No More movement) and the truth and reconciliation process for holding the state accountable for the atrocities committed on Indigenous bodies and territories.[138] "There is a spirit of outrage within Black and Indigenous communities towards a colonial system designed to destroy Black and Indigenous love and humanity."[139] The fight for Indigenous and Black humanism is an anticolonial project and important site of co-resistance connected to struggles against racialized poverty and health disparities such as that exhibited in the HIV epidemic.[140]

The HIV response has focused primarily on a state-funded treatment and prevention apparatus that has emphasized a biomedical model, which individualizes risk as a consequence of personal behaviour.[141] This approach has ignored the social determinants of HIV and injustice, and has disregarded co-resistance and activism as integral parts of the HIV response.[142] It is worthwhile to spend some time unpacking what decolonizing cross-community collaborations might entail.

In his paper titled "Decolonization and the pedagogy of solidarity," Gaztambide-Fernández reflects on three shared features of most definitions of solidarity, namely "solidarity always implies a relationship among individuals or groups, whether as a way to understand what brings people together for civic or political action."[143] Second, solidarity implies an obligation to what is "just or equitable."[144] This can include a "notion of human rights, a social contract" or struggles against oppression.[145] A pedagogy of solidarity must begin from the premise that the process is uneasy, unsettled, and even tension-filled. It "neither reconciles present grievances nor forecloses future conflict."[146] Third, solidarity always implies a set of responsibilities or "duties between those in the solidarity relationship" (e.g., treat others as you would like to be treated).[147]

Within a decolonizing framework, genuine collaboration begins by acknowledging that different groups of people have varied relationships to the white supremacist apparatus. Strategic alliances are not solely based on similarities and shared victimization because these differing relations to white supremacy are not equal or equitable to each other.[148] Counter to our neoliberally informed culture of individualism and self-interest, collaborations entail reimagining human interactions premised on the relationship between difference and interdependence.[149] This entails organizing to combat the ways we are each complicit in the oppression of each other.[150]

One proposed approach is to focus on creating a "decolonizing treaty" by turning from an understanding of treaty as a historical artefact toward an understanding of a treaty as a decolonizing process of making and keeping good relations, where power is negotiated.[151] It is to centre relationality between land, environment, people, and the state.[152] Such a relational solidarity demands that we recognize the complex and sometimes contradictory personal histories that bring us together. It is to conceptualize a common destiny where the formerly separated "races" of the world have been brought together in the epicentre of exhaustive diversity to transform social structures based on altruism," beyond the boundaries of the nation-state.[153] It entails an active orientation towards others. "To think of solidarity relationally is to ask the questions: how am I being made by others? and what are the consequences of my being on others?"[154]

Strategic alliances entail that each ally is accountable for their contribution to the oppression of others; responsive to the experiences, voices, needs, and political perspectives of others; acknowledges their stake in the struggles of the others; refrains from appropriating the voices of others; challenges colonial hierarchy; and decentres whiteness by generating theories and movements that humanize and centre Indigenous worldviews and the ties between Indigenous and racialized peoples.[155] The colonial system benefits from the fact that Black and Indigenous communities are in "perpetual states of crisis," compete for scarce resources, and struggle for daily survival.[156] These daily and more proximate battles must be taken into consideration to effectively organize co-resistance struggles between Indigenous and African diasporic communities.[157]

A decolonizing pedagogy of solidarity is the process through which we intend and create the conditions we want to live in and the social relations we wish to have.[158] This entails mutually interrogating how "stolen people (i.e., African diasporic people) on stolen land" can situate themselves in relation to Indigenous peoples who are "struggling to reclaim their relationships to that stolen land."[159] Decolonization is more than merely the liberation of "nations" along homogenous racialized and "ethnicized" boundaries.[160] Instead, decolonization consists of the liberation of people from hierarchical social relations within the larger system of globalized capitalism. Decolonization is the specific command to break the "settler colonial triad (settler, Native, slave) through the abolition of slavery in its contemporary forms,"[161] repatriation of Indigenous self-determination and land, and dismantling the imperial, raced, nationalized, capitalist, and heteropatriarchal divides that sustain the colonial project.[162]

The project of decolonization is not accountable to settlers. It cannot be "grafted" onto pre-existing "justice frameworks" (e.g., human rights, civil rights, or social justice)[163] nor can it recapitulate Western ideas of social change or "assimilationist models of liberal pluralism,"[164] whereby Indigenous and Black resistance is forced to fit within existing narratives of activism.[165] It must challenge the ideas and existence of the nation-state, imagining alliances and liberation within other possible worlds, outside of the confines of white supremacist settler states.[166]

Lastly, while there is a lot of money funnelled into the HIV surveillance and management apparatus, which focuses on the regulation of bodies and communities, there are very few resources to support critical resistance, confrontation, and civic engagement that disrupt structures of power.[167] Decolonizing alliances for HIV prevention may entail looking "beyond the non-profit and academic industrial complexes"[168] when doing decolonial organizing for Black and Indigenous communities around their health and wellbeing. Solidarity and relationship building free from state influences is after all, integral to self-determining liberation.

NOTES

1 Michael Banton, "The Idiom of Race," in *Theories of Race and Racism: A Reader*, ed. Les Back and John Solomos (New York: Routledge, 2000), 51–63; Vic Satzewich and Nikolaos Liodakis, *"Race" and Ethnicity in Canada* (New York: Oxford University Press, 2007); Audrey Smedley, "American Anthropological Association Statement on 'Race,'" American Anthropology Association, 1998, http://www.aaanet.org/stmts/racepp.htm; Eric R. Wolf, Joel S. Kahn, William Roseberry, and Immanuel Wallerstein, "Perilous Ideas: Race, Culture, People [and Comments and Reply]," *Current Anthropology* 35, no. 1 (February 1994): 1–12.

2 Satzewich and Liodakis, *"Race" and Ethnicity*.

3 Cheryl I. Harris, "Whiteness as Property," *Harvard Law Review* 106, no. 8 (1993): 1707–91; Chris Richardson, "'Canada's Toughest Neighbourhood': Surveillance, Myth and Orientalism in Jane–Finch" (MA thesis, Brock University, 2008), http://jane-finch.com/articles/files/Richardson_Thesis.pdf.

4 Alain F. Corcos, *The Myth of Human Races* (East Lansing: Michigan State University Press, 1997); Renisa Mawani, "In Between and Out of Place: Mixed-Race Identity, Liquor and the Law in British Columbia, 1850–1913," in *Race, Space and the Law: Unmapping a White Settler Society*, ed. Sherene Razzack (Toronto: Between the Lines, 2002), 47–69; Sherene Razack, "Introductions: Race Thinking and the Camp," in *Casting Out: The Eviction of Muslims from Western Law and Politics* (Toronto: University of Toronto Press, 2008), 3–22; Edward W. Said, *Orientalism* (New York: Vintage Books, 1979); Smedley, "American Anthropological Association Statement on 'Race'"; Wolf et al., "Perilous Ideas."

5 M.B. David, "Deep Racism: The Forgotten History Of Human Zoos," PopularResistance.org, 2013, https://www.popularresistance.org/deep-racism-the-forgotten-history-of-human-zoos.

6 Ibid.

7 Bonita Lawrence, *"Real" Indians and Others: Mixed-Blood Urban Native Peoples and Indigenous Nationhood* (Lincoln: University of Nebraska Press, 2004; Mawani, "In Between and Out of Place," 54.

8 Sut Jhally, Stuart Hall, and Media Education Foundation. "Race, the Floating Signifier," Media Education Foundation, 1996, https://www.youtube.com/watch?v=bMo2uiRAf3o; Bonita Lawrence, "Gender, Race, and the Regulation of Native Identity in Canada and the United States: An Overview," *Hypatia* 18, no. 2 (2003): 3–31, 8; Mawani, "In Between and Out of Place."

9 Zainab Amadahy and Bonita Lawrence, "Indigenous Peoples and Black People in Canada: Settlers or Allies?" In *Breaching the Colonial Contract*, ed. Arlo Kempf (Heidelberg: Springer, 2009), 105–36, 106; Ronald Wright, *Stolen Continents* (Toronto: Penguin Books Canada, 1993); Sylvia Wynter, "1492: A New World View," in *Race, Discourse, and the Origin of the Americas*, ed. Vera Lawrence Hyatt and Rex Nettleford (Washington: Smithsonian Institution Press, 1995).

10 Amadahy and Lawrence, "Indigenous Peoples."

11 Ibid.; Gord Hill, *500 Years of Indigenous Resistance* (Oakland: PM Press, 2009).

12 Afua Cooper, *The Hanging of Angélique: The Untold Story of Canadian Slavery and the Burning of Old Montreal* (New York: Harper Perennial, 2006).

13 Hill, *500 Years.*

14 Ibid., 37.

15 The Historica-Dominion Institute, "Black History Canada," retrieved 20 June 2015, from http://blackhistorycanada.ca/timeline.php?id=1600.

16 Amadahy and Lawrence, "Indigenous Peoples."

17 Cooper, *The Hanging of Angélique*; The Historica-Dominion Institute, "Black History Canada."

18 New France was the area of North America colonized by France from 1534–
    1763. It was part of the French-North American empire. The portion of New
    France that existed in present-day Canada had an expansive reach. New France
    spread (east to west) from the provinces we regard today as southern
    Saskatchewan and Manitoba to Newfoundland and Labrador, and (north to
    south) from the Hudson's Bay to the Great Lakes.

19 Members of the Pawnee Indian group or, as they were colloquially called,
    the Panis, were also enslaved alongside African peoples.

20 Cooper, *The Hanging of Angélique*; Mario Di Paolantonio, "Guarding and
    Transmitting the Vulnerability of the Historical Referent," *Philosophy of
    Education Archive* (1 June 2010): 129–37, https://educationjournal.web.illinois.
    edu/archive/index.php/pes/article/view/2690.pdf.

21 Cooper, *The Hanging of Angélique*, 81.

22 Cooper, *The Hanging of Angélique*.

23 Ibid.

24 Ibid.

25 L. Horne, "Real Human Being," *The New Inquiry*, 12 March 2015, http://the
    newinquiry.com/essays/real-human-being.

26 Smedley, "American Anthropological Association Statement on 'Race'"; Wolf et
    al., "Perilous Ideas."

27 Wright, *Stolen Continents*.

28 Vicki S. Freimuth, Sandra Crouse Quinn, Stephen B. Thomas, Galen Cole, Eric
    Zook, and Ted Duncan, "African Americans' Views on Research and the Tuskegee
    Syphilis Study," *Social Science & Medicine* 52 (2001): 797–808.

29 Anette J. Browne and Jo-Anne Fiske, "First Nations Women's Encounters with
    Mainstream Health Care Services," *Western Journal of Nursing Research* 23,
    no. 2 (2001): 126–47, https://doi.org/10.1177/019394590102300203; Hill,
    500 Years; Eve Tuck and K. Wayne Yang, "Decolonization is not a Metaphor,"
    Decolonization: Indigeneity, Education & Society 1, no. 1 (2012), http://
    decolonization.org/index.php/des/article/view/18630/15554.

30 Freimuth et al., "African Americans' Views"; Angela Robertson, "Who Feels It
    Knows the Challenges of HIV Prevention for Young Black Women in Toronto"
    (Toronto: Black Coalition for AIDS Prevention, 2007); Charmaine Williams, Peter
    A. Newman, Izumi Sakamoto, and Notisha A. Massaquoi, "HIV Prevention Risks
    for Black Women in Canada," *Social Science & Medicine* 68, no. 1 (2009): 12–20,
    https://doi.org/10.1016/j.socscimed.2008.09.043.

31 Adam M. Geary, *Antiblack Racism and the AIDS Epidemic: State Intimacies*
    (New York: Palgrave Macmillan, 2014).

32 Ciann L. Wilson, *Beyond the Colonial Divide: African Diasporic and Indigenous
    Youth Alliance Building for HIV Prevention* (Toronto: York University, 2016), 3.

33 Geary, *Antiblack Racism*; Juha Mikkonen and Dennis Raphael, *Social Determinants of Health The Canadian Facts* (Toronto: York University School of Health Policy and Management, 2010), https://thecanadianfacts.org/The_Canadian_Facts.pdf; Shawn Wilson, *Research Is Ceremony: Indigenous Research Methods* (Black Point, NS: Fernwood Publishing, 2008).

34 Geary, *Antiblack Racism*; Camara Phyllis Jones, "Invited Commentary: 'Race,' Racism, and the Practice of Epidemiology," *American Journal of Epidemiology* 154, no. 4 (2001): 299–304; Mikkonen and Raphael, *Social Determinants of Health*.

35 In the literature on HIV, an important distinction is made between those individuals living with the virus (people infected with HIV) and those individuals, such as family members, relatives, care providers etc., who are affected by the impact of living with (or without) and caring for someone living with HIV.

36 UNAIDS, "AIDS by the numbers," UNAIDS, 2014, retrieved June 2015, http://eprints.kmu.ac.ir/7876/1/JC2571_AIDS_by_the_numbers_en.pdf.

37 Public Health Agency of Canada, "HIV and AIDS in Canada: Surveillance Report to December 31st, 2013," retrieved 9 May 2015, http://www.phac-aspc.gc.ca/aids-sida/publication/survreport/2013/dec/index-eng.php; A.C. Bourgeois, M. Edmunds, A. Awan, L. Jonah, O. Varsaneux, and W. Siu. *HIV in Canada–Surveillance Report, 2016.* (2017).

38 Public Health Agency of Canada, "HIV and AIDS in Canada."

39 Robertson, "Who Feels It"; Audrey Steenbeek, Mark Tyndal, Richard Rothenberg, and Samuel Sheps, "Determinants of Sexually Transmitted Infections Among Canadian Inuit Adolescent Populations," *Public Health Nursing* 23, no. 6 (2006): 531–4, https://doi.org/10.1111/j.1525-1446.2006.00592.x; Williams et al., "HIV Prevention Risks."

40 Geary, *Antiblack Racism*.

41 Tuck and Yang, "Decolonization is not a Metaphor."

42 Adrian Guta, Stuart J. Murray, and Alexander McClelland, "Global AIDS Governance, Biofascism, and the Difficult Freedom of Expression," *APORIA: The Nursing Journal* 3, no. 4 (2011); Ciann L. Wilson, Sarah Flicker, Jean-Paul Restoule, and Ellis Furman, "Narratives of Resistance: (Re) Telling the Story of the HIV/AIDS Movement – Because the Lives and Legacies of Black, Indigenous, and People of Colour Communities Depend on It," *Health Tomorrow: Interdisciplinarity and Internationality Journal* 4, no. 1 (2016): 1–35.

43 Guta, Murray, and McClelland, "Global AIDS Governance," 15.

44 Guta, Murray, and McClelland, "Global AIDS Governance."

45 Ibid., 17.

46 Guta, Murray, and McClelland, "Global AIDS Governance."

47 Terry Mitchell and Dawn Maracle, "Healing the Generations," *Journal of Aboriginal Health* 2, no. 1 (2005): 14–25.

48 The relations between Indigenous and Black peoples in the Americas is historically and contemporarily fraught with complex commonalities, contradictions, and conflicts. While some Aboriginal people were enslaved along with Black people well into the nineteenth century (e.g., the Pawnee Indian nation and Indigenous peoples in California, Mexico, and the US South West), others aided the escape of slaves to lives of freedom within terrain unknown to colonialists (e.g., the Taíno of the Caribbean), adopted slaves into their family and community structures (e.g. the Iroquois Confederacy, Caribs, and Arawaks), and owned slaves themselves (e.g. the Natchez, Tawasa, Cherokee, Choctaw, and Chikasaw peoples, etc.). Cooper, *The Hanging of Angélique*; Circe Dawn Sturm, *Blood Politics: Race, Culture, and Identity in the Cherokee Nation of Oklahoma* (Berkeley and Los Angeles: University of California Press, 2002); Tuck and Yang, "Decolonization is not a Metaphor"; Rachel Beauvoir-Dominique, "Reclaiming Indigenous Heritage in Haiti: Our Taino Culture is Alive and Well," retrieved 9 September 2015, http://www.tainolegacies.com/154087477; Amadahy and Lawrence, "Indigenous Peoples"; James Brooks, *Confounding the Color Line: The Indian-Black Experience in North America* (Lincoln: University of Nebraska Press, 2002).

49 Harsha Walia, "Moving Beyond a Politics of Solidarity Towards a Practice of Decolonization," colorsofresistance.org, 2012, retrieved 25 June 2015, http://www.coloursofresistance.org/769/moving-beyond-a-politics-of-solidarity-towards-a-practice-of-decolonization.

50 Ibid.

51 Ibid.; Amadahy and Lawrence, "Indigenous Peoples."

52 J. Mokgoro, "Ubuntu and the Law in South Africa," presented at the Colloquium Constitution and Law, Potchefstroom, South Africa, 1997, 3.

53 R. Nana, "Village Rainbows: NKONSONKONSON – Unity and Human Relations," Village Rainbows, retrieved 5 January 2015, http://villagerainbows.com/cultural-troupe/nkonsonkonson-unity-and-human-relations.

54 Ibid.

55 Wilson, *Research Is Ceremony*.

56 Bernard Marshall, "The Black Caribs – Native Resistance to British Penetration into the Windward Side of St. Vincent 1763–1773," *Caribbean Quarterly* 19, no. 4 (1973): 4–19.

57 Hill, *500 Years*.

58 Beauvoir-Dominique, "Reclaiming."

59 Hill, *500 Years*.

60 Lee Maracle, "Red Power Legacies and Lives: An Interview by Scott Rutherford," in *New World Coming: The Sixties and the Shaping of Global Consciousness*, ed. Karen Dubinsky, Catherine Krull, Susan Lord, Sean Mills, and Scott Rutherford (Toronto: University of Toronto Press, 2010), 358–67.

61 European naturalists like Carolus Linnaeus defined the world's people using colour categories such as white for Europeans, yellow for Asians, black for Africans, and red for Native Americans. Importantly however, Indigenous people (especially those from the American Southeast) had long been using "redness" to define themselves according to their own creation stories of their origins from red clay, to distinguish themselves from Europeans who referred to themselves as white, and to remind Europeans of their social responsibilities to Indigenous peoples. Sturm, *Blood Politics*.

62 Hill, *500 Years*.

63 Maracle, "Red Power."

64 Paula Madden, "Indigenous/African Canadian Relations," presented at the Harriet's Legacies: Race, Historical Memory, and Futures in Canada, St Catharines, Ontario, 2015.

65 Chantal Da Silva, "Idle No More, Black Lives Matter Protesters Demand Action on Attawapiskat Suicide Crisis," CBC News, 13 April 2016, http://www.cbc.ca/news/canada/toronto/protesters-occupy-indigenous-northern-affairs-office-1.3533662.

66 Andrea Smith, "Relationships as Resistance: Dismantling Anti-Black Racism and Settler Colonialism," Plenary, Critical Ethnic Studies Association Conference, Toronto, Ontario, 30 April–3 May 2015.

67 Mikkonen and Raphael, *Social Determinants of Health*; Scott L. Morgenson, "Indigenous AIDS Organizing and the Anthropology of Activist Knowledge," *New Proposals: Journal of Marxism and Interdisciplinary Inquiry* 2, no. 2 (2009): 45–60; Robertson, "Who Feels It"; Leanne R. Simpson, "Anticolonial Strategies for the Recovery and Maintenance of Indigenous Knowledge," *The American Indian Quarterly* 28, no. 3 (2004): 373–84, https://doi.org/10.1353/aiq.2004.0107.

68 John Paul Catungal, "Ethno-specific Safe Houses in the Liberal Contact Zone: Race Politics, Place-making and the Genealogies of the AIDS Sector in Global-multicultural Toronto," *ACME: An International E-Journal for Critical Geographies* 12, no. 2 (2013): 250–78.

69 Ibid., 260.

70 Ibid., 258.

71 Ibid., 63.

72 Mikkonen and Raphael, *Social Determinants of Health*; Morgenson, "Indigenous AIDS"; Simpson, "Anticolonial Strategies"; Leanne Simpson, *Dancing on Our*

Turtle's Back: Stories of Nishnaabeg Re-creation, Resurgence and a New Emergence (Winnipeg: Arbeiter Ring Pub, 2011).

73 Morgenson, "Indigenous AIDS," 50.

74 The Toronto charter aims to: 1. Hold settler states, international bodies, and national and international law accountable for the effects of colonization and the fulfillment of treaty and constitutional obligations to the Indigenous peoples whose lands they occupy. 2. Affirm Indigenous rights, self-determination, and sovereign control over all aspects of their lives and health. 3. Argue that settler governments are responsible for ensuring equitable access to health services and health outcomes for all and must grant Indigenous peoples a "state of health that is equal to that of other people." Towards this end, the charter demands Indigenous control and management of health systems, culturally sensitive programming, and access to their own languages, cultures, and traditions to address the physical, social, mental, emotional, and spiritual dimensions of health that are necessary to prevent HIV.

75 Bonita Lawrence and Enakshi Dua, "Decolonizing Antiracism," *Social Justice* 32, no. 4 (2005): 120–43; Tuck and Yang, "Decolonization is not a Metaphor."

76 Walia, "Moving Beyond."

77 Andrea Smith, "Indigeneity, Settler Colonialism, White Supremacy Edited by Daniel Martinez HoSang, Oneka Abennett and Laura Pulido," in *Racial Formation in the Twenty-First Century*, ed. Daniel Martinez HoSang, Oneka LaBennett, and Laura Pulido (Berkeley and Los Angeles: University of California Press, 2008), 66.

78 Lawrence and Dua, "Decolonizing Antiracism."

79 Ibid.; Smith, "Indigeneity, Settler Colonialism."

80 Amadahy and Lawrence, "Indigenous Peoples."

81 Tuck and Yang, "Decolonization is not a Metaphor," 7.

82 Hill, *500 Years*; Tuck and Yang, "Decolonization is not a Metaphor."

83 Smith, "Indigeneity, Settler Colonialism."

84 Ibid.

85 Lorenzo Veracini, "Settler Colonialism and Decolonisation," *Borderlands E-Journal* 6, no. 2 (2007).

86 Nandita Sharma and Cynthia Wright, "Decolonizing Resistance, Challenging Colonial States," *Social Justice Journal* 35, no. 3 (2005): 120–38.

87 Tuck and Yang, "Decolonization is not a Metaphor," 6.

88 Iyko Day, "Being or Nothingness: Indigeneity, Antiblackness, and Settler Colonial Critique," *Critical Ethnic Studies* 1, no. 2 (2015): 102–21; Tuck and Yang, "Decolonization is not a Metaphor," 7.

89 Day, "Being or Nothingness," 106.

90 Ibid.

91 Ibid.
92 Ibid., 102; Scott L. Morgenson, "White Settlers and Indigenous Solidarity: Confronting White Supremacy, Answering Decolonial Alliances," *Decolonization: Indigeneity, Education & Society*, 26 May 2014, https://decolonization.wordpress.com/2014/05/26/white-settlers-and-indigenous-solidarity-confronting-white-supremacy-answering-decolonial-alliances; Sharma and Wright, "Decolonizing Resistance."
93 Morgenson, "White Settlers."
94 Day, "Being or Nothingness."
95 Morgenson, "White Settlers."
96 Sharma and Wright, "Decolonizing Resistance," 126.
97 Lawrence and Dua, "Decolonizing Antiracism."
98 Sharma and Wright, "Decolonizing Resistance."
99 Ibid.; Sturm, *Blood Politics*.
100 Sharma and Wright, "Decolonizing Resistance," 124.
101 Ibid., 132.
102 Ibid.
103 Smith, "Indigeneity, Settler Colonialism," 73; Veracini, "Settler Colonialism."
104 Smith, "Indigeneity, Settler Colonialism."
105 Ibid., 77.
106 Sharma and Wright, "Decolonizing Resistance"; Sturm, *Blood Politics*.
107 Day, "Being or Nothingness"; Smith, "Indigeneity, Settler Colonialism"; Tuck and Yang, "Decolonization is not a Metaphor," 7.
108 Rita Kaur Dhamoon, "A Feminist Approach to Decolonizing Anti-Racism: Rethinking Transnationalism, Intersectionality, and Settler Colonialism," *Feral Feminisms* 4 (2015): 20–38.
109 Ibid.; Day, "Being or Nothingness."
110 Sharma and Wright, "Decolonizing Resistance."
111 Day, "Being or Nothingness," 104.
112 Dhamoon, "A Feminist Approach."
113 Day, "Being or Nothingness"; Dhamoon, "A Feminist Approach."
114 Veracini, "Settler Colonialism."
115 Smith, "Indigeneity, Settler Colonialism."
116 Ibid., 84.
117 Smith, "Indigeneity, Settler Colonialism"; Dhamoon, "A Feminist Approach."
118 Maracle, "Red Power"; Andrea Smith, "Heteropatriarchy and the Three Pillars of White Supremacy," in *The Colour of Violence: The INCITE! Anthology*, ed. INCITE! Women of Color Against Violence (Cambridge, MA: South End Press, 2006).

119 Melanie J. Newton, "Returns to a Native Land: Indigeneity and Decolonization in the Anglophone Caribbean," *Small Axe* 17, no. 2 (41: 2013): 108–22, https://doi.org/10.1215/07990537-2323346; Sturm, *Blood Politics.*

120 Sturm, *Blood Politics.*

121 Amadahy and Lawrence, "Indigenous Peoples"; Wilson, et al., "Narratives of Resistance."

122 Lawrence and Dua, "Decolonizing Antiracism."

123 Smith, "Heteropatriarchy."

124 Smith, "Indigeneity, Settler Colonialism."

125 Ibid., 77.

126 Ibid., 78.

127 Smith, "Indigeneity, Settler Colonialism."

128 Ibid.; Day, "Being or Nothingness."

129 Smith, "Indigeneity, Settler Colonialism," 69.

130 Ibid.

131 Ibid.

132 Ibid.

133 Ibid.

134 Day, "Being or Nothingness" 113.

135 Ibid.

136 Ibid., 110.

137 Rubén A. Gaztambide-Fernández, "Decolonization and the Pedagogy of Solidarity," *Decolonization: Indigeneity, Education & Society* 1, no. 1 (2012); Tuck and Yang, "Decolonization is not a Metaphor."

138 Gaztambide-Fernández, "Decolonization"; Leanne Simpson, "Indict the System: Indigenous & Black Connected Resistance," leannesimpson.ca, retrieved 21 December 2014, http://leannesimpson.ca/indict-the-system-indigenous-black-connected-resistance.

139 Simpson, "Indict the System."

140 Walia, "Moving Beyond"; Jessica Wood, "#BlackLivesMatter," teaandbannock, 12 July 2016, https://teaandbannock.com/2016/07/12/blacklivesmatter.

141 Geary, *Antiblack Racism.*

142 Guta, Murray, and McClelland, "Global AIDS Governance"; Ciann L. Wilson, Sarah Flicker, and Jean-Paul Restoule, "Beyond the Colonial Divide: African Diasporic and Indigenous Youth Alliance for HIV Prevention," *Decolonization: Indigeneity, Education & Society*, 2015.

143 Gaztambide-Fernández, "Decolonization," 50.

144 Ibid.

145 Ibid.

146 Tuck and Yang, "Decolonization is not a Metaphor," 3.

147 Gaztambide-Fernández, "Decolonization," 50.

148 Smith, "Heteropatriarchy.

149 Gaztambide-Fernández, "Decolonization."

150 Smith, "Indigeneity, Settler Colonialism."

151 Gaztambide-Fernández, "Decolonization."

152 Walia, "Moving Beyond."

153 Sharma and Wright, "Decolonizing Resistance."

154 Gaztambide-Fernández, "Decolonization," 52.

155 Gaztambide-Fernández, "Decolonization"; Morgenson, "White Settlers"; Smith, "Heteropatriarchy"; Walia, "Moving Beyond."

156 Amadahy and Lawrence, "Indigenous Peoples," 131.

157 Gaztambide-Fernández, "Decolonization"; Smith, "Indigeneity, Settler Colonialism."

158 Gaztambide-Fernández, "Decolonization."

159 Amadahy and Lawrence, "Indigenous Peoples," 125.

160 Sharma and Wright, "Decolonizing Resistance" 133.

161 Tuck and Yang, "Decolonization is not a Metaphor," 31.

162 Sharma and Wright, "Decolonizing Resistance"; Smith, "Heteropatriarchy"; Tuck and Yang, "Decolonization is not a Metaphor."

163 Tuck and Yang, "Decolonization is not a Metaphor," 3.

164 Walia, "Moving Beyond."

165 Gaztambide-Fernández, "Decolonization"; Tuck and Yang, "Decolonization is not a Metaphor"; Walia, "Moving Beyond."

166 Smith, "Indigeneity, Settler Colonialism."

167 Guta, Murray, and McClelland, "Global AIDS Governance."

168 Ibid., 24.

16

Blood is a Politic of Place-Making: Blackness, Queerness, and the Construction of the Donor

OmiSoore H. Dryden

According to the published mandate letter for the Minister of Health (28 August 2017)[1] blood donation has been listed as a priority for the federal government. Specifically, the letter states that the health minister is expect to work with provinces and territories to "develop a long-term vision for blood services that ensures safety and non-discrimination in donation policies." To date, "non-discrimination in donation policies" has referred solely to the exclusion of some gay and bisexual men and some men who have sex with men (who do not identify as gay or bisexual).

Men who have sex with men (MSM) have been banned from donating blood, most noticeably, since the installation of Canadian Blood Services in 1998 (there remains some debate regarding if this ban began with the Canadian Red Cross, however with the decision of the Krever Commission, I argue that the effective ban of men who have sex with men became entrenched with the establishment of the Canadian Blood Services). Permanent deferrals from blood donation have been met with protest and legal challenges meant to encourage changes to these criteria. These deferrals are permanent unless the man involved abstains from having sex with another man (for five years or the more recent twelve-month expectation). However, in order to effectively address the concerns raised regarding MSM blood deferral, it is necessary to acknowledge the diverse nature of the MSM community in Canada.

Sexuality, race, sexual identity, gender identity, and geography are not separately occurring identity markers in the lives of men who have sex with men. MSM who are African/Black must also grapple with multiple forms of

erasure and silencing due, in part, to conditions of racism, sexism, homophobia, and transphobia both in LGBT communities and the larger imagined
community of Canada. In fact, MSM who are African/Black are uniquely
targeted for exclusion by the donor questionnaire.

Health Canada and Canadian Blood Services administer the blood system
in Canada. In particular, it is the responsibility of Canadian Blood Services
to recruit blood donors, manage blood donation and health risk, administer
quality-control standards, and create educational programs. In the aftermath
of the tainted blood crisis and the findings from the Royal Commission of
Inquiry on the Blood System in Canada, use of a donor questionnaire that
clearly and directly asked questions regarding presumed HIV transmission
elevated the questionnaire to a fundamental and mandatory component of
blood safety practices.

The design of the donor questionnaire facilitates the identification of
potential blood-borne diseases, like HIV. In fact, a number of the HIV and
AIDS-related questions focus on travel, medical background, drug use, sex,
and sexual encounters. Contemporary narratives of blood safety are intimately linked with significations of HIV, significations framed through
discourses of racism, Eurocentrism, heteronormativity, homophobia, and
sexual conservatism. As a result, certain groups of people are already
understood as deviant and a danger to the nation and, therefore, as threats
to blood safety and national security.

From imagination (in)to state regulation, blood has been used to map
the politics of belonging. Through this deployment, stories about the truth
that blood holds have been exported into official stories about national
borders and the parameters of citizenship. Blood is an enunciative site,
wherein identity can be strategically manipulated in the service of nation
(and community) building.[2] The production of space and place, and the
unequal/contested engagement with each, is informed through blood stories,
including the stories told about (and within) blood donation.

In this chapter I am interested in routing interrogations into gay blood
and blood donation through the logics and power lines of blackness.
Through the application of a Black queer diasporic analytic, I explore how
the discussions regarding blood donation participates in the politics of place
making. I examine the social construction of the ideal blood donor
and how anti-Black racism, colonialism, and racist homophobia frames
this construction.

BLOOD (DONATION) IS A POLITIC OF PLACE-MAKING

The interrogations into the mysteries of the body, including blood, did not occur as objective examinations. Scientific investigations into the body, and its blood, occur within the tapestries of colonialism, religiosity, and white supremacist logics. Science, scientific voice, scientific authority, is commissioned in the pursuit of the truth about our bodies and its blood. Nancy Stepan states, "when scientists in the nineteenth century, proposed an analogy between racial and sexual differences, or between racial and class differences, and began to generate new data on the basis of such analogies, their interpretations of human difference and similarity were widely accepted, partly because of their fundamental congruence with cultural expectations."[3] Science is not simply a colour-blind objective practice, but in fact, science exists within the social and political tapestries of homophobia, racism, misogyny, and sex phobia. Therefore, it is important to acknowledge these realities when examining scientific language and voice.

Nation-states have relied on this authoritative voice in the determination of citizenship and the cataloguing of people determined by the nation-state's interpretation of bodies. Examples of these citizen determinations can be found in one-drop dictate, blood quantum, blood protection and miscegenation laws. Each of these practices detailed norms of behaviour used to govern and regulate both the private and public sphere. The biopolitics of blood narratives affect "ratio of birth to deaths, the rate of reproduction, the fertility of a population."[4]

For example, nation-states in pursuit of maintaining colonial conquest, imposed blood quantum laws in the eighteenth century. These laws created the racial category of "Indian" which sought to evict Indigenous people out of rank of "human" whilst simultaneously erasing the diversity and distinctions between and among the already present and vibrant first nations. The nation-states insistence on these laws required the cataloguing, indexing, and recording of the levels and percentage of "Indian" blood. This cataloguing of "Indian-ness" allowed for nation-states to continue the forced dispossession of Indigenous peoples from traditional territories, while simultaneously withholding the recognition and benefits of newly established citizenship. One-drop dictates (hypodescent) and miscegenation laws are an outcome of seventeenth-century slave codes and a remnant of slave societies. These blood narratives posit that just a single drop of black or not-white blood will contaminate the purity of the white population, resulting in one's eviction from whiteness. Blood protection laws animated anti-Semitism and homophobia so that the nation-state could confirm "racial defilement" on pre-selected, already targeted "others." Blood narratives are not passive stories. The animation of this national blood narrative resulted in the nation-state sanctioned death of millions of people.

While each of these blood narratives resulted in significant deaths, the narratives also established a number of blood borders, such as, legalizing racial and sexual hierarchies, norms of behaviour, identify suitable participants in procreation, and appropriate overall surveillance measures. These state-sanctioned blood narratives impacted all daily decisions and actions and proper conduct. Through these systems, the language of purity and lineage inform nationhood, national identity, and the body politic.

Although past scientific claims may be easy to dismiss as poor and/or outdated scientific practice, the blood narratives used and produced by scientific intervention have become the constitutive framing of the contemporary nation-state and its organizations. The blood system must be considered an organization of the nation-state; therefore, it is important to acknowledge that Canadian Blood Services is also a national blood story in need of interrogation. Canadian Blood Services operates in the realm of public health – the promotion of health and prevention of disease. Within this realm, disease is considered a threat to the population. The treatment of disease occurs through a variety of initiatives including the surveillance of individual practices, actions, and behaviours. The promotion of the health of the population becomes a national concern and commitment. As Wald states, "Disease and national belonging shapes the experiences of both; disease assumes a political significance, while national belonging becomes nothing less than a matter of health."[5]

Canadian Blood Services reliance on blood narratives informs and produces public knowledge on blood safety and the ideal donor. However, this reliance on blood narratives also produces knowledge on the parameters of belonging and citizenship.

"AS IF THEIR PRESENCE IS WHAT MAKES 'US SICK'"

Dr Charles R. Drew (1904–1950), an African American cisgender man, developed procedures for collecting, storing, and transporting large quantities of blood. He began the development of these procedures while studying at McGill University, and these methods and procedures became the basis for national blood collection programs[6] in Canada, the United States, and Britain. In the 1940s, the public blood donor system began in earnest, and all blood collected was earmarked for military use only. "The first blood trans-fusion recipients were white American and British soldiers, and following the direction of the American Red Cross Society, all blood collected in Canada and the US was racially catalogued with the purpose of ensuring that white soldiers did not receive blood from not-white [people]."[7] As the creator of the modern blood donation system, Dr Charles Drew, rigorously objected to this practice of the racial segregation of donated blood, arguing that there was no scientific evidence to support such a practice. This history of anti-Black racism is often ignored when exploring the gay-blood debates and the practice of blood donation systems, including Canada's. What are also overlooked are the similar details this early blood donation practice has with other early/historical national blood practices (blood quantum, blood protection laws, miscegenation).

In each of these blood narratives/practices, bodies that are catalogued as not-white are assumed to have blood that is not quite human and therefore incompatible to white blood. There continues to be a push to connect the diversity of bodies to a racial difference in the blood. The racist, sexist, homophobic-informed symbolic of blood have come to inform the scientific truths of the biomateriality of blood – then and now.

Blood and sexuality map the terrain and territories of colonial and imperial power. As Sara Ahmed states,

> When the body of another becomes an object of disgust, then the body becomes sticky ... This is how bodies become fetish objects ... feelings of disgust stick more to some bodies than others, such that they become disgusting, as if their presence is what makes "us sick."[8]

Significations of blood safety post the 1990s tainted blood crisis have impacted the definition of the life-giving donor and reanimated the borders of the nation. The tainted blood crisis signalled a significant breach between the normative understandings of the health and the sick. It reanimated the constructed breach between the assumed healthy and vulnerable "general public" and the infected, immoral, tainted other. At the time of the tainted blood crisis, the "tainted other" was read into gay men and Haitian people (soon to be African people). AIDS was considered unusual and unknown and therefore its cause must also be unnatural and foreign. Gay people were considered outside the parameters of the "general pubic" and Haitian/African people were assumed to be not Canadian. As a result, with HIV/AIDS now scientifically understood to be tacitly carried by gay men and African, Caribbean, and Black people, the construction of safe blood was mapped onto borders – national and community.

The political and legal activism to have gay blood included in the national blood supply has relied upon claims of sexual exceptionalism (we are married and monogamous), regulation of gay identity (good gays are monogamous and practice safe sex), and the practice of racial neutrality and colour-blindness (men who have sex with men is the *only* question on the donor questionnaire that must be amended/deleted/changed). However, since sexuality, race, sexual identity, gender identity, and geography are not separately appearing identity markers, M S M, as a sexual identity, must be read through racial categories *as well as* geographic locations. It cannot be ignored that Black people in Canada are coded as "out of place" and blackness is positioned as outside the bounds of acceptable behaviour (as detailed in the above miscegenation national narrative), in other words – beyond the pale.

Canada's national identity and the geographical space/place in which it exists remains contested terrain. Therefore, a scholarship that insists upon a normative minority identity (including debates regarding "gay blood") structured within a neoliberal discourse of Canadian multiculturalism is a problem in need of rupture. Confronting racism and racist homophobia is about unsettling the antiblack conditions which frame Black queer lives.

Christina Sharpe identifies the pervasive antiblackness as "the weather." Sharpe posits, when speaking of "the weather" that, "antiblackness is pervasive as climate ... it produces new ecologies."[9] She goes on to state that, "the weather trans*forms Black being ... When the only certainty is the weather that produces a pervasive climate of antiblackness, what must we know in order to move through these environments in which the push is always toward Black death?"[10] To dismiss the weather when speaking about blood donation and gay blood is to dismiss the history of slavery[11] in Canada and the current expressions of what Saidiya Hartman calls "the afterlife of slavery."[12]

Stereotypes about Black people in Canada include, Black people as recent arrivals from the Caribbean region, Africa, and the United States, with the exception of those few who came to Canada in the 1800s through the Underground Railroad. While some of this is factual, it's overwhelming performance as the single Black people in Canada narrative occludes our long history both pre- and post- slavery. Blackness in Canada has many histories and trajectories, which insists that we conceptualize the geography of Canada anew.

The afterlife of slavery, in Canada, continues to impact the social and political realities of Black life. I would posit that the invisibility and hyper-visibility of Blackness in Canada is a notable Canadian manifestation of "the afterlife of slavery." Black people in Canada, including Black queers continue to be in peril as a result of the continued correlations between the abject and "the black;" this is experienced in the "skewed life chances, limited access to health and education, premature death, incarceration, and impoverishment."[13]

GAY BLOOD, BLACKNESS, AND QUEER
DIASPORIC ANALYTICS

Interactions with blood donation include exploration of the spaces in which we live but also how we perceive and conceive of this space. The interventions of gay blood debates is about conceiving and perceiving of blood donors and blood donation differently. Is it possible for us to think about this homo-hegemonic blood spatial practice (including the blood donor) as a "Black place/space"?

Black queer diaspora is a nuanced analytic, which allows for a "claiming of intellectual kin where we find them; speaking to, with, and through discourses appropriate to the conversation rather than those merely expected by convention, while reaching back to foundational works and projecting our imaginations forward."[14] In this work, I bring the strangeness of the symbolics of blood in conversation with black queer analytics. Rinaldo Walcott describes the analytics of black queer diaspora as "an intervention that cuts across numerous boundaries. It allows for multiple and conflicting identifications based upon a shared sense of sexual practice and the ongoing machinations of racialization, especially anti-Black racism."[15] This work in blood donation and gay blood expands the fields in which black queer analytics intervene. The interrogations into the persistent ontological problem of blackness[16] in Canada[17] must also occur in the health studies/ epidemiological field, of blood donation and the donor questionnaire. By including the symbolics of blood within black queer diasporic analytics, the examination of racialized sexuality and racist-homophobia ultimately maps the genealogy of national blood narratives. Blood narratives create(d) powerful state controls over the people within the borders, concentrating on race, gender, and sexuality. And these associations remain present in contemporary blood practices.

Thinking through the ways in which gay-blood activism is myopic, I'm curious about what is made available if, as Neville Hoad has argued, we must unsettle and make unfamiliar conceptual claims to specific identities.[18] How would differently situated bodies, people, and experiences disrupt the standardization of blood donor systems? Blood is a text in need of analysis. The donor questionnaire is the blood text I centre in this analysis.

ALL THE BLOOD IS TESTED AND THE DONOR QUESTIONNAIRE

The donor questionnaire, to reiterate, includes a variety of questions that explore sex, sexual encounters, travel, and places of birth. This "Lifestyle Question (formerly Question 30)" of Canadian Blood Services' donor questionnaire (pre–July 2015) read as follows:

TRAVEL QUESTION:
Since 1977, did you receive a blood transfusion or blood product in Africa?

LIFESTYLE QUESTION:
Have you had sexual contact with anyone who was born in or lived in Africa since 1977?[19]

Canadian Blood Services argued that it was necessary to defer from Africa for two reasons. First, that HIV-O was a specific strain only found in Africa and secondly, even though all blood is tested, there was no available or reliable test for HIV-O. On the surface, these would seem like sound science. However, this is where the interrogation into symbolics of blood safety in Canada must occur.

In the 1998 version of the donor questionnaire, the above questions were significantly different. Specifically, the question focused on people born in or who had lived in and who had sexual contact with anyone born in or who had lived in, Cameroon, Central African Republic, Chad, Congo, Equatorial Guinea, Gabon, Niger, and Nigeria.

At an in-person meeting with representatives from Canadian Blood Services and concerned Black LGBTQ people, Canadian Blood Services detailed that the move from specifically naming these eight countries to instead asking if people were born/lived in "Africa" was done for simplicity sake and donor satisfaction. In other words, the decision to conflate eight African countries to stand-in for the continent was based on *simplifying* the questionnaire because it took too long to read the question, naming each separate country. The "countrification of Africa" is a common racist practice. In addition, although it was argued that HIV-O was a strain only found in "Africa" there was accessible evidence that this strain is also found in other regions, including Europe and North America. The sanctioned narrative of blood safety has HIV-O as travelling across continental Africa but not beyond these regions. This sanctioned narrative thus places HIV-O

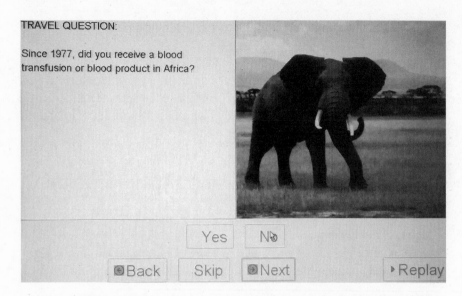

Figure 16.1 Screenshot of blood donation questionnaire from 2013. This is the "Lifestyle Question" (formerly "Question 30") from the Canadian Blood Services' donor questionnaire that was used pre-July 2015.

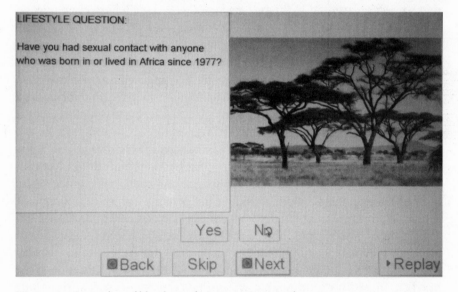

Figure 16.2 Screenshot of blood transfusion questionnaire from 2013.

into African/Black bodies.[20] In 2009, a blood test for HIV-O was approved for use in Canada and with Canadian Blood Services, however this question and the practice of banning Black people from donating blood remained until July 2015. Within that time period, Canadian Blood Services launched a computer automated donor questionnaire with attendant pictures, as seen above – an Acacia tree[21] and an elephant. These images are deployed in the geographies of blackness and remain present in the visual discourses of blood donation. The tropes of a dark and dangerous "black/not human Africa," are all too commonly used allegories. And the use of the elephant and the Acacia tree gestures to a remaining primitive time, one not yet developed as imaged through urban landscapes. HIV and AIDS endure as an African origin story – an origin story that supported(s) the permanent deferral of people connected to Africa.[22]

In 2015, these questions were adjusted. Instead of identifying Africa, these questions now reference Togo and Cameroon. No longer is the concern about the HIV-O strain, instead the justification deployed is the potential of new strains of HIV developing out of these two countries. Thus the deferrals will allow for Canadian Blood Services to develop effective testing. However, the idea that new strains of HIV will only occur in Africa/African countries continues that type of unscientific justification that was used in the 1940s when Black blood was segregated from white blood. How would the donor questionnaire shift if Canada/North America could be imaged as producing new strains of HIV?

In a very brief review of the donor questionnaire (July 2017) I am once again drawn to the images used to animate the contained information. How are questions of geography, though not specifically HIV/AIDS, imagined by Canadian Blood Services?

Overall, the questions that speak to the United Kingdom, France, and Europe are accompanied with the following images: a picture of the union jack, the Eiffel Tower, and a picture of the globe with the European region highlighted. For the questions regarding travel outside of Canada and the United States there are images of a cruise ship, a passenger train, and a passenger plane. The use of the flag, landmarks, and modes of travel gestures to long, vibrant, and evolved nation-states. In particular, separation of animal and nature (deemed primitive and crude) from the nation-state (use of flag), advanced technology (Eiffel tower and modes of long-distance travel) signals the breach in how blood is determined to be safe and tainted.

Moving onto the questions regarding Mexico and Central and South America, images become more disturbing. A picture of the globe accompanies a question regarding if one is born in Mexico, Central America, or

South America with *only* South America highlighted. A picture of a pyramid accompanies a follow-up question regarding length of stay. Moving southeast across the globe, an image of a sandscape, presumably the desert,[23] accompanies a question about length of stay in Saudi Arabia.

The images accompanying questions referencing Togo and Cameroon no longer include that of an elephant; however, the Acacia tree remains. For Canadian Blood Services, African/Black blood is properly represented only through the image of an elephant or of a tree. It is necessary to note that the Acacia tree is *not* indigenous to Togo or Cameroon. These trees are indigenous to the southeastern region of the continent (in the countries Mozambique, Botswana, Swaziland, for example) not the west where the countries of Togo and Cameroon are located.

The choices made in the animation of these questions demonstrate how logics of white supremacy continue to inform the blood system's science and medical practices. The animation predetermines who is the ideal donor (person) and what is the tainted other (non-human object).

As discussed elsewhere[24] "sexual contact" remains a phrase used only in relation to Africa, Togo, and Cameroon. At an August 2015 meeting with Canadian Blood Services representatives, they suggested they didn't realize there was a difference in the language used (sex[25] versus sexual contact). They argued that this was an oversight that would be corrected in the new, upcoming version of the donor questionnaire. However, the new version has been released since that meeting and the language has not been changed. So one must ask again, does the use of "sexual contact" with this question on Togonian and Cameroonian (née African) blood speak to a particular type of "Togo and Cameroon (nee Africa)" sexual practice?

Canadian Blood Services' donor questionnaire, much like miscegenation laws earlier, educates the nation on the immorality of having "sexual contact" with (not quite human) people from Africa, Togo, and/or Cameroon. In fact, the donor questionnaire suggests that if too many people engage in this sexual contact not only would the blood system collapse (again) but also the nation.

The ease with which HIV/AIDS continues to be attributed to Africa/Black people continues to animate, as evident in the above images, that the African/Black body is bestial/plant life/not human (incompatible) other. I posit that these colonialists and racist disorientations is "the weather" in which the Canadian blood system (and gay blood activists) operates.

GAY BLOOD IS NOT THE WAY

Blackness in Canada matters in the political and social interventions into gay blood and blood donation practices. My interest and commitment to Black life *in Canada* insists upon the interrogation of the Canadian colonial project, anti-Black racism and the afterlife of slavery. Blackness in Canada exists, and the positioning of Blackness in Canada matters, particularly within the discourses of blood donation. As such, through the application of a black queer diasporic analytic, I am able to identify the ways in which the Canadian colonial project is supported and preserved through the seemingly objective field of gay blood and blood donation. The donor questionnaire is used to differentiate life-giving donors from harmful death-bringing objects.

When thinking through the social construction of the ideal gay blood donor, it is not simply enough to have one or two Black people stand in for the empty signifier of the diversity of men who have sex with men. Nor is it productive to simply represent gay people as sexually moral and virtuous Canadians, as demonstrated in the #EndTheBan political campaign.

Inclusion (as it is normatively operationalized) is not freedom, and sameness (as far as homophobia and identities are imagined) is actually a social *in*justice. Hope for inclusion (and legal, political, and social commitment to securing inclusion) does not ultimately disrupt[26] the anti-Black practices of homophobia, and the racism and sexism inherent in that homophobia.

There is a conflation between the visual presence of racial diversity (no matter how tiny) with a broader celebration of inclusion and diversity. The homonormative work of gay blood inclusion continues to make itself known is one that expects blackness to fall into line and thus disappear into a larger, flatter, experience of homophobia. José Esteban Muñoz calls this "normativizing protocols." In fact, to be included in the nation-state not only furthers the barriers to Indigenous sovereignty but specifically, to deploy Marco's image in this inclusion campaign, occludes the anti-Black racism that is embedded in the nation's colonial project. Thus, erasing the experiences of African, Caribbean, and Black men who have sex with men. In other words, ACB are sacrificed in the process of making some gay people acceptable blood donors. In the article, "Resisting Inclusion: Decolonial Relations between Peoples of Afrikan Descent and Original Peoples," Moyo Rainos Mutamba states,

> History shows how the white supremacist colonial state of Canada strategically desires our inclusion at times, to further its colonial agenda, only to exclude us to sustain its racist, anti-black agenda.[27]

Marco has been in a monogamous
relationship with his boyfriend for over 6
years and has perfectly healthy blood, so

Figure 16.3   Canadian Federation of Students postcard from #EndTheBan Campaign.
This image was used as both a poster and a postcard available for distribution.

As Treva Ellison, Kai M. Green, Matt Richardson, and C. Riley Snorton
posit, "blackness as 'unknown' … promotes a way of viewing blackness as
belated arrival or addendum."[28] The inclusion of Marco in this political
campaign, without taking up the anti-Black realities of homophobia in
Canada, means that the only way to read this campaign is one in which
Marco's Black life (and the Black life of men who have sex with men)
remains "unknown." Gay blood narratives also participate in the regulation
of identities and ultimately the organization of the nation-state and its
approved subjects.

Citizenship and belonging are framed through the logics of anti-Black
racism and white supremacy that are found in the construction of the ideal
blood donor, safe blood, and the gay blood debates. Blood simultaneously
facilitates the production of space while perpetuating continuing inequalities. Blood becomes deployed and therefore maps the parameters and limits
of inclusion/exclusion, boarders, and regions, regulating identities and is
ultimately used in the organization of the nations and its subjects.

In order to rethink the blood system, there must be a serious engagement
with colonialism and the afterlife of slavery. The continued interrogation
into Canadian Blood Services, gay blood, and blood systems remains

important in light of Canadian Blood Services's role within the Alliance of Blood Operators. This organization is responsible for advising blood systems operators worldwide. In addition, the World Health Organization has argued that in order to respond to serious health consequences a global strategy of national blood systems must be implemented in Africa. We must be concerned with how the social construction of the good blood donor will be deployed globally.

NOTES

1 Justin Trudeau, "Minister of Health Mandate Letter," pm.gc.ca, 4 October 2017, https://pm.gc.ca/en/mandate-letters/2017/10/04/ archived-minister-health-mandate-letter.

2 Homi K. Bhabha, *Nation and Narration* (Milton Park, UK: Routledge, 1990).

3 Nancy Leys Stepan, "Race and Gender: The Role of Analogy in Science," in *Feminism and Science*, ed. Evelyn Fox Keller and Helen E. Longino (Oxford: Oxford University Press, 1996), 121–36, 125.

4 Michel Foucault, *Society Must be Defended: Lectures at the Collège de France, 1975–1976* (New York: St Martin's Press, 1997), 243.

5 Priscilla Wald, *Contagious: Cultures, Carriers, and the Outbreak Narrative* (Durham, NC: Duke University Press, 2008), 67.

6 Charles W. Carey Jr, *African Americans in Science: An Encyclopedia of People and Progress*, vol. 1 (Santa Barbara: ABC CLIO, 2008).

7 OmiSoore H. Dryden, "'A Queer Too Far': Blackness, 'Gay Blood,' and Transgressive Possibilities," in *Disrupting Queer Inclusion: Canadian Homonationalisms and the Politics of Belonging*, ed. OmiSoore H. Dryden and Suzanne Lenon (Vancouver: UBC Press, 2015), 116–32.

8 Sara Ahmed, *Cultural Politics of Emotion* (New York: Routledge, 2004), 92.

9 Christina Sharpe, *In the Wake: On Blackness and Being* (Durham: Duke University Press, 2016), 106.

10 Ibid.

11 Slavery in Canada lasted for more than two hundred years; however, because Canada's slave institution was much smaller in scope than the slave institutions in the United States, Latin America, and the Caribbean it is often deemed "too small to warrant intellectual or political consideration" and is subsequently (dis)appeared. Katherine McKittrick, *Demonic grounds: Black Women and the Cartographies of Struggle* (Minneapolis: University of Minnesota Press, 2006), 97. However, to dismiss slavery in Canada is to dismiss the historical, and therefore the contemporary, presence of black people in Canada.

12 Saidiya Hartman, *Lose Your Mother: A Journey Along the Atlantic Slave Route* (New York: Farrar, Straus and Giroux, 2007).

13 Ibid., 6.

14 Jafari S. Allen, "Introduction: Black/Queer/Diaspora at the Current Conjuncture," GLQ: *A Journal of Lesbian and Gay Studies* 18, nos. 2–3 (2012): 211–48, 215.

15 Rinaldo Walcott, "Homopoetics: Queer Space and the Black Queer Diaspora" In *Black Geographies and the Politics of Place*, ed. Katherine McKittrick & Clyde A. Woods (Toronto: Between the Lines, 2007), 233–46, 234.

16 My use of the term blackness allows for an acknowledgment of the impacts and effects of colonization and the after-life of slavery while simultaneously exploring the diasporic nature of Black people. I also use the term blackness in conversation with other Black queer/trans Canadian/North American scholars, including in the work of Rinaldo Walcott. Walcott states that blackness is "a sign, one that carries with it particular histories of resistance and domination. [B]lackness is also a sign which is never closed and always under contestation … allow[ing] for a certain kind of malleability and open-endedness which means that questions of blackness far exceed the categories of the biological and the ethnic." Rinaldo Walcott, *Black Like Who: Writing Black Canada* (Toronto: Insomniac Press, 2003), 27.

17 Canada's national identity and the geographical space/place in which it exists remains contested terrain, a scholarship that seeks a normative minority identity as structured within a neoliberal discourse of Canadian multiculturalism is a problem in need of rupture.

18 Neville Hoad, *African Intimacies: Race, Homosexuality, and Globalization* (Minneapolis: University of Minnesota Press, 2006), 16.

19 These screenshots are from the very early/first implemented computer-animated Canadian Blood Services' donor questionnaire. When I contacted Canadian Blood Services in February 2017 for an e-copy of this first animated questionnaire, the Access to Information office informed me that they no longer had this version on file. As such, I am the using screen-shots from a video, recorded on a colleague's smart phone. This colleague shared the video with me in 2013.

20 It was acknowledged in the Krever Commission that during the tainted blood crisis, nurses, in an attempt to screen out tainted blood, would begin to flag blood for removal if they felt that someone "looked" unwell. With the signification of HIV/AIDS focusing on gay men and Haitian people, it is reasonable to believe that the donations from Black people in general were flagged for removal.

21 The Acacia tree is not indigenous to Togo or Cameroon. It is indigenous to the southeastern region of the continent (in the countries Mozambique, Botswana, Swaziland, for example), not the west, where the countries of Togo and Cameroon are located.

22 It must be noted that not all people from continental Africa were banned. Over the course of my research, a number of white people who were born in Africa and/or lived in Africa were instructed to answer "no" to these questions "because these questions were not about them." In this action, the blackness of Africa was operationalized.

23 Not the capital city centre or an image of the Kingdom Centre.

24 See OmiSoore H. Dryden, "Canadians Denied: A Queer Diasporic Analysis of the Canadian Blood Donor," *Atlantis: A Women's Studies Journal* 34, no. 2 (Spring 2010): 77–84; OmiSoore H. Dryden, "A Queer Too Far," 116–32; OmiSoore H. Dryden, "Blood Out of Bounds," *NoMorePotlucks,* issue 40, *Self,* http://nomorepotlucks.org/site/blood-out-of-bounds-omisoore-h-dryden.

25 In the last 6 months have you had sex with anyone who has taken clotting factor concentrates? In the last 12 months have you had sex with a sex trade worker or anyone else who has taken money or drugs for sex? In the last 12 months have you had sex with anyone who has ever taken illegal drugs with a needle? In the last 12 months have you had sex with another man? Have you had sex with anyone who has AIDS or tested positive for HIV or AIDS? versus Have you had sexual contact with anyone who was born in or lived in Togo and Cameroon since 1977?

26 For some white gay men, the desire to be included has meant they are willing to abstain from sex for twelve months in order to be able to participate in the practice of donating blood. This is not an option that is available to everyone, and it presupposes that the blood donated will be included in the larger blood system.

27 Rainos Moyo Mutamba, "Resisting Inclusion: Decolonial Relations between Peoples of Afrikan Descent and Original Peoples," *Decolonization: Indigeneity, Education & Society* (2014): n.p.

28 Treva Ellison, Kai M. Green, Matt Richardson, and C. Riley Snorton, "We Got Issues: Toward a Black Trans*/Studies," *TSQ: Transgender Studies Quarterly* 4, no. 2 (May 2017): 162–9, 164.

Creation is Legacy:
Creativity and Futures

17

The Story of Sister Vision:
Black Women and Women of Colour Press

Makeda Silvera

WE HAD TO FIGHT, CUSS,
AND KICK EVERY INCH OF THE WAY

As far back as I can remember I have had a passion for writing and an interest in publishing. Before Sister Vision came into being, my first job – part-time in the 1970s – was as a typesetter and proofreader at the Black newspaper *Contrast*. Royston James's tribute "I Stand on Al Hamilton's Shoulders," reminds us what that paper meant:

> At a time when black folks were dismissed as troublemakers not worthy of Canadian citizenship, *Contrast* was a bulwark, a shelter against a storm of media criticism and unfair caricature and representation. Before the Jamaican Canadian Association and other community agencies found root, Contrast was community centre, information hotline, ombudsman, integrity commissioner, human rights provocateur.[1]

At *Contrast*, I covered the protests of Caribbean-born domestic workers from the beginning. In one of my first ventures into activism, I joined in their demonstrations. The women were at a disadvantage because of their race, class, sex, and status as migrant workers. These women had come to Canada to work as household help and babysitters under a Canadian government scheme and wanted to bring their children to Canada as permanent residents.

Six decades have passed since the scheme began in 1955 – to be replaced with the temporary employment visa in the late 1970s and 1980s. To qualify for the original scheme, a woman had to be single and between eighteen and thirty-five years old. Many of those who qualified were sole-support mothers who had left their children behind with their own mothers, aunts, cousins, or best friends. Years later, when the mothers wanted their children to join them, the federal government rejected their applications. The same standard did not, however, apply to Caribbean-born men. Many of these mothers retained lawyers, some of whom worked pro bono. But what made the difference was the women themselves, who with the backing of community leaders and people from the broader public, took their fight to the streets, and in time the mainstream media could no longer ignore them and they achieved their goal.

I decided to leave *Contrast*, for although it gave me training in journalism and although I agree wholeheartedly with Royston James's praise of the paper, working in a male-dominated newsroom also meant working in a sexist workplace, replete with unwanted sexual overtures. After I left *Contrast* newspaper, I sojourned with a fellow editor of *Contrast* who had a different vision of a Black/Caribbean newspaper. Shortly, I became an assistant editor. It sharpened my skills, but it was not without sacrifices – bounced cheques, long working hours. Still it excited me. I was in the middle of community, I knew communities, met old-timers who worked on the trains, heard stories of having to say "yes sir" and bowing to white men. I heard first-hand stories.

My point here is that I was aware, as a Black woman working at both newspapers, that in the celebrations of their wonderful historical achievements, women were rarely mentioned. The only woman editor of *Contrast* was not recognized in the celebration of the paper's past. I, as an assistant editor of *Share* was erased from that history and from their anniversary. It begs the question again and again, "where have all the women gone?"

In 1983 I published my first book: *Silenced: Talks with Working-Class Caribbean Women about Their Lives and Struggles as Domestic Workers in Canada*.[2] The second edition, with a new introduction, was published in 1989. Not much has changed for foreign-born domestic workers since *Silenced*. The only substantive change – a small but important one – is that they can choose to live on their own. Stephen Harper's Conservative federal government "balanced" that change by enacting a law to limit the numbers of workers who can enter Canada. Women who come to Canada to do domestic work still face sexual and other forms of assault by their employers and they still live in fear of being deported if they report those crimes. At the time of writing this (2018), we have a Liberal federal government, but having observed the issue for more than thirty years – through various changes of government – I have seen that it doesn't matter what political party comes into power: things remain much the same. To date, I have not heard a single politician speaking out on behalf of Filipina domestic workers. Unless the women organize themselves, and can count on the strong backing of allies among feminist, community organizations, and the general public, I don't see prospects for them changing their working conditions – and that means their day-to-day lives – for the better.

In *Briarpatch*'s labour issue (2016) Tiana Reid revisits both editions of *Silenced*.[3] She refers to my use of the phrase "female sensibility" and to my use of oral history as a methodology and examines what the phrase and the methodology mean. I chose to move away from traditional social research methodology. I listened to the women, sought out their experiences and perspectives, urged them to speak in their own languages, and to speak about what mattered to them. With that as the framework, it's not surprising that what would come to light would be the racism, sexual assault, and the class bias they faced, the longing they felt for their children, their relatives, and their friends, the loneliness of living among strangers in a strange land. In her article, Reid also refers to the Harper government's policy on foreign-born domestic workers. She, too, finds that nothing much has changed and that it doesn't matter which party is in power. For Reid, the only change is in the "landscape of punitive laws" within a system that "upholds racialized and sexualized violence in its labour law."[4]

Two early influences on Sister Vision's work and on my own were the oral histories by the late anthropologist Oscar Lewis: *Four Women* and *The Children of Sanchez*.[5] I was so intrigued with Lewis's work – especially the story-telling aspects. I wanted to bring that story-telling approach to *Silenced*. As Lewis had done with those he interviewed, I taped each woman and offered each her typed transcript to review. Many of the women had grown up in a place and at a time where story telling was still valued. I wanted the individuality of their voices. I sought concrete details about their individual experiences and encouraged them to talk about the "feminine." These stories mattered because few readers seem to realize that no girl-child dreams of growing up to go away to clean other people's toilets. The women spoke of what it was like to be a Caribbean-born domestic worker in someone else's home: the hours of looking after other people's children, hand-washing other people's underwear, dealing with the sexual advances of employers, labouring for long and poorly paid hours. They also spoke about their own children, about what they did on their all-too-brief days off, about their friends, about their churches, about all that mattered to them. My priority was to preserve that history. In so doing, I also wanted to work with working-class women and feminists, inside and outside the Black community.

In 1983 I was also invited to join the previously all-white feminist collective that produced the quarterly *Fireweed*. Initially, I was excited – I was learning a lot, reading manuscripts and debating their merits. I soon began to find out first-hand about white middle-class feminism and about its resistance to incorporating an analysis of race and class within feminist thought. Eventually, another woman of colour joined the collective. The other collective members asked the two of us to co-edit *Fireweed 16*, an issue on women of colour, and to pull together a guest collective to work on that issue.

A year and a half before I joined *Fireweed*, a fellow writer and I had approached the collective about editing a women-of-colour issue, which would have been a first for Canada. The collective declined. So when the prospect of co-editing *Fireweed 16* came up, my colleague and I were puzzled at the timing. We decided to go ahead, to counter the collective's claim that it previously could not find writers of colour. During the production of *Fireweed 16*, my co-editor and I had to fight to retain editorial control. White members of the collective – and all were white but two of us – did not understand the day-to-day workings of race and class – not among themselves and not in the world at large. Thus, for example, they did not understand a group of women's account of racism, an account that my co-editor and I found unexaggerated but that the rest of the collective found over-the-top.

To counter their assumptions we titled *Fireweed 16*'s editorial "We Were Never Lost" and in it we spelled out how we "found" the contributors.[6] This was long before the rise of social media and before the Internet itself had burgeoned. We placed flyers in locales frequented by women of colour: libraries, community agencies, immigrant women's centres, bookstores. And, of course, we used word of mouth. Many victories came with that issue. Most significant was that there was no question that women of colour could write. We were never lost.

Later in 1983, I was invited to Vancouver as one of four keynote speakers for the first Women and Words Conference, which drew women from across Canada. As keynote speakers we were asked to address the question "How Far Have We Come?" I responded "Not Far Enough" and began my speech with, "For each step that we take as Black women, we had to fight, cuss, and kick every inch of the way." I ended with, "Stop correcting our voices."[7] There were gasps, followed by silence in the large auditorium. I overheard a well-established white woman writer ask another, "Why don't they start their own journals and presses and stop complaining?" When I got back to Toronto I was determined to establish a press by and for women of colour. At the time, I could count on one hand the number of Black women who had published single-author books or were featured in anthologies.

Sister Vision, which I co-founded with Stephanie Martin in 1984, was born out of the need to exert the autonomy of women of colour. We looked close to home for a name, in other words, at who we were – two sistas – two feminists with a vision. And so, the press was named Sister Vision. Initially, we asked two other feminist sisters to join us. They hesitated, then said no – their reasoning was that Black men would think we were fighting against them. That did not deter us. I knew enough to know to keep firmly to the path we had chosen and had already read and found affirmation in "The Combahee River Collective Statement," first published in 1977. This is what the women said: "Above all else, our politics initially sprang from the shared belief that Black women are inherently valuable, that our liberation is a necessity not as an adjunct to somebody else's ... We realize that the only people who care enough about us to work consistently for our liberation are us. Our politics evolve from a healthy love for ourselves, our sisters, and our community which allows us to continue our struggle and work."[8]

In 1985, we began to produce provocative, challenging, and risk-taking books by and for Black women, Indigenous women, Asian women, and women of mixed-race heritage – books that were independent of white male literary conventions and independent of white feminist presses. As we were setting up Sister Vision, I kept in mind the problems I had had finding a publisher for *Silenced*. Publishers had wanted good-news stories about domestic workers, not accounts of the long hours they toiled, not accounts of sexual harassment, not accounts of racism on the job, and not accounts of being disparaged for being working class. They did not want to read the narratives of Black working-class women speaking about what it was like to work for white middle-class families. And publishers wanted the women's voices to reflect CBC-standard English throughout, not their various Creole languages.

Setting up Sister Vision and actually doing the business of publishing was hard work. We knew very little about the nuts and bolts of book publishing, and we were trying to do the jobs of roughly ten people while holding down full-time jobs and raising our two children. In addition, we had decided to open up our three-story home to LGBTQ of colour tenants who were committed to feminism and to living as a collective where we shared cooking, childcare, and household responsibilities. We added two other mothers, one Métis and the other, African Caribbean Canadian. Debbie Douglas, one of the mothers who shared the house, sums up the atmosphere best in her article, "That Collective House on Dewson Street": "The house was traffic central, with folks dropping by to borrow a book, drop off flyers, attend late-night meetings about a protest ... or an editorial meeting ... and conversations about feminism, organizing, writing, music, identities and, of course, gossip."[9]

It was an exciting time, with rarely a dull moment, for spontaneous get-togethers would spring up with lots of food on the kitchen stove and music and the pitter-patter of children's feet for accompaniment. In the summertime there were always people hanging out in the backyard or on the front steps. Food and politics were always in the air.

But over the years, running the press from the house became harder and harder. With eight adults and four children living in the house, it could be chaotic, and some authors did not understand boundaries and would call us at seven in the morning or after midnight to chat about their books or their personal lives. In the beginning, we had no idea that the boundaries of the personal, the professional, and the parent would become increasingly blurred and that this blurring was of no service to anyone. In 1992 we moved the press into shared space with *Our Times*, an independent labour magazine.

In the beginning, we stored our files in cardboard boxes and ran the press from our basement. Sometimes, during production, we also used the dining table. We knew little about finances and little about the market. We did know that we had to come up with fund-raising ideas and that we had to reach out to women of colour who had completed manuscripts or had ideas for books. We had to learn the trade's many conventions – for example, the number of pages for a book of poetry or a children's book. We also knew that we wanted to strengthen our links with women outside of Canada. We were "crazy" – "crazy" with desire, "crazy" risk-takers.

Ever optimistic, sometimes we would over-print books, not knowing just what the market would be. We assumed we could just take a box of books to any bookstore and they would put them on their shelves. The only two bookstores to operate that way were the Toronto Women's Bookstore and Third World Books and Crafts. (The latter, an important institution in Toronto, opened in 1968 and was owned by Gwen and Lenny Johnson. It thrived for thirty years, not only as a bookstore but a place for public meetings and hosted radical guest speakers from the United States. Its final home was on Bathurst Street.)

We realized very quickly that we needed a paid distributor and a paid sales representative to represent Sister Vision's books in the marketplace. We also realized that with only a few books under our belt, we would not be seen as a legitimate publisher and no distributor or sales reps would take us up. Once we had enough books for sales reps to represent us, we were faced with another problem – very few, if any, had represented books produced by a press owned and operated exclusively by women of colour. It was a steep learning curve for many reps – all were white, needed to understand our books, and needed to figure out how to hook on to a sales angle. We learned by trial and error, realizing that it would be a long climb up the ladder. Hope and determination kept us climbing.

We did massive amounts of fund-raising: dances, bake sales, yard sales, and poetry and short-story readings at the house. We invited writers from the United States to read, and we held concerts. One of our most successful fund-raisers featured a female duo from the US: J. Casselberry and Jacque Dupree, whose repertoire ranges from gospel, to reggae, to jazz, to rhythm 'n' blues and which apportions feminism with entertainment. Some twenty years later, they are still singing. Our next concert brought the famed Bernice Johnson Reagon, founder of Sweet Honey in the Rock, an internationally known, award-winning, African American female *a capella* ensemble, which performed for us twice, each time filling the University of Toronto's Convocation Hall to capacity. The logistics proved to be hard, hard work: catering to five women with differing dietary needs, booking hotels, arranging transportation, selling tickets, advertising, getting press coverage. Cheryl Clarke – an African American poet, essayist, educator, and lesbian feminist activist – also graced us with a stellar evening of her poetry. We were on our way to building a strong vibrant community of women of colour who volunteered to work on fund-raising events and who were eager to learn about building a publishing house.

Stephanie Martin and I divided up our work, partly based on our skills and partly on our personalities. Because of my previous work with *Fireweed*, I took on the managing editorship, which included commissioning single-author books and anthologies, working with the writers, working with the freelance editor we contracted, and going over contracts with the writers. I also looked after a large part of promotion and publicity, including organizing book launches, reaching out to and organizing volunteers, and eventually working with our sales representatives. I helped with cover design, including the images chosen for our book covers and found people to write blurbs for the back covers.

Stephanie Martin, a trained visual artist, took charge of the major design elements and of production and dealing with our distributor. Initially, she designed many of the covers herself, but as we got more established, we contracted designers who understood that our priority was always that the images reflected the content of the books.

From the beginning, potential authors met us with enthusiasm. Both women of colour and white feminists who shared in our vision helped to fundraise and volunteered. This volunteering cannot be stressed enough: without that we could not have survived. The media was sceptical and the basic assumption was that we would never survive as a woman-of-colour press. Sister Vision, the first press by and for Black women and women of colour in Canada survived for sixteen years. In those years – 1985–2001 – we published more than seventy-five first-time writers in single-author books and more than two hundred women in anthologies. We had to wait a long time to get mainstream media attention.

Our first book, *Speshal Rikwes*, poetry by ahdri zhina mandiela, was published in 1985.[10] "Speshal rikwes" is Jamaican Patois for "appreciation and respect." *Speshal Rikwes* was a co-operative effort, involving the author and many volunteers who gave their time generously in all aspects of its production, including proofreading, typesetting, cover art, and the monies raised to make that first book possible. Its experimental form and language made it a bold challenge to white-owned and -run women's presses. Earlier, Jamaican Canadian dub poet Lillian Allen's *Rhythm an' Hardtimes*[11] had faced similar criticisms and scrutiny. At the time, mainstream publishers as well as white feminist publishing houses did not understand that Patois is (as are all Creole languages) a full and complete language, not degraded or corrupted English. Both *Speshal Rikwes* and *Rhythm an' Hardtimes* were written in post-colonial times and both writers were influenced by Garveyism and Rastafarianism. There has been no stopping the form, and it is slowly being recognized as legitimate. For example, in 2012 the Jamaican English poet Jean "Binta" Breeze, who brought her feminist voice to dub poetry, became the first female dub poet to be made a Member of the Order of the British Empire (MBE) for her services to literature.

As I mentioned earlier, when Sister Vision was founded, very few Black women and other women of colour were being published in Canada. Armed with that knowledge, as managing editor I decided to make anthologies a significant part of what we published. In that way, more women would gain exposure; "sister-women" could compare experiences, could think about the differences among women of colour, could learn from each other, and move forward towards coalition building.

One inevitable challenge of producing an anthology is that the work will be uneven because most likely it has new or first-time writers, unsure of their abilities and in need of mentoring. New or first-time writers often must be reminded to take their work seriously, to heed deadlines, and most important, they need to be reminded that they're not in school or university, where a paper can be written in one night. They also need to be reminded that their writings will have implications and that there may be repercussions. But the joys far outweigh the challenges. For the anthologizer, it's a chance to discover new and different voices. For the reader, anthologies are like short stories – you can read a piece while on the bus or train, while doing laundry, or while eating alone. There's also the joy of reading varied writing styles and the mix of familiarity and discovery. Anthologies also encourage dialogue and offer varied forms of writing for reading clubs.

Here is a sampling of anthologies that were published by Sister Vision: *Piece of My Heart* (1991, reprinted 1993)[12] was the first lesbian of colour anthology in North America. The anthology gained much attention and praise. It was nominated for the Stonewall Book Award – Barbara Gittings Literature Award. The anthology celebrated diversity among lesbian Caribbean-born women, Indigenous women, Asian women, and other women of colour. It was published at a time when white lesbians often assumed that all Black women, all women of colour, all Indigenous women were heterosexuals – especially if they had children. *Piece of My Heart* stood proudly beside the (then) ever-growing body of white queer literature.

Because I was Sister Vision's managing editor, I was also reading other manuscripts, working with other writers, and promoting books we had previously published. Not surprisingly, *Piece of My Heart* took six years to complete. It was a far different world then than today – much of the time I devoted to the anthology was spent easing many contributors' fears of "coming out" in print – fear of family anger, fear of repercussions by employers (if indeed they in fact turned the pages out of curiosity). *Piece of My Heart* broke the silence and laid bare the isolation and loneliness of many queer women of colour. The book exploded white folks' assumptions about us as a homogeneous group; it highlighted our multiple realities and explored the connections between race, ethnicity, class, gender, sexuality, and more as it delved into the concomitant overlapping and interdependent discrimination we face.

The Colour of Resistance: A Contemporary Collection of Writing by Aboriginal Women, anthologized by Cree writer Connie Fife (1993, reprinted 1994) features more than forty non-fiction and fiction writers and poets.[13] In the reader, it encourages an understanding of the struggles of Indigenous women and an appreciation of their joys and respect for their hard-won battles. For many non-Indigenous women, it serves as a starting point for doing away with stereotypes, for listening, and for taking action.

Miscegenation Blues: Voices of Mixed Race Women (1994),[14] was anthologized by Carol Camper, who is of Black, white, and Indigenous ancestry, and includes more than fifty women, many of whom describe the paradox of living in two worlds – and find themselves at home in neither. They are often objectified, fetishized, and exoticized. Camper herself writes of being adopted by a white family and of her "extreme cultural isolation." This anthology was groundbreaking and an important first in North America.

Plural Desires: Writing Bisexual Women's Reality (1995)[15] was edited by a bi-sexual women's collective made up of women of colour and white women. It explores the contributors' race, ethnicity, dis/ability, binary divisions, heterosexuality, queerness, and desire.

Black Girl Talk (edited by The Black Girls, 1995)[16] is a project I initiated. It brought together the poetry, fiction, essays, and artwork of young Black women. The contributors explore the confusion of young adulthood, including love, jarring urban racism, male power and dominance, interracial relationships, lesbian relationships, substance abuse, sexual abuse, conflicts with parents, and death. The contributors are proud, loud, and bold.

That year Sister Vision also published *The Other Woman: Contemporary Canadian Literature*, which I anthologized and which presents interviews of twenty women of colour about their lives as writers.[17] It was an extraordinary experience for me to bring these women together between the book's covers. I am honoured and proud, too, that many Indigenous women gave time from their busy schedules to be a part of this anthology. Among the authors are Métis writers Maria Campbell (author of *Halfbreed*[18]) and Beatrice Culleton (author of *In Search of April Raintree*[19]). Culleton now writes under her birth name, Beatrice Mosionier. As well there is Cree writer Beth Cuthand (author of *The Little Duck/ Sikihpsis*);[20] Mi'Kmaq elder and residential school survivor (1936–1947) Isabelle Knockwood (author of *Out of the Depths: The Experiences of Mi'Kmaw Children at the Indian Residential School at Shubenacadie, Nova Scotia*);[21] and Anishinaabekwe writer Lenore Keeshig-Tobias of the Chippewas of the Nawash Unceded First Nation on the Bruce Peninsula (formerly known as the Cape Croker Reserve). This impressive collection also features Black women, Asian women, and other women of colour.

We were also proud of our single-author books. Many of these women published for the first time with Sister Vision. Guyanese Canadian writer Norma De Haarte's novel *Guyana Betrayal*[22] explores the friendship between two young girls in the lead-up to Guyana's independence and offers a riveting glimpse into the growing tensions between Indo-Guyanese and Afro-Guyanese in what was then British Guiana. Sister Vision was not De Haarte's first choice. She shopped the manuscript to many publishers, all of whom hesitated for fear that the readership would be too small (on the groundless assumption that few people of colour read – never mind buy – books). Such blinkered thinking was not uncommon at the time. Potential publishers also told De Haarte they would not take the book unless she rewrote the Creolese passages in Received Standard English.

As managing editor, I heard the same story from countless other writers who worked with Sister Vision. At the time, publishers assumed that a book written in Patois – the Jamaican Creole language – would not sell. Thirty years later, in 2015, Jamaican-born and -raised novelist Marlon James would win the American Book Award and the £50,000 Man-Booker Prize for the *New York Times* best seller *A Brief History of Seven Killings*, in which numerous characters speak Patois.[23]

In 1992 and 1995, respectively, we published *The Invitation* and *Sage*,[24] novels by Cyndy Baskin, a woman of Mi'Kmaq and Irish descent. Her work explores the power of traditional Indigenous culture and spirituality to make broken lives whole.

Chinese Canadian Yan Li's manuscript *Daughters of the Red Land*[25] came to us unsolicited, as many manuscripts did. As I read through the manuscript, I knew immediately that we had to publish it. Although it was rough and in need of work because the author's first language was not English, we decided to put time and money into it. This first novel is a riveting saga of three generations of Chinese women – before, during, and after Mao's regime. The strength and complexity of characters torn between a new politics and traditional values was recognized publicly when it became a finalist for *Books in Canada*'s First Novel Award in 1996.

China Dog and Other Tales from a Chinese Laundry, by Chinese Canadian Judy Fong-Bates[26] published in 1997, also arrived unsolicited. As managing editor, I read it and asked other manuscript readers for comments. Because the collection showed promise, I assigned the book to an editor and worked with Fong-Bates on the manuscript for two years. Her vivid and richly textured characters are Chinese immigrants who lived from the beginning of twentieth century to the mid-1990s. The stories focus on the complexities of adjusting to life in small-town Ontario while trying to live up to traditional family values.

Vanessa Alleyne's *There Were Times When I Thought I was CRAZY: A Black Woman's Story of Incest* (1997),[27] is a first-person true account of the physical, sexual, and psychological abuse that Alleyne suffered at the hands of her stepfather, of the aftermath, and of her attempts to bring him to justice. The book was a real risk-taker for us. Incest and rape happen in our various communities and in many of our families, too. But it is taboo, not to be talked about, considered "unpleasantness" to be swept into the corner or under the rug. So, it wasn't a surprise to Sister Vision when many people advised us not to publish the book. We were fortunate to have Melba Wilson, author of *Crossing the Boundary: Black Women Survive Incest*,[28] endorse the book on its back cover: "This is an important addition to the growing swell of Black women who are refusing to remain silent." Opal Palmer Adisa, award-winning novelist, poet, and performance artist, also endorsed the book: "Vanessa Alleyne is a warrior in the tradition of Harriet Tubman and Jamaica's Maroon Nanny; she is a brave heart who refuses to be a victim, triumphant ... in a system that all too often does not help children who are voiceless."

We also published books for young people of colour. As a mother, I found that books with texts and illustrations that reflect children of colour were hard to come by. If, by chance, I found one in a bookstore, it would inevitably be about African American children. Although such books were a blessing, we decided that Sister Vision would fill that void. *Coloured Pictures* (1989, 1991, 1993),[29] by Bengali Canadian Himani Bannerji, recounts the responses of Sujata, a South Asian girl and her friend when local bullies attack them. Sujata takes the problem to her classroom, where she and her classmates learn the power of organizing.

The idea for *Growing Up Black: A Resource Manual for Black Youths*[30] came to me through my work with the Black Youth Hotline, a project of Toronto's Immigrant Women's Centre. I was one of the resource workers at the hotline. After the publication of the manual, I went on to do numerous workshops with after-school programs, libraries, and community centres. The manual was designed as a workbook for participants to write down their answers for later reflections, sharing, and discussion. During many of the workshops I was struck at the participants' honesty. Many were misinformed about many things: for example, their legal rights, how to work out a career path, and how to avoid streaming in schools.

The Ojibway (Anishinaabekwe), storyteller and writer Lenore Keeshig-Tobias's bilingual children's book *Bineshinh dibaajmowini/Bird Talk* (1991)[31], is written in Ojibway and English, with illustrations by Keeshig-Tobias's daughter Polly Keeshig-Tobias. One day at recess, a young Indigenous girl is startled to find that the other children want to play cowboys and Indians. She tells them that she's Indian and that it's not nice to play that game, only to have them ask, "If you are an Indian, where are your feathers then?" She goes home very sad but draws comfort and strength from her mother's stories of *Mishomis* (The Grandfather) and from hearing the real facts about Christopher Columbus. The Canadian Children's Book Centre recommended the book, which also won the Manhattan County School's MLK Living the Dream Book Award. The award celebrates the work and life of Martin Luther King Jr.

In 1996 Lenore Keeshig-Tobias (storyteller), Polly Keeshig-Tobias (illustrator), and Rose Nadjiwon (translator) teamed up to create *Emma and the Trees/Emma Minwaah Mtigooh*.[32] In this delightful story that teaches urban children the magic and beauty of trees and of the environment, Emma is in a bad mood and does not want to go out with her mother. She cries and screams. Instead of becoming angry, Emma's mother points to the trees and tells her, "Look, the trees are waving at you." Emma looks up and waves back at the trees and never cries about going out again.

In 1992 we published Trinidadian Canadian Lynette Roy's *Brown Girl in the Ring*,[33] a biography of feminist and peace activist Rosemary Brown, the first Black woman elected to the Canadian House of Commons after having served as an NDP MLA for the riding of Burrard-Vancouver in the British Columbia Legislative Assembly 1972–79. Brown was also first woman to run for leadership of a federal party. She lost to Ed Broadbent on the fourth ballot.

Antiguan-born Althea Prince's *How The East Pond Got its Flowers* (1991)[34] is set in Antigua. It tells of a girl born with a caul, who learns from a healing woman both to plant seeds for pond flowers and that she, the child, is destined for great things. It is a delightful story of hope.

Ninja's Carnival, by Trinidadian-born Ramabai Espinet (1993),[35] introduces seven-year-old Ninja, born in Trinidad but enduring his first Canadian winter and feeling very grumpy about it. His mother reminds him it's Carnival time in Trinidad. Memories of the revelry of Carnival, of its music and of its smells put him to sleep with a smile.

Crabs for Dinner (1995),[36] by Ghanaian Canadian Adwoa Badoe, proved to be another favourite with children. A mother comes home with big brown crabs bought at an African shop, but her children prefer hamburgers. When their grandmother arrives from Ghana for a visit, they learn there is a lot of family tradition to love, including eating crabs.

Over the years we shared what we learned about publishing with a number of Indigenous women's groups. In 1994, we teamed up with the Turtle Island Publication group to bring out two books: *Onkwehon Neha/Our Way*[37] (written by Mohawk writer Sylvia Maracle and illustrated by Chilean Canadian artist Carlos Freire) and *The Seven Fires: An Ojibway Prophecy*[38] (written by Sally Gaikezheyongai and illustrated by Polly Keeshig-Tobias), as part of a series on Indigenous life and culture.

We also published three playwrights, knowing full well that their work would be welcomed by many readers but would not be bestsellers. *Afrika Solo*[39] (1990) by Djanet Sears, who – like the heroine is herself – is of Caribbean parentage and was raised in England and Canada. The often painful but also humorous piece explores a young Black woman's voyage of self-discovery. Having been assailed with the word "nigger," and shouted at to "go back to where you come from," she takes the audience on a four-hundred-year journey through Africa. *Dark diaspora ... in dub: a dub theatre piece*[40] (1991, 1992), by ahdri zhina mandiela, fuses exploration with celebration. It is being remounted in 2018. In Diana Braithwaite's one-act play *Martha and Elvira*[41] (1993), two formerly enslaved women share with each other their memories of slavery. Each of the three playwrights have by now had long careers; in the theatre for Sears and mandiela; in music for Braithwaite.

Sister Vision also published a significant amount of poetry. We were well aware that women and girls of colour wrote poetry in part because poems can be short and are often seen as the best way to express emotion. *All Words Spoken*[42] (1992), by two Japanese Canadian writers, Tamai Kobayashi and Mona Oikawa fuses the tough humour of "street-wise dykes" with lyrical descriptions of Japanese culture, histories, and memories.

Kaushalya Bannerji's *The Faces of Five O'Clock*[43] (1996) presents passionate and sensual poems that invite the reader to accompany her on her many journeys, whether by airplane or on foot. *Utterances and Incantations: Women, Poetry and Dub*[44] includes eleven dub poets. As managing editor, I commissioned the anthology: I wanted Sister Vision to publish a collection of poetry that featured local poets, both established and emerging along with others who were known internationally and were also rooted in the oral tradition. The collection, includes, among others, Louise Bennett, Lillian Allen, Jean "Binta" Breeze, and Anilia Soyinka.

As I stated at the outset, we committed ourselves to publishing women outside of Canada whenever feasible, particularly writers in the diaspora. We steadfastly maintained that the women we published were interconnected and that we would strengthen those links whenever and wherever we could. We acted as if there were no borders, even if we could do that only in our imaginations. For those who are unfamiliar with Canadian publishing, it is important to know that given Canada's very small national market for books, Canadian publishers, of necessity, rely on government grants and those grants do not cover all the costs of producing a book. Thus, the Canada Arts Council and the Ontario Arts Council provide funding to offset the publication costs of books by writers living in Canada. To qualify, a book must be deemed to be "75 percent Canadian," which meant that we were on our own with any book we published that did not meet that criterion. Nonetheless, we forged ahead.

Here is a sampling: Nikky Finney's poetry collection, *Rice*[45] (1995) explores the complexity of that grain in South Carolina, its connections to slavery, its role in the economy, and its culture. It sold well. We owe that success to her high profile and her large Black readership in the United

States. The back cover blurbs featured two Americans: poet Nikki Giovanni and composer Bernice Johnson Reagon, the founder of Sweet Honey in the Rock and a founding member of the Student Non-violent Coordinating Committee's (SNCC) Freedom Singers in the Albany Movement.

Creation Fire: A CAFRA Anthology of Caribbean Women's Poetry[46] (1990), edited by Trinidad-born writer Ramabai Espinet, fits into the category of "international." We worked with Espinet, who lives in Canada, and with the Trinidad- and Tobago-based Caribbean Association for Feminist Research and Action to develop the anthology. The book was a long time in the making. Our writers spanned the Caribbean and its languages (English, French, Spanish, as well as a number of Creole languages). At the time, few people used e-mail and Skype was the stuff of science fiction. Letters went back and forth, so did long distance calls, and it sometimes meant travelling to Trinidad and Tobago. It took years to pull this anthology of more than one hundred contributors together and it was also a privilege to be part of strengthening the bonds.

Among the books for which we had no government grants were *Lionheart Gal: Life Stories of Jamaican Women*[47]; *Blaze a Fire: Significant Contributions of Caribbean Women*[48]; *The Very Inside: An Anthology of Writing by Asian and Pacific Islander Lesbian and Bisexual Women*[49]; and African American Nikky Finney's poetry collection, *Rice*, which, as I commented earlier, sold well.

Lionheart Gal (1991, edited by Honor Ford Smith) presents fifteen powerful stories by Patois-speaking Jamaican working-class women. All were a part of the internationally renowned Sistren Theatre Collective. *Blaze a Fire*, by Nesha Haniff (1988) also profiles Caribbean working-class women. Many years later, Haniff would say, "[T]his book is used at funerals whenever any of the women in the book dies as very little is written about them anywhere else." *The Very Inside* (1994, edited by Jamaican-born Sharon Lim-Hing) brought together more than fifty contributors. The first book of its kind, it was nominated for the Lambda Literary Award, which celebrates the best in LGBTQ books.

Sister Vision: Black Women and Women of Colour Press took risks. We published books by women of colour, many who would have never called themselves writers, established a community of writers, and changed the landscape of Canadian literature. Sister Vision rooted its approach to publishing in an appreciation of those who came before us and in the celebration of the lives and work of "ordinary" women. The power of language – particularly the power of storytelling – was the focal point for my vision for the press. Both were key in my upbringing. I grew up on storytelling. Both my grandmother and great-grandmother were native speakers of Patois and were wonderful storytellers, recounting stories that had been handed down for generations. From an early age I heard folk tales: sometimes in bed; other times, other children joined us on the veranda; or at night, under the big almond tree in the backyard, lit only by lamplight. From an early age, I understood that each character in the stories had a voice. Sometimes the stories dealt with values, such as the importance of respect for elders, or the importance of being proud of being Jamaican and of being proud of growing up working class.

Always the stories were entertaining. For example, there was Br'er Anancy – the Trickster, a liar who gets out of – or tries to get out of – trouble by telling more lies. Or Br'er Rabbit, who wants to please his friends and can't think on his own. Or River Mumma, who lives in the rivers of Jamaica with all her children and was the figure who served to warn us to beware of greed: an attempt to steal her golden table from the water becomes the ruin and death of the greedy. Or the duppy stories, which tell of the Good Duppy and the Bad Duppy. As children, we believed that the dead turn into duppies after they are buried, that they roamed the cemeteries at night, and would even sometimes come out and roam the streets looking for trouble. The Ol'Hige stories were scary. Ol'Hige, a witch, sheds her skin at night and takes the form of a cat. She would suck people's breath while they sleep. To this day, many Jamaicans are scared of or dislike cats. The Roll'n Calf, with its fire-red eyes, was the most dramatic character and the scariest. If we were coming home at night and passing our curfew, the Roll'n Calf could spring out of nowhere and block our way, with bells clanging around his neck. So we would grab each other's hands and run fast-fast to home, always looking out for the fire-red eyes. Duppies and the Roll'n Calf originated in folk tales from West and Central Africa. My short story "The Funeral," from my collection *Remembering G and Other Stories*, refers to duppies and to the Roll'n Calf.[50]

My writing draws on a story-telling tradition. My foremothers are often at the centre: their resilience, their strength, their spirits are all suns in my blood. My grandmother, the late Lucille Johnson, was my role model. Too often, those closest to us seem too "ordinary" to look up to; instead many look to the rich and famous for inspiration. My grandmother's strengths, her vulnerabilities, her political work, her generous-to-a-fault nature, her pride in her Afro-Caribbean heritage are what I look up to. An avid reader and consummate storyteller, she nurtured the writer in me. As if all that wasn't enough, she also knitted and crocheted countless pieces, from baby clothes to bedspreads, and she embroidered pillowcases, tea towels, and centrepieces. She baked cakes, adding intricate decorations of icing. She also baked gizzadas (a coconut pastry), picking and then grating the coconut from the trees in our yard, and plantain tarts, plucking the ripe and sweet plantains from our vegetable garden.

She never spoke about herself as an artist, which takes me back to Alice Walker's groundbreaking collection *In Search of Our Mother's Garden*,[51] where Walker considers what it meant for a woman to be an artist in our grandmothers' time. Walker writes that our grandmothers were "creators … women burdened with the weight of racism and class bias, raising too many children, cooking too many meals." She concludes that they "handed on the creation sparks, the seed of the flower they never hoped to see." My grandmother did live to see the flowering of the seeds she planted in me.

Not surprisingly, whether I am writing fiction or non-fiction, I always feel that I am telling a story, and because working-class Black women's experiences are often forgotten, and even lost, I try to retrieve some of those experiences through my work. In Nancy Kang's essay "In Memory of Our Foremothers," she writes that my work brings "the foremothers to the fore."[52] She is right on about that. *In Remembering G and Other Stories*, the grandmother, called Mama, is the one my unnamed narrator goes to for advice, guidance, and protection.[53] In my second collection of short stories, *Her Head a Village*, the title story introduces a spirit-woman, Maddie, who lives in a young writer's head and gives her direction and clarity when she is beleaguered and confused.[54] In my novel *The Heart Does Not Bend*, the rhythms of Jamaican Patois are very present. The book delves into mother-daughter-grandmother relationships in a working-class family led by a Jamaican matriarch and the changes that migration brings to those relationships, as well as exploring the narrator's sexuality, which is at odds with what her mother and grandmother hold to be proper and correct and is silenced in the family. But in times of loneliness, the narrator remembers her grandmother's sky-blue Jamaica and other consoling memories.[55] Both *Her Head a Village* and *The Heart Does Not Bend* break of some of the silences that Sister Vision Press itself broke for women of colour – the naming of one's self as writer, pride in one's ethnicity, sexuality, class, and dis/ability.

Sister Vision's most enduring legacy is that it was the first Black women and women of colour press in Canada and that it lasted for sixteen years. It passes on an impressive inheritance in its challenging of the dominant literary landscape of Canada, a challenge that crossed Canada's border. It created spaces in books where writers of colour met. It remains a beacon, signalling that such a vision can be realized.

Every now and then I wonder about the future of publishing for women of colour, particularly for marginalized women. I am aware of what social media offers, but my views on it are mixed. To begin with, the new media cannot take the place of the feel of a book in one's hands, the comfort of lying back and reading a book that resonates with one's reality, one's socio-geographic location, and with one's identity. The pleasure of reading and rereading a certain passage of a story or a certain line of a poem can be breath taking. Of course, blogs and platforms like Instagram and Facebook offer a means of communication for groups that have remained on the margins. More important, these platforms offer a connection to and for new audiences. There are some great Black feminist blogs, written in a collective voice, with a plethora of opinions and perspectives, full of off-the-cuff arguments, insults, and so on. Some such sites become battlegrounds. Some encourage the sharing of ideas and perhaps educate their readers, to a certain extent. But I also find that sometimes there is a lack of awareness about the variety of lives and experiences. I would say that social media doesn't offer either the depth or breadth of discussion and reflection that face-to-face writing forums provide.

As far as creating the conditions necessary in setting up a press like Sister Vision, I tend to be optimistic – it is possible, but it demands hard work, very long hours, extreme patience and persistence, a mountain of dedication and then some. It calls for women who can work together to make difficult decisions, who can leave their egos at the door and focus on the tasks at hand and on the goal. The time is ripe and I am hopeful that Sister Vision Press will light the way.

NOTES

1 Royston James, "I Stand on Al Hamilton's Shoulders," *Toronto Star*, 27 February 2012, https://www.thestar.com/news/city_hall/2012/02/27/royson_ james_i_stand_on_alhamiltons_shoulders.html.
2 Makeda Silvera, *Silenced: Talks with Working-Class Caribbean Women about Their Lives and Struggles as Domestic Workers in Canada* (1983: reissue, Toronto: Sister Vision Press, 1989).
3 Tianna Reid, "Silenced," *Briarpatch*, 23 October 2016, https://briarpatch magazine.com/articles/view/silenced.
4 Ibid.
5 Oscar Lewis, *The Children of Sanchez: Autobiography of a Mexican Family* (New York: Vintage Books, 1961); Oscar Lewis, Ruth M. Lewis, and Susan

Rigdon, *Four Women: Living the Revolution: An Oral History of Contemporary Cuba*. (Urbana: University of Illinois Press, 1977).

6 Nila Gupta and Makeda Silvera, "The Issue Is 'Ism: Women of Colour Speak Out," *Fireweed: A Feminist Quarterly* 16 (1983).

7 For one account of this gathering see "One Thousand Women Writers Gather to celebrate their words" in *Dalhousie Gazette* vol. 116, issue 9, 3 November 1983, https://findingaids.library.dal.ca/uploads/r/dalhousie-university-archives/a/c/e/acedef597b73446d1a49b6ab4561ab8d647b8adc-2699c6b70b52b508daca4031/dalhousiegazette_volume116_issue9_november_3_1983.pdf

8 Combahee River Collective, "A Black Feminist Statement," in *But Some of Us Are Brave*, ed. Akasha (Gloria T) Hull, Patricia Bell-Scott, and Barbara Smith (New York: The Feminist Press, 1982), 13–22.

9 Debbie Douglas, "The Collective House on Dewson Street," in *Any Other Way: How Toronto Got Queer*, ed. Stephanie Chambers, Jane Farrow, Maureen FitzGerald, Ed Jackson, John Lorinc, Tim McCaskell, Rebecka Sheffield, Tatum Taylor, and Rahim Thawer (Toronto: Coach House Books, 2017), 176–7.

10 ahdri zhina mandiela, *Speshal Rikwes* (Toronto: Sister Vision Press, 1985).

11 Lillian Allen, *Rhythm an' Hardtimes* (Toronto: Domestic Bliss, 1982).

12 Makeda Silvera, ed., *Piece of My Heart* (Toronto: Sister Vision, 1991).

13 Connie Fife, ed., *The Colour of Resistance: A Contemporary Collection of Writing by Aboriginal Women* (Toronto: Sister Vision Press, 1993).

14 Carol Camper, *Miscegenation Blues: Voices of Mixed Race Women* (Toronto: Sister Vision Press, 1994).

15 Bisexual Anthology Collective, *Plural Desires: Writing Bisexual Women's Reality* (Toronto: Sister Vision Press, 1995).

16 The Black Girls, eds., *Black Girl Talk* (Toronto: Sister Vision Press, 1995).

17 Makeda Silvera, ed., *The Other Woman: Contemporary Canadian Literature* (Toronto: Sister Vision Press, 1995).

18 Maria Campbell, *Halfbreed* (Toronto: McClelland and Stewart, 1973).

19 Beatrice Culleton, *In Search of April Raintree* (Winnipeg: Pemmican Publications, 1983).

20 Beth Cuthand, *The Little Duck/Sikihpsis* (Penticton, BC: Theytus Books, 2013).

21 Isabelle Knockwood, *Out of the Depths: The Experiences of Mi'Kmaw Children at the Indian Residential School at Shubenacadie, Nova Scotia* (Black Point, NS: Roseway Publishing, 1992).

22 Norma De Haarte, *Guyana Betrayal* (Toronto: Sister Vision Press, 1991).

23 Marlon James, *A Brief History of Seven Killings* (New York: Riverhead Books, 2014).

24 Cyndy Baskin, *The Invitation* (Toronto: Sister Vision Press, 1992); Cyndy Baskin, *Sage* (Toronto: Sister Vision Press, 1995).

25 Yan Li, *Daughters of the Red Land* (Toronto: Sister Vision Press, 1995).

26 Judy Fong-Bates, *China Dog and Other Tales from a Chinese Laundry* (Toronto: Sister Vision Press, 1997).

27 Vanessa Alleyne, *There Were Times When I Thought I was CRAZY: A Black Woman's Story of Incest* (Toronto: Sister Vision Press, 1997).

28 Melba Wilson, *Crossing the Boundary: Black Women Survive Incest* (Seattle: Seal Press, 1993).

29 Himani Bannerji, *Coloured Pictures* (Toronto: Sister Vision Press, 1989)

30 Makeda Silvera, *Growing Up Black: A Resource Manual for Black Youths* (Toronto: Sister Vision Press, 1989).

31 Lenore Keeshig-Tobias, *Bineshinh dibaajmowini/Bird Talk* (Toronto: Sister Vision Press, 1991).

32 Lenore Keeshig-Tobias, *Emma and the Trees/Emma Minwaah Mtigooh*, illus. Polly Keeshig-Tobias, trans. Rose Nadjiwon (Toronto: Sister Vision Press, 1996).

33 Lynette Roy, *Brown Girl in the Ring* (Toronto: Sister Vision Press, 1992).

34 Althea Prince, *How The East Pond Got its Flowers* (Toronto: Sister Vision Press, 1991).

35 Ramabai Espinet, *Ninja's Carnival* (Toronto: Sister Vision Press, 1993).

36 Adwoa Badoe, *Crabs for Dinner* (Toronto: Sister Vision Press, 1995).

37 Sylvia Maracle, *Onkwehon Neha/Our Way*, illus. Carlos Freire (Toronto: Turtle Island Publication, 1994).

38 Sally Gaikezheyongai, *The Seven Fires: An Ojibway Prophecy*, illus. Polly Keeshig-Tobias (Toronto: Turtle Island Publication, 1994).

39 Djanet Sears, *Afrika Solo* (Toronto: Sister Vision Press, 1990).

40 ahdri zhina mandiela, *Dark diaspora ... in dub: a dub theatre piece* (Toronto: Sister Vision Press, 1991).

41 Diana Braithwaite, *Martha and Elvira* (Toronto: Sister Vision Press, 1993).

42 Tamai Kobayashi and Mona Oikawa, *All Words Spoken* (Toronto: Sister Vision Press, 1992).

43 Kaushalya Bannerji, *The Faces of Five O'Clock* (Toronto: Sister Vision Press, 1996).

44 Afua Cooper, ed., *Utterances and Incantations: Women, Poetry and Dub* (Toronto: Sister Vision Press, 1999).

45 Nikky Finney, *Rice* (Toronto: Sister Vision Press, 1995).

46 Ramabai Espinet, *Creation Fire: A CAFRA Anthology of Caribbean Women's Poetry* (Toronto: Sister Vision Press, 1990).

47 Sistren with Honor Ford-Smith, *Lionheart Gal: Life Stories of Jamaican Women* (Toronto: Sister Vision Press, 1991).

48 Nesha Haniff, *Blaze a Fire: Significant Contributions of Caribbean Women* (Toronto: Sister Vision Press, 1988).

49 Sharon Lim-Hing, ed., *The Very Inside: An Anthology of Writing by Asian and Pacific Islander Lesbian and Bisexual Women* (Toronto: Sister Vision Press, 1994).

50 Makeda Silvera, *Remembering G and Other Stories* (Toronto: Sister Vision Press, 1991).

51 Alice Walker, *In Search of our Mothers' Gardens: Womanist Prose* (New York: Harcourt Inc., 1983).

52 Nancy Kang, "'Revolutionary Viragoes': Othered Mothering in Afro-Caribbean Diaspora Literature," *Women's Studies* 42, no. 6 (2013): 696–719.

53 Silvera, *Remembering G.*

54 Makeda Silvera, *Her Head a Village* (Vancouver: Press Gang, 1994).

55 Makeda Silvera, *The Heart Does Not Bend* (Toronto: Vintage Canada, 2002).

18

Dub and the Right to Exist:
An Interview with Lillian Allen

Lillian Allen

with Natalee Caple and Ronald Cummings

No one exceeds Lillian Allen's longstanding and ongoing commitments to poetry, music, broadcasting, education, and activism. Allen's artistic practice has won her two Juno awards and has been central to situating Toronto, Ontario as one of the international hubs for the historically important interdisciplinary form of dub poetry (beside Kingston, Jamaica and London, England). Allen is referred to as one of the Godmothers of Dub. As a leading cultural strategist, Allen has worked with all levels of government in Canada to promote equity and engineer social change. As a professor at OCAD University Allen initiated and led the development and design of a creative writing undergraduate degree. Allen is a mentor and educator in the field of cross-cultural and experiential learning, anti-bias curriculum, popular culture, and creative writing, empowering under-represented voices and democratizing artistic and cultural processes.

In her 1993 collection *Women Do This Everyday*, Allen includes "Nothing but a Hero," a tribute poem for Harriet Tubman. In her verse, she celebrates Tubman's heroism, describing her in layered, superlative terms as "a really cool / super duper visionary / revolutionary shero." Allen's poem, in effect, offers what might be read as a scripting of Tubman in an epic register. Her use of this exultant language, in this instance, emerges both from a deep admiration of Tubman, of her actions and accomplishments, but also from a keen understanding of the poem as a tool for teaching the public about Tubman's historic importance. The poem is one of Allen's verses for children, with significant resonances for a wider public, and effectively uses devices such as repetition and rhyme as poetic tools for recollection and teaching.

While Allen lauds Tubman's "skill" and "lifelong dedication," it is important to note that this celebration does not offer an individualistic vision of heroism. Instead, heroism becomes conceptualized as a practice of working towards collective liberation. In this interview we return to consider, once again, the significance of Harriet Tubman and her meaning for a poet like Lillian Allen. We revisit some of the themes and concerns of Allen's poem and her wider body of work, raising key questions about liberation and, in particular, the liberation of the body. As it is in the poem referenced above, in this discussion liberation is articulated and understood as collective possibility. The self is represented in intergenerational and communal terms, and as embedded in a tradition of "Sheroes, dreams and history." We also talk here about how these concerns with freedom and with history shape Allen's ongoing work as a writer, performance artist, educator, community activist, and mother.

RC: Activism, poetry, teaching, are all part of your work in helping to construct a liveable present, but they are also part of engaging with legacies and histories.

LA: Yes, for me, a primary concern is to liberate the Black body and to cross and transgress all the boundaries and borders intended to confine us.

RC: I am struck by your poem "Nothing but a Hero," which is a dub poem about Harriet Tubman.[1] It is a poem about her heroism, but you importantly note that her heroism is not just a onetime act of resistance; her heroism is ongoing in that she keeps returning to and crossing borders. I wonder if you might talk about the practices of women's everyday resistance and existence within patriarchy, colonialism, neocolonialism, and capitalism and what lessons we can learn from Tubman?

LA: Dub poetry is about asserting the right to exist, not unlike Tubman's impulse to free herself and other enslaved people. That right to exist means not asking for or negotiating with anyone for permission. Dub is about what is fundamental to humanity. What comes to the surface in dub is the skin you see: Blackness. But there are a lot of things that go on beneath that surface, there is a lot of struggle, there is a lot of dialogue, there is a lot of deep thinking, there is a lot of strategizing, because dub is also a political act. Politics are the primary reason for and the primary mode of dub. In the language are not just the ideas and the stance but also cultural and linguistic elements that are brought to bear to form resistance.

So it is not like you are coming to language, and then you are doing the politics, they are interwoven.

NC: You talk about revolution. I was thinking about this idea of revolution as something of a kind of a turning. So, revolution is an ongoing right to turn and confront the forces that surround you.

LA: Yes, all the forces, in the political sense, in the aesthetic sense, in everything. In another sense, I would say the right to exist is not just an individual right but it is also a collective right. We cannot be political and be alone in our own little spheres. Politics is relational. Our collective values are our life blood. Our spiritual and vibrational blood is our determination to resist and transform ugly forms of inequality and injustice. That's why it becomes social and political. Harriet Tubman is one of my heroes because in the face of the constructed reality, in the face of what they say is law ...

NC: In the face of a whole economy based on this effacing of humanity ...

LA: In the face of what you are supposed to be a part of and uphold, that which keeps society going, and puts your food on your table, Tubman basically said, "No." One big fat NO! And went on to make her revolution. That was something seriously profound. Because when we talk about civil society and regulations, rules that are unjust and hurt other human beings, we need to put our lives on the line so that we can bring about change. For me, what Harriet Tubman demonstrated is what's greatly lacking in the world today: courage. I don't know where it has gone, where it is hiding, but there is such a dismal lack of courage in this world. Even from people who seem not to have much to lose. Appearing to be on the appropriate side of an issue, dialoguing it to death, instead of actually doing something seems to be the "thing" these days.

RC: Recently I saw a picture of you speaking at a protest in 1979, at Harbourfront in Toronto, and one of the things you noted in relation to that picture is that it has been a long time since we have been trying to call the police into account for the shooting of Black people. So, I wondered if you could talk more about how do we engage social justice but also what kind of political work does poetry do or might it do in relation to ongoing revolution and ongoing experiences of social violence?

LA: In the early days, people had to scream or bang something to be heard. We had to do something to break through to the mainstream public, and then when you do that you are immediately labelled and ghettoized. You are put in a little box and there is a border around you again. Getting a forum of our own to include our many voices and struggles is what's important to me. Talking to our hearts is important to me.

Many young writers want to talk about the things that affect them the most. They have many concerns about our society but they also want to talk about their fears and heartbreaks, abandonment, betrayals, their parents' break up, feeling loss in a world with changing goal posts, wondering what to aspire for. Is there a space outside "the gaze"? We have a society that has allowed a sliver of our voice to be heard, mostly the one responding to the "tractor on our ankle." As a social and political being with conscious ties around issues of racism, decolonization, feminism, classism, I want to use my voice to address or at least to point out some of these complex inequalities. In terms of where you are in the culture, there comes a point where you make some decisions about your life and what you'll do about it. I always thought that culture is very key in terms of all the things that it can do for community. Things that go beyond communication, like holding aspects of history, customs, collective vision, connectivity in the now and throughout the ages across time and space, providing rituals, and so on, and usually in spirited and joyous terms. We are community because we have culture. To me, culture is that one thing that can change the world, by raising consciousness en masse. Culture is a collective thing. Note that education is part of culture also.

NC: What do you mean by raising consciousness?

LA: Raising people's own sense of justice and injustice and them becoming aware of what is happening in the world, that they feel connected and that they understand the roots to inequality and injustice, and what are the possibilities for change and that there is an engagement that can make them a better human. That goes to the heart. That's when consciousness is raised.

NC: Tubman embodies this by going back for people, over and over, she saw her own self as something other than a commodity. She is evidence of what a raised consciousness can do.

LA: Yeah, dear revolutionary Harriet was living a life outside of material trappings, those were no longer important to her. She was driven by what she thought was just. People talk about the arc of justice and the way the universe bends towards justice. It is really fundamental to strive for justice. That's the consciousness of the universe. Competitive societies have socialized people out of that consciousness.

Outside of our material trappings, this consciousness is a greater calling. Harriet Tubman had this calling and the interesting thing about that kind of work, working for the rights and liberation of others, is that the more you do it, the more important it becomes, the more it resonates with who you are inside. So, it's not just that Tubman was doing this because justice and the freedom of her people were important to her, it is clear that her life, as she lived it at the time, had a certain gravitas and importance. No wonder we are still talking about her now.

NC: We see this resonating with multiple movements in the present that are asserting the right of people to exist and be protected, not be shot at, not be disappeared in the case of missing and murdered Indigenous women and children. It feels very much that those kinds of assertions were central to the actions taken by Tubman and are essential to the ongoing practices of revolution and art. Maybe particularly with dub.

LA: Going back to talking about Harriet again, about the body and the self, and this extension to the community, and the extension to race. Certain bodies exist always under the notion that they can be disappeared and that whole processes have been employed to disappear them, to disappear their culture, to disappear their voices, to disappear their contributions. Revolution comes when we operate in this context that we are being disappeared. So, dub says we'll deploy words, utterances, signifying, language, musicality, embodiment in performance, and the poet's presence in community, as part of resistance and revolution.

The logical process of this colonial project of disappearance can be clearly seen in the West Indies/Caribbean. Take a place like beloved Jamaica, Indigenous territory of the Arawak-speaking Taínos and Carib peoples. We call ourselves Jamaicans, Africans kidnapped, forcibly and brutally brought by the colonizers ... to supplant the Indigenous peoples. The disappearing of Indigenous peoples was so seamlessly done by the colonial system, and then we were placed on that land. Yes, we have replanted our ripped up roots, but we cannot be neutral about the bones on which we are allowed to thrive.

RC: The colonial project was a project of genocide. Some did survive in Maroon spaces and blended with the Maroon communities. Or so the history goes, or so one version of the history goes.

LA: The struggle has been to resist disappearance. To just assert your right to exist, to assert your right to bring the body back, and to reappear cultures and to be visible in the arena.

NC: And to continue to exist as a living body of community, not as one monument.

LA: Right. Presence is important. Tokenism is one thing. I think that Black folk are entitled to be tokenized if they so wish, they are entitled to be whatever, as is any other group of people. That's an aside. But I think we are talking about asserting a presence that's meaningful. Although that is not the kind of demands we make on white folks. They are just there.

NC: Because white people's presence is already encoded in the economy as meaningful; it is not a demand because ...

LA: It is just there. But there is this extra thing you need to engage with if you are Indigenous people or Black folks or people of colour, or people who are marginalized, then you have to come with some kind of additional credentials to exist.

In the Academy, in our universities, I believe that one of the biggest barriers to progress, and hence a main cause of subverting justice and equality is, has been, and continues to be entitled white folks who resist the changes necessary to make transformation possible. Sometimes you can't even get to dialogue about equity concerns, moreover get beyond dialogue to action. Who is stopping any individual professor from decolonizing their curriculum or their syllabi? Not Administration. Try to get some kind of antiracist policy or women's equality rights on the table. It's not the administration fighting it; the administration lets it get by because it suits them. The people I see who are actively pushing back against change and who are doing nothing and are also sometimes turning the clock back, for whatever reason, are those everyday colleagues. Those are the everyday white folks that we sit around and talk to, that teach us, that we go out to coffee with. That, to me, is an insidious aspect of racism.

NC: Yes, as educators, I agree very much, especially when we talk about creative writing. The first thing you do is look at what you can do. To look at your own syllabi and what you have failed to do and what you still can do. I think you have to release some authority. You have to say, "OK, I want you also to look to other places for knowledge and not just to me and my experience. I want you to understand that the knowledge base isn't only in the classroom. You come from communities and that there is knowledge in those communities." You have to listen to your students and support their vulnerable grappling with what you mean. You have to help them to cultivate their own personal relationship with the world, and their own personal relationship with writing.

LA: Yeah, a couple of things there. I think that the most valuable thing that we can teach them, and you use the word cultivate. It is for them to develop, or have, or cultivate in themselves an obligation to transform society. I don't think there is a more important task for a teacher.

NC: And to value their peers and the well-being of their peers. I had a student the other day who was saying "it's nice we learn all these different things but I want to be taught how to be like the greats, like Hemingway. I want you to teach me how to be famous, like one hundred years from now." I said, "but you will be dead one hundred years from now." And he said, "I want to know how to be great," and I said "well you are doing this right, and you are doing this right." And he said "well how do I know that," and I said "well your peers are telling you, you are in the workshop sharing with each other, and listening to each other. The hierarchy of the canon is damaging to your self-esteem, but it is also damaging your ability to listen to your peers, and to value them."

LA: In my teaching of poetry, it is about developing the whole human being. I am not just building writers. I am building human beings who will use the beauty and power of language to "write" and write well and contribute to creating a better world. That should seep into the granularity of their being. We have to understand this as fundamentally important in educating young people.

NC: And the way that those play out in institutionalized forums as well. I often think about how dub has a complicated relationship to the page because of inequality. Dub practices exist both on and off the page because there isn't this assumption of access to traditional print and publication but there also isn't the assumption that the page is enough. There is no assumption that what is printed does all the work and is permanent. There isn't this, "what's going to happen in one hundred years?" It is about where am I writing now? Who is in the room with me right now?

RC: Lillian, you have talked about this in your own work. In your essay, "Poems are not meant to lay still"[2] you have talked about some of your own artistic practices and choices in terms of publishing your work and significantly you frame recordings as one publishing of your work.

LA: Dub has a lineage, a genealogy, and in each generation, each moment, it rises to deal with the specific conditions. Urgency and making visible our connections and inter-connections, even on the psychic level, are part of the poetics of dub. Dub poets never set out to be bestsellers. We weren't in that world. We were doing community work. That's what had meaning for us. We knew that, for example, one of the best ways to reach the people that we wanted to reach was through a kind of communality, meaning they are present with us. So, contact was important to us. We are not rejecting publishing but it's a different mindset in terms of somebody who would dream of being picked up and made famous. Our dream was to be subversive, to get out to the community, and to have people interrupting our shows and repeating our poems. When the work started moving in different directions, starting to get through to all the critics, it was a mega surprise; we were not focused on that at all.

NC: When was that?

LA: Mid to late seventies, maybe early eighties, early on in my career. It was a big surprise, I mean, getting my work studied in school, read at assemblies is still one of the greatest things.

NC: The goal or the dreaming of success is staying in a community versus breaking out. Success means being part of this space that you share with everybody as opposed to the elevation of the singer on the stage of the opera house; do you know what I mean?

LA: To use the analogy of reggae musicians or pop music and classical music, there are some reggae musicians playing and they have got their audience, they are grooving, and then people are starting to see them. They don't say, "Well, I need to be in a symphony."

RC: But there are multiple legacies in your work. In your writings about your work you note different connections to your poetry. These influences emerge in really interesting ways. I note that the title of your book *Psychic Unrest*,[3] for instance, references Gloria Anzaldúa's *Borderlands*.[4] So there are connections across oral and scribal traditions but also connections across different geographies and cultures, which converge in your work.

LA: It's not the way I was thinking about it when it was happening. In retrospect, you are putting a frame on it, and you are bringing a certain kind of analysis and a methodology in your analysis of thinking about it. But what was happening at the time I was writing was that there was this movement that I was a part of. That movement existed with movements about equality, justice, the anti-apartheid movement, Black liberation movement, Black power, civil rights, women's movement, feminist movement, union movement, etc. And what was clear was that in each of these movements, they were addressing similar things from their own viewpoint. What was important was that at some given point, we knew that we were a political movement. Part of that vision was that if we are connected/networked then the voice is louder, stronger, more powerful. We could see the way that unequal accumulation of wealth, as well as weapons of discrimination affected folks, different communities, and groups differently and in diverse ways. We also began to understand different cultural responses to similar conditions. Although, I have to say, that race has never been adequately attended to in all the movements I've been involved with. In North America, race remains one of the most stubborn forms of discrimination, that cuts across every single thing, the very air we breathe.

NC: And compounds in the case of issues around economic prosperity, around gender, around sexuality, race, intersex, but also often compounds the difficulties of people ...

LA: Well that's the thing; we are trying to get back to the body. The Black body is so marked. So are the bodies of diverse sexualities marked. You cannot escape it if you wanted to. We can think here about Harriet's legacies and Black bodies. It is our concern to liberate the Black body; this remains the major concern of dub poetry and the Black community. Our concern in Canada, for example, as a Black community, is about the inescapable Black body, which is marked, marginalized, categorized, and targeted.

NC: Is still not able to move freely.

LA: It is said that in the United States every gesture is informed by race. For me, this carries over to Canada but framed differently to acknowledge the overbearing context of Colonization, its mission, and its ongoing effect on Indigenous peoples in their own land. And also to think about the intersectional nature of the Colonial and capitalist tools of oppression. But the statistics fall the same way here as in the United States around employment, opportunities, policing, health care, day-to-day commerce. Here in Canada, every Black person knows the experience of having a marked body.

RC: I wanted to go back to something you were saying about the body and the presence of the body, and I wondered how this might also be related to the question of dub and work of dub as an art form?

LA: I think it is important that when we work we know that we have to transform our societies and build institutions differently and think about things that people can build on and how we want things to be sustained. We are doing this for ourselves too, and it's important that we are using our time to express ourselves and to build culture. It is very important that we build a new rich culture. We don't acknowledge as much as we should that having diverse art and culture takes great personal sacrifice from a lot of people. So, I think we are talking about the internal life and how do you live that well every day. And that is the primary thing for me. It's just my little humble kind of thing.

I remember when my kid became a teenager and I was travelling a lot and I cursed going to this and that, and I realized that my presence away from home was having a kind of negative effect on my daughter and there was no question in my mind, was I going to be a good mother or a good dub poet? I began studying her books, staying up at night, because it was important to me that this human being and this young Black woman got all she needed to be able to live a good life in the world. So, for me to write instead of doing that would be disastrous. It would be disastrous if I had gone on to win more prizes and wrote five hundred more books than I did instead of being there with her. I remember no choice, no contradiction. And people tell me I am great all the time.

NC: That's what I mean by talking about the future when we consider how to act in the present. You talk about it in terms of your daughter, but it is also a kind of mentorship. You aren't mentoring your students to become famous and competitors but to become people whose lives work for them and have a relationship with writing and community.

RC: One of the ways in which you address questions of legacy and futures is with your writing of children's books. I am wondering if you could talk about the process and impetus behind your work in writing books for children?

LA: One impetus for writing for children came when I used to go around and do poetry for them, perform for children. There's a lot of stuff I have that isn't published or printed. But I remember distinctly at activist events there would be childcare. We got that one right. But what would the children be looking at while we met? "Cinderella," "Beauty and the Beast." And I thought this is absolutely ridiculous, this is counter to everything we are fighting for. I remember there was a conversation, and I said that someone should pay attention to what the kids are learning from this material. As there was very little material to nurture young children's intellect, I thought I must make some of the ideas we're engaged with accessible to them.

By that time, I remember, my kid was playing "Meetings" with other activist friends' kids; they would have conversations about who was going to be the chair and who was going to take minutes. It was a scene to watch, better than turning into a chariot or a pumpkin at midnight to escape one's true identity or whatever, or having the responsibility of turning a beast into a prince. I figured that young people could be brought into the conversation of what their parents were passionate about. I think that when our children are young we have to engage them in our world view and they have to understand what we stand for. They will rebel at some point but you know what, those people, those kids who were raised by activists, they are some of the best human beings. They did not all go on to do what their parents did, but they have a sense of fairness, the importance of human dignity, and fearless compassion. I think that there is a bunch of us that did a really good job. I mean we didn't know it was a great job then. But now, those kids are awesome.

NC: You need to give them a central place in community at the beginning. You don't teach them as adults how to recognize others and be empathetic towards issues of equity. You have to be including them and discussing issues with them on an ongoing basis.

RC: One of the things you have returned to throughout this conversation has been the need to strategize solidarities and build different and indeed new kinds of collectivities and institutions. Our relationships to the institutions in which we work as academics and artists are complex ones.

How do we also possibly imagine futures outside of our current institutional structures?

LA: I actually don't have a lot of faith in institutional contexts or processes. It is hard work and sometimes brutal work when it comes to change in the academy. There is no way that you can bring all of your full self to any of these tables. It is simply too treacherous. Vulnerability is not an asset. You have to armour up. The missiles are subtle and poisonous. There are infinite ways and excuses to subvert a progressive agenda, and infinite ways to undermine BIPOC existence. Colleagues often complain about "top down" changes. I point out to them that it only seems top down because they made themselves oblivious to the battles we were/are fighting, sometimes for decades, and that they stayed neutral on struggles and the daily grind we have to face, and that they were not there in the trenches with us to understand that we brought it to the point that Administration is forced to act. When you are at the table with these same people there is no sense that they are interested in addressing equity issues, no sense of cultivating input or BIPOC voices, nothing important you say can land anywhere. I think that we've got to do better in our educational system and the justice system. Thinking about the Truth and Reconciliation Commission and how they talked about the school system being the perpetrator of violence. The stuff they talk about is just a physical manifestation of what they perpetrated. The mental stuff is still ongoing. We need a total overhaul from early education to the university level in terms of just looking at where people are and how they got there, thinking and teaching about a different kind of national culture, and expanding that vision. I think that's what we need to do. We need redress and recontextualization and a dynamic expanding vision of possibilities.

In our very flawed institutions at the moment, I think we need more of a certain kind of courageous leadership to address pressing issues of inequality and discriminatory practices on which the institutions are built. We also need to be turning out more engaged people, more active people, more questioning people, more people willing to take on these social and political issues. More people who are ready to change the world. In talking about the future within the context of what we have, we need to demand and ensure functional infrastructure for Indigenous communities, to imagine sovereign, independent, and self-determined communities. I am thinking about this in terms of independent institutions like the Watah School, it is in jeopardy because its visionary founder d'bi.young doesn't have the resources.[5] Where is the infrastructure for ten more? More community activation, more culture, I say. So that's some of what I want to see in terms of a new future.

NOTES

1 See Lillian Allen, *Women Do This Everyday* (Toronto: Women's Press, 1993), 50.
2 See Lillian Allen, "Poems are not meant to lay still," in *The Other Woman: Women of Colour in Contemporary Canadian Literature*, ed. Makeda Silvera (Toronto: Sister Vision Press, 1995), 253–62.
3 Lillian Allen, *Psychic Unrest* (Toronto: Insomniac Press, 1999).
4 Gloria Anzaldúa, *Borderlands: The New Mestiza* (San Francisco: Aunt Lute Books, 1987).
5 For one discussion about structural aims and challenges of the Watah School (an independent arts mentorship and performance program) see the account of its founding offered by d'bi.young anitafrika in "Black Plays Matter: Watah Theatre, Creating Safe Space for Black Artists in these Dangerous Times," *Canadian Theatre Review* 165 (Winter 2016): 26–31.

19

Dub Pedagogies:
An Interview with d'bi.young anitafrika

d'bi.young anitafrika, with Ronald Cummings

d'bi.young anitafrika is a writer and performer who has been a significant presence on the Canadian cultural scene. d'bi's work has been published both on the page and in recordings. She has also performed extensively on stage in Canada and internationally. d'bi is the author of four collections of poetry: *Art on Black* (2005), *Rivers … and Other Blackness … Between Us* (2007), OYA (2015) and *dubbin poetry* (2019) and has recorded several albums of music and dub.[1] These works have effectively positioned her as a recognizable part of the dub poetry community and as a key inheritor of the dub legacies forged by an earlier generation of poets – in particular, a community of radical women poets – including Lillian Allen, Afua Cooper, ahdri zhina mandiela (and others anthologized, for instance, in the book *Utterances and Incantations: Women, Poetry and Dub*) and which include her mother Anita Stewart (also published in that book under the name Anilia Soyinka).[2] In addition to poetry, d'bi is widely known as a theatre practitioner. She has written no fewer than eight plays including the plays that constitute the Sankofa trilogy (*bloodclaat, benu, word.sound.powah*) and the Orisha Trilogy (*Esu Crossing the Middle Passage, She Mami Wata and the Pussy WitchHunt,* and *Lukumi: A Dub Opera*).[3] She has also worked as an actress and as a director in several major Canadian productions. Her other writings include the comic book *Shemurenga: Black Supah Shero* which she produced in collaboration with the visual artist Ronald Kayima.[4] d'bi is also the lead singer for the Afro-Fusion-Reggae band d'bi & the 333.

We did not have a chance to talk about all of these various creative practices and pursuits. However, in this interview we talked in-depth about d'bi's poetry and theatre practice. We explored her embodied, spiritual, and artistic relationship to these different forms as well as how language and the body are central to her understanding of these creative practices. In our discussion, d'bi offers accounts of her early experiences, her transnational formation as an artist, the influences and sources that have shaped her work, and the diasporic legacies and artistic traditions and meanings that converge in her creative practice. Legacy emerges as a central theme here. Not only does d'bi talk about how she is located in a line of Black women artists but she also explores the desires she has for her work to change the world and engage the work of shaping community. We also discussed her relationships to a range of artistic and activist communities. As revealed here, the question of community for d'bi is a complex one. It is an active process negotiated through practices of pedagogy and formed in relation to those with whom we might share vision, ethics and purpose. It is also discussed here as shaped through connections with the living and with ancestors. Mortality lingers at the edge of this discussion both in terms of relationships to the ancestors but also in terms of the dreams and legacies for the future.

RC: Your work spans several genres. Which did you come to first and how?

d'bi: I grew up in Jamaica, watching my mother perform on stage. I can't remember if I saw her as an actor or doing dub first, but I say the poetry came first because that is my first love. She started at the School of Drama in Kingston, in 1982, when I was five.[5] I watched her perform in a newly formed group called The Poets in Unity. And I can remember her giving me a copy of a book by one of the best-known dub poets, Mikey Smith. You can see my little six and seven-year-old drawings in that copy of the book, which I still have. It has become my permanent companion.[6] I went to the theatre and watched my mother do her student pieces, and she also took me to the Little Theatre, and to Ward theatre, to see Pantomimes and other productions. So she introduced me to both theatre and poetry at the same time.

RC: So perhaps a related question is how do you think about the relationship between your theatre work and your poetry? You are working on a piece now that you call a Dub Opera and it seems to me that there are always these hybrid or cross-generic moments and texts in your work. So, how do you think about the relationship between these practices?

d'bi: So much of what I am and what I do comes out of my specifically lived Jamaican reality. If you zoom out from me and look beyond the formal poetry, theatre, and performance and at tapestry of life in Jamaica, you will see that poetry – in terms of parables, pithy sayings and in terms of the way that we communicate – is actually culturally embedded, and that is an African retention. So, growing up in the yard, my experience of metaphors and similes (that English has decided to name and claim), are really parts of speech structures found in the fabric of African and West African languages. In Jamaica, our use of what Kamau Braithwaite calls nation language is heavily influenced by English.[7] But we also realize that it is a language that comes out of many other languages. Nation language shows the influence of West African languages including their syntactic and grammatical structures. Nation language even includes vocabulary from enslaved African peoples. English itself, in countries other than England, is basically an immigrant language. And so, within that complex, there are many traditions of storytelling that are heavily metaphoric and full of similes.

Dub poetry brings our attention to this. That is what dub is. You take how people speak regularly and then you give it a particular focus and you highlight certain elements and you have a form, you have a genre. That's how I feel about it. It feels natural in my body. This is very important. We are given this idea that we have to struggle with art but the amazing thing about Jamaican culture is that it is overflowing with artistic expression, not because people are trying to be artists but because it is an embodied reality. So, poetry and theatre for me are an embodied reality, amplified by the education that I received in various, more formal environments. My mother sent me to the School of Drama every summer as a child. Between summers I worked on theatre when people would come into my neighbourhood and teach us. I had access to thinkers like Blacka Ellis, who recently directed *She Mami Wata and the Pussy Witch Hunt*.[8] Blacka would come to Maxfield Avenue when I was ten, eleven, twelve and teach us theatre.[9] So, growing up I had my mother as an example and access to some formal ways of training.

Getting back to the original question about what I feel the relationship is between poetry and theatre, what I feel I am doing is political. I am a political person by condition, by design, by choice, by experience. It is important to me that the art I do reflect my politics as womanist, as feminist, as a queer person, immigrant, working class/middle class person, as a mother, as someone who has taken the Buddhist vows. I am also trying to expand on my mother's work because she was specifically asking the question "how can dub be theatricalized?" Dub was really young at the point when she was part of that pioneering movement and she wanted to know as a practitioner and a poet, how do we theatricalize poetry? She was a young mother, she had me at fifteen. But already, at that age, she was trying to get access to theory and to theorize, in her working class, Jamaican, womanist body, survival for the people. My mother wanted theory to help people better understand the impacts of colonialism on Jamaican society. Her commitment fascinates me to this day. I soaked that up, and being around her made theory accessible to me. I love academics who insist on being revolutionaries because I think that there is a crucial place for that kind of action, for developing ways to help us make sense of our world. I don't like theory or art when they are not accessible to the people or used to create new borders and boundaries and hierarchies. But I see my mother as one of those theorists who are on the ground; they are my heroes. I try and continue that kind of work to honour her.

All that I do is all I have ever been taught to do. That's important because sometimes we are keen to say we have no tradition. So I feel that whenever I am in that space and when I feel like there is nothing, when I look in the mirror, I am looking at the product of an amazing (this doesn't mean unprob-lematic) circular legacy of mentorship. That started off in Jamaica and when my mother moved here and my father moved here they continued to be connected with different communities. For my father, being in Brampton he was connected to a working class and middle class Jamaican community of people who were really proud about coming to Canada and working hard and their Sunday barbeques and maintaining certain traditions in the new country. For my mother, it was being a part of the dub poetry community and also being a part of the womanist, Black feminist community here and the artistic intersections of these communities. When I came here (I visited here before I actually moved and every time I visited) my mom put me in the same kind of programming she did in Jamaica. Here it was in programs like Fresh Arts doing visual arts with Winsom Winsom and theatre and eventually when I moved here, she put me in an antiracism, anti-oppression theatre program at Theatre in the Rough whose artistic director was Amah Harris.[10] At that point I was fifteen, and for two months I was studying theatre from a feminist, antiracist and anti-oppressive lens with sixteen other multiracial, but predominantly Black, young people. That program was a rite of passage. Leading up to this I was exposed to all kinds of things politically, but that program radicalized me in terms of race, gender, and sexual politics. At the time, I was also making the transition to go to Jarvis Collegiate. And Jarvis is right there in the village. Many of my friends were in that theatre program – Yaya was in that theatre program, Paul Osbourne who is now one of the heads of Woodgreen Community Services doing Rights of Passage programs with young teens was in that program. So there were several of us who were in that program at sixteen being radicalized by Black theatre practitioners in the city of Toronto. We had a number of people coming in and teaching us; Ivor Pecou, my mother, Amah Harris, Star Jacobs. We had workshops around police accountability; it was radical by every stretch of the imagination. That was part of the Fresh Arts, JOY (Jobs Ontario Youth) Program.[11]

That period (early to mid 90s) was a huge transition into Canadian society; on the one hand I was experiencing serious cultural shock (feeling the pressures of assimilating, feeling not beautiful, being called lesbian because of the way my body was structured). I was going through this really challenging adolescence. But on the other hand I had this radical Black feminist, Black nationalist awakening, I shaved my head for the first time, I went vegetarian, and I was wrestling with these internal knowings, like knowing that I was queer, realizing there was a community that could hold me but which was still homophobic, negotiating my language in terms of not wanting to speak nation language but being in a community of people who celebrated that language, it was really intense. I wasn't sexually active because I grew up being told that I would get pregnant, and there were a lot of expectations from my family. There was a lot going on. But what an incredible childhood. It was a fantastic childhood because all of that led to this. So at sixteen, and seventeen, I was being socialized at Jarvis Collegiate, which was a great space for me. I did really well. I graduated as an Ontario scholar; I got scholarships and awards. Even though internally there were a lot of things going on, externally I was excelling and becoming and at the same time becoming very radicalized. And then I decided to go to McGill University to study and I moved away and that was also excellent because it just built on the foundation that I had. I met David Austin, Adrian Harewood, who is now at the CBC, and they were running study groups just like the Black Panthers had. We would study C.L.R James, Kamau [Brathwaite], Amílcar Cabral, Frantz Fanon. We would study Black literature and talk about it. We were being radicalized in this circular tradition but then I dropped out of McGill. I continued to study with Dave and he was like my big brother and it is really in Montreal where my rebirth as a poet happened. In the middle of all the studying Dave said to me one day that he noticed that I did not speak nation language. He said, "you have permission to do that." So this was about six or seven years after coming here and going through different spaces of Black nationalism, feminism, womanism, and trying figure it all out. I had studied people like bell hooks and Audre Lorde. After Dave told me this, it turned me back to look at Jamaica in a different way and at myself in a different way. I rewrote all the poetry I had written up to that point in English. I rewrote them in nation language. And then shortly thereafter I moved to Cuba. I did a lot of soul searching. I spent my late teens and twenties soul searching and I was just surrounded by amazing mentors and people who guided me along the way. My whole conditioning was in that circular pedagogical model.

I am almost forty ... That is forty years of being socialized in a very specific way. I have made choices along the way, and I recognize that, but I feel I have to give credit to the ancestors and the community because I feel like I have been guided.

RC: I am interested in the insistence on art as theory practice. In that insistence is also sense of the communal function of art as something that helps us understand our world. And perhaps one of the concepts that I want to bring into this conversation is that of dub pedagogies. Which for me is a process of learning with, learning from, and learning through others. And I am not suggesting that this question of pedagogy is not important to other forms of art and poetry or to other poets but it seems to be particularly important in the context of dub poetry. So, I am wondering if you could say more about how not only theory but also pedagogy, and a concern with speaking with communities, informs your work.

d'bi: I don't know if this is some childhood love affair with my mother. I keep coming back to her story. She was also a teacher at Drama school, at the Cultural Training Centre. This was how brilliant this space was, she was able to study as an actor and as a poet to become a teacher. These are all the areas for me that are important. You express yourself through the creative arts, but you simultaneously have a responsibility to teach and also infuse those spaces with your political, philosophical and spiritual positionings. You have to live what you believe. She modelled that for me.

As an artist you are going to express yourself, but know that that expression has to be inspired and influenced and heavily connected to the community. In that regard, you are a teacher and a leader but that doesn't mean you are at the head of the group. We are trying to work with non-hierarchical models. That's theatre for the people, that's popular theatre, that's a circular model, which is like an Indigenous approach. So, once you get into these theories and pedagogies, and these ways of working, you realize that these are old ways. These are established models of human acculturation and there are countless historical examples of social evolution through circular models. Yes, sometimes we have to dig deep for them because of patriarchy and misogyny and systems of kingdoms and monarchs and wars and this 150-year system of capitalism in Canada. But even within systems that colonize, conquer, and steal there are other models of being.

So where does pedagogy and theorizing come into this? What theory means for me is simple. How can I understand, using multiple lenses, my potential positioning in society, and from that how to change my positioning, how to impact and empower myself and other people? From there, I can work on equality, equity, humanity, fighting patriarchy, fighting capitalism, fighting colonialism. Theory is an equation that helps me calculate how to get from point A to point B. How do I learn and teach these equations that will help me understand my positioning in society? And the "how" is not a "why." A lot of elders have talked about the significance of asking "how" as opposed to "why." How are we are going to have a conversation across boundaries? How are we going to get young people to care more about their humanity rather than their gadgets and social media? How are we going to run a program with no money? That's what I am interested in. And the "how" is intrinsic to the theory. When I think of pedagogy, I think of how are people who self-define as leaders, going to make impactful change?

RC: One of the things you have obviously been talking about here, as well, is legacies. Firstly, in terms of your mother but also the influence that others have had on your social and artistic formation. And you have also been talking about the impact that you hope your art will have in the world. I am really interested in the idea of archiving as part of your practice. I want to link this to the idea of Black women's legacies. We might talk about this in terms of a genealogy of women's resistance but also practices of making space. Mothering is certainly a big part of this. I want to ask about the question of mothering as part of that larger question of legacies. You have talked about the ways in which your mother modelled mothering. And I wonder about your own experiences of mothering and creating spaces for your others.

d'bi: It is really crucial to recognize, research, and learn about these legacies of Black women who have observed and then named through their own tongues their own theories that then help me. Audre Lorde is one of those women. bell hooks is one of those women. Jean Binta Breeze, who is a dub poet, is one of those women. My mother is one of those women. ahdri zhina mandiela is one of those women. I love turning attention in my work to that. That brings me so much joy. I love writing and shouting-out those women because that's how I come to know myself. That is mothering. For me, when I think of my two children and I think of the community, I actually have them in the same position. I feel the same kind of urgent, unrelenting commitment to community that I do with my children, which makes me work really hard and which makes me prioritize the work I am doing in the community over my own career. For me, the way I feel it in my body is not in terms of either/or. If I am a successful artist, then it means that I have to teach and have to lead. They go together. That is also the example that has been given to me. So that is the legacy and tradition that I have observed in the people who have come before. In these women who have been doing that and whose personal, political, and family lives are all together, that is the circular model which is not compartmentalized. That's a model that's really deeply life fulfilling. It may not be a model that leads you to be the richest person on the planet or the most popular but it feels like a model that makes life worth living. That's the example in terms of how Audre led and how Harriet Tubman led.

RC: So how does this relate to the question of Black futures? I raise this question because in your most recent work, you are arguably thinking about the future. In your most recent trilogy – the Orisha Trilogy (*Esu Crossing the Middle Passage*, *She Mami Wata and the Pussy Witch-hunt*, and *Lukumi: A Dub Opera*) – there is a kind of clear trajectory in terms of looking at the past, present, and the possibility of futures. I am intrigued by the fact that you continue to return to the trilogy as a formal structure. The Sankofa trilogy moves through the story of three generations of a family and now the Orisha trilogy, which is writing past, present, and future. Am I right in saying that your use of the trilogy might allow us to think about futures through the question of form but also the in relation to the actual lived realities and possibilities of Black futures?

d'bi: As Black people, we have to think about our past because our reality currently is so heavily influenced by it. Where I am as a woman, as a black body, as a queer body, as an immigrant body, my past is constantly working on my present, which will work on my future. I don't have the luxury of not thinking about my past. But when we think philosophically and spiritually as Black people and as African people, we are very much about the Sankofa bird – looking to the past to learn so that we can move into the future. We are poised to think about our past and I feel like I have the responsibility to do that. I feel like I don't know how to make art and not think about the past. I don't know how I would do that. The first trilogy was very much about navigating this legacy of Jamaican-ness as it moves into Canadian-ness and it moves back into Jamaican-ness. That movement is like water. And I very much looked at my own childhood and the childhood of my mother.

RC: That temporality isn't linear.

d'bi: No, it is not. Which the trilogy reflects. We start out in Jamaica, we go to Canada, go back to Jamaica. We are moving people, by forced movement and by choice. And then this new trilogy. *Esu Crossing the Middle Passage* is about the Middle Passage of then and the goddamn Middle Passages of now. The way that *Esu Crossing the Middle Passage* ends, the play comes full circle. The child is with her mother and grandmother. She is weeping. She has come to a point where she has this rite of passage and they hold her hand through it. In one final scene, we see a life cycle. The play opens with people, and we see Esu in the belly of the ship and then we see all these Black people going through various things and then we see this little girl, at the end, asking "What's fear grandma?" She grows in that scene to be a woman and the mother and the grandmother are holding her hand. By the end of it she is doing that Esu crossing ritual, coming into herself, and it ends on that journey. It says, yes we will die, and that's okay. We don't have to be afraid because then another will come and then another.

She Mami Wata, the second in the trilogy is set in Jamaica and deals with feminism, religion, spirituality, and queerness. There are real people who have to deal with their real friendships. Of the plays in this trilogy it is the one that engages most with theatre of realism. But there is also lots of symbolism. In the end, the people set fire to the church and then the goddess comes in and there's water and fire and brimstone, and they all die. But where do they go? That just makes me want to weep because when I think of Black people and I think of all my ancestors at the bottom of the Atlantic, I ask, "where did they go?" There are so many traditions and stories of ancestors flying away or that they went to the bottom of the sea and that for me, is part of my negotiation of my own mortality. At the end of *She Mami Wata and the Pussy Witch hunt* they die but for me it's like liberation, just like our ancestors felt sometimes on plantations that they had to kill their children and themselves. Because sometimes you have to do that.

In relation to *Lukumi*, that word comes out of the Ifa tradition that was globalized through the passages of the transatlantic slave trade. I am using the word "Lukumi" for that character to have a subliminal dialogue about that passage. But in that play, we are in the future. A nuclear apocalypse has happened and we have these descendants of Black Lives Matter (and they have to be decedents of Black Lives Matter because that is what we are dealing with now, this is who is talking for us now even if we don't agree with all of their methods) and they are trying to get back to the old practices because no children are being born and science can't figure anything out, science is not the way. And the central character goes onto a rite of passage and they have to deal with the animals and trees. For me, the play is about a relationship to this natural world, this organic world, and but also our relationship to the spiritual world and the way in which our ancestors have used that relationship to come through. We have always used relations with the organic and spiritual to make it through our trials and tribulations. I am still rewriting *Lukumi* so I don't know what happens, but I know that for me the answer will always lay in the journey. Who knows what the answer is? But we are people who journey, so for me Black futures is constantly recognizing and acknowledging that the direction is inward, we go inward to go outward. We go inward to make revolution outward. We go inward to change lives and refuel. It's always that direction. Whatever the result is, we see the future ancestors going inward in order to go back outward.

RC: One of the interesting things in your work is the centrality of goddess figures. I think your plays are often ritual spaces. And I am wondering if you want to say something more about spirituality and ritual as a part of your art.

d'bi: I feel like I have a million questions. I don't need to know in order to practice and believe. I will simultaneously be asking a million questions and still be practicing. That for me is not a dichotomy. So I have a million questions about Ifa and Buddhism and Daoism, and I have such a deep and profound respect for all kinds of spiritual traditions because we know that this is how we continue and grow. So I don't know but I practice. So what is practice? Practice for me is setting up an altar when I need to, and meditating, putting water and food, when I need to do that, and I am constantly learning, so I will go to the elders and sit with them and they will expose me to a few things and I will read and do my research and continue to practice. But what I don't do and choose not to do, politically, is go out and say "this is how you do this. This is the way." I cannot do that and I don't want to do that. I don't have enough information for that because I am afraid of the spirit realm because I don't know it or understand it and I just humble myself. So I try not to invoke and incant things that I don't know about. I have a relationship to the goddess Oya (who is considered the defender of women in the Ifa spiritual tradition) and Yemoja (who is considered the mother goddess in that tradition and goddess of the sea and ocean) and to Oshun, (who is the goddess of sexuality and childbirth and she is a river goddess). And some of these shift depending on where you are in the world but I take my relationship to those three goddesses very personally. And even if I look at them intellectually as archetypes, I am so strengthened by what they represent. And emotionally, they allow me access to certain ideas that they represent. For example, Oshun deals with sexuality, and Oshun helps me negotiate through my sexualities. And Yemoja deals with mothering and she helps me with my mothering. And Oya, who is the wrath and the fire, helps me to accept and negotiate my anger. I am a very angry person. I experience a lot of anger all the time and Oya gives me space to be angry but she also asks that I am accountable and responsible for my anger. So Oya says don't just be angry and destroy yourself; that will not make sense. So Oya says be angry but direct your anger. Have some "inner-standing" of your anger, use it to let you know what is truly right and truly wrong, don't just be an idiot and let your anger flare all over the place. So they help me to negotiate my day to day. And so they appear in my work.

RC: One of the other recurring figures in your work is the figure of the child. I am thinking back to early poems like "Children of a Lesser God"[12] as well as your first play *blood.claat*.[13] But children also become central in the latest trilogy. What is their significance?

d'bi: I am a child. I really experience myself like that. I don't know what that is but I feel very childlike in relation to the world and learning. So I am watching these grey hairs increase daily and I am watching and feeling my body shift and change. And I am still a child. It is a very accessible place for me. I am very celebratory of that. You know what that space also does? It allows me access to my deepest vulnerabilities. That is very important to me. It also allows me to not have to know everything. The pressure of having to know everything, I simply cannot deal with. My students come to me and I have to be able to say, "I don't know." And the only way I can is by being a child. Now that does not mean I am not a mature, adult woman. Again, those two things are not a fork in the road going into different direc-tions. I am a mature adult woman who is a leader in the community, who takes her responsibilities very seriously, who is very serious, and people perceive me to be very serious. But balance and intersectionality, which makes me able to be a child, and so that child-like energy is all over the work because it is a space that I occupy and embody and that I really love. Because it makes me able to be playful and relate to my children. I wish I could say it is intellectual but it is way more visceral.

RC: I was struck by this again when I saw you recently on stage in Soulpepper Theatre's production of Ntozake Shange's *For Colored Girls who Have Considered Suicide/When the Rainbow is Enuf*.[14] We think of that work as such a grown up play. And in the last monologue you did, there is a moment in which you so clearly embody the figure of the child. You took the child on stage with you. That was really interesting to me.

d'bi: Every opportunity that she gets to speak she does. Everybody has an inner child. When I reflect now on the little girl that I was, she was really cool. I remember her saying, "I wish they could see all of who I am." And I am sure that is an experience that we all have because we have this internal world and the adult world can't really see it and our friends can't because it is our internal landscape. The feeling of not being seen in our totality is a very interesting feeling. I still remember it. And so recently I had a nervous breakdown, and so my girlfriend who was there at the time, Raven, came from upstairs and she started doing some spirit work. And in this moment, I can see I am having a breakdown. I know I need to have a breakdown in order to have a break through. Because I am stuck. And so I am seeing myself and I am going along with it because it is like purging. You actually have to burn everything down to move past it. And so she calls my other friends who actively work on African [spiritual] models of support, and they work on me for the whole night. They are doing a laying on of hands, church style, like by the altar. And as they are doing the work, my little girl-self comes and asks "are you alright?" I am like "I am alright, are you?" She said, "I am alright but you need to get this healing. Because I am okay." And as they were working through this healing I was able to have a conversation with her. Through this, she was telling me, the adult woman having the breakdown, that I could let things go. But that would not have been possible without the ritual of the laying on of hands, to clear the energy. So she was able to come and I was able to see her, adult to little girl, and hear her say, "I know you have things up in your heart, but it is okay. I am telling you, I am okay. You have been doing the work over the last twenty years. I am good. Now I need you to be good. So let's go through this so you can be good." And it was such a confirmation of what we always suspected and known about Black people's mental health and wellness, and the ways in which systematic oppression can send us crazy but also the ways in which our own systems can heal us. African systems can heal us when these systems send us into a place of mental un-wellness. Which is really a need for clearing the mind and body from systems of oppression. You need to have community and unconditional love and powerful energies to clear you out. It is not an individual thing. It is not just that moment, not just a ritual but consistent work. I felt like all the work led to that moment and all the work after. That spiritual work also has to be brought into the academic, intellectual space where we are theorizing. Because it is part of the theory.

RC: This spiritual work also seems to be about ways of negotiating survival. One of the other things you have also talked about elsewhere, in relation to survival, is the question of art as survival. I don't know if you want to expand on that here.

d'bi: That is exactly what it is. It's survival, complete human embodiment, self-actualization, self-knowledge, accessing your deepest integrity. There is an urgency around that for us. I do believe that it is a gift that we get to experience our lives in an urgent way. I am not talking about frantic and anxious and nervous, I am talking about urgent in the sense that there is an awareness that you will transition so your time here is to be used in the ways that you feel most deeply, passionate about. I feel like we have access to that as Black people because of what we have lived through. And I am very grateful to have access to that because it makes me waste less time. Spending time with my friends one-on-one is important and crucial to me. That is a revolutionary act in a capitalist system that tells you that all you need to do is work. I see my friends more now that I live in the country than when I lived in the city because now they make time to come up to the country and when they come up for an hour, they do not use or necessarily have access to social media, instead they have to engage in dialogue. These are revolutionary things for me. So is the action of organizing, so is creating spaces and not just talking that things don't exist. Creating space so that we can survive and thrive. The nucleus of that for me is a sense of urgency. Urgency for me simply means, an awareness that I will die and therefore I have to live accordingly.

NOTES

1 d'bi.young anitafrika, *Art on Black* (2006; reissue, Toronto: Women's Press Literary, 2013); d'bi.young anitafrika, *Rivers … and Other Blackness … Between Us* (Toronto: Women's Press, 2007); d'bi.young anitafrika, OYA (Toronto: Spolrusie Publishing, 2015); d'bi.young anitafrika, *dubbin poetry: the collected poems of d'bi.young anitafrika* (Toronto: Spolrusie Publishing, 2019).
2 Afua Cooper, ed., *Utterances and Incantations: Women, Poetry and Dub* (Toronto: Sister Vision Press, 1999).
3 d'bi.young anitafrika, *Sankofa: blood.claat, benu, word.sound.powah* (Toronto: Playwrights Canada Press, 2017); d'bi.young anitafrika, *Dubbin Theatre: The Collected Plays of d'bi.young anitafrika* (Toronto: Spolrusie Publishing, forthcoming 2021).

4 *Shemurenga: Black Supah Shero* which she produced in collaboration with
   the visual artist Ronald Kayima

5 The Jamaica School of Drama (formerly the Theatre School) was established in
   1968. It was part of what might be called the post-independence cultural project
   of decolonization in Jamaica. In its early years, it operated as a part-time institution run by the Little Theatre Movement (which was founded by Henry and
   Greta Fowler). In 1976, it was incorporated into the Cultural Training Centre –
   an arm of the Institute of Jamaica. The Cultural Training Centre brought
   together schools of visual arts, music, dance and drama. During this period, the
   institution trained several graduates who would become major cultural contributors in the field of dub poetry including Mikey Smith and Jean Binta Breeze.
   In 1995, the institution was renamed The Edna Manley College of the Visual
   and Performing Arts.

6 The influence of dub poet Mikey Smith's work on d'bi's artistic practice can
   be further noted in the fact that d'bi organized the Mikey Smith Raw Works
   Festival each year. The festival ran annually in December between 2014 and
   2018 and constituted a key part of the program of the Watah School – an artistic residency, training, and mentorship program initiated by d'bi for young Black
   artists in Toronto. The Watah School is a space that was conceptualized to help
   mentor individual artists in as much as it is also meant to function as part of
   ensuring and supporting a culture of Black artistic production in Toronto. For
   more about the structure and aims of the program, see the moving and thoughtful examination of its founding offered by d'bi in "Black Plays Matter: Watah
   Theatre, Creating Safe Space for Black Artists in These Dangerous Times,"
   Canadian Theatre Review 165 (Winter 2016): 26–31.

7 Kamau Brathwaite, *History of the Voice* (London: New Beacon Press, 1984).

8 In May 2016, the show *She Mami Wata and the Pussy WitchHunt* – the second
   in the sequence of the Orisha Trilogy – was staged in Toronto. The show was
   directed by Owen "Blacka" Ellis. d'bi received an award for best actress for her
   performance in that production and the show was also nominated for a Dora
   Award for Best New script.

9 Maxfield Avenue is an urban community in Kingston. d'bi's representation of life
   in Maxfield Avenue can be seen in her first play *blood.claat* (Toronto: Playwrights
   Canada Press, 2005).

10 In 1985 Amah Harris founded Theatre in the Rough. The company was known
   for its production of youth theatre and school plays as well as using theatre for
   public education. Theatre in the Rough toured and performed all over Ontario
   and Canada and internationally including South Africa.

11 In the wake of the 1992 Yonge Street Uprising in Toronto, the Fresh Arts program
   was instituted as an initiative of Jobs Ontario Youth (JOY) for Black and urban

youth in the city. The program was short-lived. It lasted for three years. However, it contributed much to the cultural life and future of the city. Not only has it produced well-known and influential alumni such as d'bi.young anitafrika, Kardinal Offishall, as well as others who are listed by d'bi in this interview, but it has also offered an important model for the arts-based initiatives in the province and in Canada. In many ways, this important initiative warrants a cultural-historical study that might usefully delineate its interventions, influence, and afterlife as part of a history of Black Canadian cultural production. For a further account of her experience in Fresh Arts and its influence on the development of the Watah School, see d'bi.young anitafrika, "Black Plays Matter."

12 anitafrika, *Art on Black*, 15.

13 anitafrika, *blood.claat*.

14 In May 2017, Soulpepper Theatre staged a production of Ntozake Shange's *For Coloured Girls Who Have Considered Suicide/When the Rainbow is Enuf*. The cast of the production included d'bi.young anitafrika as Lady in Red, Ordena Stephens-Thompson as Lady in Purple, Karen Glave as Lady in Yellow, Tamara Brown as Lady in Brown, Evangelia Kambites as Lady in Orange, Sate as Lady in Blue. The production was directed by Djanet Sears.

20

Spoken Word:
A Signifying Gesture Toward Possibility

Andrea Thompson

We die. That may be the meaning of life.
But we do language. That may be the measure of our lives.
                    Toni Morrison, Nobel Lecture, 7 December 1993[1]

Once upon a time. It is these words, spoken aloud, that so often mark the beginning of our experience of literature. Through stories, we are initiated into the world of metaphor, symbols, and language used to convey the values, traditions, and history of our society. In this way, oral lore becomes psychosocial artefact – transitory in its transmission, yet serving as the thread of knowledge passed from generation to generation. Each time we hear these familiar refrains, we are taken deeper into the realm of the symbolic, where the act of language meets the evolution of our cultural psyche.

The legend of Harriet Tubman demonstrates one of the most foundational aspects of the Black Canadian experience. Tubman understood the value of human connection as a vehicle for emancipation. As much as it was her life mission to escape to freedom, she returned – to wander through a terrain of danger, to risk her life for family, friends and then strangers. We are connected together through this strength of character – a DNA strand of resilience that has kept our people moving forward. It is this refusal to swallow the silence of servitude and insistence on exercising our right to speak out that has kept the backbone of the Black community strong.

During slavery, we sang out in rebellion. We found a communal language of connection and a way to celebrate our dreams of freedom by letting the wind carry our voices forward. We used rhyme, rhythm, metaphor, and cadence as a means of covert insurgence. We sang spirituals about Moses (as Tubman was known throughout the network of the Underground Railroad). We sang of Canaan, of Egypt, and Israel, anthems encoded with tempo-driven direction – when to lay low, when to head north again.[2] We freed ourselves – voice first, used language and rhythm as a medium for political action. We shared information, we sang and we made our plans – to follow the North Star all the way to the Promised Land. This is the story of how Black North American spoken word began.

Once upon a time ... In her acceptance speech for the 1993 Nobel Prize for Literature, African American writer Toni Morrison began with storytelling's most familiar refrain.[3] The narrative Morrison chose to share on the day she spoke before the Swedish Academy was a folk story of a blind old woman who, in spite of her physical handicap and her station as solitary outsider, had become a wise elder. Morrison's story begins as a group of young people approach the woman, seemingly to test the breadth of her knowledge. They stand before her, telling her that one of them has a bird in their hand and posing the question: is the bird living or dead? Like Tubman, Morrison embraces the position of elder and guide in her explanation of this tale and the true motivation behind the question the children are raising. To Morrison, the old woman represents a practiced writer, while the bird she views as language. Using this metaphorical framework, Morrison goes on to interrogate the current uses and abuses of language as a means of degradation and disempowerment. Morrison's comments can be used as a meta-narrative framework to investigate the intellectual colonization of language in Canada, as reflected through the journey of the art of the spoken word – from the bondage of marginalization, to the freedom of exaltation.

You trivialize us and trivialize the bird that is not in our hands.
Is there no context for our lives? No song, no literature, no poem full
of vitamins, no history connected to experience that you can pass
along to help us start strong?[4]

Spoken word is enigmatic. An umbrella term that refers to a hybrid genre that includes forms such as performance poetry, dub, jazz, and hip-hop; each branch of spoken word has its own historical lineage and as such reflects the diversity of the Black diaspora. While some spoken word artists use traditional elements of literary verse (or page poetry, as it is often referred to in the spoken word community), this adherence to poetic norms is not required in order for a spoken word piece to be successful. Many spoken word artists draw inspiration from a different palette – blurring the lines between poetry and performance art, theatrical monologue, stand up comedy, sermonic rhetoric, and storytelling. Most spoken word artists use a blend of varied influences, creating their own unique aesthetic – the common denominator being that each artist writes and performs pieces that are focused on creating a sense engagement with an audience through the use of combination of sound-play, word-play, and an unlimited range of other performative techniques.

Spoken word is a paradox. While some audiences are just beginning to become acquainted with this dynamic "new" oratory, spoken word is one of the oldest forms of creative expression. A natural evolution of the oral traditions, with an ancestry deeply rooted in preprint literature, spoken word is as primeval as prehistoric petroglyphs. This ancestry can be traced back past the European troubadours of the eleventh century, *Beowulf*, and the Homeric epics, to the more primordial poetic oratory of the West African Griot and other indigenous traditions that use storytelling, mantras, and chanting as a central part of the development and continuity of culture.

Narrative is radical, creating us at the very moment it is being created.[5]

The history of spoken word in Canada consists of many creative and cultural streams that feed into the sea of our communal language. The First People of this land had deep traditions of orature, expressed through stories and myths passed down through generations.[6] Subsequent cultures that arrived in what was to become Canada each carried with them their own firmly established oral literary traditions. Of these cultural contributors, the influence of the Black diaspora has had a profound and lasting impact on the evolution and revolution of contemporary spoken word.

Dub poetry – a Caribbean literary tradition closely related to the social activist lineage of reggae music and most often performed over reggae instrumentals – is one of the most popular manifestations of performative literature in Canada, with Toronto in particular having gained an international reputation as one of the leading hubs of dub. Much of the inspiration behind this reputation comes from the foundational work performed and published by feminist dub poets Lillian Allen, Afua Cooper, and ahdri zhina mandiela. Allen helped bring dub poetry into the lexicon of popular culture with her two Juno Award winning albums, *Revolutionary Tea Party* (1986) and *Conditions Critical* (1988), as well as through her collaborative album with Devon Haughton and Clifton Joseph, *De Dub Poets* (1985). In a recent interview about this time in history, Joseph recalls, "There was a scene going on Queen Street. We were playing at those clubs, performing at different cultural events with a lot of different artists and Queen Street became in some ways our home. There was a whole sweltering rise of culture at the time. Queen St became this place where there was a lot of cross pollination."[7]

This cross-pollination also seems to have had a palpable effect on the publication of performative texts, with the early eighties marking an era when the boundaries between page and stage became increasingly blurred. Poets once thought as primarily performative broke through barriers as they began to publish in larger numbers. Allen's *Rhythm an' Hardtimes* and Joseph's *Metropolitan Blues* were both released in 1982, with Afua Cooper's *Breaking Chains* published the following year. Shortly after this, Jamaican born women Makeda Silvera and Stephanie Martin co-founded Sister Vision Press, a publishing house dedicated to producing "innovative, challenging and provocative works by Canadian women of colour."[8] Notably, it was towards the end of this dub r/evolution of the eighties that Caribbean storyteller and cultural icon, Louise Bennett – affectionately known as Miss Lou – relocated from Jamaica and began to call Toronto her home.

> Be it grand or slender, burrowing, blasting, or refusing to sanctify; whether it laughs out loud or is a cry without an alphabet, the choice word, the chosen silence, unmolested language surges toward knowledge, not its destruction.[9]

By the early 1990s, as Morrison joined the ranks of Nobel laureates, the spoken word movement all across North America was undergoing a similar momentum – with slam poetry events in particular drawing audiences in unprecedented numbers. In the US, many marked the emergence of oral forms into popular culture as being rooted in a renewed interest in the Beat poets of the fifties and sixties, and their rejection of the norms of both the literary establishment and society as a whole. Allen Ginsburg commented on the similarity between the Beats and the growing spoken word movement in an article that appeared in a 1995 issue of *The New Yorker*: "This movement is a great thing: the human voice returns, word returns, nimble speech returns, nimble wit and rhyming return."[10]

One of the results of this momentum was the establishment of a weekly poetry slam in Vancouver. From this dynamic performance event organized by Graham Olds and James P. McAuliff, the first national slam team emerged. The team, consisting of me, Cass King, Justin McGrail, and Alexandra Oliver, travelled to Portland Oregon, where we reached the semi-finals in the 1996 National Poetry Slam Championships and witnessed a new style of vibrant spoken word. The history of slam in the US goes back to the mid-eighties, when poet and activist Marc Kelly Smith created the form of competitive performance poetry as a method to inspire poets to share their work in a way that was engaging and to integrate the audience into the process of determining literary merit by appointing them as judges. In a 2009 article in *The New York Times*, Smith declared that his intention was to challenge the current literary establishment with a form of poetry that was both democratic and subversive.[11] Slam was, and continues to be, popular with youth and as such, often represents a microcosm of youth culture. As the thoughts, feelings, and perceptions its practitioners express are a direct reflection of the experiences and preoccupations of their generation, slam pieces often gesture towards themes of disenfranchisement and social justice. For many Black youth, the local slam series offered a rare outlet – for not only their budding literary talents but also for unexpressed feelings of isolation, disillusion, and disempowerment.

This spoken word revolution of the nineties was a national phenomenon. Poets such as Mercedes Bains and Roger Blenman lit up West Coast stages with their unique brand of spoken word-play while others such as d'bi young and Dwayne Morgan have been igniting the spoken word scene in Toronto since then. In 2002, Wayde Compton mapped the path of Black writing on the West Coast through *Bluesprint: Black British Columbian Literature and Orature*[12] – a comprehensive anthology that traces the influence of Black writers in the province from the 1800s to the early 2000s. Despite its vibrancy, by the end of the decade the spoken word scene still lacked a cohesive sense of self-definition. Many of us called ourselves performance or action poets. Spoken word was one of several new terminologies used for this renegade oral literature. In the introduction to their 1998 anthology, *Poetry Nation: The North American Anthology of Fusion Poetry*[13] Regie Cabico and Todd Swift coined the term "fusion poetry" as a way to provide a framework for this hybrid art form and as "a way of approaching the myriad of poets at the end of the millennium and their numerous positions and personae."[14] A few years later, in 2002, Swift and Phil Norton expanded on this definition with the publication of *Short Fuse: The Global Anthology of New Fusion Poetry*.[15] "The fusion poets define these complex times through new forms of performance and text by mixing the best of the oral and written traditions."[16] Swift and Norton also emphasized the fusion of this new poetry with cultural influences such as the use of rapidly changing computer-based technology, which offered poets access to both new avenues for creation and publication, as well as the ability to connect with a global creative community. While the term "fusion poetry," successfully captured the hybridity inherent in spoken word, it did not become common terminology.

As the spoken word community continued its creative exploration and self-definition, a palpable shift began to occur between those who practiced the oral presentation of poetry and those who focused on the written word.

Many of us who came to the stage from the page felt pressured to declare allegiance. Some viewed spoken word, and slam in particular, as at best a cheap trick of theatrics and at worst a toxin to the body poetic. Spoken word artists had become literary other, and as such, many experienced anxieties of marginalization and self-representation as we practiced a form viewed by some of our peers to be terminally transgressive.

> Oppressive language does more than represent violence; it is violence; does more than represent the limits of knowledge; it limits knowledge.[17]

By 2003, the voices of protest against this new wave of spoken word had moved beyond barely audible grumblings at poetry events to a full frontal attack. In response to the sudden growth and popularity of spoken word and the slam performance format in Canada and around the world, many detractors viewed the genre not as an evolution of the oral tradition but as a sub-standard poetic, the creation of which was indefensible. Shortly after his appointment as the first Canadian parliamentary poet laureate in 2002, a reporter from *The Globe and Mail* asked George Bowering if he thought there were any connections between the successes of BC poets in the award circuit that year and the growing proliferation of spoken word in the province. Bowering replied, "Horseshit," adding that spoken word artists and slams were "abominations" and that "To treat poetry as performance is crude and extremely revolting."[18] The public lambasting of spoken word was not merely a Canadian phenomenon, as Jonathan Galassi, then honorary chairman of the Academy of American Poets, referred to poetry slams as "a kind of karaoke of the written word."[19] Literary critic Harold Bloom declared them "the death of art" in the Spring 2000 issue of *The Paris Review*.[20] This condescension towards spoken word and the positioning of oral poets as fundamentally inferior has helped to perpetuate the page versus stage dichotomy and has furthered the conceptualization of spoken word artists as literary other. Yet, this view of spoken word as literary lesser is by no means new or exclusive to the English language. The concept of an oral literature that is different yet equal was encapsulated by Ugandan linguist Pio Zirimu in the early seventies when he coined the term "orature" in response to the growing sentiment in African literature that the oral traditions were inferior, less evolved forms than their printed counterparts.[21]

In response to this criticism, some artists in the Canadian spoken word community began to volley their own condemnation in response, many viewing traditional "page poets" as out of step with the times. In a 2010 blog post entitled "The Living Language of Spoken Word," [22] poet and activist

Chris Gilpin noted, "Each old guard tries to expel the work of the avant-garde before inevitably embracing it," citing the early criticism of Ginsberg and Robert Frost's dismissal of free verse as "playing tennis with the net down," as historical examples. Gilpin goes on to chastise poets "entangled in academia and its publish-or-perish credo" for creating work "so insular and cryptic, so divorced from broader society, that they have alienated a generation from their brand of poetry." South of the border, poet and critic Victor D. Infante stated in an essay in *oc Weekly*, "[The death of art] is a big onus to place on anybody, but Bloom has always had a propensity for (reactionary) generalizations and burying his bigotries beneath 'aesthetics,' insisting – as he did in his prologue to the anthology *Best of the Best of American Poetry* – that the 'art' of poetry is being debased by politics." Infante goes on to say, "The irony, of course, is that denying politics a place in poetry is itself a political position, one undeniably born of class and privilege."[23]

Official language smitheryed to sanction ignorance and preserve privilege is a suit of armor polished to shocking glitter, a husk from which the knight departed long ago.[24]

In her interpretation of the story of the blind old woman, Morrison spoke of the misuse of language by those in positions of power, claiming that this type of authoritative expression is, "ruthless in its policing duties (with) no desire or purpose other than maintaining the free range of its own narcotic narcissism, its own exclusivity and dominance." Morrison added that the abuse of language was "crafted to lock creative people into cages of inferiority and hopelessness." In this respect, I believe that the lack of respectful dialogue and polarization between "page" and "stage" poets created what Morrison calls, "lethal discourses of exclusion blocking access to cognition for both the excluder and the excluded."[25]

This fracturing in the literary community leads to the consideration of more general questions of power and inclusion. In an essay entitled "Language and Agency," linguistic anthropologist Laura M. Ahearn offers a provisional definition of agency as "the socio-culturally mediated capacity to act" and defines language as a "social action." Ahearn provides an overview of current theoretical perspectives on the relationship between the two and the ways that language is used to either encourage or hinder that capacity. According to Ahearn, over the past few decades, postmodern criticisms within the academy "have called into question impersonal master narratives that leave no room for tensions, contradictions, or oppositional actions on the part of individuals and collectives."[26] This trend indicated dangerous repercussions in terms of the nurturing and development of Black writers and spoken word artists within the academy who wished to express themselves on their own terms.

But who does not know of literature banned because it is interrogative; discredited because it is critical; erased because alternate? And how many are outraged by the thought of a self-ravaged tongue?[27]

Indeed, what groundbreaking poetry movement was not, in its inception, plagued by cries of public outrage at the onset? The Tish Poets of the sixties, for example, were well known for their anti-establishment sentiments. In *From Cohen To Carson: The Poet's Novel In Canada*, author Ian Rae tells us that the name of the group came about as a playful reference to an anagram for "shit," adding that "the scatological connotations of Tish underscore the collective's anti-establishment irreverence."[28] However, the poets of the Tish collective were serious about Charles Olson's theory of poetry "as an energy discharge," a theory outlined in his essay "Projective Verse."[29] Ironically, Bowering was a key member of this radical youth movement, disenchanted with the then current state of Canadian poetics and driven by a desire to move beyond the conventional parameters of poetic discourse.

Displaying a dismissive literary ethnocentrism, many critics of spoken word have overlooked the cultural and sociopolitical influences on the genre's roots. Dub, hip-hop, and jazz poetry have all been influenced by the Harlem Renaissance of the 1920s and 1930s and the Black Arts Movement of the 1960s. These movements emphasized the upliftment of the Black community by encouraging a literature that was both cultural vessel and vehicle for social justice and equality.

As Modernist poets of the early twentieth century experimented with fragmentation and a desire to "make it new" rather than emulate the traditional forms of realism, the poets and writers of the Harlem Renaissance, such as Zora Neale Hurston and Langston Hughes, were creating a writing aesthetic that emphasized inclusiveness and strove to bring the traditions of the past forward. Literary scholar Houston A. Barker cites this impulse as the foundation of Afro-American Modernism; a movement "concerned pre-eminently with removing the majority of the black population from the poverty, illiteracy and degradation that marked southern, black, agrarian existence in the United States ... Rather than bashing the bourgeoisie, such spokespersons were attempting to create one. Far from being rebellious dissenters against existent Afro-American expressive forms, they sought to enhance these forms and bring them before a sophisticated public."[30] This motivation created a poetic which often blended the iambic patterns of traditional forms such as the sonnet, the ballad, or lyric with the musical cadences that arose from the lexicon of common Black vernacular and the blues and jazz music of the day.

Forty years later, fuelled by the activist passion of the Civil Rights and Black Power movements, the Black Arts movement continued the momentum of the Harlem Renaissance. Based on a politic that rejected the concept that Blacks would ever achieve full equality through passive integrationist methodologies, the Black Arts movement insisted on an imperative that sought to unearth racial inequities in both American culture and the academy through a realistic representation of the realities of the Black community.[31] This rapid advancement in the Black literary aesthetic introduced audiences to poets such as Sonia Sanchez, Amiri Baraka, Gil Scott-Heron, and Ntozake Shange. These writers were radical, militant, and unapologetic as they advocated a poetic based on rebellion against the inaccessible, elitist use of language and encouraged social, economic, and psychological empowerment. This revolutionary, populist philosophy became an expression of a Black postmodernism that expanded upon the modernist theoretical foundations of the Harlem Renaissance. Didacticism, a dirty word in traditional poetry, furthered this political agenda and was encouraged in both content and delivery as an extension of what Gwendolyn Brooks referred to as "preachment," a sermonic oracular style rooted in the history of Black sermons, gospels, and spirituals. The immediacy of performance was often punctuated by a call-to-action or the use of call-and-response or dialect to further the imperative of audience accessibility and engagement. Colloquial speech, slang, and profanity served to challenge traditional syntax, spelling, and grammar while representing the rhythmic patterns of the Black vernacular.

In the groundbreaking book *Understanding the New Black Poetry: Black Speech and Black Music as Poetic Reference* (1973) Stephen Henderson referred to this sort of blending of cultural influences as entering one's "Soul Field." Based on the concept of psychological Field Theory, which investigates patterns of interaction between an individual and their environment, Henderson saw the African American Soul Field as "the complex galaxy of persona, social, institutional, historical, religious and mystical meanings that affect everything we say or do as Black people sharing a common heritage."[32] To Henderson, this Soul Field offered the Afro-centric writer "a kind of continuum of Blackness – at one end instantly identifiable in all of its rich tonal and rhythmic variety, at the other indistinguishable from that of the whites."[33] Within this continuum, the Black literary aesthetic has blossomed, from seeds sown in the soil of what Henderson described as "a complex and rich and powerful and subtle linguistic heritage whose resources have scarcely been touched."[34]

> Be it grand or slender, burrowing, blasting, or refusing to sanctify; whether it laughs out loud or is a cry without an alphabet, the choice word, the chosen silence, unmolested language surges toward knowledge, not its destruction.[35]

The development of the Black creative aesthetic encouraged a cross-pollination between all forms of creative expression but particularly between music and poetry. During the Harlem Renaissance, the evolution of blues into jazz was documented through poems that mimicked the musical cadence and phrasings of both forms, such as in Langston Hughes's "The Weary Blues" which explores the subject of a blues pianist using the cadence of early jazz.[36] During the Black Arts Movement, the jazz-infused Black Nationalist poetry troupe the Last Poets and poet/musician Gil Scott-Heron not only continued the tradition of adopting musical rhythms and phrasings in their poetry, they also helped contribute to the initiation of another consequential evolutionary leap in Black music. Scott-Heron specifically (who cites Langston Hughes as a key influence) is often referred to as "the godfather of rap"[37] because of his inspiration of early creators of the form. The revolutionary early eighties track "The Message" by Grandmaster Flash and the Furious Five, not only helped to bring rap music into mainstream culture, it constituted a vital link between Scott-Heron and, by extension, the Black Arts Movement and Harlem Renaissance. Historian James B. Stewart says of "The Message," "it has that melodic dimension, streetwise poetic lyrics, and even the beat was very similar to some of Gil's productions."[38] Though Scott-Heron eschewed the title, preferring to refer to himself as a "bluesologist,"[39] his politically driven poetic has been touted as foundational for artists such as Public Enemy, KRS-One, and Mos Def.[40] Since its inception, rap has, in return, become a significant influence on the development of spoken word, with contemporary Canadian artists such as Motion, Jemini, J-Wyze, and Little X, drawing from the cultural, political, and stylistic characteristics of rap for inspiration.

Rap (most commonly believed to be an acronym for rhythm and poetry), dub, and jazz poetry all use the technique of "signifying," which is the practice of using devices such as homonyms to explore the complexity of allusion that arises from the use of common vernacular to imply a deeper meaning or what Louis Henry Gates Jr calls a "verbal strategy of indirection that exploits the gap between the denotative and figurative meanings of words."[41] In his landmark book *The Signifying Monkey: A Theory of African-American Literary Criticism*, Gates investigated the roots of the use of signifying as one that goes back to the days of slavery and the development of a communally based use of language that allowed slaves to communicate to each other without their meaning being deciphered. Gates summarizes the confluence of these sorts of historically based speech patterns with the evolution of its speaker's literary aesthetic by stating, "A vernacular tradition's relation to a formal literary tradition is that of a parallel discursive universe."[42]

Though Gates's subsequent examination of Black writing, which he refers to as "reading the tradition,"[43] focuses exclusively on the work of fiction writers, his theory can be even more aptly applied to the examination of oral literature. Specifically, his observation of what he terms as "speakerly text"[44] – a page-bound literary work that captures the essence and cadence of everyday dialogue has become one of the trademarks of much of contemporary Black poetry – most notably in the oral tradition of spoken word. In addition, Gates's discussion of the "trope of the talking book"[45] – a kind of Black reactive archetype that arose from the sense of alienation and exclusion that most Black slaves experienced through observing their masters in the act of reading – serves as a fitting allusion to reflect the disenfranchisement that many contemporary spoken word artists feel when attempting to have their work valued or understood by the gatekeepers of the literary establishment. In reflecting on the writing and the reaction to the writing of the few early Black authors to emerge while in the bondage of slavery, Gates wrote, "What seems clear upon reading the texts created by black writers in English or the critical texts that responded to these black writings is that the production of literature was taken to be the central arena in which persons of African descent could, or could not, establish and redefine their status within the human community."[46] This observation not only serves as a foundational understanding of the attitudes that may still resonate within the contemporary Black responsive legacy, it also emphasizes the psycho/social legitimacy offered through the elevation of the written word over oral literature as one that is deeply rooted in the "soul field" of Black consciousness.

Tell us ... What moves at the margin. What it is to have no home
in this place. To be set adrift from the one you knew. What it is to live
at the edge of towns that cannot bear your company.[47]

In the book, *What Moves At The Margin: Selected Nonfiction*, Toni Morrison and Carolyn C. Denard elaborate on Morrison's interpretation of the motives of the children with the bird in their hands. The children were not attempting to humiliate the old woman; rather they were offering her an invitation to impart some of their wisdom – an invitation that Morrison refers to as "a gesture toward possibility."[48] The silence the old woman offers in response is indicative of neither indifference nor condemnation. It is offered as a sign of respect and a willingness to learn and listen. Further insight into Morrison's interpretation of the tale of the old woman can be inferred from a slam performance series that the Nobel laureate organized in 2006 when she served as guest curator at the Louvre in Paris. This event centred on the theme of "The Foreigner's Home" and investigated the concepts of identity, exile, and belonging. Moved to action by the anger and alienation felt by youth in Parisian suburbs – a sentiment which sparked violent rioting in the predominantly working-class immigrant communities that lived there, Morrison wanted to give the youth a venue for free creative expression. In an interview in *Libération*, Morrison stated that "From my experience in the United States, I know that the music of outsiders, those who are discriminated against, have historically become very powerful … I have come here to listen to the young people; it is not for me to tell them anything."[49]

Over the past few decades, oral literature has solidified its place in the collective consciousness of mainstream culture, as spoken word artists continue to move the form forward on their own terms – taking their work into the areas of community building and youth engagement, using the form as a tool for personal empowerment and the development of literacy skills. Spoken word artists are often invited to perform and speak at community centres, libraries, high schools, and post-secondary institutions across Canada, and spoken word components have been a part of an increasing number of university creative writing courses. Notably, there are still only few post-secondary institutions that teach spoken word theory, history, or practice as a designated credit course. Lillian Allen, now a tenured creative writing professor teaching a fourth year dub, spoken word, and performance writing course at the Ontario College of Art and Design University states that one of the problems in academic circles is that spoken word seems like too much fun to be taken seriously. "Spoken word artists also have an unapologetic appreciation of media and multimedia technologies, and the methods they afford to further creative expression," she says. "The book isn't quite dead, but it's no longer the only train leaving the station." Allen also sees the dichotomy created between the stage and page communities as artificial. "It's a spectrum," Allen states, adding that the need for people to reduce the issue to a polarity is due to the urge to categorize, define and marginalize what they don't understand or perceive to be "other."[50]

One strategy to bridge the gap between spoken word artists and the traditional literary establishment is to aim for mutual appreciation and respect. Across the country, literary organizers have put this strategy into action through the curation of events that provide the opportunity for cross-pollination. The Toronto Poetry Slam proudly featured poetic elder George Elliott Clarke shortly after his appointment as Toronto poet laureate, and festivals across the country are increasingly showcasing a mix of both published poets and spoken word artists. Though, perhaps even more progressive an approach would be to take a page from the past, breaking down the page versus stage dichotomy altogether as an outdated construct that fails to serve the whole.

> Sexist language, racist language, theistic language – all are typical
> of the policing languages of mastery, and cannot, do not permit
> new knowledge or encourage the mutual exchange of ideas.[51]

Spoken word artists are the personification of the notion of speaking truth to power. Our subject matter is as old as human emotion and as new as the most current regional and global events. Today, the national spoken word scene in Canada has blossomed from coast to coast. From the Banff Centre of the Arts Spoken Word residency program, to Montreal, where innovative artists like Kaie Kellough – whose poetry bridges experimental and spoken word theory and practice – and musical fusion performances by the Kalmunity Vibe Collective are redefining the parameters of the genre, to the East Coast where artists such as Shauntay Grant, El Jones, and the Word Iz Bond collective continue to create work that inspires, ignites, and reflects Halifax's complex racial climate. Nationally, the slam scene has grown from its West Coast roots in the mid-nineties, to a flourishing network with over thirty regional venues (including youth slams) now taking place across the country.

Spoken word is and will always be the voice of the people – rooted in community particularly at a grassroots level. Each year, spoken word events across Canada draw crowds in the hundreds who come in order to listen to a form of orature that is both old and new and which is fed by a variety of cultural and artistic streams. As our Afro-Canadian literary canon is as diverse as the diaspora of Black people around the world, there is an ocean of influences affecting our artistic praxis. In his book *Odysseys Home: Mapping African-Canadian Literature,* George Elliott Clarke makes clear the problem that generalizations create when discussing African Canadian writing. "To speak about an 'African-Canadian' literature, then, I must be 'essentialist' enough to believe that an entity describable as 'African Canada' exists ... In fact, I hold that African Canada is a conglomeration."[52]

It's quiet again when the children finish speaking, until the woman breaks into the silence. "Finally," she says, "I trust you now. I trust you with the bird that is not in your hands because you have truly caught it. Look. How lovely it is, this thing we have done – together.[53]

As Harriet Tubman served as guide, leading her people to freedom, so does Toni Morrison offer instruction on how to move language forward – beyond the shackles of ethnocentric colonization into a future where our voices can be used as a tool for emancipation. Each spoken word artist is an explorer of a new literary landscape – on a journey which will take them beyond the bondage and limitations of categorization, into a territory of experimentation, not restricted by tradition – but informed by it as a compass point. Our elders are our North Star – guiding us towards the Promised Land of authentic creative expression. Spoken word is a fluid, ever-evolving form – it is poetry politica, guerrilla literature, a verbal transmission of culture. It is a breathing document and testament to the enduring resilience of the Black diaspora – transferred from performer to audience, word by word.

A SELECTED HISTORY OF SOUL SPEAK

Seemingly innocent spirituals
to both master and overseer
they were merely words
simple lyrics, ingenuous
halleluiah ballads.

Swing low sweet chariot
Coming for to carry me home[54]

But these words were charms
incantations chanted
in secret freedom code
surreptitious melodies

sung by restless slaves
chariot became train
became a rumbling
underground
echoing over plantation field
of cotton, tobacco and cane.

Gospels, for safety
for shouts – never mind battle cries
would leave a brother dead cold in a heartbeat.

Mothers with babies, strapped to their bent to near
snapped backs, sung under
the unrelenting sun of the Old South
and men with bodies worked hard, then raw
till they were little more than meat and bone
recounted these so-called silly spirituals, to both
each other and God.

God, they asked for strength
each other, they asked for directions
where to cross over that river
where to board that subterranean
north-bound train to freedom.

Then came the blues
belting out anguish over injustice
after emancipation failed
to deliver the promised land
instead, sending clansmen
who strung-up till lifeless
one brother after another
as law enforcers turned away
and crosses burned till dawn.

Dallas Blues, Memphis Blues–
I ain't had nothin' but bad news.
Crazy Blues.[55]

Unabashed, these words
laid claim to the pain of generations
love was sought, found, then
– gone, gone, gone
Ye shall overcome if ye faint not[56]
our victory will not be undone.

And so the young entered, at their peril
the guarded gates of academia
living the vision of Booker T. Washington
where scholarly success meant abandoning
one's own language, meant
adopting the mother tongue
of Uncle Tom.

When a hunger for our own vernacular
mingled with the passion of romanticism
a new language was born, on the page
on the stages of smoky coffee houses
deep in the heart of Harlem.

In this Renaissance, we began to reclaim ourselves.
Began to own our newly found freedom
to simply read and write, en mass
in public, to make love and meaning
from our suffering, to live out loud
word by word, on our own terms.

Langston left a language
deep as the Euphrates[57]
that flowed into the ocean
of Gwendolyn, bestowing
permission for preachment
as Baraka and Sanchez
re-loaded the cannon[58]
with unapologetic verse
fueled by didacticism.

While up here, in the true
north beyond that 49th parallel
Clifton Joseph and Lillian Allen
waged a Rub-a-Dub revolution.

George Elliott Clarke taught us
the maritime equation of
Black + Acadia = Africadian[59]
and Wayde Compton mapped
the path of B.C. Bluesprint.

While all across the country
Slam and Hip Hop brought
the acronym of
Rhythm-And-Poetry[60]
back to the streets, and
ghetto speak became fodder
for heightened verbal artistry.

These are our ancestors of verse.
This is our legacy.

And still this history is incomplete
so diverse is the lineage
unsung are so many
who first spoke the words
that birthed the language
of Soul Speak.

(*A Selected History of Soul Speak*, Frontenac Press, 2021)

NOTES

1 Toni Morrison, "Nobel Lecture," Nobel Prize, 7 December 1993, http://www.
   nobelprize.org/nobel_prizes/literature/laureates/1993/morrison-lecture.html.
2 Kate Clifford Larson, "Harriet Tubman Myths and Facts," *Bound For the
   Promised land: Harriet Tubman, Portrait of an American Hero*, accessed
   15 April 2017, http://www.harriettubmanbiography.com/harriet-tubman-myths-
   and-facts.html.

3 Morrison, "Nobel Lecture."

4 Ibid.

5 Ibid.

6 "Storytelling," *First Nations Pedagogy Online*, accessed 15 April 2017, https://firstnationspedagogy.ca/storytelling.html.

7 "A Brief History of Reggae in Toronto," *Blog TO*, 24 December 2014, http://www.blogto.com/music/2014/12/a_brief_history_of_reggae_in_toronto.

8 "Celebrating Women's Achievements," *Collections Canada*, accessed 5 January 2017, http://www.collectionscanada.gc.ca/women/030001-1212-e.html.

9 Morrison, "Nobel Lecture."

10 Henry Louis Gates Jr, "Sudden Def," *New Yorker*, 19 June 1995, 40.

11 Larry Rohter, "Is Slam in Danger of Going Soft?," *New York Times*, 2 June 2009, https://www.nytimes.com/2009/06/03/books/03slam.html.

12 Wayde Compton, *Bluesprint: Black British Columbian Literature and Orature* (Vancouver: Arsenal Pulp Press, 2001).

13 Regie Cabico and Todd Swift, *Poetry Nation: The North American Anthology of Fusion Poetry* (Montreal: Véhicule Press, 1998).

14 Ibid., 25.

15 Phillip Norton and Todd Swift, *Short Fuse: The Global Anthology of New Fusion Poetry* (New York: Rattapallax Press, 2002).

16 Ibid., back cover.

17 Morrison, "Nobel Lecture."

18 Alexandra Gill, "A Little the Verse for Wear," *The Globe and Mail*, 1 January 2003.

19 Diana Jean Schemo, "After the Beats: A New Generation Raises Its Voice in Poetry," *The New York Times*, 26 September 1994, http://www.nytimes.com/1994/09/26/arts/after-the-beats-a-new-generation-raises-its-voice-in-poetry.html.

20 David Barber, "The Man In the Back Row Has A Question VI," *The Paris Review* 154 (2000): 379.

21 "An Approach to Black Aesthetics," in *Black Aesthetics: Papers from a Colloquium Held at the University of Nairobi, June, 1971*, ed. Pio Zirimu and Andrew Gurr, East African Literature Bureau, 1973.

22 Chris Gilpin, "The Living Language of Spoken Word," *Poetry Is Dead* 1, no. 1 (2010–11), http://www.poetryisdead.ca.

23 Victor D. Infante, "Yaaay! The Death of Art!," *OC Weekly*, 27 July 2000, http://www.ocweekly.com/arts/yaaay-the-death-of-art-6400316.

24 Morrison, "Nobel Lecture."

25 Ibid.

26 Laura M. Ahearn, "Language and Agency," *Annual Review of Anthropology* 30 (2001): 109– 37.

27 Morrison, "Nobel Lecture."

28 Ian Rae, *From Cohen To Carson: The Poet's Novel In Canada* (Kingston and Montreal: McGill-Queen's University Press), 140.

29 Charles Olson, "Projective Verse," University of Pennsylvania, accessed 5 January 2017, http://writing.upenn.edu/~taransky/Projective_Verse.pdf

30 Houston A. Baker, *Afro-American Poetics: Revisions of Harlem and the Black Aesthetic* (Madison: University of Wisconsin Press, 1996), 4.

31 "Black Creativity: On the Cutting Edge," *Time*, 10 October 1994, http://content.time.com/time/subscriber/article/0,33009,981564,00.html.

32 Stephen Henderson, *Understanding the New Black Poetry: Black Speech and Black Music as Poetic Reference* (New York: William Morrow & Company, 1973), 41.

33 Ibid., 32.

34 Ibid.

35 Morrison, "Nobel Lecture."

36 Cheryl A Wall, "A Note On 'The Weary Blues,'" *Lenox Avenue: A Journal of Interarts Inquiry* 3, (1997): ii–vi.

37 Marcus Baram, "How Gil Scott-Heron, Battling His Record Label and Cocaine, Became the "Godfather of Rap," *Vanity Fair*, 4 November 2014, http://www.vanityfair.com/hollywood/2014/11/gil-scott-heron-book-excerpt.

38 Ibid.

39 Ben Sisario, "Gil Scott-Heron, Voice Of Black Protest Culture, Dies At 62," *New York Times*, 28 May 2011, http://www.nytimes.com/2011/05/29/arts/music/gil-scott-heron-voice-of-black-culture-dies-at-62.html.

40 Baram, "How Gil Scott-Heron."

41 Henry Louis Gates Jr, *The Signifying Monkey: A Theory of African-American Literary Criticism* (New York: Oxford University Press, 1989).

42 Ibid., XXII.

43 Ibid., 125.

44 Ibid., xxv.

45 Ibid., 127.

46 Ibid., 129.

47 Morrison, "Nobel Lecture."

48 Carolyn C. Denard and Toni Morrison, *What Moves at the Margin: Selected Nonfiction* (Jackson: University Press of Mississippi, 2008), xii.

49 Jennifer Allen, "Toni Morrison 'Slams' the Louvre," *Artforum*, 27 November 2006, http://artforum.com/news/id=12117.

50 Lillian Allen, phone interview, 15 November 2014.

51 Morrison, "Nobel Lecture."

52 George Elliott Clarke, *Odysseys Home: Mapping African-Canadian Literature* (Toronto: University of Toronto Press, 2015), 7.

53 Morrison, "Nobel Lecture."

54 "'Swing Low, Sweet Chariot' – The Fisk University Jubilee Quartet (1909), Library of Congress," accessed 1 August 2017, https://www.loc.gov/programs/static/national-recording-preservation-board/documents/Swing%20Low%20article.pdf.

55 "Blues," *Wikipedia*, accessed 1 August 2017, https://en.wikipedia.org/wiki/Blues.

56 Inspiration for the sixties protest song "We Shall Overcome," "I'll Overcome Someday," was a hymn written by the Reverend Charles Albert Tindley. Epigraph from the published text reads, "Ye shall overcome if ye faint not," a quote derived from Galatians 6:9; "We Shall Overcome," *Wikipedia*, accessed 1 August 2017, https://en.wikipedia.org/wiki/We_Shall_Overcome.

57 Langston Hughes "The Negro Speaks of Rivers," in *The Weary Blues* (New York: A.A. Knopf, 1926).

58 Klyde Broox, "re-loading the caNnon," *My Best Friend is White* (Toronto: McGilligan Books, 2005).

59 "George Elliott Clarke," *Wikipedia*, accessed 2 August 2017, https://en.wikipedia.org/wiki/George_Elliott_Clarke.

60 Hasan Khan, "RAP: Rhythm and Poetry," *Huffington Post*, 23 January 2014, http://www.huffingtonpost.com/hasan-khan/rap-rhythm-and-poetry_b_2023837.html.

wordsoundsystemsengineering: Meta-dub and Creation

Klyde Broox

"Introdubtion"

You are reading a written voice, imagine yourself hearing it.
Creation was a "wordsoundengineering" operation.

Big Bang Version!

"Abrakadabra!" "Arbadakarba!"
Voice of Creator like lightning and thunder!
Wordsound explosion! "Big Bang version!"
Genesis was a performance poetry event.
I think that's how it went.
The Universe was created before English was invented.
"Let there be light" doesn't sound quite right.
"Abrakadabra!" sounds like a better idea
of the very first word that God uttered. "Abrakadabra!"
"I create as I speak!" God said, "dubrakadabra-ing'
everything, out of nothing, into be-ing within one week!

Jah Almighty is a dubpoet and the entire Universe is
a dubpoem. Upon such a cosmological foundation,
this article posits dubpoetry as both oral and scribal
"wordsound-and-shape-systemsengineering,"
a natural technology of the voice.

Voice is: Sign of Life

Dead bodies cannot speak; ghosts and corpses are not identical.
Breathing orchestrates utterance, voice is "wordsign" of life!
Language expresses existence. All living bodies possess voice.
Globally portable and universally recognizable, wordsound
is a veritable rhizome of human identity.

"Meta-dubstract"

"wordsoundsystemsengineering: Meta-dub and Creation!" is a
"performance essay" designed more for stage than page. This article
demonstrates dubpoetry's discursive instrumentality and metanarrative
propensity. It also provides evidence that "Canada Dub" is beginning
to command a cardinal location within the Black Atlantic cultural milieu
and is also becoming a significant engine of emerging global "neopoetic"
conventions.[1] Dubpoets usually import customized discursive platforms
and frames of references, often including self-explanatory neologisms,
into each context. The expository text was composed during sessions
of "performance writing" while reading out loud as if delivering an
extempore lecture to a live audience. Dub discourse generally
relocates contemporary poetics, in all languages, within the domain
of neoliterature. This article will weave, fuse/merge, and dub prose
and poetry (even music as background for live delivery) into a composite
articulation of the idea that human languages are primarily scribalized
orality or "wordsoundandshapesystems." The poems provide
"textimony" of dubpoetry's facilities for scribalizing orality and
oralizing scribality.

Journey of the Voice

Perhaps, if no one spoke there would be no need to write.
Scribal literature must have begun as an echo of the oral, the literation
of the narrative utterances of the earliest campfire storytellers.[2] Through
the lens of such an ontological vision, one can envision a universal,
tellurian, orally rooted, and technologically routed, literary tradition that
evolved proportionately to keep pace with developments in technology.
In essence then, the evolution of literature is a Journey of the Voice.[3]

Tongues speak essences of being.
AfroAsiatic linguistic origin, migratory routing,
echoes out of Africa overflowing; journey of the voice.
Landscapes shape soundscapes, topographical acoustics. Chirography,
calligraphy, typography; geocultural accentuation, babel-ization
of the word; European imperialist expansion.
Roman template of erasure; set fire to the library of Alexandria!
Transcontinental attempted murders of cultures, Columbus syndrome,
you did not exist until I "discovered" you. He re-scripted our hi-stories
as his story only, fabricating even "West Indians,"
errors as corrections, diss/curse/ive domination.
De-rooting to reroute evolution of writing, *whitening the written voice*,
colon/i/zation came in claiming, de-naming, re-naming,
shaming, blaming, power gaming; colon-eye-sation to rehearse.
Paper *colo/noise/ation of verse*; Anglophonic impositions,
reinvent mode, style, content; continents of diss/content.

Struggles of the tongue, chemistry of culture-mixtures,
the hatching of pidgin, bodies in passage got to keep on moving,
portable engines span centuries.

Journey of the voice journals travelogues of collective autobiographies.
Wormseyeviews birdseyed inscribe hybrid vibes multiplied worldwide.
Tellurian emotions exchanged, digitally updated meta-mentality
augmented imaginational territory. Dear diary, today I feel very
ultramodern and also, neoliterary;
Blended potencies shatter genre barriers!
Deconstructing cultural imprinting, I and I un/colonize id in entity,
R/evolutionary Tea Party I/Deed entity, Blackvoice victory!
DecolonIzation of verse, colonoise-ation in reverse,
counter colonial portrayals reverse coloneyesation.
Wordsoundshapesensengineering renew meanings of being
Conductor, amplifier, reflector, magnifier; re-encoding
abrakadabra within wordsoundpower!
Spectacular vernacular, words of a feather figure together
flocking in whatever weather. The voice is a time-traveler.
W/Rap me your heart's story within (y)our rhyme,
Flexible circle of literature paradigm.

Digital technology has returned us full circle forward to the virtual campfire of computer-screened interface via web camera, enabling the re-ascendancy of orality in literature. Dubpoetry is integral to this process because it emphasizes presence of body and inscribes voice directly upon memory via sounds and vibrations of the spoken words.

Utterance vibrates resonance, performs dominance
Poem on page: bird in cage; spokenword: flying bird
Uncage page-birds; dub wings on words!
More poems uttered; more poems heard
More poems heard; more poems remembered
Dubscapes expound sound as sight; incite sounds out of shapes
I am the voice that rules the pen; I am the pen that schools the voice
The voice, the voice of a body dubs wordsounds of the body in voice!

The wordsounds of bodies of colour are usually relegated to subaltern status within the colour-coded context of the Canadian literary continuum, reflecting the racially stratified mosaic of power configuration within Canadian society. Hence, Canadian literary discourse generally mirrors the mainstreaming of whiteness and side streaming, or undergrounding, of "unwhiteness." Remarkably, despite the filters, the Black Canadian poetic voice has applied dubpoetry's dynamic scribal orality to inscribe monumental archives of blackness upon the pages of Canada's literary memory. Poetic voices of colour have uttered their way into Canadian national public attention. Dubpoetry literally instigated Canada's Spokenword movement when Lillian Allen and De Dub Poets chanted down the League of Canadian Poets' colour-coded barrier against "performance poetry."[4]

One can reasonably assert that dubpoetry has substantially transformed the literary imagination of Canada. Significantly, when the Black Canadian poetic voice imprinted its legitimacy within the CanLit canon; it instrumentalized utterance by literally applying wordsound as power to illustrate a pathway from resistance to self-deliverance. Dub's instrumentalization of the word can conceivably serve as a template for broad application across a transcultural, intersectoral, multilingual, spectrum/continuum in any given society. The trajectory of this idea extends discourse on the Black historical presence in Canada outside the parameters of the Underground Railroad narrative.

Underground Railroad; that link I don't download
That's not my story; when I came to Canada I was already free
Via airway; that's how I came; passport and visa with my name
I came with my voice and tongue to tell that I can count and spell, well.

Narratives of colour in Canada are usually perceived through a screen
of "cultural specificity." This screen of cultural specification has impeded
perception of the fact that dubpoetry invests the spoken word with
transcendental status as a common denominator among tellurians, by
focusing primarily on each word uttered as basically another unit of sound,
wordsound. Are you seeing what I am saying, tellurian being? Despite the
cultural specificity of my voice, I am the poet whose village is this entire
planet. The sound of my word, my wordsound, is my power, sayeth a
dubpoet. I talk what I live and live what I talk, even if I sound to you
as if I'm talking with a Foreign Accent.

My native voice is my trademark. I feel fluent when I talk.
When I talk, when I talk is talk I talk is not bark I bark.
My accent is no accident, is nat some ting-dat-I-invent.
It is not recent but ancient. Don't resent. Skip value judgment.
Stat-us, stay-tus, forget fuss; no need for us to ack facetious,
self-conscious, supercilious, suspicious or anxious,
when I sit beside you in di bus / shed-ule, schedule; whose rule?
Jus cool, I went to a really good school: mandaytory, mandetory,
why worry? No rush, no hurry; my goat well curry.

While the goat is being curried, let's take a time-out from the poem to
reiterate that the definition of languages as "wordsoundsystems" detaches
language from the various partitions, differentiations and specificities
signified by the parameters of national borders with their corresponding
language and literature domains and barriers.

Bab-el, ba[y]-bel: every tongue has a tale to tell. Ears have their
own doubts to dispel. Id-E-ology, I.D.-ology, comparative orthography:
cert-if-icate, surf-it/icket, get suspect, inspect, disrespect, reject;
nigglected immigrant intellect.
Foreign accented narrative, no need to be negative.
Language is relative. Distribution of syllabic stress
should not create ethnic distress.
Tomayto, tomahto; potayto potahto, eeda, ida, dayta, data, zed or zee;
same vocabulary con-tro-versy, controv-er-see.
Build a bridge across di sea; level out hire/archy.

The Queen's English is her own. Let har speek it fram har trone.
If she doan min' speekin it aloan. I know my English is fine;
my tongue makes it mine, strong blend of vintage wine in moonshine.
Borderlines intertwine into grapevine.

There is no foreign accent when listening to tellurian voices as
vessels of wordsounds. In hearing each language as a
wordsoundsystem we can listen to our world as it actually is, covered
only by the imaginary canopy of our single sky.

A-li-en, a-li-an? I am not one, no relayshan.
I doan fit dat diss-skryption. I have di wit to prove it
in a written exa/mi/nayshan. I am a born tellurian.
My place of birth is planet Earttttthhh.

Wordsounds are common to the voices of all peoples because all
peoples utter their narratives in wordsounds. Dubpoetic emphasis on
the sonic identity of all words (both spoken and written) creates an
operational space of multilingual equalization where language differences
are neutralized by the common denominators of sound and shape. Thus,
dubpoetry frames poetry as a transculturally portable platform for the
stylization of "wordsoundshapesystems." Dubpoets focus on the sound
of stylized wording to empower and enhance our occupation of social
and psychological space. Dubpoets believe that the primary role of poets,
in any society, is to interrogate the society's use and abuse of language.
Therefore, dubpoetry generally addresses the power relationships that
gave rise to, or seem to arise from, the state of language in a society.
Dubpoetry's overarching raison d'être is to echo, instrumentalize,
amplify, historicize, and memorialize the voices of people who probably
have been misled into believing that they are voiceless. Dubpoetry
inspires, empowers, and activates the silent, or silenced, to utter, literate
and self-advocate in choral communal solidarity.

Interestingly, the global rise of orality from Beat, Dialect Verse, to Dub,
Rap/Hiphop/Spokenword/Slam suggests the resurgence and functional
fusion of elements common to historically influential oralities such as
griotic, shamanic, and bardic traditions.[5]
I consider this twenty-first-century ascendancy of orality as a victory
of the voice. Print dominance had circumcised wordsound from
wordshape, causing the academic invention of an oral-scribal divide,

resulting in what I define as "sp/literature," where scribality was gradually disconnected from orality to the detriment of literature in general. Print's circumscription of the uttering voice severely muted orality in poetry and encouraged poets to try to mystify solitary readers with supposed profundities mused in silence.

Dub demystifies poetry and returns it to its original role as a very vocal and lively, politically influential, form of public art and a viable instrument of cultural communion, social mediation, collective literation, and public education. Dubpoetics can also provide transformative interpersonal resources with which to animate compassion within others, reinforce mental health programs, and support anger management. The genre offers powerful opportunities for poetry to become actively engaged in intellectually reinvigorating social imaging and political messaging because dubpoets instinctively challenge official narratives and discourses. Dubpoetry bridges the oral–scribal divide in the same way that the edge of a coin joins its two sides. From the perspective of this article, literature is a two-headed coin. One side is oral, the other scribal. Dubpoetry's location at the edge of the coin rationalizes its scribal orality. Within this paradigm, dubpoetry is written as it is spoken as one word. Dubpoetry signifies the "dub" being contained in the poetry.

Dubpoetic focus on uttered word as sound, frames all forms of poetry as "wordsoundengineering." In the domain of dub, all languages are "wordsoundandshape systems." Thus, poetry is the stylization of "wordsoundshapesystems" for instrumental as well as ornamental purposes. Dubpoetry involves wordsound engineering, wordshape configuration, and "wordsoundsystemsengineering." Principles of dubbing are applicable to all wordsoundsystems.

Due to the historical dynamics of its emergence, the originating mystique of dubpoetry has been framed as culturally specific. However, the techniques of dubbing are globally portable because "dub" is a fundamental operational sound engineering and sound processing word. Those are just a few of the reasons reinforcing the notion of dubpoetry as a main engine of the emerging neoliteratures of the twenty-first century. Generally, dubpoetry facilitates the poetic packaging of ideas and concepts into concise, precise, and vivid language. Dubpoets stylize and simplify content to widen the audience for the ideas and concepts as well as to facilitate comprehension by the widened audience. Therefore, dub not only makes it easier for people to comprehend and embrace poetry, but the genre also illustrates the sociocultural utility of poetry as a potential wideband transmitter of ideas and concepts.

The principles and practices of dubbing as wordsound (and shape) engineering, and also as the chemistry of emotional vibrations, make dubpoetry a "neopoetic" genre. Dubpoetry mends the rifts of sp/literature by giving primacy to orality rather than scribality in an oral scribal binary but also assigning equal value to both as integral and vital aspects of literature. Interestingly, orthography and typography are approached with particular specificity in dubpoetry because writing is the lettering of wordsound.

Writing and printing were vital developments in the evolution of literature. I imagine that before the advent of print, one could only have retained as much as one could remember. To forget a word heard would have been to lose it forever. Therefore, the entirety of one's personal literary canon had to be contained between the ears, within the library of memory. Clearly, print was an important word-memory-technology that would have been like the Internet of its time. Imagine how exciting it must have been for people to experience their very first book. I expect that level of excitement to have been very similar to the thrill that I felt, that pregnant moment, in the early nineties, when I heard the dial-up Internet modem sound for the first time. I remember the tingling in my veins, the sense of adventure to enter Apple's e-world, as if Scotty had actually beamed me up and I was now standing on the terrain of Mars or star hopping my way there. Now, on the wheels of technology, the unwitting tyranny of print is being digitally toppled. The camera is challenging the pen as the main mode of cultural documentation. Image is text and vice versa. These are times for talking bodies, alphabets of gestures, and dancing voices. These times require poets to blend speech of figures with figures of speech.

Mutiny of the Subaltern[6]

During the seventies, tides of cultural revolt stirred "Carried Beyon" streams of literatures in English and churned up dubpoetry to revive the tradition of the tongue as the ultimate tuner of the pen. Dubpoetry illustrates cultural hybridity and multimodal artistry. Its creativity embraces digitality vigorously. Dubpoetry simultaneously echoes ongoing struggles of the tongue even as it pronounces the victory of the Black voice. Dub is the voice of epistemological mutiny. ·

It vocalizes global oral and scribal "decolonoisation" of language. Most importantly, dub declares diminished Eurocentric dominion over the "Englishes," also the "Spanishes," the "Frenches," and other colonial languages. Since dubpoetry's trans-Black-Atlantic-wide emergence, there has been an undeniable uprising of popular poetic orality and the world has been witnessing a gradual Literary Coup.

Voices of subalterned bodies, salvoes of anomies,
military coup: power for a few; literary coup: people power renew!
Our little neoliterary coup is too huge to be a haiku
Entry point without return; mutiny of the subaltern,
neomodern pith in pattern, profile me as "superaltern!"
To Whom It May Concern; memory library didn't burn! I know
it's my turn to teach and you learn! *Mosquito one, mosquito two,*
mosquito jump inna hot callaloo Cocka-doodle doo, Timbuktu!
Déjà voodoo; parlay view Morning dew is vintage brew.
Literary coup; people power renew! Highbrow, lowbrow,
no, I and I know that's not so. Alter-native narratives overthrow,
underthrow, throwout, topple, trample, transfigure
pyramid & triangle. Restructure hire/archy as power circle.
Reshuffle puzzle into miracle. Create spectacle; make people marvel!
Mosquito one, mosquito two; mosquito jump inna hot callaloo. Cocka-
doodle doo, Timbuktu! Déjà voodoo; parlay view Morning dew
is vintage brew. Literary coup; people power renew!

I encourage you as reader/viewer/listener, virtual or actual audience, to
"profile me as superaltern" because "I know it's my turn to teach and you
learn." Slavery was an entry point without return. Dubpoetry represents
the "mutiny of the subaltern," and is largely characterized by the
"neomodern pith in [its] pattern." But, dubpoetry does not signify
a "departure"[7] from literary traditions; it signifies a returning of
literature, via digitality, to its original oral-based identity, where voice,
tongue, and body are fundamental literary resources. "Morning dew
is vintage brew."

And even as this current interface is occuring. Tides of times flow
without ebb. World Wrapping Web,
Web Wrapped Worl, pages of ages further unfurled,
official denials hurriedly hurled. Behold another former
emperor; minus an expired empire, staring down his stuff-up nose
striking a supposed power-pose, as if no one knows
state secrets have been exposed He's lost all titles,
even his clothes!

Graduate gown-wearing sometimes impedes seeing and hearing.
Spivak the Penguin; dubbing moistens stiffened listening.

Who is who? I will dub U a clue
Penguins can't fly where the phoenix flew
Never heard a parrot who could outsing a cuckoo.
Classic phantoms skew academic critic's review
Dubbers dubbing to do long overdue neoliterary coup
Didn't come out of the blue; we came thru Timbuktu!
(Refrain)

Living bodies house chronologically archived libraries of memories.
Memory library is a province of imaginational territory. Literary
production requires cooperation between memory and imagination.
Initially, scribality has less natural intimacy with memory than orality.
However, scribality eventually becomes ultimately more intimate with
memory because writing dredges memory, reviews it constantly,
manipulates it repeatedly to generate narration.[8]

Memory is a basic building block of imagination. We cannot imagine
anything outside of realities that we have experienced. Dubpoetry
is a particularly useful tool for exercising memory and instigating
spontaneous leaps of radical imagining because the discursive
dissidence of dubpoets disrupts the domination of public imagination
by official narratology.

Dubpoets typically embody the radical imaginary of our communities,
wielding power of voice to "poemize" and historicize the daily lives
of ordinary people. As self-empowering narrators of mental liberation,
dubpoets deploy the power of voice to occupy social and psychological
space. Dubpoetic techniques harness and transmit colloquially encoded,
grassroots-grounded, sociopolitical energies. Dubpoetry implodes and
explodes language. It excavates artifice, eviscerates subterfuge, and
exposes camouflage by radically interrogating semiotics and mimetics.

Dubpoets manipulate (and "womanipulate") semantics with
counter-systemic rhetoric to deconstruct existing hegemonic narrations
in order to construct unorthodox narratives and discourses that
challenge institutionalized cosmologies and mythologies. As this art/icle
has already asserted, dubbing transcends language barriers, cultural
borders, and national literatures because the sonic identity of words
is common to all languages. In the context of our "cyber-spatial"
interconnectedness, digitally technologized voices can be specifically
instrumentalized to serve the purposes of intellectual liberation and
advance the notion of a global compassion revolution.[9]

And so, as the journey of the voice continues in contemporary
(neo)literary reality, dubpoetry pitches poems as
WorldWideWordsounds: and weapons of massliberation.

multivocal Intraterrestrial Sonar Pulsations reverberate in
WorldWide Wordsoundversions convocate translingual oral flow
to and fro Person Per Person voice-to-mind-dialing
vibrating earth-echo in h/art/beatriddim
transmitting sim-of-vim mirroring vivid dubbing grid
Domain Naming System override verified
internal cranial hard drive initialized configuring
self-authenticating truth sifting searchengines receiving/sending
cultural signals blending no matter what's trending
online grapevines can soulscape macromeaning
matrixed autofix of belief systems errors
demystified mirrors minimize terrors render
acrobatic reader enabled idea distiller @ speed of thought
in streams of art launch live RawTruthFiles
click ok to insert vital grassroots styles
check yes to output communal spontaneous smiles
hover over shortcut to laughter clear headspacebar
block avatar pop-up window, debug ego!
Dub/ble clicks input natural mysticality enhance mentality
activate algorithmic biodigital audiovisual
basic Common Gateway Interface
retrace subsurfacespace read race in lower case
embrace interrogatives delete derogatives
bleep expletives repeat imperatives perceive alternatives
believe relative reality registries weave tellurian metanarratives
Earthanchored crossplatformed mainframe of references
unlimited broadbonding frequencies
portable neonetworking preferences, random log in recognition
compassion unlocks encryption, easy log out option
OneLove password seen and heard Holy Talk Magic Language
Hyper Truth Transmission Process Flexible Transfer Protocol
registration optional no catch nor hidden cost attached
opensourceservers 360-degree vision monitors inner ear amplifiers
original thought generators Universal Resonance Locators
Reciprocal Access Memory I and I are we

instant messaging global villagers sharing animated GIFs
skip filters of proxies bypass differences link priorities
bridge culture gaps swap homebrewed remixed javascripts
E-trade harmless homemade cookies buffering humbugging buzzes
and hisses of hits and misses of eked out E/businesses: icon-aliases
flashing big k, meg, gig, WYSINWYG: What You See Is Not What You Get
some things slip thru any net: upload download unload reload
data overload! infinite forks in the road encrypt decode
pre-set browser mode embed mental filter install intellectual firewall
reinforce wit secure Central Psychological Unit emotions to administrate
upgrade update hardware software freeware shareware spyware
spamware shamware scamware malware madware gladware sadware
good wear bad wear tupperware in there somewhere footwear headwear
daymare nightmare everywhere; beware! computers can think
quicker than a blink but for compassion or common sense,
Artificial Intelligence still too dense hence Garbage In Garbage Out
face to face erases doubt anti-virus anti-bug alt/escape exit shutdown
unplug.

Under the Influence of Dub!

The rise of the machine, as the central intermediary in the interface
between persons, facilitates communication but it also simultaneously
simulates direct person-to-person interaction. Consequently, as our rates
of virtual interpersonal interactions increase, we risk incurring the social
disadvantage of our rates of actual interpersonal interactions gradually
decreasing. Dubpoetics and "dubpoetriology" can offer openings to
approaches that might balance the proliferation of simulated
interaction.[10] It seems necessary to emphasize here that the word dub
can also be easily read as blending, joining, integrating, synergizing,
combining, and so forth and so on.

Since the 1970s, dubpoets have displayed principles and practices that
can be easily linked to more than one of the many meanings of the word
"dub." Some relevant meanings of dub include "to name," "to forge
keys," "to invest with a dignity," "to moisten leather," and, "to smooth
down; as to dub a spar or timber with an adze." Dub is also onomato-
poeia as well as metaphor of the "flub-dub" of heartbeat. Figuratively,
orality is the literal lifeblood of language. Indeed, when people stop
speaking a language, history pronounces it dead. Dub is a film word,

in terms of dubbing one language in place of another as movies travel across cultures. Similarly, dubpoetry dubs poems out of daily life to dub poetry into daily life. Dubpoets often dub dialogue, different languages, ambient sound, and gestures into the poetry writing and performance. This feature makes dubpoetry very multimedia-friendly. Dub means also "to make a copy of an audio or video recording." Each dubpoet usually aims to dub/imprint/stamp a copy of a particular worldview onto audiences. Actually, as was noted earlier, dubpoetry generates portable discursive platforms and imports them into performances to influence discourse formation. Such a practice suggests that dubpoets can be particularly useful as community development facilitators.

In general practice, dubpoetics merge both analog and digital muses to fuse retro and neo devices in creative domains of "neo-imaginational" territory that chart contemporary departure routes that return us to ways of literary artistry that we thought we had long-parted company with. For example, the oral cultural ritual of call and response has repeatedly demonstrated a potential to infuse communal vibrations into the flow of interpersonal interaction to frame juxtaposition as apposition instead of opposition. Adjusting individual vibrations adjusts the vibrations of interactional environments. Designing a composite from opposites out of the chaos of sound-clashing resonances, assonances, and dissonances, dubpoetry harnesses and unleashes the soul of the Earth amidst the noises of the world. Essentially, (dub) the poetry has been providing literature with gifts as useful as those with which (dub) the music has gifted global musical sensibilities.

Dubpoetry is at once a musical/literary/political/social/cultural platform. Its principles and practices embrace music, straddle theatre, step into dance, and paint verbal imagery reminiscent of visual, or video, art. For dubpoets, the stage is a page and the page is a stage. This chiasmic reality is evident in voice as pen/pen as voice, uttering to write/ writing for utterance, agonies of comedies/comedies of agonies, sound of dub/dub of sound, poetic body/body poetic, dub as poetry/poetry as dub. Incidentally, dubpoetry continuously critiques itself with informal action research to retain its sense of self-authentication and radical epistemological and pedagogical unorthodoxy. Dubpoets interrogate social issues and cultural conundrums, often positing innovative solutions for problems and alternative approaches towards positive change.

Dubpoetry's artistic visioning is rooted in a focus on art as more of an instrument than an ornament. Dubpoets view artistic endeavours as being as valid as industrial activities in the workday rituals of society.

The works of dubpoets are rooted in the issues of such realities.[11] The dubpoet generally projects self as an informal public intellectual, cultural activist, political catalyst, social worker, educator, and community builder. Under the Influence of Dub,

soulbruising blues ooze in and out of moods
fuse in muse as wordsounds pounding pole to pole!
raw soul Creole, raw Creole soul; Creole rawsoul, soul raw Creole
Southern noise in the North, southernoising the North!
under the influence of Dub, under the influence of Dub
under the influence of Dub
bodyspeakers demolish language barriers
interrogate ivory and ebony towers
illuminate innate angles of insight
obscurity obliterated by spotlight
under the influence of Dub
under the influence of Dub
dubbed dubbers dub di Dub dubbin dubs of Dub
dub di-di, di-di Dub; Dub, Dub?
dubculture is not scrubculture, nor shrubculture
neither grub-culture, pub-culture, nor paystub culture
not much of a hot-tub fan club culture
Dub, di Dub di-di, di-di Dub, Dub
dubculture is more than jus' subculture
is hubculture, voice signature, live literature
altercultural capital; ancestral oracular revival
conquering continual spiral under the influence of Dub
under the influence of Dub bodies politik talk louder
gesture people power, utter live to camera
arouse browser, engender close encounters of an oral kind
open windows and doors to new states of mind
we have our world to re-design within and between daily grind
under the influence of Dub
under the influence of Dub
under the influence of Dub
dubbed dubbers dubbed in di Dub
dub di Dub dubbin dubs of Dub
di Dub di-di, di-di Dub, Dub
dub di Dub, dub
Dub dub-in ...
dub-outtttttttt ...

NOTES

1 See Paul Gilroy's important work *The Black Atlantic: Modernity and Double Consciousness*, (Cambridge, MA: Harvard University Press, 1993).

2 Although I do not quote directly from his work, the idea of orality's primacy in literary evolution is theoretically rooted in readings from Walter J. Ong, *Orality and Literacy: The Technologizing of the Word* (London: Methuen & Co. Ltd, 1982).

3 This phrase refers to Kamau Brathwaite's *History of the Voice* (London: New Beacon Press, 1984). However, the idea of journey as used here invokes an embodied experience of the word.

4 See Lillian Allen, "De Dub Poets: Renegades in a One Poet Town," *This Magazine* 21, no. 7 (December 1987/January 1988): 14–21; Allen recounts how the League of Canadian Poets refused membership to herself and two other "dub poets" in 1984 because, they were "not poets but performers." For a discussion of this see Brenda Carr, "Come Mek Wi Work Together": Community Witness and Social Agency in Lillian Allen's Dub Poetry" *ARIEL: A Review of International English Literature* 29, no. 3 (July 1998).

5 Common ground exists between dubpoetic and bardic traditions. Both include the work of poets, chroniclers, satirists who are highly trained in their craft and who pay attention to and consciously extend the limits of language. Dubpoets and bards are steeped in the histories and tradition of their respective communities and verse traditions and forms and might be said to each perform a range of roles some of which are traditional and at the same time reinvented in relation to particular social and temporal contexts. Their work also effectively functions both to "praise and damn." Furthermore, in both traditions, a poet can be defined as a practitioner of a literary medium that offers functionality in daily community life. (For more on bard traditions, see: https://en.wikipedia.org/wiki/Irish_bardic_poetry).

Both dubpoets and griots occupy multiple positionalities as simultaneously, "historian, storyteller, praise singer, poet and/or musician." They are each respectively a "repository of oral tradition ... often seen as a societal leader ... an advisor to [power]." What might also be usefully known in marking connections between griots and dubpoets is their "ability to extemporize on current events, chance incidents and the passing scene." Their wit can be devastating and they "have to keep up to date on current events." These storytellers are "a living archive of the people's traditions." "Griot," *Wikipedia*, https://en.wikipedia.org/wiki/Griot.

The shamanic connection is less obvious and more complex. It is linked to a wider argument, which is attached to the "magico-religious" dimensions of the oral ritualization of the spoken word with specific historical reference to "abracadabra/abrakadabra." Also, both shamanistic and dubpoetic traditions are concerned with "mending the soul" and facilitating balance between spirit and flesh, tangible and intangible, visible and invisible. The idea of praise or curse, benediction and malediction, is also applicable here. Furthermore, both traditions are considered engines of the "counter-cultural movement" that afford prominence to the influence of indigenous intuition. Significantly, a dubpoetic perspective is discursively and epistemologically resistant to the cultural misappropriations of "neoshamanism" and "neo-pagan practices." "Shamanism," *Wikipedia*, https://en.wikipedia.org/wiki/Shamanism; "abracadabra," *Wikipedia*, https://en.wikipedia.org/wiki/Abracadabra.

6 The idea of mutiny of the subaltern is directly derived from and engages with the seminal postcolonial studies essay, Gayatri Chakravorty Spivak, "Can the Subaltern Speak?," in *Marxism and the Interpretation of Culture*, ed. Cary Nelson and Lawrence Gosberg (Basingstoke: Macmillan Education, 1988) 271–313.

7 Linton Kwesi Johnson ... described "dub poetry" as "a new departure in Jamaican protest poetry. Here the spoken/chanted word is the dominant mode. People's speech and popular music are combined, and the Jamaican folk culture and the reggae tradition provide both sources of inspiration and frames of reference." Linton Kwesi Johnson, "The New Englishes," in *The Story of English*, Robert McCrum, William Cran, Robert MacNeil (London: Faber, BBC Publications, 1987), 311.

8 Despite the absence of a direct quote, my discourse on memory in the cited segment is significantly influenced by Ong, *Orality and Literacy*, 14.

9 To the best of my knowledge, the notion of a global "compassion revolution" is my original idea. It envisions the ascendancy of empathy and the framing of a "neoworld" where economic competition gives way to international cooperation. Dubpoetry is linked to the global compassion revolution as an effective multimodal delivery system of wordsounds of people power framed as weapons of massliberation. The notion of a compassion revolution also involves upgrading individual resistance to collective self-deliverance. The poem "Worldwide Wordsounds" illustrates the potential of the Internet to initiate the compassion revolution.

10 Dubpoetriology, the "ology" of dubpoetry, is another of my original concepts. It widens the ontology and expands the taxonomy of the genre. Dubpoetriology is functionally linked to numerous denotations and collo-quial usages of the word dub. I applied phenomenology to uncover a

common set of features, principles, and practices that support the widening of ontology and expansion of taxonomy.

11 Dubpoets are generally known for instrumentalizing poetry as a community development tool. Poets In Unity pioneered the practice in the late seventies in Jamaica. LKJ set the standard in England. Lillian Allen, Michael St George, and I have also been recognized for such work in Canada. There are also Cherry Natural and Yasus Afari in Jamaica, Malachi Smith in the US, Ras Mo in Dominica, Brother Resistance in Trinidad, and Winston Farrell in Barbados, to name a few. Evidence of Allen's work: https://journalhosting.ucalgary.ca/index.php/ariel/article/download/34070/28109. Broox: https://www.thespec.com/news-story/7290105-gaining-voice-through-verse-poems-for-mental-health. St George: https://www.yardedge.net/art/the-turn-around-project-tap-at-work-in-jamaica.

Contributors

LILLIAN ALLEN is a professor of creative writing at OCAD University where she spearheads the establishment of Ontario's only BFA in creative writing. Considered a cultural deprogrammer, she is an award-winning internationally acclaimed poet/performer and language innovator and works at the intersection of dub, sound, and rebel poetics. She has several award-winning recordings and several critically acclaimed books of poetry to her credit. Lillian has been a strategic initiator of programs, networks, and arts organization in the city of Toronto for several decades. She is a longtime arts activist now in her sage years and focuses on mentoring the mentors and on intensifying her work to decolonize cultures as she remains an instigator of all things radical.

KLYDE BROOX is an internationally seasoned, seventies-vintage, Jamaican-born, Hamilton-based dubpoet. A 1992 University of Miami James Michener fellow, Broox won the 2005 City of Hamilton Arts Award for Literature and the 2011 John. C. Holland Award for Arts Achievement. He has published *Poemstorm,* (Swansea, Wales, 1989) and *My Best Friend is White* (McGilligan Books, 2005), an Amazon.ca bestseller. Klyde's performances "inspire audiences to experience poetry as social communion."

DANN J. BROYLD is an assistant professor of public history and African American history at Central Connecticut State University. He earned his PhD in nineteenth-century United States and African diaspora history at Howard University in 2011. His work focuses on the American-Canadian borderlands and issues of Black identity, migration, and transnational relations as well as oral history and museum-community interaction. Broyld was a 2017 Fulbright scholar at Brock University and is currently working on a manuscript with the University of Toronto Press.

NATALEE CAPLE is the author of nine books of poetry and fiction and the co-editor, with Michelle Berry, of an anthology of interviews and short fiction titled *The Notebooks*. Her work has been nominated for the KM Hunter Award, the RBC Bronwen Wallace Award, the Gerald Lampert Memorial Award, the ReLit Award, and the Walter Scott Prize for Historical Fiction. Her latest novel, *In Calamity's Wake*, was published in Canada by HarperCollins and in the US by Bloomsbury. The novel in translation was published by Boréal and has been sold separately for publication in France. Her third book of poetry, *Love in the Chthulucene (Cthulhucene)*, was published by Wolsak and Wynn in 2019. Natalee is an associate professor at Brock University.

GEORGE ELLIOTT CLARKE is the fourth Poet Laureate of Toronto (2012–15) and the seventh Parliamentary/Canadian Poet Laureate (2016–17). He is a revered artist in song, drama, fiction, screenplay, essays, and poetry. Born in Windsor, Nova Scotia in 1960, Clarke was educated at the University of Waterloo, Dalhousie University, and Queen's University. Clarke is also a pioneering scholar of African Canadian literature. A professor of English at the University of Toronto, Clarke has taught at Duke, McGill, the University of British Columbia, and Harvard. He holds eight honorary doctorates, plus appointments to the Order of Nova Scotia and the Order of Canada at the rank of officer. He is also a fellow of the Royal Canadian Geographical Society. His recognitions include the Pierre Elliott Trudeau Fellows Prize, the Governor General's Award for Poetry, the National Magazine Gold Award for Poetry, the Premiul Poesis (Romania), the Dartmouth Book Award for Fiction, the Eric Hoffer Book Award for Poetry (US), and the Dr Martin Luther King Jr Achievement Award. Clarke's work is the subject of *Africadian Atlantic: Essays on George Elliott Clarke* (2012), edited by Joseph Pivato. Finally, though Clarke is racialized "Black" and was socialized as an Africadian, he is a card-carrying member of the Eastland Woodland Métis Nation Nova Scotia, registered under Section 35 of the Charter of Rights and Freedoms. He is, at last, a proud Afro-Métis Africadian.

AFUA COOPER was born and raised in Jamaica; Afua Cooper moved to Canada as a young woman. Cooper has a PhD in history, and she has written extensively on the history of Black peoples in Canada. The author of four books of poetry, her non-fiction book, *The Hanging of Angélique* was nominated for a Governor General's Award. Cooper is the James Robinson Johnston chair in Black Canadian studies at Dalhousie University, Nova Scotia.

JULIE CROOKS is curator, Global Arts of Africa, at the AGO, and her first exhibition in that role was *Free* Black North (29 April–20 August 2017). She received her PhD in the Department of History of Art and Archaeology at the School of Oriental and African Studies (SOAS), University of London, where her research focused on historical photography in Sierra Leone, West Africa, and the diaspora. Prior to joining the AGO, Crooks curated and co-curated a number of exhibitions in Toronto including *No Justice, No Peace: From Ferguson to Toronto*, in February 2017 (co-curated with Reese de Guzman and co-organized by the Ryerson Image Centre and BAND). Julie is also the co-curator for the *Of Africa* project at Toronto's Royal Ontario Museum. Her most recent exhibitions include *Here We Are Here: Black Canadian Contemporary Art* (2018), co-curated with Silvia Forni and Dominique Fontaine, and *Cutting a Figure: Black Style Through the Lens of Charles "Teenie" Harris* (2018).

PILAR CUDER-DOMÍNGUEZ is professor of English at the University of Huelva (Spain). Her research interests are the intersections of gender, genre, nation, and race. The author of three books and editor of eight collections of essays, she is currently lead investigator of the research project "Bodies in Transit 2: Mobilities, Genders, Interdependencies" (bodiesintransit project.com).

RONALD CUMMINGS is associate professor in the Department of English and Cultural Studies at McMaster University. His work has been published in the *Journal of West Indian Literature*, *Small Axe*, *sx salon*, *Cultural Dynamics*, and *Transforming Anthropology*. His research focuses on critical maroon studies, Black diaspora studies, gender and sexuality studies, and on Caribbean literary historiography.

OMISOORE H. DRYDEN, PhD, a Black queer femme, is the fourth James R. Johnston Chair in Black Canadian Studies (https://www.dal.ca/faculty/jrj-chair.html) in the Faculty of Medicine at Dalhousie University, and an associate professor in the Department of Community Health and Epidemiology. Dryden engages in interdisciplinary scholarship and research that focuses on Black LGBTQI communities, blood donation systems in Canada, systemic/structural issues that affect health and well-being, medical education, and Black health curricular content development. Dryden, the principal investigator of #GotBlood2Give/#DuSangÀDonner (https://gotblood2give.weebly.com), has innovative and unique research that identifies the anti-Black homophobic barriers Black gay, bisexual, and trans men encounter with donating blood and the blood system in Canada. She is the co-editor (along with Dr Suzanne Lenon) of *Disrupting Queer Inclusion: Canadian Homonationalisms and the Politics of Belonging* (Vancouver: UBC Press, 2015). Dryden is the co-lead of the Black Health Education Collaborative (https://www.bhec.ca), a member of the Black Feminist Health Science Studies Collective (https://blackfeministhealth.com), and the past co-president of the Black Canadian Studies Association (2019–21, http://www.blackcanadianstudiesassociation.ca).

SARAH FLICKER is an associate professor at the Faculty of Environmental Studies at York University. Sarah has a track record of success in engaging communities in community-based participatory action health research with racialized and Indigenous communities. Sarah has spent the last ten years working with Indigenous youth in Canada on a variety of HIV-prevention research projects.

ALEXIS PAULINE GUMBS is the author of *M Archive: After the End of the World* (Durham: Duke University Press, 2018), *Spill: Scenes of Black Feminist Fugitivity* (Durham: Duke University Press, 2016), and the co-editor of *Revolutionary Mothering: Love on the Front Lines* (Oakland: PM Press, 2016). She lives in Durham, North Carolina where she is forever cultivating Eternal Summer of the Black Feminist Mind, The Black Feminist Bookmobile Project, and the Mobile Homecoming Living Library Archive and Trust. She is also the 2017–19 Winton Chair in the Liberal Arts at University of Minnesota.

NATASHA HENRY is a historian and has been an educator for twenty-two years. She is the president of the Ontario Black History Society. Natasha is an award-winning author and an award-winning curriculum developer, focusing on Black Canadian experiences. Through her various professional and community roles, Natasha's work is grounded in her commitment to research, collect, preserve, and disseminate the histories of Black Canadians. Natasha Henry is currently completing a PhD in history at York University, researching Black enslavement in early Ontario.

KAIE KELLOUGH is a novelist, poet, and sound performer. His first novel, *Accordéon*, was shortlisted for the Amazon First Novel Award. His book of poetry, *Magnetic Equator*, was published by McClelland and Steward in 2019. In 2020 he was awarded the prestigious Griffin Poetry Prize. He is currently near the equator working on new and old ideas.

SONNET L'ABBÉ, PhD, is the author of *A Strange Relief* and *Killarnoe* and was the 2014 guest editor of *Best Canadian Poetry*. Her chapbook *Anima Canadensis* was published by Junction Books in 2016 and won the 2017 bpNichol Chapbook Award. The poems in *Harriet's Legacies* are from her next collection, *Sonnet's Shakespeare*, in which L'Abbé writes over all 154 of Shakespeare's sonnets. L'Abbé is a professor of creative writing and English at Vancouver Island University.

NALINI MOHABIR is an assistant professor in the Department of Geography, Planning and Environment at Concordia University. Her teaching and research interests focus on postcolonial historical geographies.

JEAN-PAUL RESTOULE is Anishinaabe and a member of the Dokis First Nation. Jean-Paul's research focuses on Indigenizing and decolonizing teacher education, supporting Indigenous student success, Indigenous pedagogy in online learning environments, and Indigenous research methodologies and ethics. He is professor and chair of Indigenous education at the University of Victoria.

NELE SAWALLISCH is a senior lecturer at the chair of American Studies at Catholic University Eichstätt-Ingolstadt, Germany. She studied English, French, and education in Germany, France, and Quebec and holds an MA and a PhD from the University of Mainz in American studies. Her first monograph, *Fugitive Borders: Black Canadian Cross-Border Literature at Mid-Nineteenth Century* (transcript, 2019) looks at autobiographical writing by former slaves who settled in Canada West in the 1850s and their community-building processes in pre-Confederation Canada.

WINFRIED SIEMERLING is professor of English at the University of Waterloo and an associate of the W.E.B. Du Bois Institute at Harvard University. He won the Gabrielle Roy Prize for *The Black Atlantic Reconsidered: Black Canadian Writing, Cultural History, and the Presence of the Past* (2015, French translation forthcoming 2022). Earlier books include *Canada and Its Americas: Transnational Navigations* (co-edited, 2010), *The New North American Studies: Culture, Writing, and the Politics of Re/Cognition* (2005, French translation 2010), and *Discoveries of the Other* (1994). He has contributed chapters to *The Oxford Handbook of the African American Slave Narrative* (2014), *The Cambridge History of Postcolonial Literature* (2012), and *African American Literature in Transition* (Cambridge University Press, 2021).

MAKEDA SILVERA was born in Jamaica and has lived in Canada for more than thirty years. She is the co-founder and managing editor of Sister Vision Press and is the author of two collections of short stories, *Her Head a Village* (1994) and *Remembering G* (1990). She is the editor of *The Other Woman: Women of Colour in Contemporary Canadian Literature* (1994), *Ma-Ka: Diaspora Juks* (1997), and the groundbreaking *Piece of My Heart: A Lesbian of Colour Anthology* (1991). *The Heart Does Not Bend* is her first novel. She lives in Toronto.

KAROLYN SMARDZ FROST is an archaeologist, historian, and award-winning author. Karolyn's biography of Toronto-based freedom-seekers Lucie and Thornton Blackburn, *I've Got a Home in Glory Land*, won the Governor General's Literary Award in 2007. In 2016, she coedited with Veta Smith Tucker the groundbreaking *A Fluid Frontier: Slavery, Resistance and the Underground Railroad in the Detroit River Borderland*. Karolyn's newest book, *Steal Away Home* (2017), tells the story of Cecelia Jane Reynolds who fled Kentucky slavery by way of Niagara Falls in 1846. Karolyn Smardz Frost holds a PhD in history: race, slavery, and imperialism from the University of Waterloo and is both an adjunct professor at Acadia University and senior research fellow for African Canadian history at the Tubman Institute, York University.

CAROLE LYNN STEWART is professor of English where she teaches American and African American literature at Brock University. She also has taught a course on the Underground Railroad in the Canadian American studies graduate program at Brock. Her publications include *Strange Jeremiahs: Civil Religion in the Literary Imaginations of Jonathan Edwards, Herman Melville, and W.E.B. Du Bois* (2011) and articles on civil religion and civil society, and nineteenth-century literary and historical figures such as Melville, Du Bois, George Moses Horton, William Wells Brown, Frances Ellen Watkins Harper, and Amanda Berry Smith. Her second book, *Temperance and Cosmopolitanism: African American Reformers in the Atlantic World* was published in 2018 (paperback 2021), with Pennsylvania State University Press.

ANDREA THOMPSON is a writer and educator who has performed her poetry across the country for more than twenty years. In 1995 she was featured in the documentary *Slamnation* as a member of the country's first national slam team, and in 2005 her CD *One* was nominated for a Canadian Urban Music Award. She is the author of the novel *Over Our Heads* and co-editor of *Other Tongues: Mixed Race Women Speak Out*. A graduate of the University of Guelph's MFA Creative Writing Program, Thompson currently teaches fiction through Brock University and spoken word through the Ontario College of Art and Design University and the University of Toronto's Continuing Studies departments. Thompson is the author of two critical essays on spoken word: "Committing the Act of Language: The (R)evolutionary Tactics and Hybridist Anxieties of Spoken Word's Third Wave" (*More Caught in the Act*, 2016), and "Spoken Word: A Gesture Towards Possibility" (*Creative Writing in the 21st Century*, 2018). She is currently working on a new CD and print collection about spoken word. For more information: www.andreathompson.ca.

CIANN L. WILSON is an associate professor at Wilfrid Laurier University where her areas of interest build off her community-engaged work to include critical race theory, anti-/de-colonial theory, African diasporic and Indigenous community health, HIV/AIDS, sexual and reproductive wellbeing, and community-based research. Her body of work aims to utilize research as an avenue for sharing the stories and realities of African diasporic and Indigenous peoples and improving the health and wellbeing of those communities.

SHAUN WINTON graduated with a BA in history from Grand Valley State University in 2011. Winton returned to academia years later at Central Connecticut State University (CCSU), in its Public History Master's Program. He has worked on oral histories with the Center for Oral History Research at Columbia University, CCSU's Veterans History Project, and the New Haven Preservation Trust. He currently works as a librarian in Los Angeles, California.

D'BI.YOUNG ANITAFRIKA is a triple Dora award-winning published playwright-performer, director-dramaturge, and emerging scholar. She was one of two hundred Canadian artists to receive a New Chapter Grant to produce her critically acclaimed environmental musical entitled *Lukumi: A Dub Opera*. anitafrika's other awards include Canadian Poet of Honour, YWCA Woman of Distinction in the Arts, Mayor's Arts, Vital People, KM Hunter Theatre Award, and The Golden Beret Award. She was also a finalist for the 2017 Ontario Premier Arts Awards for Theatre and Literature. She is an internationally celebrated arts-educator and the founding artistic director of the Watah Theatre as well as the instigator of Spolrusie Press, a unique micro-press that publishes original works by Black and QTIPOC creators.

anitafrika is the originator of the creative leadership praxis and intersectional decolonialist framework the Anitafrika Method which has been utilized by the Stephen Lewis Foundation, the Banff Centre, University of Toronto, MARS, and Women's College Hospital, as well as other institutions globally. She is the published author of seven books, nine plays, and seven dub albums and has toured her work nationally and internationally. Addressing issues of gender, sexuality, race, class, and the human experience through her vast field of artistic knowledge, anitafrika is pursuing postgraduate studies in London, UK, researching the use of theatre to address generational trauma in the Black body through the Anitafrika Method.

Index